Engraved for Dr. Fuller's History of Berwick.

Drawn by A. Carse

Engraved by R. Scott

LONDON BOROUGH OF LEWISHAM
LIBRARY SERVICE

Author

Title

Books or discs must be returned on or before the last date stamped on label or on card in book pocket. Books or discs can be renewed by telephone, letter or personal call unless required by another reader. After library hours use the Ansafone Service (01-698 7347). For hours of opening and charges see notices at the above branch, but note that all lending departments close at 1 pm on Wednesday and all libraries are closed on Sundays, Good Friday, Christmas Day, Bank Holidays and Saturdays prior to Bank Holidays.

THE HISTORY
OF
BERWICK UPON TWEED

by

JOHN FULLER

FRANK GRAHAM
6 Queen's Terrace, Newcastle upon Tyne 2

First published 1799
This edition 1973

S.B.N. 902833 08 1

Printed in Great Britain by
The Scolar Press Limited, Menston, Yorkshire

THE

HISTORY OF

BERWICK UPON TWEED,

INCLUDING A SHORT ACCOUNT

OF THE VILLAGES OF

TWEEDMOUTH AND SPITTAL, &c.

By JOHN FULLER, M. D. Berwick.

EDINBURGH:

PRINTED FOR BELL & BRADFUTE, J. DICKSON, W. CREECH, P. HILL, MANNERS & MILLER, AND A. CONSTABLE, EDINBURGH; W. EMBLETON, BERWICK; CADELL & DAVIES, AND J. FAULDER, BOND-STREET, LONDON.

1799.

DEDICATION.

TO

Sir JOHN SINCLAIR

of Ulbster, Bart. M. P. &c.

SIR,

I presume it will be allowed, that the chief object of all ſcientific purſuits ought to be the promoting of uſeful knowledge.

Holding this principle in view, it will appear evident, that every author ſhould diveſt himſelf of all ſiniſter views, and ought to chooſe a perſon for the ſubject of his *Panegyric* who is intereſted in ſuch purſuits, and whoſe *patriotiſm* has entitled him to the reſpect and eſteem of all good men.

If

If this is admitted, I have little doubt but the world will agree with me, that, in this respect, I could not have fixed on any person to dedicate this work to, whose character stands so eminently distinguished for unabated ardor in every pursuit tending to promote the general interests of society and the happiness of mankind, as yourself.

Those persevering and unremitting exertions which you made, and which were crowned with success, even though seemingly opposed to insurmountable obstacles, in the establishment of the BOARD OF AGRICULTURE, will immortalize your name, and will serve as an illustrious example of a great and active mind.

Permit me then, Sir, to submit the following sheets to your consideration as founder of

the

the above Inſtitution, which, for your honour and the proſperity of my native country, I moſt ſincerely wiſh may flouriſh for ever.

If this work ſhould fortunately meet with your approbation, I ſhall conſider my labour amply rewarded.

I have the honour to be, with the moſt profound reſpect and eſteem,

SIR,

Your moſt obedient,

And faithful humble ſervant,

JOHN FULLER.

BERWICK,
Aug. 17. 1799.

ADVER-

ADVERTISEMENT.

THIS Work is of the ſame nature with that of the Statiſtical Account of Scotland. It is the firſt attempt of the kind made in England, and is to be conſidered as conſtituting the firſt part of a ſecond great national undertaking, the importance and utility of which do not fall to be here inveſtigated.

It was firſt drawn up in a ſmall compaſs, at the requeſt of Sir John Sinclair, then Preſident of the Board of Agriculture, but the writer ſuggeſting to him that, to do juſtice to the publication, he conceived it ſhould be written on a more extenſive ſcale; Sir John, after having peruſed the papers, was of the ſame opinion; and accordingly wiſhed that the details might be lengthened, and the obſervations made more copious. This being complied with, the manuſcript, when nearly finiſhed, was ſhown to the Preſident, who thought it ſhould be printed in chapters and ſections, which he had the goodneſs to draw up from the ſimple arrangement preſented to him by the Author: At the ſame time Sir John requeſted that the work ſhould be publiſhed in the writer's name, which the latter was prevailed on to agree to.

From the Author's reſiding at a diſtance ſeveral errors have unavoidably crept in to the work, which, it is hoped, the candid reader will readily pardon.

INTRODUCTION.

THE Town of Berwick upon Tweed is one of the moſt celebrated in the Hiſtory of Great Britain. From its having been a frontier garriſon town, long before the glorious æra of the union, and from its being ſituated cloſe by the ſea, and upon the banks of an unfordable river, it was conſidered, when in poſſeſſion of the Engliſh, as a key to England; and, when in poſſeſſion of the Scots, as a key to Scotland. Having of courſe become a bone of contention between thoſe once contending kingdoms; it was but too often productive of ſcenes of the moſt cruel devaſtation and blood ſhed.

As

As its ancient hiſtory may ſerve to throw conſiderable light upon thoſe great events which formerly agitated and convulſed theſe two nations, we deem it incumbent upon us to give, in the following work, as ample a detail of it as is conſiſtent with the limits of our publication. But the principal object of this work, is to lay before the public as complete an account as could be drawn up from the well authenticated materials which we have been able, with much induſtry, to collect, reſpecting its preſent ſtate, and the means of promoting its future improvement.

CON-

CONTENTS.

CHAP.

CHAP. II.

Hiſtory of the Town.

CHAP. III.

Public Buildings.

CHAP.

CHAP. IV.

Conſtitution and Government.

CHAP. V.

Population.

CHAP. VI.

Eccleſiaſtical State.

CHAP.

CHAP. VII.

Charitable Inſtitutions.

CHAP. VIII.

Education.

CHAP. IX.

Revenue Department.

CHAP. X.

Military Department.

CHAP. XI.

Manufactures and Trade.

CHAP. XII.

Fisheries.

CHAP. XIII.

Police.

CHAP. XIV.

Manners, &c.

CHAP.

CHAP. XV.

Country part of the Diftrict.

CHAP. XVI.

Mifcellaneous Obfervations.

CHAP. XVII.

CON-

CONCLUSION.

Advantages and Means of Improvement.

APPENDIX,

THE

HISTORY

OF

BERWICK UPON TWEED, &c.

CHAP. I.

Preliminary Obſervations.

IN the Introduction to this Work, we have pointed out that the principal and ultimate object it has in view, is the future increaſe and improvement of Berwick.

How univerſally great ſoever the applauſe which the publication of the Statiſtical Account of Scotland has moſt meritoriouſly obtained from the public, and which may be looked upon as a demonſtrative proof of the great advantages to be derived from ſtatiſtical purſuits, thereby rendering any future diſcuſſion on the merits of proſecuting theſe inquiries unneceſſary; we humbly conceive it behoves us here, in conſideration that the Statiſtical Account of Berwick is the firſt attempt of the kind made in England under the auſpices of the Board of Agriculture: In the *firſt* place to make a few brief obſervations on agriculture, trade, and commerce; and, *ſecondly*, to offer ſome curſory remarks on ſtatiſtical inveſtigations, with a view of removing any prejudices to works of this ſort, which may ſubſiſt in the minds of thoſe who have not beſtowed that attention upon them to which they are evidently entitled.

Though the mental powers and faculties of man, (an imperfect and finite being,) muſt ever continue limited while he exiſts in this ſublunary ſtate, which renders him incapable, with all the poſſible reſearches and full energy of his ſoul, to bring any of the arts and ſciences to complete perfection; yet the all-wiſe and beneficent Author of the human race has endowed the mind of man with powers, which,

which, when diligently and richly cultured, judiciously exercised, and properly directed to suitable objects of improvement, have, in a variety of instances, enabled him to bring some branches of the arts and sciencies to a very high state of improvement.

Man, in a state of nature, it would appear, can only lay claim to one step in the chain of being superior to the brute creation. But when his mind is duly and highly cultivated, and his manners receive the finest polish, he then rises with a degree of transcendence in the scale of comparison, that not only dazzles our imagination; but overpowers the whole soul. What a grand and luxuriant theme for the theologist and philosopher! but which would lead us to an endless digression. We beg leave only to remark, that, from the foregoing observations, we are constrained to admire the wisdom and benevolence of Omnipotence, in his having, for the great happiness of mankind, along with the limited mental powers given to him, left the cultivation and improvement of his mind to his own will and choice.

choice. At the ſame time it is likewiſe proper to obſerve, that God has tied him down by his laws, and thoſe of nature, to improve thoſe talents which he has beſtowed upon him to the utmoſt of his power, both for his own good and alſo for that of ſociety, the neglecting which conſtitutes a crime of great magnitude. For what would have been the conſequences if the powers and faculties of the human mind had been ſo conſtituted, that they expanded, and ſpontaneouſly improved in regular progreſſion, in all branches of knowledge, in the ſame manner as the body of man is evolved, and gradually grows up to perfection. If ſuch had really been the ſtate of man, and that he were poſſeſſed of the ſame ideas and propenſities which are congenial to his preſent nature, human ſociety, (if under ſuch circumſtances ſociety of any kind had been poſſible to have been formed,) could not have long exiſted. For all denominations of men having in this caſe an equally univerſal intuitive knowledge of all ſubjects and profeſſions, complete anarchy and confuſion muſt

muſt have taken place in ſuch a community, which could not have failed ſoon to have terminated in its extinction, ariſing from cauſes which are completely obvious.

The Author of nature has, no doubt, for the wiſeſt of purpoſes, compoſed the corporeal parts of man of materials which are ſubject to decay; to ſucceſſive proceſſes of decompoſition; and ultimately to complete diſſolution; thereby leaving behind, of that once perfectly ſymmetrical and moſt beautiful fabric, only its elementary parts. That though, having conſtituted his body an animal machine of the moſt exquiſite texture and mechaniſm, and alſo ſuperadded thereto a principle of animation or rational ſoul, whereby, through the medium of the brain and nervous ſyſtem, all its organs derive the power of performing their various and reſpective functions; (ſome of which are voluntary and others involuntary: by means of theſe producing the involuntary and alternate contraction of the right and left ventricles of the heart, there is a conſtant circulation of the blood carried on throughout

throughout the whole body: and, from the unceasing action of the lungs, there is, during each inspiration, a quantity of atmospheric air *, most essential to the preservation of life, conveyed into the sanguiferous system. Yet, notwithstanding these extraordinary and wonderful resources provided by Nature for the continuation of vitality, the constant waste and exhaustion that takes place in the body, arising as an unavoidable consequence of the numerous secretions from the blood which occur in the course of its circulation through particular organs, it has been found that human existence cannot be long prolonged, unless a regular supply either of vegetable or animal substances,

* The reader ought to be informed, that the air of the atmosphere, when uncontaminated, has, by the test of chemical analysis, been discovered to consist of two distinct airs or gasses, the one called *vital*, the other *azotic*. The vital air, being what is absolutely essential to the support of animal life and combustion, is that portion alone which is absorbed from the air-vessels of the lungs into the mass of blood; the other, or azotic, being rejected as totally unfit for the maintenance both of animal life and flame.

ſubſtances, or part of both, be taken into the ſtomach. And it is to be remarked, that theſe ſubſtances, by the aſtoniſhing powers of the organs of digeſtion, become aſſimilated to the nature of the human body itſelf, for the direct and obvious purpoſes of nutrition. Hence appears the primary neceſſity of cultivating the ſurface of the globe to obtain food and clothing, for the preſervation and ſupport of the human ſpecies, as well as to procure ſuſtenance for the other animals which are ſubſervient to the uſe of man.

This circumſtance, of man's depending wholly for the ſupply of the waſte of his body on vegetable and animal matter, is moſt wonderfully and beautifully diſplayed in the new-born infant, almoſt immediately upon its coming into the world, diſcovering an eager deſire to ſuck its mother; which propenſity conſtitutes what has been called the *inſtinctive principle of animals*.

To thoſe readers unacquainted with the nature of milk, it may be proper to ſtate, that it partakes partly of a vegetable, and partly of an animal nature; this fact affording a strong presumption, that Nature intended the food of man should consist of both, in such proportions as might be found by experience most suitable to individual constitutions.

Thus, by the improvement of the natural powers of the mind, man may acquire such degrees of knowledge as are not only sufficient to enable him to conduct himself with ability in the common transactions of life, but are even capable of exalting his nature, and reflecting lustre on the human character, acting at the same time as a strong incitement to the exertion of others. We have also observed above, that, by the laws of Nature, we are particularly bound to cultivate our minds for the purpose of acquiring knowledge, first, with the view of providing our FOOD, and, secondly, our CLOTHING. And as the obtaining of the first depends upon the produce of the surface of the earth, so the culture of it becomes of all other terrestrial objects the first and most important to mankind; and, as the second is absolutely necessary for the protection

protection of our bodies from the inclemency of the atmosphere, as well as for the adorning of our frame, it is therefore of all others next entitled to our consideration. An attention to the article of clothing naturally leads to an extension of our manufactures as well as of our trade and commerce. All the other subjects of the arts and sciences, compared with these, are of subordinate moment, not only when viewed in themselves individually, but also when considered in a national point of view. These facts appearing to us so obviously incontrovertible, it follows of course, that, next to the government, religion, and laws of a nation, that agricultural, manufacturing, and commercial improvements ought to be its primary objects; that is, every kingdom or state should direct its attention, first, To the melioration of the soil; second, To the improvement of manufactures; third, To the improvement of trade and commerce; and that these three national objects ought, in our opinion, to form the basis of all statistical inquiries and investigations.

That the attempting to reduce to practice the culture of the earth, on ſcientific principles, by means of national and other inſtitutions, ſhould have lain neglected ever ſince the creation of the world until lately, ſurely conſtitutes one of the greateſt wonders of the preſent age, and cannot but be conſidered as juſtly ſubjecting man to ſevere animadverſion. What art but itſelf can boaſt of a divine original! An art of all others the moſt natural, as well as the moſt ſalutary: An art that even in the earlier periods of the world was thought worthy the attention of the greateſt of men. We find that Virgil, the moſt celebrated of the Roman poets, formed his elegant precepts of huſbandry upon a publication of Magos the Carthaginian general, which conſiſts of 28 books on the ſubject of agriculture. The Romans were impreſſed with a laudable pride in being conſidered huſbandmen. So remote as the reign of King Numa, public encouragement was beſtowed on thoſe who promoted agricultural knowledge. Cato the Cenſor publiſhed a volume on the ſame ſubject. Colu-

mella

mella left to the world 12 books on rural affairs. Varro alſo wrote an eſteemed treatiſe on agriculture. Beſides theſe, many other Greek and Latin authors might be adduced to prove, that the cultivation of the ſoil has ever been attended to both by the enlightened philoſopher, and the patriotic citizen.

The celebrated Sully ſtiles agriculture one of the breaſts from which a ſtate muſt draw its nouriſhment. A more happy ſimile than this could not be thought of. By inſtructive precepts and ſtimulating rewards this great man prevailed on his countrymen to cultivate this art, though theſe his induſtrious exertions were but of ſhort duration, as the public troubles of thoſe times ſoon put an end to the arts.

The French nation have meritoriouſly paid great attention to the ſubject of improving the ſurface of the earth; and men of the moſt elevated ranks in that country have not diſdained to cultivate their own lands. Even one of their renowned monarchs, Lewis XIV. with a view to obtain an account of his exten-

ſive

ſive provinces, eſtabliſhed a BOARD, and appointed *Intendants* for this laudable purpoſe. But the board being very much limited in its powers, only the Province of Languedoc was particularly deſcribed. If the reader wiſhes for a more full account of this praiſe-worthy attempt of the French king, we refer him to Voltaire's Age of Lewis the XIV. vol. II. p. 127, 128. edit. 1752.

Our wonder is again excited, when we reflect, that notwithſtanding the diſcoveries of ſuch luminaries as a Bacon and a Newton, who (like reſplendent ſuns) aroſe in the hemiſphere of ſcience, and who diſpelled thoſe almoſt impenetrable clouds, which till then had obſcured true philoſophy, but which are now eſtabliſhed on the baſis of eternal truth; yet, that not only the general body of farmers, but likewiſe gentlemen farmers, poſſeſſed of great landed property, acute diſcernment, and a conſiderable ſhare of general knowledge, ſtill followed the old beaten unſyſtematized track; which, having no conſiſtent theory to ſupport it, rendered every attempt

tempt to accelerate the progreſs of agricultural improvements precarious and uncertain, which often muſt have been attended with great loſs, but which, till lately, few farmers could well bear; and this conſtituted, and ſtill conſtitutes, (though in a leſs degree than formerly), one of the greateſt obſtacles to the eſtabliſhment of a complete ſyſtem of agriculture founded on the baſis of demonſtration. Let us here inquire how this important object is moſt likely to be attained: And we preſume it is neither to be acquired in the field alone, nor in the ſchools: It ſurely muſt be ſought for in a happy combination of what is to be learned in both. The philoſopher ſhould ſeduloufly follow the plough, and with the moſt minute attention obſerve its effects, and regiſter them carefully in his mind.

When we contemplate the faculty which this incomprehenſible ſtore-houſe of ideas and of knowledge poſſeſſes, in that the more it receives and lays up, its capacity and deſire for receiving more, eſpecially if the matter be pure and inſtructive, increaſes in proportion,

and

and the powers of retention are thereby enlarged and ſtrengthened ; our ſouls are filled with aſtoniſhment and a ſoothing awe. The huſbandman ought, in his turn, to go into the ſchools, and, taking up the pen and compaſſes, make himſelf maſter of the elements of mathematics, with their application to mechanics; he muſt afterwards reſort to the chemical elaboratory, where, plying diligently until he acquires a thorough knowledge of the moſt eſſential doctrines of chemiſtry, let him attend the academical chair on agriculture in the Univerſity of Edinburgh; after all which, he will return to the culture of the earth furniſhed with a ſtock of geometrical and chemical information, which, being founded on certain data, ſtanding the teſt of demonſtrative proof, he will thereby be enabled ſcientifically to comprehend the conſtruction and powers of all the utenſils uſed in huſbandry, and by which he will be enabled to add to their improvement. By chemical analyſis it will be greatly in his power to evolve and diſcover the nature and properties of of which the different ſoils are compoſed, and alſo the chemical principles of all the various manures. From theſe acquiſitions, and the knowledge he will derive from the profeſſor's lectures, he will thence be enabled to determine what manures are adapted to certain ſoils, and in what proportions they ought to be uſed. By all which, combined with the knowledge to be derived from experience, he will then find himſelf capable of forming a more fixed and regular ſyſtem, founded on the principles of conſiſtency and truth, which muſt lead to a more ſucceſsful practice of farming.

By purſuing ſuch a plan, farmers in general would become men of ſcience; and thus the practice and theory, by being united and acting reciprocally on each other, would certainly tend to the improvement of both.

The profeſſion would then acquire ſuch an acceſſion of reſpectability as could not fail to excite the attention of all ranks of men, which might be productive of the happieſt diſcoveries, leading not only to the increaſe

of

of individual, but alſo of national wealth. The riches thus acquired, too, though they might excite the jealouſy of ſurrounding nations, yet that power and grandeur, which generally accompany their poſſeſſion, become, at the ſame time, the ſtrongeſt bulwarks againſt the incurſions of foreign foes. But beſides theſe eſſential and moſt deſirable acquiſitions, ariſing as the fruits of our induſtry, there are other important advantages which would naturally flow from this propoſed plan of improving agriculture, and which relate to the ſubject of religion and morality. Theſe being intimately connected with the growing riches of a country, and the ſucceſs of agricultural purſuits, we humbly apprehend they fall briefly to be noticed here. Though it muſt be admitted, that affluence, by affording the luxuries of life, too often has proved the ſource of vice and immorality; yet riches, acquired by men of cultivated and enlightened minds, will in general be found to be leſs likely to lead to depravity and diſſipation, than if acquired

quired by persons not possessing those mental endowments.

Hence the great advantages which might likely accrue to a nation, were farmers to receive a philosophic education, such as we have proposed. There is no profession better fitted, nor none that has a greater tendency, to inspire the mind with devout and sublime ideas, than the occupation of cultivating the inanimate clod, for the purpose of bringing forth corn and grass for the use of man and those animals which are subjected to his dominion. What an excellent and inexhaustible subject for the exercise of the contemplative mind does not this afford! *Consider the lillies how they grow; they toil not, neither do they spin; and yet I say unto you, that Solomon, in all his glory, was not arrayed like one of these!*

In every well regulated government, the circumstances above alluded to will be likely to prove the surest and most effectual means of preserving its constitution inviolate;—of commanding a due respect for, and obedience to its laws;—the greateſt and moſt natural ſecurities of public tranquillity and domeſtic peace;—the firſt objects of a great empire.

In taking a more comprehenſive view of agriculture, it appears to us that its ſlow progreſs in improvement, until of late years, is chiefly to be attributed to the following cauſes:

1. To the want of a theory founded on rational principles.

2. To the want of a ſufficient capital in the general body of farmers.

3. To the native indolence of the human mind.

4. To prejudice, and a bias to old modes, as alſo to a general averſion which ſubſiſts in man to innovation of every kind.

5. To a modeſty and timidity ariſing from the fear of being ſubjected to deriſion.

6. To the ſucceſsful exertions of individuals not having been made publicly known.

7. The ſcience of agriculture not having become, till lately, the object of accademical purſuits.

8. To gentlemen of fortune not having combined a conſiſtent theory with a practical knowledge,

knowledge, and profecuted the fubject upon an extenfive fcale with unremitting affiduity.

9. To the art not having been patronifed by civilifed ftates in the eftablifhment of national boards of agriculture, except in the ifland of Great Britain, which took place in May 1793.

10. To the land proprietors having formerly been in the practice of granting either too fhort or too long leafes to their tenants.

To enter upon a difcuffion of the various caufes above enumerated, which have chiefly operated towards retarding the progrefs of agricultural acquirements, would occafion us to exceed the limits of this publication; the bare recital which we have already given of them, it is to be hoped, will be deemed fufficient to the candid and intelligent reader.

Had the whole of the arable foil of the globe been originally of the fame nature, the climate and feafons in all the different regions alike, not fubjected to fudden changes and violent tempefts; and all the articles of manure in each diftrict equally abundant, and

of

of the ſame quality; the art of cultivation, eſpecially if the ground had been naturally rich, would probably have been very ſoon ſimplified, and an univerſal ſyſtem ſpeedily raiſed and confirmed on ſcientific principles; provided, however, that the luxuriance of the earth, and the perpetual ſtate of weather favourable to vegetation, would not have led men to indulge themſelves in that averſion to laborious ſtudy and active exertion, which is inherent in, and congenial to, their nature; and where their daily ſuſtenance is, as it were, poured down upon them from Heaven. But, as a very mixed and oppoſite ſtate in every reſpect has neceſſarily ſubſiſted ſince the primeval days of the world, and which muſt ever remain as long as the preſent condition and arrangement of the ſolar ſyſtem exiſts, the fertilizing the various kinds of ſoils in climates of oppoſite tendency, comes to be very perplexed and difficult; which calls not only for the utmoſt energy of the huſbandman individually, but even for the united efforts of a whole nation, as far as it is poſſible

to

to obviate them. And this leads us to direct our attention to an aera propitious to our hopes of living to ſee a ſyſtem of agriculture brought to a very high ſtate of improvement—the offspring of reſearch, diſcovery, and experience. The arrival of this auſpicious epoch, which, we truſt, is not far diſtant, will, in all probability, be much forwarded by the eſtabliſhment of the National Board of Agriculture in Great Britain, which, in the dedication, we have ſtated was effected principally by means of the moſt arduous, unremitting, and truly patriotic exertions of its preſent Preſident. * To enter upon a detail of the riſe and progreſs of this wiſe and moſt important inſtitution would lead us into an unpardonable and unneceſſary prolixity. We therefore refer the reader to an elegant work on that ſubject, publiſhed by Sir John Sinclair lately. We ſhall therefore confine our obſervations to its uſeful tendency, with a view to explain the nature and propriety of ſtatiſtical purſuits.

The

* Theſe Preliminaries, and moſt part of the Work, were written anno 1797, and beginning of 1798, when Sir John Sinclair was Preſident.

The perſevering and undaunted ſpirit of the Preſident of the Board of Agriculture having, in ſpite of many and ſeemingly unſurmountable obſtacles, brought this inſtitution to be eſtabliſhed on the broad and firm baſis of a National Board, which having fortunately obtained his Majeſty's patronage, Great Britain has begun a career of unexampled glory, in what relates to the arts of peace,—induſtry,—improvement of the ſoil, —manufactures,—trade and commerce,—the arts and ſciences. Other nations may imitate or come up to, but cannot eaſily ſurpaſs an inſtitution which has for its objects whatever a truly dignified, enlightened, and benevolent mind can dictate, or the fineſt feelings of the heart can point to. As it cannot be preſumed it is, in general, in the power of one ſingle man, in the courſe of his life, to bring any of the arts to great improvement, it becomes neceſſary for men to form themſelves into ſocieties for the purpoſe of combining their efforts to accompliſh ſuch objects. Independent of the native benevo-

lence

lence of the minds of the members of which ſuch ſocieties are compoſed impelling them to contribute every thing in their power to promote the ſucceſs of their purſuits, that ſpirit of emulation which is more or leſs inherent in every man's breaſt becomes a powerful additional ſtimulus to the exertions of his inventive faculties, whereby a body of men, thus aſſociated, act reciprocally on one another, in a double ſenſe, towards the attainment of objects of improvement; and it has been found, in a great variety of inſtances, that where ſocieties have been judiciouſly arranged and properly conducted, many great and uſeful diſcoveries have been brought to light. But if ſuch are the advantages reſulting from ſingle ſocieties compoſed of but a few men, what is not to be expected from the united efforts of a whole nation? Great Britain has taken the ſtart, and leads the van, not of an army hoſtile to humanity, but of a powerful phalanx, compoſed of many of the nobles of the land, and other gentlemen of profound erudition and true patriotiſm. Hav-

ing

ing a virtuous and magnanimous Prince for their patron, and one of the moſt celebrated philanthropiſts of the preſent age for their Preſident, and each of this choſen band holding as it were an olive branch in his hand, (ſweet emblem of peace, and portentous of every good that can attend mankind), calls aloud and fervently invites every individual, and alſo ſocieties compoſed of men intereſted in the various ſubjects of improvement above ſpecified, to exert their utmoſt endeavours to accompliſh, more or leſs, ſuch important objects, and from time to time to communicate to this inſtitution their progreſs and ſucceſs; and there can be no doubt but the Board of Agriculture, with a liberal ſpirit, will reward ſuch individuals or ſocieties not only with their own marked reſpect and eſteem, but (through the medium of their publications) do every thing in their power to ſecure to them the approbation of the world, thereby defending them againſt the prejudices and invidious calumnies of their illiberal opponents. Admirable inſtitution that combines ſo many

incentives

incentives to induſtry, and a perſevering application to objects of improvement! To bring our obſervations nearer to a cloſe on this eſtabliſhment, we have to remark, that, as in medicine the collection of well authenticated facts, with regard to the ſucceſsful effects of particular remedies in certain diſeaſes and conſtitutions, tends to lead, if not to the diſcovery of ſpecifics, yet to a conſiſtent and rational theory, and, founded upon that, to a practice generally ſucceſsful. In like manner, the Board of Agriculture, which is to be conſidered as a national and general repertory, placed in the focus of an immenſe circle, whence it is ſucceſſively, and almoſt conſtantly receiving from its correſpondents uſeful communications, which, together with the Statiſtical publications, are by this means enabled, (as with the effulgence of noon-day), to tranſmit and diffuſe into all the regions of civiliſed ſociety, every eſſential improvement and diſcovery which the Honourable Board may find they contain, together with their own obſervations, thereby contributing to bring ſuch improvements and discoveries to a still greater degree of perfection. These last remarks apply, in general, to elucidate the nature and expediency of statistical pursuits;—rich sources flowing from their original fountain, the Board of Agriculture.

To put this matter in a more forcible and clearer point of view, we beg leave to add the few following general observations:

Statistics, we presume, may briefly be defined the ascertaining the actual state of cities, towns, and the various districts of a country, with regard to their situation, extent, population, climate, diseases, religion and laws, customs and manners, local advantages, public and private institutions, education, agricultural state, trade and commerce, &c. &c. &c.—together with a variety of other subjects connected with, and in a great measure dependent upon, those we have just enumerated. Publications of this sort, we conceive, could not be considered (even *a priori*) but as leading to the discovery and establishment of many useful and important facts, which other-

wise

wiſe might lie concealed. But if, in works of this nature, the ſtatiſtical writer gives a correct detail of every improvement which, from time to time, has been made, and by whom, and by what means effected in all the different ſubjects that comes under his diſcuſſion, and, at the ſame time, alſo points out (and which we think ſhould always be the caſe in ſtatiſtical publications and agricultural reports of the counties) thoſe improvements they are ſtill capable of, that appear to himſelf, and may be ſuggeſted to him by others, the nature and uſeful tendency of ſuch purſuits will be evident to every man of candour and reflection.

Surely a more natural and more rational plan, leading to the improvement of a country in every reſpect, than the one adopted by the Board of Agriculture, could ſcarcely be deviſed by human wiſdom. For, as we formerly obſerved, the mind of man is averſe to innovation of every ſort, and that, unleſs he is convinced, either by ocular demonſtration, or from works printed, of the ſuperior

ſucceſs

fuccefs of his neighbours or others, by means of profecuting fome new and improved fyftem, he will naturally go on in his old beaten track; but fhould he perceive his cotemporaries both enriching themfelves, and, at the fame time, rifing into reputation and fame in confequence of their following improved modes, he will thereby be ftimulated to make the greateft efforts not only to acquire riches, but that principle of emulation to excel, and which, more or lefs, pervades every man's breaft, will tend to aroufe his dormant powers into active exertion. This principle of human nature applies not only individually but will be found to extend alfo to affociations of men formed for promoting objects of improvement.

We would therefore propofe, in order to give an additional fpur to the innate propenfity of the mind to rife to diftinction and celebrity, that in all ftatiftical publications, agricultural reports, &c. the names of thofe individuals who have rendered themfelves confpicuous in advancing any of the branches of fcience, ſcience, ſhould be announced in terms adequate to their reſpective merits.

We apprehend that the prodigious maſs of information acquired to the nation reſpecting ſo many important objects, through the medium of the ſtatiſtical publications, as well as the publiſhing the agricultural reports of the different counties, cannot fail, under the auſpices and guidance of a well regulated inſtitution of this kind, to be productive of the moſt ſolid advantages to this empire *. And after

* In order to corroborate what has been advanced in theſe preliminaries reſpecting the utility and importance of the eſtabliſhment of the board of agriculture, on its preſent plans, we have judged it proper to inſert the following copy of a letter from that truly great and patriotic character General Waſhington to Sir John Sinclair.

Agriculture.—" I have read with peculiar pleaſure and " approbation, the work you patroniſe ſo much to your " own honour and the utility of the public. Such a ge-" neral view of the agriculture in the ſeveral counties of " Great Britain is extremely intereſting, and cannot fail " of being very beneficial to the agricultural concerns of " your country, and to thoſe of every other wherein they " are read, and muſt entitle you to their warmeſt thanks, " for after what we have ſaid in various parts of theſe preliminaries, it is ſurely unneceſſary to add

"for having ſet ſuch a plan on foot, and for proſecuting "it with the zeal and intelligence you do.

"I am ſo much pleaſed with the plan and execution "myſelf, as to pray you to have the goodneſs to direct "your bookſeller to continue to forward them to me, ac- "companied with the coſt, which ſhall be paid to his or- "der, or remitted ſo ſoon as the amount is made known "to me. When the whole are received, I will promote, "as far as in me lies, the reprinting of them here.

"I know of no purſuit in which more real and import- "ant ſervice can be rendered to any country than by im- "proving its agriculture; its breed of uſeful animals, and "other branches of a huſbandman's cares; nor can I con- "ceive any plan more conducive to this end than the one "you have introduced, for bringing to view the actual "ſtate of them in all parts of the kingdom, by which "good and bad habits are exhibited in a manner too plain "to be miſconceived. For the accounts given to the Bri- "tiſh board of agriculture appear, in general, to be drawn "up in a maſterly manner, ſo as fully to anſwer the ex- "pectations formed in the excellent plan which produced "them; affording, at the ſame time, a fund of informa- "tion uſeful in political œconomy, and ſerviceable in all "countries."

add more here by way of carrying conviction to the minds of our countrymen *.

To ſecure ſucceſs to this grand enterpriſe, every ſenſible and patriotic perſon will (there can be little doubt) join in opinion that this inſtitution ought to be liberally ſupported and cheriſhed by the Britiſh legiſlature, to which ſupport it ſeems entitled (as its birth right) in order to carry into effect its various and important national objects.

We cannot take our leave of this ſubject without ſaying that the illuſtrious character who

* *The following letter was alſo ſent to Sir John Sinclair by General Waſhington.*

" I cannot but expreſs myſelf highly pleaſed with the " undertaking in which you are engaged, (that of draw- " ing up the Statiſtical Account of Scotland), and give " my beſt wiſhes for its ſucceſs.

" I am fully perſuaded, that when enlightened men " will take the trouble to examine ſo minutely into the " ſtate of ſociety, as your inquiries ſeem to go, it muſt " reſult in greatly ameliorating the condition of the peo- " ple—promoting the intereſts of civil ſociety—and the " happineſs of mankind at large.—Theſe are objects truly " worthy the attention of a great mind, and every friend " to the human race muſt readily lend his aid towards " their accompliſhment."

who has been the principal means of giving birth to this ſociety (ſtill in its infancy) deſerves to have his name engraved not only on pillars of marble, but on ſtatues of gold, to perpetuate, to the lateſt ages, his memory and well earned labours, and to keep alive this ſpirit of true patriotiſm, without which a nation may exiſt and loiter, age after age, without ever advancing one ſtep towards perfection. But the ſervices done by individuals to their country can only be truly appretiated by poſterity. For that principle of jealouſy which rankles more or leſs in every man's breaſt, inſtead of leading him (with the breath of liberality and candour) to approve and admire, in but too many inſtances has been found to exhauſt itſelf, if not in calumny and deriſion, yet in throwing in the way obſtacles to improvement that have no foundation in truth, being only the offspring of an improper bias—Prejudice and Malignity.—Baſe ſacrifice of the powers of an enlightened and intelligent mind, degrading to the human character. When by a reſolute exertion

of

of thoſe generous faculties of the ſoul, which ſtand oppoſed to thoſe vile propenſities of the mind, he would be led not only to acquieſce in, but alſo to co-operate with, every laudable ſcheme tending to promote the happineſs and proſperity of his native country, which, next to the principle of ſelf-preſervation, is undoubtedly what he owes to Nature and to God.

SECTION I.

Origin of the Name.

BERWICK is evidently of Saxon or Teutonic original. *Vic* or *Wick* is a name very commonly given to any town or village ſituated on a corner or angle where a ſtream or river terminates its courſe. Cambden derives it from the Saxon Beopnicapic, which ſignifies the town of the *Bernicians**. Among

* "The limit of Bernicia, on the ſouth, is ſometimes "ſaid,

the various etymologies given of the name of Berwick, that of *Aberwick* is not the leaſt probable; for *Aber* ſignifies the mouth of a river, and *Wick* a town at its mouth; hence Berwick, dropping the A, which is retained in Aberdeen, Aberbrothick, &c.—Some ſuppoſe that it takes its name from the Bar at the entrance of the Tweed, *q. d.* the town on the Bar. Others from Bear, founded on a notion that the neighbourhood was formerly infeſted by that animal; hence it is, that a bear, in the midſt of trees, makes the ſupporters, and part of the arms, of the corporation.

It is called Berwick *upon Tweed* to diſtinguiſh it from North Berwick in Eaſt Lothian, and a village called Berwick in Shropſhire; in the ſame manner as the birth-place of Shakeſpear is termed Stratford upon Avon, to diſtinguiſh

" ſaid, by the ancient Engliſh writers, to be the Tyne, " and ſometimes the Tees. In the ſame manner its " northern limit is ſometimes ſaid to be the Frith of " Forth, at other times the Tweed. It is probable that, " at different periods of time, its actual limits did thus " vary."—See Border Hiſtory, page 15.

tinguiſh it from other Stratfords, properly Strait-fords, in England.

SECTION II.

Situation and Extent.

BERWICK is pleaſantly and beautifully ſituated on the north* ſide of the river Tweed, long celebrated both in hiſtory and ſong, within half a mile of where it empties its waters into the German Ocean in the Bay of Berwick. It lies in 55 degrees 48 minutes north latitude, and 1 degree 45 minutes weſt longitude; being diſtant, by the great poſt-road which paſſes through the City of York, 336 miles north by weſt from London; 54 miles ſouth-eaſt from Edinburgh, by the ſame road which runs through Dunbar; and

* Berwick was originally a Scotch town.—See Chap. II. Sect. I.

and 56½ miles by the road through Greenlaw, the county town of Berwickſhire.

The ground, on which the town is built, has, in general, an eaſy aſcent from the river, though, in ſome ſtreets, ſuch as part of Hide-hill, Eaſtern and Weſtern Lanes, and Bank-hill, the acclivity is ſomewhat more conſiderable. From its facing the ſouth it fully enjoys the enlivening rays of the ſun. Its circumference, within the preſent walls, is one mile, one quarter, and two hundred and ſeventy-two yards; but taking the admeaſurement in the ſcite of the old walls, which will include the ſuburb of Caſtle-gate, the circumference will be found to extend to two miles and two hundred and eighty-two yards.

SECTION III.

Description of the Town, and Scenery of the Neighbourhood.

IT is not our intention here to enter into a deſcription of the *Public Buildings*, or the *Walls*, which every where completely ſurround the town, as they will be fully deſcribed in future ſections of this work. We ſhall, therefore, content ourſelves with giving, in this place, a general account of the town and neighbouring ſcenery, referring the reader, at the ſame time, to the ground plan of the town, which will afford him more clear ideas of the width and relative ſituation of the ſtreets than can be otherwiſe given.

The *figure* of Berwick, which is ſomewhat circular, approaches however nearer to that of an oval than that of a complete circle.

Independent of the public buildings, the town conſiſts of the following principal ſtreets and lanes; viz. High Street, formerly known

by

by the name of Mary-Gate, Hide-Hill, Sand-Gate, Bridge-Street, Church-Street, Wool-market, Silver-Street, Palace-Street, Backway, Eaſtern and Weſtern Lanes, with ſome other lanes of inferior note; beſides an imperfect ſquare, generally called the Palace, we have the Parade and Golden Square.

The *Buildings*, which generally are of free-ſtone covered with red tyles, extend in many places not only to the walls, but, in ſome parts, are really built on them. The houſes, particularly in the High-Street and Hide-hill, are, for the moſt part, three ſtories in height; and many of them are not only highly commodious within, but thoſe of modern erection are handſomely fronted: Nor are theſe improvements in building ſolely confined to the two ſtreets now mentioned, but this laudable ſpirit is to be diſcovered in other parts of the town.

A conſiderable number of the *Shops* exhibit an appearance of neatneſs and elegance greatly ſuperior to what they did a few years ago. And the taſte of the ſhopkeepers in ornament-

ing

ing their ſhops, and in diſplaying their goods, is ſuch as to rival ſimilar ſhops in the metropolis of either kingdom.

It would give us pleaſure could we ſay with truth, that a proper attention to the laying out of the *Streets* in a regular manner had been originally attended to. All of them are not only irregular, but intolerably ill paved; while ſome others, though labouring under the ſame diſadvantages, yet are ſufficiently wide and commodious. The principal ſtreet, however, and one through which there is conſtantly a very conſiderable thorough-fare, is ſhamefully cramped at the bottom, by the town-hall being injudiciouſly placed in the middle of it: And, near to the other end of the ſame ſtreet, a ſimilar obſtruction is occaſioned by the building called the Main Guard.

Notwithſtanding the general cenſure which we have thrown out on the negligence ſhown in the pavement of the town, yet candour requires that we ſhould beſtow much commendation on ſeveral individuals, who lately ſtepped forward, and, at their own expence, have paved the ground in the front of their own premiſſes

premiſſes. Examples highly worthy of the imitation of their fellow townſmen!

With regard to the *Lighting* of the town. The perſon who is under the diſagreeable neceſſity of walking the ſtreets in the dark winter's evening, will here and there meet with a glimmering lamp, whoſe faint light aſſiſts him but little in avoiding nuiſances. For ſome winters paſt, the High Street and Hidehill have been tolerably well lighted by means of a ſubſcription. More of this, however, when we come to treat of the police of the place. The *Bridge* will be deſcribed under the head of Public Buildings; and the *Reſervoir for water*, and the manner in which Berwick is ſupplied with that moſt uſeful article, will be detailed in Section 7. Chap. XVI.

Before entering upon a deſcription of the *Scenery* of the neighbourhood, this ſeems to be the proper place to notice the ſuburb of *Caſtle-gate* ſituated without the walls, near the north weſt part of the town. It conſiſts of one long broad ſtreet running nearly north, being the outlet to the great north road;

and a long range of houſes ſtretching from the further end of Caſtle-gate eaſtwards, called *Greenſes*, principally inhabited by fiſhermen and labourers.

Monſieur Jorvin wrote a deſcription of England and Scotland, publiſhed at Paris, A. D. 1672, which the editor of the Antiquarian Repertory thought worthy of being inſerted in that work. The account given in it of Berwick, and the adjoining country, contains ſeveral particulars which appear to be highly entitled to a place here.

" Berwick is the firſt town by which I re-
" entered England; and, being a frontier to
" England, has been fortified in different
" manners. There is in it at preſent a large
" garriſon, as in a place of importance to this
" kingdom. It is bounded by the river
" Tweed, which empties itſelf into the ſea,
" and has a great reflux, capable of bringing
" up large veſſels, was it not prevented by
" ſands at the entrance into its port. I ar-
" rived here about ten of the clock on a Sun-
" day; the gates were then ſhut during

"church time, but were opened at eleven, as "is the caſe in all fortified places. *Here is* "*an upper and a lower town*, which are both "on the ſide of a hill that ſlopes toward the "river. *On its top there is a ruined and aban-* "*doned Caſtle*, although its ſituation makes it "appear impregnable; it is environed on one "ſide by the ditch of the town; *on the other* "*ſide, by one of the ſame breadth, flanked by* "*many round towers and thick walls, which* "*incloſe a large palace; in the middle of which* "*riſes a lofty keep, or donjon, capable of a long* "*reſiſtance, and commanding all the environs* "*of the town.*

"The High Town incloſes within its walls "and ditches thoſe of the Lower, from which "it is only ſeparated by a ditch filled with "water. In the Upper Town the ſtreets are "ſtraight and handſome; but there are not "many rich inhabitants, they rather prefer-"ring the Lower Town, in which there are "*many great palaces*, ſimilar to that which "has been built near the great church; and "*in all the open areas are great fountains*, and "in one of them, the guard-houſe and pub-

"lic

" lic parade, before the town-hall or feffions-
" houfe, over which is the clock-tower of the
" town; fo that, by walking over Berwick,
" I difcovered it to be *one of the greateft and*
" *moft beautiful towns in England.*

" The greateft part of the ftreets in the
" Lower Town are either up or down hill,
" but they are filled with many rich merchants,
" on account of the convenience and vicinity
" of its port bordered by a large quay, along
" which the fhips are ranged. There is not
" a ftone bridge in all England longer or
" better built than that of Berwick, which
" has fixteen large and wonderfully wrought
" arches; *it is confidered as one of the moft re-*
" *markable curiofities in the kingdom.* I paffed
" over it in leaving the place. Adjoining to
" it is a large fuburb, *from whence* the coun-
" try is covered with heath and briars to
" Afhton, where there is a caftle: Bowklin,
" where the fea appears on the left, and a
" fmall ifland not far off, which forms a pret-
" ty good harbour, near a village, having a
" caftle.

* This appears to have been Holy Ifland, 12 miles fouth eaft from Berwick.

" caſtle. All this ſea coaſt is covered with " ſand banks, *and the interior country to Bel-* " *ford an entire deſert, as it is far above* 20 " *miles round about*, being only fitted for " feeding cattle, occaſioned by divers rivulets " which run through meadows, where great " herds of all ſorts of cattle may be ſeen feed- " ing."

How laviſh ſoever Nature has been in having beſtowed upon Berwick many ſingular and important local advantages, She has (confining ourſelves to the immediate neighbourhood of the town) but with a ſparing hand, appropriated to it much of the richneſs of rural ſcenery, affording only a very limited ſcope for the pencil of the delineator in landſcape, or for the deſcriptive powers of the writer in that branch of ſcience. Notwithſtanding the truth of this general obſervation, yet, when we inveſtigate this ſubject on a more comprehenſive ſcale, it appears to us to be by no means ſo ſterile as not to entitle it to our conſideration and particular diſcuſſion. The land proſpect, both

both to the ſouth and north, is extremely limited, and ſo barren, as in both of theſe directions, not to lay claim either to be called a romantic or a ſmooth placid ſcene. Sunnyſide hill, ſituated about a mile and a half ſouth from the town, obſtructs the view of the country farther in that direction. All of this high ground (between which and Berwick, Tweedmouth is interpoſed) is a common. A great part of its ſurface is broken and deſtroyed by roads that have led, and thoſe ſtill leading, to coal pits, ſtone quarries, and brickeries, &c. that are every where lying in large confuſed heaps. The luxuriant hand of nature is much reſtrained in clothing this ſpot with verdure. Hence, when viewed from Berwick, it preſents a diſguſting object to the eye, and impreſſes the mind of the ſtranger that he is in the neighbourhood of a poor and but thinly inhabited country. Were this moor to be divided, and the arable parts of it cultivated, incloſed, and trees planted in the hedge rows, and all the more barren parts planted with firs, it would ſoon impart

part to this neglected diftrict fuch a wildnefs and richnefs of fcenery, as would more than compenfate for the want of the wide extended view of Northumberland lying beyond this hill. This, at any rate, affords but a bleak and unrich profpect, arifing from the fcantinefs of plantings, and part of the lands in that neighbourhood having a poor foil, and much of the face of the country being broken in a zig-zag manner by coal pits and lime-ftone quarries, and the great many roads leading to them. We may here obferve, however, that the produce of thefe pits and quarries have made up moft amply for the defect of foil and fterility of the landfcape, they having been the principal means of enriching this quarter of Northumberland. The higheft weftern part of Sunnyfide hill is reforted to by military troops for exercifing upon, for which it is excellently well adapted. This part commands a very extenfive profpect of the furrounding country, overlooking almoft all the flat part of Berwickfhire, we enjoy from it a captivating view of that rich

county.

county. The town of Berwick appears to great advantage from every part of this high ground, and cannot but be confidered (including the bridge, river, and bay) as forming a very rich and picturefque piece of fcenery. It exhibits London in miniature. This is formed by the Tweed refembling the Thames, Berwick and Tweedmouth, London and Southwark. The author of this publication would rejoice to live to fee it rival London in extent, population, trade, and commerce. There is no view of the country from the town to the north and north by weft, as the walls completely intercept it in thefe directions. From the northern parts of the ramparts we have but an imperfect profpect of the fea in that quarter, and Caftlegate, with the rifing ground beyond it, ftretching towards Hallydown hill, obftruct it on that fide. From the Bell Tower, and fome fields contiguous to it, the low lying lands of Berwick, next to the German Ocean, appear to us. This fcene, which terminates at Lamberton race-ground, five miles diftant, excepting the ſea, has nothing in it peculiarly intereſting. The neat farm houſe and offices lately built at Lamberton, the property of Lieutenant Colonel Renton, which we have here in full view, enlivens the diſtant proſpect, and leſſens the gloomy effect of the moor. Travelling the road between Berwick and Lamberton is very pleaſant, as we have a full view of the ſea all the way, and rich fields on both ſides of the road. There are no trees to be ſeen in this tract, except at Marſhall Meadows, and a few at Newfarm. From the weſtern parts of the walls, and particularly from the Weſt Mound and Old Caſtle, we enjoy a proſpect extending both into Northumberland and Scotland upwards of 30 miles with the naked eye. In this wide range we comprehend many rich and beautiful tracts of country on both ſides of the Tweed. We have a diſtinct view of Hume Caſtle, in the county of Berwick, darting as it were its apparently lofty and magnificent towers among the encircling clouds. The celebrated Eildon Hills in the county of Roxburgh, next preſent themſelves to the enraptured

enraptured eye, and impreſs the mind of the beholder with admiration and awe.—May we not compare theſe towering verdant hills to ſiſters rivalling each other in richneſs of dreſs, beauty, and majeſtic ſtature? In turning a little to the left, and directing our eye to the ſouth by weſt, and allowing it to range between that point and ſouth weſt, we behold the renowned mountains of Cheviot, whoſe magnitude and immenſity of height entitle them to Alpin or Andean rank, and afford to the contemplative mind a grand and impreſſive inſtance of the wonders of Creative power. The bloody battle fought near theſe celebrated mountains, between the two illuſtrious heroes, Earls Piercy and Douglaſs, upon which the famous ballad of Chevy Chace is founded, ſtands recorded in the annals of the Hiſtory of Great Britain, and affords one among the too many ſhocking inſtances of wars having been in thoſe times carried on between the two nations with brutal ferocity, without having for their objects either the equilibrium of power, the balance of commerce, the policy of ſtates, or the peace of Europe. Inflamed with national pique, and impelled by an unſatiable thirſt of revenge, the armies of theſe contending kingdoms ruſhed to battle with a ſavage cruelty; and but ſeldom was the bow unbent, the ſword ſheathed, or the ſpear laid aſide, until the arms, which wielded them, could no longer excercife them to the farther effuſion of human gore. In thoſe rude and barbarous ages, wars were often levied on the principles of robbery, rapine, and plunder, ariſing from a loſt ſenſe of religious oaths and moral obligations, of the ſacred ties of honour and honeſty and compacts of nations. We are afraid we have made an unpardonable digreſſion, and ſhall, therefore, not proceed to contraſt the preſent happy ſtate of theſe two kingdoms (now, by the bleſſing of heaven, united in one) with that in which they were at the aera above alluded to. We ſhall only ſay, happy Britons, thrice happy Iſlanders, only think you are happy, and you and your poſterity (following your example in each ſucceſſive generation) will be really ſo.

"O

"O fortunatos nimium, ſua ſi bona nôrint,
"Agricolas! quibus ipſa, procul diſcordibus armis,
"Fundit humo facilem victum juſtiſſima tellus."

In looking up the Tweed from the Old Caſtle, and many other places near it, we cannot but admire the beautiful windings of that majeſtic ſtream, which we gradually, though reluctantly, loſe about two miles diſtant among ſome ſcattered trees beyond New Water Haugh.

The luxuriant verdure of the banks of the Tweed and adjoining fields, together with Spring Gardens, enrich and embelliſh this intereſting piece of ſcenery.

Theſe gardens are ſituated about half a mile from the farther extremity of the ſuburb of the town, and ſtretch along the ſteep banks of the north ſide of the river. They enjoy much of the genial warmth of the ſun from their ſo completely facing that animating luminary. From whatever quarter theſe Gardens are viewed in the vernal and ſummer months, the ſeveral little clumps of planting, which are irregularly interſperſed through them,

them, ſome being ſituated on projecting eminences, and others ſhooting forth their exuberant foliage, from natural excavations, impart to the whole a conſiderable degree of rural ſimplicity, and no ſmall ſhare of a romantic and pictureſque appearance.

The ſcenery of this diſtrict of the Tweed will, in the courſe of a few years, derive much additional richneſs and ornament from thoſe plantations which have lately been made by Sir Francis Blake, from the banks at New Water Haugh along the ſide of the river, and which extend nearly to thoſe young plantings ſituated on the weſt ſide of Spring Gardens. Hallydown Hill, famous in the Hiſtory of Berwick, is diſtinctly ſeen from many parts of the walls and the immediate vicinity of the town, being diſtant from it two miles north by weſt. This eminence fully commands the whole of the town and quay: Were the top of it planted with trees, it would become an uſeful object, as it would afford an excellent land-mark for ſhips at ſea, and would alſo greatly heighten the ſcenery

of

of the neighbourhood. The rich inclofed fields intervening between Tweedmouth and Ord Houfe, through which there is a pleafant foot road leading to the village of Eaft Ord, look beautiful and enlivening viewed from the ramparts and other places of the town.

In looking down the river, either from Spring Gardens or the Old Caftle, we are prefented with a fcene truly picturefque and captivating, compofed of the Bridge with its fifteen arches, feveral windings of the Tweed, moft part of Berwick, and all Tweedmouth and Spittal. Standing in either of thefe fituations, and extending the view farther in the fame direction, we diftinctly behold Holy Ifland, with its caftle, fituated at the extremity of the bay, about ten miles diftant by fea, and twelve by land. In a clear day, we plainly perceive the houfes, the fandy beach, and the foaming furf on the weftern parts of the ifland. In fome ftates of the atmofphere, the caftle appears in the figure of a large cone, fufpended between heaven and the ocean, forming a fingular and romantic object, from which

which the eye cannot withdraw itſelf without reluctance. In exerciſing the powers of viſion in a ſouth-eaſt direction from the iſland, Bamborough Caſtle, built on ſtupendous perpendicular rocks, overlooking the ſea, twenty miles diſtant from Berwick by land, appears in all the ſolemnity of rude magnificence. From all the northern and eaſtern parts of the ramparts, we have a moſt complete and intereſting view of the bay, German Ocean, the iſland and caſtles juſt now noticed. Acroſs the Tweed, near its junction with the ſea, the lands to the ſouthward opens for ſeveral miles upon the view, but the variegated colourings of nature, ſucceeding to cultivation, are loſt in the diſtant proſpect. The beauties, too, of the landſcape lie in confuſed arrangement; and frequently the whole is enveloped and totally obſcured in ſea vapour. The richeſt proſpects which Berwick has to boaſt of are thoſe from the Bridge, particularly during the time of fiſhing ſalmon; the richneſs of theſe views conſiſts, in the firſt place, in the tranſparent Tweed, with ſtately majeſty,

majeſty, gliding down between its proud, luxuriant, and graſſy banks. This enchanting river, after making many artleſs and beautiful windings, diſembogues its waters into the German Ocean, and thereby produces a conflux and ſeeming diſcord with it; the point of which may be ſaid to be manifeſted in the raging and roaring billows on the bar.

2dly, In the great number of boats employed both above and below the Bridge in bringing to land thouſands of ſalmon of equal quality to any in the world.

3dly, In the perpetual hurry and buſtle on the quay in loading and unloading ſmacks and other veſſels.

4thly, In viewing the building of ſhips, both on the Berwick and Tweedmouth ſides of the river, that are allowed to be the faſteſt and ſafeſt ſailers which go to ſea.

The proſpect we enjoy in looking up the river from the Bridge is enlivening; the ſcenery here terminates in Spring Gardens and ſome farm houſes ſituated on elevated fertile grounds,

grounds on the north ſide of the Tweed. From the Bridge we plainly diſcover Holy Iſland in the ſkirts of the horizon. Bamborough Caſtle is alſo diſtinctly ſeen from this place, and reſembles a huge mortar raiſed to an angle of 45 degrees. From a great many places ſituated within the liberties, we have very extenſive and intereſting proſpects both of the ſea and the ſurrounding country; the principal of which we ſhall only ſtate in a curſory manner, as a minute deſcription of them would run out to an unpardonable length.

At Letham farm, two miles from the town, enchanting views of various extent are to be found. This healthy ſpot fronts the Tweed, with many faſcinating peeps of which we are highly gratified. We here diſcover objects upwards of thirty miles diſtant; among theſe are the following hills, viz. Rubers Law, Dunyeon, Minto Craigs, Wiſp, with ſeveral others of inferior note. Theſe hills are ſituated in the neighbourhood of Jedburgh. Seven caſtles can be counted from this place; viz. Berwick, Holy Iſland, Bamborough, Norham,

ham, Hume, Twiſel, and Dunſe Caſtles. The eighth is only about a mile and a half diſtant, namely, Edrington Caſtle, the property of Joſeph Marſhall, Eſq; but an intervening piece of high ground prevents it from being ſeen. The beautiful villa of Sanſon Seal, belonging to Burnet Roger Greive, Eſq; which is built on a delightful riſing piece of ground, fronting the ſouth, ſituated about a mile north by weſt from Letham, enjoys all the proſpects laſt deſcribed in a pre-eminent degree. To the north of Sanſon Seal, at a very little diſtance from it, ſtands Hallydown Hill. When we arrived at the ſummit of it, and began to exerciſe the powers of viſion, our attention was inſtantaneouſly arreſted, and a great degree of admiration excited upon viewing the numerous highly picturеſque objects which, except towards the north, every where ſurrounded us.

The ſtupenduous Cheviot, with his ſnowy cap, commanded much intereſt, as well as the chain of inferior mountains, which run acroſs the iſland almoſt to the weſtern ſeas. From this high ground, the extent of profpect in feveral directions is very great. It would fill many a page to enumerate all the different objects that here prefent themfelves to the eye, and to defcribe the great variety of rural fcenery which diverfify and grace the landfcape.

From the top of the hill, near to Riddell's Stead, about a mile north by eaft from Hallydown Hill, we command the moft extenfive view of the German Ocean to be found in all the liberties of Berwick.

We cannot, in juftice to this fubject, but remark, that the traveller, in going from Berwick towards Dunfe, muft, in fine weather, be much gratified with the beautiful fcenery which exhibits itfelf all the way to the extremities of the boundaries. In approaching near Berwick, by this road, to the beauties of the country which are there to be feen, we have to add thofe of the town—the Bridge—the Tweed—the Bay and German Ocean—Holy Ifland—Bamborough Caftle, &c. &c. The whole together form a more interefting

and

and enlivening piece of ſcenery than is moſt-ly to be met with. To conclude this ſubject it may be added, that from the higheſt bal-luſtrades of the Town-hall we were for ſome time almoſt loſt in admiration at the numerous captivating objects which preſented themſelves to us in whatever direction we turned. To attempt ſuch a delineation of their ſeveral beauties as they are well entitled to would far exceed the limits aſſigned to this part of the work. We ſhall therefore take our leave of the ſcenery of Berwick, recommending theſe laſt faſcinating views to the attention of the pencil.

SECTION IV.

Climate.

THE Town of Berwick and its Liberties have very univerſally obtained the cha-racter of being ſituated in a healthy climate, which opinion (from certain circumſtances reſting upon the teſt of experience, and that will

will be taken notice of in another part of this work) appears to be well founded. This diſtrict, however, experiences all that inconſtancy of weather which may be ſaid to characteriſe the iſland; for it is not uncommon to ſee in the ſame day a viciſſitude of temperature diſplayed of the moſt oppoſite tendency and effect.

The air of Berwick is generally ſaid to be cold and penetrating, which obſervation is perfectly juſt when we compare its atmoſphere with thoſe of other towns ſituated in the interior parts of the country.

As it ſtands almoſt immediately on the ſea, and on the banks of a very wide river, running from the weſt, and from its not being ſheltered by any plantings, it is much expoſed to the north, eaſt, and north-eaſt winds, as well as to thoſe which blow from the weſt and ſouth by weſt. The latter frequently ruſh with ſuch violence down the Tweed, that between the under part of Caſtle-gate and the Scotch-gate, where there are no buildings, perſons are ſometimes carried off

their

their feet, while others are thrown upon the ground. Theſe occurrences take place alſo on the Bridge, beyond the north toll-bar, oppoſite to the Old Caſtle.

From the high and inclined ſituation of moſt of the principal ſtreets, and from all of them, as well as all the lanes of any note, being thorough fares, the town in general participates of a very free circulation of air, particularly the High-Street, Hide-Hill, upper part of Church-Street, Woolmarket, Back-way, and Parade.

The effects of thoſe frequent gales that occur here from the weſt and ſouth-weſt, and of ſuch an uninterrupted circulation of air, which the town ſo generally enjoys, contribute, no doubt, to rendering it healthy;—ſo ſalutary a conſequence would be derived in a ſuperior degree were it not for the walls, which extend from the weſt to the moſt eaſterly mound, obſtructing a freer admiſſion of the air into the town.

The generally acknowledged healthineſs of Berwick, joined to its local advantages, have frequently

frequently induced families, as well as individuals retiring from bufinefs, to fettle here.

This climate appears to be a medium between thofe too wet and thofe too dry. It is not peculiarly liable to fogs. As in other parts on the fea coaft, fnow does not lie long in this neighbourhood.

When it rains very heavily in the weft, accompanied with violent gales from that quarter, Tweed rifes fuddenly in thefe parts, (particularly if the ground has been previoufly very wet or covered with much fnow), that upon fome occafions rolls down, as it were in huge columns, with great majefty, threatening to fweep every thing before it, which irrefiftibly impreffes the mind of the fpectator with refpectful awe, and a filent dread leading him, at the fame time, to contemplate the unlimited and uncontroulable powers of the Author of the univerfe, as well as of his great goodnefs in having fcattered rivers, rivulets, and fprings all over the earth for fertilizing the foil and many other important and ufeful purpofes.

SECTION V.

Boundaries and Extent of the Liberties of Berwick.

THE form of the pariſh of Berwick approaches nearly to an equilateral triangle, two ſides of which being fully three miles each, and the other ſide ſome what more. One ſide of the triangle extends from the entrance to the harbour northwards, terminating at the grounds of Lamberton; a ſecond runs from thence weſt by ſouth, and paſſing the houſes of Mordington and Edrington, and afterwards croſſing the river Whitadder, terminates at the Tweed, a little way above Gainſlaw-houſe; the remaining third ſide goes down cloſe by the river all the way to its termination at the Bar. In the eaſt, theſe liberties are bounded by the German Ocean to the north-weſt; and ſouth-weſt, by the lands of Lamberton, Mordington, Edrington,

Edrington, and Paxton, all lying in the county of Berwick; and in the south by the river Tweed. Several small estates lie within the liberties of the corporation, viz. Castlehills, belonging to Mrs Askew; Letham, to Sir Francis Blake, Baronet; New Water Haugh, to Watson Balderston, Esq; Gainslaw, to Robert Ogle, Esq; on the Tweed; Sanson Seal, to Burnet Roger Greive, Esq; Bates Cross, to Blake Stow Lundie, Esq; and Cumberland Bower, to Robert Romer, Esq; those on the west side of Hallydown Hill; and Marshall Meadows, at the extremity of the parish, on the German Ocean, the property of George Hogarth, Esq; Mandlin (or Magdalene) Fields, close to the walls, the property of Lord Lisburne.

CHAP.

CHAP. II.

Hiſtory of the Town.

SECTION I.

Ancient Hiſtory of the Town.

IT would require a volume to detail, with minuteneſs, the hiſtory of this ancient and celebrated frontier town, and the various important and memorable tranſactions connected with it: A ſhort ſketch or abſtract of them (drawn from authentic ſources) is all that is conſiſtent with the nature of ſuch a work as this. Beſides, did the limits of this volume admit of it, moſt of our readers, inſtead of peruſing, with pleaſure and amuſement, a minute narration of the ſavage barbarities which are every where to be met with in the ancient hiſtory of this place, would turn from it with horror and diſguſt. Should any one, however, wiſh for a more particular detail of the ſcenes of bloodſhed and devaſtation which were carried on in this town and its vicinity, during the frequent wars between England and Scotland, which raged with ſuch ferocity for many centuries, his wiſh may be fully gratified by peruſing Leland's Collectanea, or an excellent work publiſhed about twenty years ago by Mr Hutchinſon, entitled, A View of Northumberland, in two volumes quarto. The border hiſtory of England and Scotland, by Mr Redpath, may alſo be conſulted with advantage. The antiquity of the town of Berwick is, beyond all doubt, very great. Its very early hiſtory, however, is ſo much blended with fable and contradiction, that we ſhall not attempt to inveſtigate it, nothing reſpecting its hiſtory being known with truth, whilſt the country was poſſeſſed by the ancient Britons, or was held under the dominion of the Roman Empire. It is mentioned, however, as a place of ſtrength in

the

the reign of Osbert, one of the last kings of Northumberland, who died in the beginning of the ninth century; and it is said to have been the place where the Danes, in one of their invasions, under Hubba, landed about the year 867.

It continued in the possession of the Saxons for some time; and afterwards in that of the Danes; until the Scottish King, Gregory, who was cotemporary with Alfred, and like him was justly surnamed the Great, took it by assault. The garrison consisted of Danes and Picts. The former he put to the sword, but spared the latter. From Berwick, Gregory pursued the Danes into Northumberland, where he defeated them; and then passed the winter in Berwick. This Prince died in the year 892. About the year 1098, Berwick, having for many centuries constituted a part of the dominions of the Scots Crown, was given by Edgar to the See of Durham (as is related by the historians of these times) in honour of St Cuthbert; owing to whose interposition, he obtained a victory over the forces

ces of Donald, who had ufurped the Scottifh Throne. This donation was foon after refumed, in confequence of the ingratitude of Ralph Flambert, who had been confecrated Bifhop of that See.

William the I. of Scotland (known by the appellation of William the Lion) who, in 1174, had joined Henry's three fons, and others of the Englifh nobility, in a rebellion againft their Sovereign, was taken prifoner at Alnwick Caftle, whether he had retired, and was carried in chains before Henry. Soon after this, an accommodation took place between Henry and his fons; and the prifoners on both fides were fet at liberty, William only excepted: Who bore his confinement with great impatience. Of this, Henry took advantage; and obliged him to pay homage for the whole kingdom of Scotland, and acknowledge that he held it only as a feu of the Crown of England; and, as a fecurity, he was forced to deliver up to Henry the Fort of Berwick, together with all the other principal Forts of Scotland; William agreeing to

fubfift

ſubſiſt the Engliſh garriſons which were put into theſe Caſtles. David, the King's brother, with twenty barons, who were preſent at the ſigning of this ſhameful compact, were put into the hands of Henry, as hoſtages for William's good faith: After which the King was ſet at liberty, and returned to Scotland. The Scots continued in ſubjection to the Engliſh till 1189, when Richard I. ſtiled Richard *Coeur de Lion*, previous to his undertaking an expedition to the Holy Land, relieved William and his ſubjects from that ſubjection, which even the Engliſh theirſelves conſidered as forced and unjuſt, but not before he made William pay him 10,000 marks (about twenty thouſand pounds of our preſent money) which he accepted as an equivalent for the releaſe of the vaſſalage of Scotland, and the Fortreſſes of Berwick and Roxburgh. William I. was ſucceeded in the Scottiſh Crown by Alexander II. who revived his claim to Northumberland, and the other northern counties; but John not only refuſed to accede to the demands of Alexander,

ander, but made preparations for invading Scotland. Accordingly the latter fell upon Northumberland, which he eaſily reduced, while the former entered the Scottiſh nation. Alexander retired to defend his own country; upon which John, after burning Alnwick and ſome other towns, took Berwick. He afterwards directed his operations againſt Edinburgh; but being oppoſed by Alexander, at the head of an army, he precipitately marched back. Alexander did not fail to purſue; and John, to cover his retreat, burnt the towns of Coldingham and Berwick; the inhabitants of which latter place, he treated with the greateſt cruelty. In this retreat, the King of England himſelf ſet his men an example of barbarity and ingratitude, by ſetting fire every morning to the houſe in which he had lodged the preceding night. In ſhort, ſuch deſolation did John ſpread all around him, that Alexander found it impoſſible to continue his purſuit; for which reaſon, he marched weſtward, and invaded England by the way of Carliſle. This place he took, and fortified;

after

after which, he marched ſouth, as far as Richmond, receiving homage from all the great Barons as he went along. At Richmond, he was again ſtopped by John's ravages, and obliged to return through Weſtmoreland to his own dominions.

Berwick was afterwards rebuilt and fortified by the Scots; and a meeting took place here, in the year 1216, of the Archbiſhop of York and the Biſhop of Durham, to abſolve, from a ſentence of excommunication, Alexander, who attended in perſon.

On the 2d. day of Auguſt 1291, the States of England and Scotland, with Edward I. aſſembled at Berwick, in order to determine the claims of Robert Bruce and John Baliol, who, during the inter-regnum, had appeared as competitors for the Scottiſh crown; but this important point was not decided till after ſeveral adjourned meetings of this aſſembly, when, in the great hall of the caſtle, upon the 17th day of November in the following year, the king appointed John Baliol ſucceſſor to the crown.

Yet

Yet the reſtleſs and ambitious ſpirit of Edward was productive of much calamity to this place. For Berwick having remained more than two thirds of a century in the undiſturbed poſſeſſion of the Scots, John Baliol, provoked by his haughtineſs, in 1295, paſſed the Tweed with his army, and committed conſiderable depredations in England: His career however, was ſoon checked by the forces of Edward, who, in the ſpring of 1296, obliged Baliol to reſign his crown, and took the town and garriſon, which he ſtormed both by ſea and land. In the town, there was a building called the *Red-Hall*, which certain Flemings poſſeſſed by the tenure of defending it at all times againſt the King of England. Thirty of theſe maintained their ground for a whole day againſt the Engliſh army, but at night, the building being ſet on fire, all of them periſhed in the flames. The ſame day the caſtle capitulated; and the garriſon, conſiſting of two thouſand men, marched out with all the honours of war, after having ſworn never to bear arms againſt England.

Some

Some idea may be formed of the population of the town from the ſlaughter attendant upon the aſſault. According to Boethius, 7,000; according to the Scottiſh hiſtorian, Fordun, 7,500, and, if we were to credit Mathews of Weſtminſter, no ſmaller a number than 60,000 were cruelly butchered on that occaſion. Previous to the reduction of the town and caſtle, three ſhips, belonging to the Engliſh navy, were burnt in the haven by the townſmen; and, it is ſaid, that the others, which were much diſabled, had conſiderable difficulty in eſcaping, owing to their having imprudently ſailed over the bar into the harbour, their crews wiſhing to participate in the glory of the army. What number of Edward's troops were ſlain is not particularly mentioned either by the Scottiſh or Engliſh hiſtorians of theſe days. Hutchinſon mentions, that this carnage may be aſcribed to a reſentment of the cruelties committed the preceding year by the men of Berwick, and the fighting men of Fife, in attacking certain Engliſh veſſels that had entered the port, ſetting fire to the ſhips, and putting the ſeveral crews to death.

Berwick, after this cataſtrophe, became filled with Engliſh inhabitants, and the king received the homage * of the Scots nobility here, on

* Moſt of our readers will, we doubt not, be gratified with a ſight of the oath of fealty then adminiſtered; for which reaſon, we here tranſcribe it at length. "Becauſe "we are under the ſubjection of the thrice noble prince, "and our dear Lord Sire Edward, King of England, Lord "of Ireland, and Duke of Aquitain, we do faithfully "promiſe for ourſelves, and for our heirs, upon pain of "body and eſtate, that we will ſerve him truly and loyally, "againſt all manner of people that may live and die, "whenever it ſhall be required or commanded by our "ſaid Lord, the King of England, or his heirs. That "we will hinder him from damage as much as we can, "and ſet upon his enemies with all our forces, wherever "they may be found; and to the end that we may firmly keep and hold theſe preſents, we do bind ourſelves, "our heirs, and our goods, and we have ſworn to this "upon the bleſſed Evangeliſts. Beſides, all we that are "preſent, and every of us ſeparately, have done homage "to our Lord, the King of England, in theſe words.

"I will be true and loyal, and bear true faith and allegiance to Edward, King of England, and his heirs, "and ſerve him with life and limb, and do him all earthly honour againſt all manner of people that may live and "die on the 24th of Auguſt 1296, in the preſence of an Engliſh Parliament ſummoned for that purpoſe. An Exchequer, for the receipt of the Scots revenue, was eſtabliſhed here the ſucceeding year, on the ſame principles of that at Weſtminſter.

It would appear as if fate had decreed, that the Engliſh ſhould not remain long in poſſeſſion of this garriſon town in theſe ages; for the renowned Sir William Wallace, † in the year

" die; and from henceforth, I will not bear arms, nor be " aiding in council againſt him, or againſt his heirs, on " any cauſe whatſoever. So help me God and all the " Saints. In witneſs of theſe things, we have made theſe " letters patent, and ſealed them with our ſeals. Given " at Berwick upon Tweed, the 28th day of Auguſt, in " the year of the reign of our ſaid Lord the King of Eng- " land 24."

† His ſtature and ſtrength were gigantic; his aſpect and addreſs pleaſing and attractive; he was ſubtile in deviſing, and dexterous in the execution of the moſt adventurous and perilous projects. In an old poem, he is thus deſcribed.

Wallace

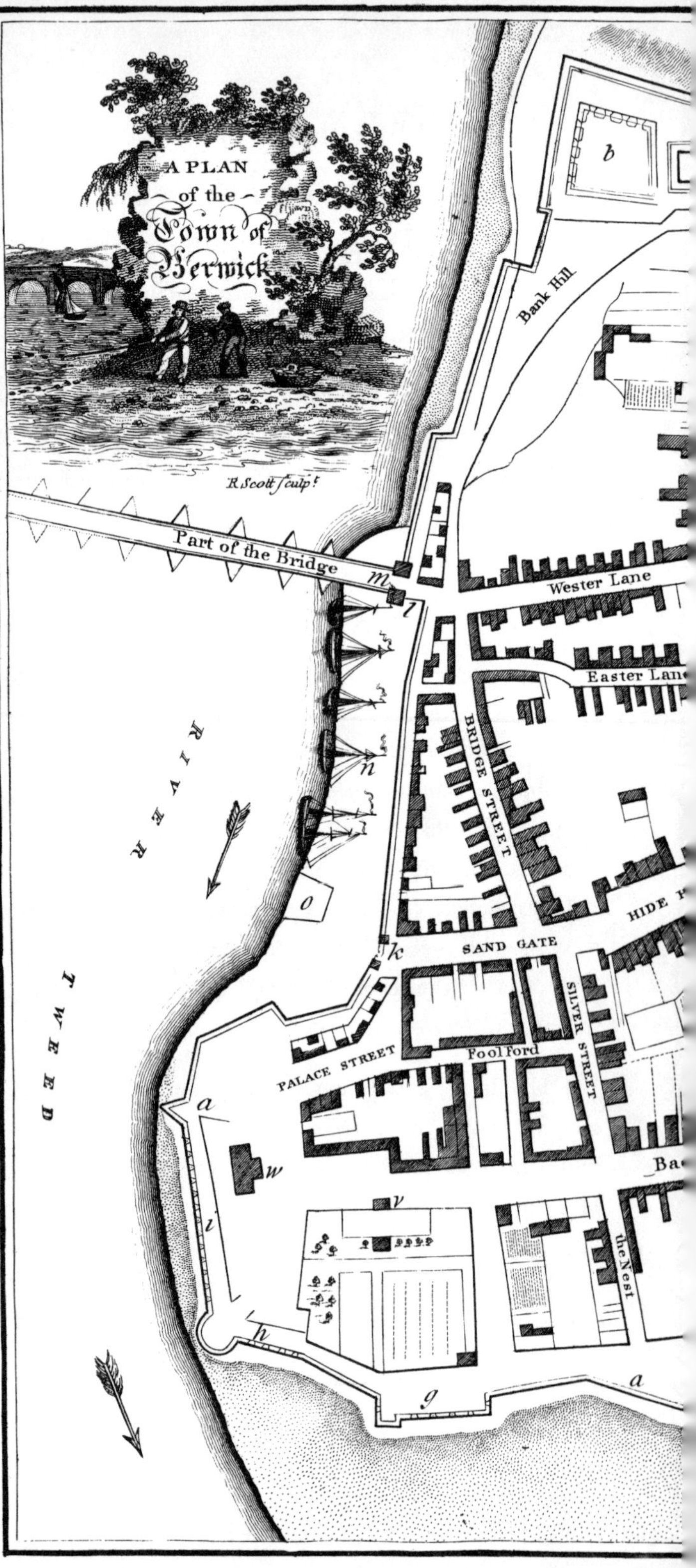

A PLAN of the Town of Berwick
R.Scott sculp.t
Part of the Bridge
Bank Hill
Wester Lane
Easter Lane
BRIDGE STREET
RIVER
TWEED
HIDE H
SAND GATE
SILVER STREET
PALACE STREET
Fool Ford
the Nest

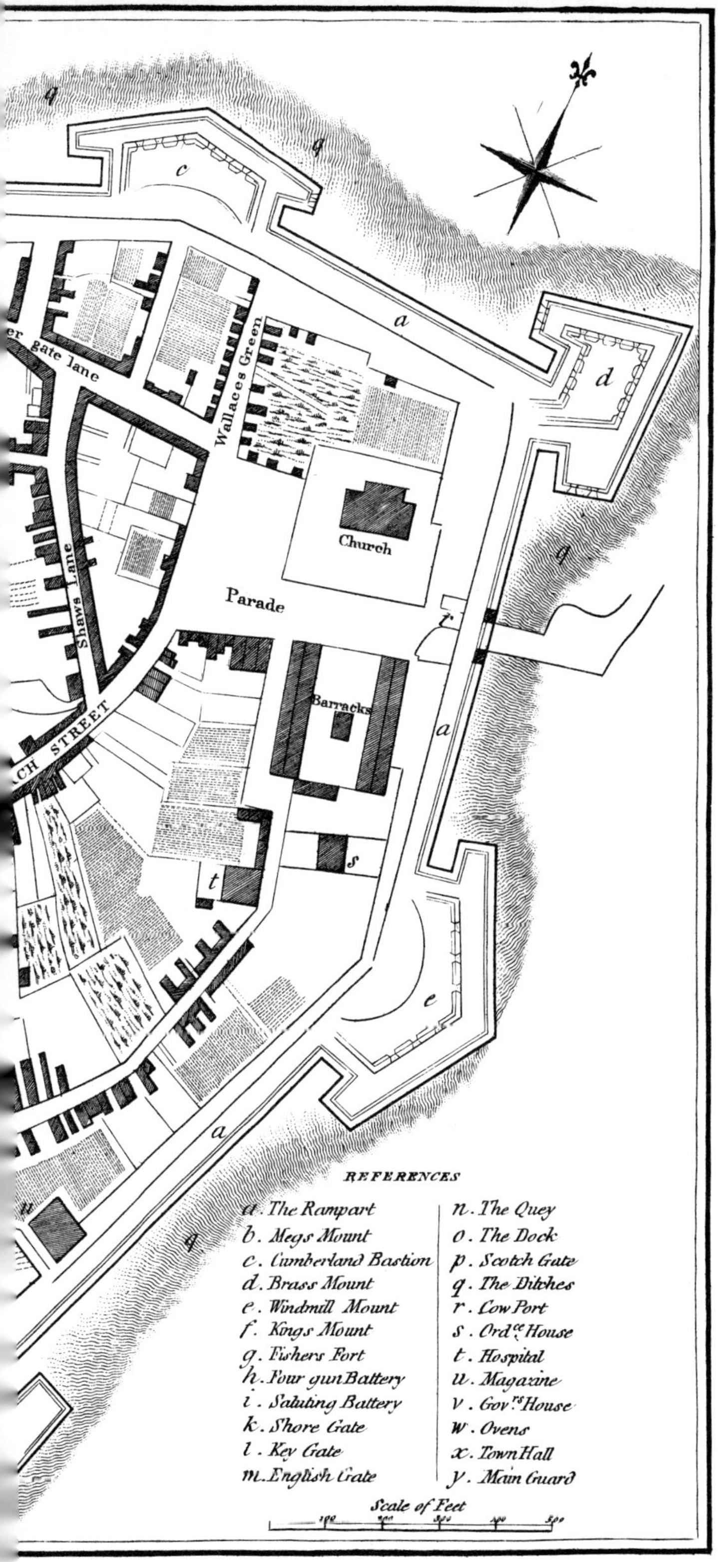

gate lane
Wallaces Green
Shaws Lane
Church
Parade
Barracks
CH STREET
REFERENCES
a. The Rampart
b. Megs Mount
c. Cumberland Bastion
d. Brass Mount
e. Windmill Mount
f. Kings Mount
g. Fishers Fort
h. Four gun Battery
i. Saluting Battery
k. Shore Gate
l. Key Gate
m. English Gate
n. The Quey
o. The Dock
p. Scotch Gate
q. The Ditches
r. Cow Port
s. Ord^ce House
t. Hospital
u. Magazine
v. Gov^rs House
w. Ovens
x. Town Hall
y. Main Guard
Scale of Feet
100
200
300
400
500

year 1297, took arms in defence of the kingdom; and having appeared with his forces before the

Wallace ſtature of greatneſs and of height
Was judgéd thus by diſcretion of ſight,
That ſaw him both on Cheval and in Weed, F. I.
Nine quarters large of height he was indeed. 6 $11\frac{1}{4}$
Third part that length in ſhoulders brode was he,
Right ſeemly ſtrong and luſty for to ſee;
In limmes great, with ſtalwart pace and ſound,
His brands hard, with armes long and round;
His hands made right like to a palmeir,
Of man-like make, with nails long and cleir.
Proportioned fair and long was his viſage,
Right ſad of ſpeech, and able of courage.
Both breaſted high, with ſturdy craig and greet,
His lippes round, his noſe ſquare and neat.
Burning brown hair on brows and brees light,
Cleir aſper eyes like diamonds full bright.
Under his chin, on his left ſide was ſeene
(By hurt) a wan, his colour was ſangueene.
Wounds he had, in mony divers place,
But fair and whole well keeped was his face.
Of riches als he keept no proper thing,
Gave that he wan, like Alexander the King.
In time of peace meek as a mind ſhould bee,
When war approached the right Hector was hee.
To Scotſmen right and good credence he gave,
But known enemies they could him nought deceive.

the place, the inhabitants quickly evacuated it. Some writers blame Creſſingham, the king's treaſurer, for this unfortunate event, in having neglected to fortify the garriſon, agreeable to the expreſs orders of Edward himſelf. The caſtle, however, which was ſtrong and well maintained, after a long blockade, was happily relieved by an immenſe army of horſe and foot ſent by the regency.

Wallace, notwithſtanding the ſucceſs with which his inſurrection was at firſt crowned, after experiencing different reverſes of fortune, was ſhamefully betrayed into the hands of his enemies; and in 1305, he was executed, and one half of his body ordered to be expoſed on the Bridge of Berwick. Many perſons of note, among whom was Neil, the brother of Robert Bruce, were taken priſoners and ſent to Berwick, where they were condemned, and ſentenced to be hanged, drawn, and quartered.

King Edward ordered the Counteſs of Buchan to be ſhut up in a wooden cage, in one of the towers of Berwick Caſtle, for hav-

ing

ing crowned Robert Bruce King of Scotland at Scone; arrogantly aſſuming to herſelf the office of her brother the Earl of Fife, whoſe duty only it was, by hereditary right, to execute that high office. During ſix years ſhe continued in this confinement, when, by the royal clemency of Edward II. ſhe was releaſed.

The year 1307 was productive of an event which filled the Scottiſh nation with joy, namely, the death of Edward I. at Carliſle in the month of July.

Berwick was honoured with the company of King Edward II. his Queen, and nobles, during the winter of the year 1310, his Majeſty being on his return from an invaſion of Scotland *.

A

* During this invaſion, the cauſe of the Scots was favoured, and the progreſs and operations of the Engliſh greatly retarded, by a ſcarcity which prevailed at this time in Scotland; for, as magazines and other reſources of modern war were then unknown, the Engliſh army were much impeded in their operations, and found it impoſſible to ſubſiſt in the country. Hutchinſon ſays, that the dearth was ſo great, that the people fed on horſe fleſh and other carrion.

A ſhort period, of leſs than two years, after the departure of the Engliſh Monarch, was diſtinguiſhed by a daring attempt on Robert Bruce, the grandſon of him who ſtood in competition with Baliol. He endeavoured, in 1312, by a ſcalade, to take the town and fortreſs of Berwick. The attack was made in the night, and had nearly ſucceeded, the ſcaling-ladders having been all fixed, when the barking of a dog gave the alarm to the garriſon, who repulſed the aſſailants with great loſs.

The progreſs of the Scots, headed by Robert, became the object of general reſentment and indignation to the Engliſh nation. Edward reſolving, if poſſible, completely to check their inroads, aſſembled the whole military force of England, which, according to the Scots writers, amounted to one hundred thouſand men, but which was probably much inferior to that number.

Theſe he rendezvouſed at Berwick. Meanwhile Robert collected his army, not exceeding thirty thouſand combatants; it being, however,

however, composed of men who had distinguished themselves by many acts of valour, who were rendered desperate by their situation, and who were inured to all the varieties of fortune, might justly, under such a leader, be deemed formidable.

The Scottish Monarch chose, as the field of battle, a piece of ground about three miles south-west from Stirling on the banks of Bannock-burn. Thither Edward, who, with a view of relieving Stirling Castle, which at that time was blockaded by the Scots troops, marched with his army, which was allowed to be the finest that England had ever produced. The particulars of the bloody conflict which ensued, we have not here room to relate. Suffice it to say, that it ended completely in favour of the Scots; securing to them their independence, and establishing Robert Bruce on the throne of that kingdom. The number of slain, on these occasions, are usually magnified; most authors, however, admit that it was the most complete overthrow which the English monarchy had ever sustained fustained fince the time of William the Conqueror.

Bruce, after the rout of the enemy, ordered the fortifications of Stirling Caftle to be levelled with the ground. This battle, which lafted feveral days, commenced on mid-fummer-day, in the 1314. Upon this occafion, the remarkable lofs of the Privy Seal caufed Edward to iffue a proclamation advifing his fubjects of this circumftance; and it is afferted that it was dated from Berwick the third day after his defeat.

The King of the Scots, defirous of availing himfelf of the fucceffes he had lately obtained, fent his armies the fame year into England, and, meeting with no oppofition, ravaged the northern counties. He befieged Carlifle, which was faved by Sir Andrew Harcla the governor. According to fome hiftorians, he was more fuccefsful in an attack againft Berwick, which yielded to his affault. But writers of more credit inform us, that Berwick, after remaining in the poffeffion of the Englifh twenty years, was betrayed, by the Commander of the town, into the hands of the Earl of Murray, who headed a body of Robert's forces ſometime in 1318.

An attempt to recover this place by a ſcalade (ſeldom now adopted ſince gun-powder came into general uſe, and the walls of towns have been flanked) was made by Edward II. in September, the following year. On the firſt of the month, he approached the town with a numerous body of troops, which were well ſupplied with proviſions, by means of a fleet fitted out for that purpoſe. On the ſeventh, an eſcalade was attempted in different places at the ſame time; and an exertion likewiſe was made to ſcale the walls next the harbour, by means of an engine which had been carried there in a ſhip. But this proved abortive; and the ſhip, being ſtranded, was burnt. A more general aſſault was made on the 13th; and, with a view to undermine the wall, a huge machine called a *ſow* *, (unknown to modern engineers),

* This is the firſt occaſion where we have any mention made of this engine, which, in many particulars, reſembled the

gineers), built ſo as to protect a number of men, was placed cloſe to the wall: but the Scots contrived to ſplit the ſow, and diſlodge its contents. It is reported that the attack on Mary-Gate *, when the draw-bridge was burnt down, had nearly ſucceeded, the gate (known by the name of Scots-Gate) being almoſt deſtroyed; but the detachment of troops employed on that ſervice were neceſſitated to give it up, owing to a ſtrong force which was ſent from the caſtle to defend that quarter. Meanwhile, the ſoldiers employed within the walls being nearly exhauſted, by the continual haraſſments of their enemies for almoſt a fortnight, would (as is almoſt commonly the fate of the beſieged ſooner or later) moſt probably have capi-

the *teſtudo arieteria* of the ancients. It appears to have been a large fabric, compoſed of timber, and well roofed, having ſtages within it; and in height ſurpaſſing the wall of the town, which at that time was of no inconſiderable elevation. It was moved upon wheels, and ſerved for the double purpoſe of conducting the miners to the foot of the wall, and armed men to the ſtorm.

* Now called the High-Street.

capitulated, had not the Earl of Lancaster, who had been suspected of holding a secret correspondence with the King of Scots, withdrawn his Majesty's forces, owing to a pique which he had long had against the King his master, and which his malevolence led him very unpardonably to display upon this occasion. This circumstance added to an invasion of England, which was then conducted by the Earl of Murray and Lord Douglas, prudently weighed with Edward to cease renewing any further attack upon the garrison.

Edward's Queen, who at this time had taken refuge in the city of York, escaped narrowly being taken prisoner by the forces of the Lords Murray and Douglas, who had penetrated nearly so far south.

After the siege of Berwick was raised, Robert, elated by his prosperity and entertaining hopes of making some very important conquests on the English, raised and strengthened the walls of Berwick, added many towers, and put the fortifications in a more complete state of defence against future besiegers;

well

well aware that this was a place of no leſs conſequence to the Scots than to their more ſouthern neighbours.

In the year 1323, May 30th, Robert Bruce confirmed at Berwick the treaty of peace entered into with King Edward II. by his plenipotentiaries at Biſhop Thorpe near York.

In 1328, Edward III. renounced all right to the dominion or ſovereignty of Scotland, which he and ſome of his predeceſſors had endeavoured to obtain. In conſideration of which, and as a compenſation for the loſſes ſuſtained by England through Robert and his ſubjects, Edward received from the King of Scotland, and the eſtates of his kingdom, letters patent, binding themſelves to pay to him, at three different terms in three years, at Tweedmouth, the ſum of 20,000l. Sterling, ſubjecting themſelves to the coercion of the Apoſtolic See for fulfilling theſe ſtipulations.

A ſhort time after this, in the ſame year, Joan, ſiſter to King Edward III. having entered into a contract of marriage with David, ſon and heir of Robert Bruce, was conveyed

to

to Berwick with great pomp and ſplendor, where ſhe was received by Earl Murray and Lord Douglas, the repreſentatives of the King, he himſelf being then ſick; and the nuptials were celebrated with great joy and magnificence. She obtained the appellation of *Make Peace;* and brought with her the Ragman Roll, and all the records which had been carried off by Edward I. to be again depoſited among the Archieves of Scotland.

Upon occaſion of this royal marriage the nobles of both nations made a magnificent ſhow;—and a ſumptuous diſplay of their numerous attendants crowded the place with that oſtentatious ſolemnity which, in thoſe days of chivalry, embelliſhed public ſpectacles. What conſtituted the chief objects, which more eſpecially attracted the attention of the numerous ſpectators, who eagerly preſſed forward to witneſs this ſplendid cavalcade, were long trains of horſes ſuperbly capariſoned; men arrayed in glittering armour, and ſtiffened in coats of mail, reſembling effigies of ſteel, and,

being

being ſtrapped to their ſaddles, had more the appearance of inanimate than living beings.

Lord Mortimer's retinue alone conſiſted of nine ſcore of knights, richly capariſoned, with their eſquires, gentlemen, and yeomen.

The ſucceſsful expediton of Lord Henry Beaumont and his aſſociates into Scotland in the year 1332, rouſed the attention of the Engliſh Monarch.

Edward Baliol, who derived ſupport from this party in the pretenſions he had to the Crown of Scotland, as ſucceſſor to his father John Baliol, having taken the caſtle of Roxburgh, King Edward received his letters patent, in which he acknowledged the King of England ſupreme Lord of Scotland, and, at the ſame time, ceded to him the town, caſtle, and county of Berwick, to be annexed to his kingdom, with many other advantages. Edward called a Parliament to meet at York; and it was agreed upon to inſtruct commiſſioners to require homage and fealty from the Scotch King, but theſe demands were rejected with the utmoſt diſdain. During this time Baliol made a nar-

row

row eſcape from Annan, and was forced to fly into England, his party having been thrown into great diſorder. King Edward being too far advanced in the cauſe to recede, accepted thoſe terms propoſed by Baliol at Roxburgh, and ratified them on his part *.

The Engliſh did not recover Berwick till the ſeventh year of the reign of Edward III. after the memorable battle of Hallydown Hill. King Edward, on being refuſed the homage of David Bruce, and the reſtitution of Berwick being with-held from him, commanded his herald to proclaim his defiance of the Scotch King, which, in theſe times, was equivalent to a declaration of war. This incited the Engliſh army to beſiege Berwick, which commenced on the 12th of April 1333.

The Scots, convinced that the reduction of this

* Edward Baliol gave up Berwick, Roxburgh, Dedinburg, Pebilles, and Dunfres, to King Edward, and promiſid to make hym homage for the reſideu, after that the hole Engliſch hoſte had faughte with the Scottes, and had ſo great a victory of the toune of Berwick, was gyven up to King Edward.—*Lel. Col.* v. 1. p. 554.

this town would be one of the firſt objects of their enemies enterpriſe, put it into as complete a poſture of defence as poſſible; and, in order to reſiſt the formidable attack they dreaded it would ſuſtain, they threw into it a garriſon of choſen veterans, appointing Sir William Keith their governor, and Patrick Earl of Dunbar keeper of the chief fortreſs or citadel. The King of England, animated with all the enthuſiaſm and ardor of a young hero, repaired to the ſcene of action, before the walls of Berwick, where he remained in perſon about a month, when perceiving, from the ſtrength of the garriſon and the reſolute defence it made, that the place could not eaſily be reduced, he led part of his army into Scotland. In this roaming expedition, after taking and garriſoning Edinburgh Caſtle, he croſſed the Firth at Queensferry, and overran the country as far as Scone and Dundee, carrying carnage and devaſtation in his train. Not ſatiated with theſe enormous cruelties, he puſhed thoſe ſhocking ravages of war ſo far weſtward as into the neighbourhood of Dum-

† M barton

barton Caſtle, whether King David and his Queen were placed for ſafety.

Glutted with the blood of his fellow creatures, and loaded with ſpoil, Edward, with his army, returned to Berwick, which place he found ſtill held out. He then changed the ſiege into a complete blockade both by ſea and land.

The beſieged, ſuffering by having their ſupplies cut off, made many vigorous ſallies, either with the view to drive off their enemies, or to force a paſſage through their lines. They made a deſperate attack upon the fleet, by which the greater part of the navy, at that time lying before Berwick, was burnt. In this aſſault Sir William Seton, natural ſon of Sir Alexander Seton, was drowned in endeavouring to leap from one veſſel into another; and in a ſally by land one of his legitimate ſons was made priſoner.

The brave garriſon ſtill did not deſpair of receiving relief, and therefore would not accede to terms of capitulation.

Lord

Lord Douglas had raiſed a mighty army, with which he marched to the neighbourhood of Berwick; but how great was the aſtoniſhment of the garriſon, when, in full hopes of almoſt an immediate deliverance, inſtead of his falling upon the Engliſh, Douglas croſſed the Tweed, and, in full view of the town, proceeded along the coaſt towards Bamborough Caſtle, which having been deemed impregnable, was fixed on by Edward as affording a reſidence of great ſecurity for his Queen, who at that time was lodged there. The eagerneſs of the Scotch ſtill to retain poſſeſſion of Berwick, impelled Douglas to block up the former fortreſs for ſeveral days, and to commit depredations in the neighbourhood, flattering himſelf that King Edward's regard for his Queen would induce him to raiſe the ſiege of Berwick; but the Engliſh Monarch remained inflexible, and could not be moved from his determined purpoſes.

The garriſon being now reduced to a ſcarcity of proviſions, and ſinking under the apparent neglect of Douglas, propoſed to treat, which King

King Edward attended to; and the capitulation was concluded on the 15th July, under the following conditions: That the town and caftle fhould be delivered up to King Edward on the 20th, provided it fhould not be relieved by 200 men at arms, or by a battle; that in this interval a ceffation of arms fhould take place; that, in the event of a furrender, the lives and properties of the inhabitants fhould be protected; that the governor fhould be permitted to refort to the Scotch army to communicate the articles.

Sir William Keith repairing to the Scotch camp, there prevailed that the relief of the place fhould not be attempted.

This meafure was greatly difapproved of by feveral of the old and moft experienced of the Scotch army.

During this time a tranfaction is reported to have taken place which fullies the luftre of Edward's military fame, and fixes an indelible ftain on his memory. It ftands upon record to the following purport, by Buchanan and Boece, and other Scotch authors of great credit.

credit. Hoſtages were delivered by the Scots for the performance of what related to them in the treaty, one of whom was the eldeſt ſon of Sir Alexander Seton, who was deputy governor, and who took command on Keith's reſorting to the camp. King Edward had alſo at this time in cuſtody Seton's younger ſon, who had been taken priſoner during the aſſault made on the navy.

The King ſtrongly impreſſed with an apprehenſion, that if the Scotch army approached he might fail in the capture of Berwick, an object of ſo great importance; ſoon after Keith departed, in direct oppoſition to the faith of kings—the ſacred ties of treaties—the common policy of nations—and independent of all private honour, inſiſted upon the inſtant ſurrender of the town, threatening, if the governor refuſed, he would inſtantly hang up his two ſons, the hoſtage and the priſoner, in front of the ramparts.

This unexpected and barbarous meſſage excited a panic in the breaſt of the governor, which was followed by a conflict ſo agoniſ-

ing

ing between the ſtrongeſt and nobleſt paſſions of which the mind of man is ſuſceptible, reſulting from the bonds of nature, and a nice ſenſe of duty and honour that ſets at defiance all the powers of language juſtly to deſcribe. In vain did Seton remonſtrate; for Edward, deaf to all the charges urged againſt him for ſo flagrant a violation of public faith, ordered a gibbet to be erected in full view of the town to carry into execution his moſt deteſtable threat.

Seton, nobly ſtruggling between contending impulſes that put every ſentiment on the rack, it would appear would have yielded to nature, and thereby ſaved the lives of his children by ſacrificing his country's honour and his own, had not the mother, with a degree of heroiſm worthy of a Roman matron, and equal to the greatneſs of the moſt exalted mind, ſtepped forward, and, with the moſt forcible eloquence, argued to ſupport his principles and ſuſtain his trembling ſoul; and, while the bias of parental affection yet inclined him to relax, ſhe withdrew him from

the

the ſhocking ſpectacle that he might preſerve his rectitude though at the ineſtimable price of his two ſons. Edward, with an unrelenting heart, put them both to death, and Seton kept poſſeſſion of the town. Engliſh hiſtorians, almoſt without exception, deny the perpetration of this deed. This denial of theirs, however, ſeems to be futile in oppoſition to that uniformity which is found to prevail among the Scots hiſtorians. The truth of this execution is farther confirmed by a tradition that has continued in Berwick down to this day. This fatal ſpot, on the ſouth ſide of the river, a little above the bridge well, accords with the account given by hiſtorians of its being full in view of the ramparts of the town. The author was ſhown this place by a very old perſon of reſpectability. It is a conſiderable eminence, ſituated about 100 yards diſtant from, and oppoſite to a fiſhing water formerly called the Pool. But ever ſince that dire event has been ermed Hang-a-dyke-nook: Moreover the remains of two human ſkulls are to be ſeen at

this

this day in the poor-houſe of Tweed-mouth, which the oldeſt and moſt reſpectable inhabitants of that village affirm to have been handed down from generation to generation, as being the ſkulls of Sir Alexander Seton's two ſons.

On the 18th July *, Lord Douglas marched his army over the Tweed, and encamped at a place called Dunſe-park, Bothull or Bothville. The Engliſh occupied Hallydown-hill, a very conſiderable eminence about two miles and a quarter north-weſt from Berwick. This high ground, fully commanding a proſpect of all the approaches to the town, afforded a moſt advantageous poſition for attacking an army advancing againſt it on the ſide of Scotland.

The Scots, however, not intimidated by this evident advantage, determined to engage the Engliſh on the Scots ſide of the hill, with a view, as it would appear, not only to ſecure a ſafe retreat, but alſo, in caſe of ſubduing their enemies, by taking the advantage of the flow of the tide when the Tweed is impaſſible, to

* Vid. Border Hiſtory, p. 306.

to render the escape of the English impracticable.

The Scotch army was formed into four grand bodies; *John Murray* commanded the first, with Lord *Andrew Frazer* and his sons *Simon* and *James;* the second was commanded by *Robert*, *Lord High Steward of Scotland*, with the principal men of his kindred, and the *Earl of Monteith;* the third by the *Earls of Ross*, *Sutherland*, and *Strathern*; and the fourth by *Lord Archibald Douglas*, guardian of the kingdom of Scotland and commander in chief. Their whole army, according to historians, amounted to 68,000; but this is doubted: The number of King Edward's is not positively stated by any author; but many historians are of opinion that the two contending parties were nearly equal in numbers.

When both armies were ready to commence the attack, the shock of battle was for a short time suspended by a Scotchman of gigantic stature, who had obtained the name of Turnbull on account of a magnanimous exploit by which King Robert Bruce was refcued from the attacks of a wild bull that had unhorfed him while he was hunting. Turnbull, accompanied by a great maftiff*, fallied forth with terrific ftrides, and, approaching the Englifh army with an invincible air, challenged any perfon in it to clofe with him in fingle combat. After a fhort paufe, which fuch a novel occurrence produced; the challenge was accepted by Sir Robert Benhale a young Norfolk knight. Though inferior in ftature to the Scots champion, yet he was of uncommon bodily ftrength, and furpaffed by none for adroitnefs in military atchievements. The maftiff with the utmoft ferocity darted forward, and the undaunted knight, receiving him with a fkilful blow upon the loins with his fword, cut him in pieces.

The Scotch hero advancing, Benhale with aftonifhing agility and addrefs, eluded the weighty blows aimed at him; and firft cutting off

* Some of the Borderers, on the weftern marches, kept maftiffs or bull dogs, which were let loofe on the ravaging parties.—Nicholfon and Burn's Hift. Weft.

off the left arm of his antagonist, then struck off his head.

Notwithstanding this disaster, the Scotch army made a vigorous effort to gain the summit of the hill. To animate the troops, and render the danger equal, their leaders and chieftains dismounted. But the impetuosity with which they ascended the steep put them soon out of breath.

The English archers who were skilfully stationed in different parts of the hill, pouring down showers of arrows on the close battalions of the Scotch troops, made a shocking slaughter among them. They also suffered greatly by the rolling down of large stones from the height, and in a short time were thrown into confusion. The English commanders, perceiving this, ordered their spearmen and men at arms instantly to attack, by which the Scots, being pressed whilst breathless and dispirited, multitudes of them fell immediate victims to their blood-thirsty opponents. This forced the Scots often to retreat, but they always rallied again, and with great bravery

returned

returned to the field, firmly maintaining the conflict, till Douglas their general was mortally wounded by a ſpear, which fatal cataſtrophe reaching the ears of the Scotch forces, they became panic-ſtruck, and a total rout enſued. The carnage which followed was dreadful, for the ſervants entruſted with the care of the horſes fled, leaving behind them their maſters a prey to the devouring ſword of a conquering foe. Edward commanding in perſon a choſen brigade of cavalry and archers equipped on horſeback, attended by Lord D'Arcy with his Iriſh troops, led on the purſuit, and conducted the ſlaughter, ſo that the country, for the diſtance of five miles from the field of battle, was ſtrewed with the carcaſes of the ſlain. The Engliſh hiſtorians ſet forth, that the Scots loſt on this fatal day eight Earls, 90 Knights, 400 Eſquires, and 35,000 privates.

Among the perſons of diſtinction in the Scotch army, there fell the *General*, the *Earls of Roſs*, *Sutherland*, *Carrick*, *Athol*, *Lennox*, and *Monteith*, three *Stewards*, uncles of Ro-

bert

bert the Lord High Steward, three *Frazers*, *Sir John Graham*, *Sir Duncan Campbell*, and *Sir William Tudway*. Among the prifoners were *Sir William Keith*, *Sir William Douglas*, *Sir Robert Kirkpatrick*, *Sir William Campbell*, *Sir Gilbert Wifeman*, *Sir Alexander Graham*, and *Sir Oliver Sinclair*.

It is juftly doubted whether the whole number of the Scottifh army amounted to fo many; feveral, however, of the Scotch nobility, and a great number of the gentry were taken prifoners, which Boece charges Edward with having barbaroufly put to death the day after this bloody battle. Douglas, before he fell, difplayed many ftriking proofs of true bravery and diftinguifhed heroifm ; the fpot where he met his fate is to this day called Douglas Dyke. The Englifh hiftorians diminifh the number of their flain beyond all bounds of probability. The Scots writers admit of the Scots having loft 10,000 men. The day after this battle, the caftle and town of Berwick was furrendered to King Edward, who faithfully obferved the articles of capitulation: He remained

ed ſome days in Berwick to refreſh himſelf and his army, and ordered a public thankſgiving to be obſerved throughout his dominions; and, as a farther monument of pious gratitude, he made a donation of 20l. *per annum*, to the Ciſterian Nuns, near to whoſe Convent the battle was fought, together with complete reparation of all damages done to the Conventual Church, and other buildings: According to the author of the Border Hiſtory. "Thus
" affecting, like moſt other conquerors, to
" draw heaven to his party, and to regard
" the ſucceſs accompanying the moſt unjuſt
" enterpriſes as a proof of the peculiar favour
" of the Deity."

King Edward being determined to retain Berwick, appointed Lord Henry Percy governor of the Caſtle, and gave a commiſſion to him and the Earl of March to act as joint-wardens of all the country on this ſide the Scottiſh ſea, where the terms of peace had been received. For ſecuring the town of Berwick in his allegiance, he demanded twelve hoſtages to be choſen out of the children of the families of the beſt

rank

rank and reputation in the place; eight of whom he placed at Newcaſtle upon Tyne, and four at York. Edward Baliol, the tool of faction and ambition, did homage to King Edward at Newcaſtle upon Tyne, in June 1334; his Parliament having ratified the treaty of Roxburgh, by which the caſtle, town, and county of Berwick, with their appendages, were to be annexed to the crown of England for ever.

In October 1335, King Edward being at Berwick, appointed the reward promiſed William de Preſſen for ſeizing the Earl of Murray, guardian of Scotland*. Before Edward left this town, he alſo granted letters of protection for ſix convoys, with a retinue conſiſting of 40 horſemen coming from David de Bruce out of France to treat with the nuncios and ambaſſadors. He alſo gave orders on his exchequer

* By a deed, dated at Berwick 10th October, Edward grants to William Preſſen and his heirs, the village of Eddrington, the fiſhing water of Eddermouth, the mills of Berwick and Eddrington, with the griſts belonging to them. The whole eſtimated at 107l. 3s. 7d. *per annum*, in

quer there for the payment of five merks a day to Baliol, his vaſſal king, to aſſiſt him in his daily expences.

In the year 1339, Lord John Mowbray was governor of Berwick. His garriſon conſiſted of 120 men at arms, 100 halberdiers, and 200 archers.

In 1340, King Edward the III. was at this place with an army of 40,000 foot and 6000 horſe. Next year he celebrated the feſtival of Eaſter here, and held a tournament in which twelve Scottiſh Knights entered the liſts with twelve of Edward's train. This ſpectacle was exhibited with that ſolemn pomp and great magnificence peculiar to thoſe times; but, unfor-

in time of peace, for the yearly rent of one hundred and ten merks. The ſurplus of the value of the premiſſes, above the ſaid rent, being fifty merks ten ſhillings and threepence yearly ; the King gives to the ſaid William Preſſen, for his good ſervice, until he puts him in poſſeſſion of land in England, to the amount of twenty pounds a year ; but, as ſoon as William Preſſen receives land to that amount, he is required to pay the whole yearly eſtimation, viz. 107l. 3s. 7d. for the above named village, fiſhing water, and mills.

fortunately, from the animoſity which had long ſubſiſted between the two nations, this mock-encounter was carried on with ſo much rancour and inveteracy, that two Scottiſh Knights were ſlain, as alſo Sir John Twiford, an Engliſh Knight, A. D. 1354. November 12th, a treaty was held at Berwick, for the purpoſe of ranſoming David Bruce King of Scotland, taken priſoner at the battle of Durham, on the 26th of October 1346; and on the 3d of October 1357, all the articles of it, for delivering him up, were concerted there. Beſides, it was agreed upon, that the ranſom money ſhould be paid at Berwick, Norham, or Bamborough. On failure of performing theſe articles, a ſecond treaty ſucceeded, with a truce of 14 years, which ſtipulated that 56,000 merks were to be paid by yearly inſtalments of 4000 merks each. In the 29th year of the reign of King Edward the III. that is in the year 1355, he then being on an expedition to France, the Scots ſurpriſed Berwick in the month of November. Thomas Stewart, Earl of Angus, in concert with the

Earl of March, procured a great number of ſhips, and filled them with veteran warriors, whom they diſembarked in a dark night on the northern ſide of the Tweed. They thence moved unobſerved to the foot of the wall; and, in the firſt dawn of returning day, applied their ſcaling ladders at the port called Cow-gate. William Towers, the firſt who gained the top of it, being bravely followed by his companions, the Engliſh on guard were very ſoon overpowered, but not without making a forcible reſiſtance. Sir Alexander Ogle, captain of the town, with two other Engliſh Knights were ſlain. The conquerors loſt ſix Knights of note, beſides a conſiderable number of inferior rank. Upon this, moſt of the townſmen fled in the greateſt conſternation by the gates or over the walls. The whole wealth of the place, reported to have been very great, * fell a prey to the Scots. The Engliſh in the Caſtle concerting with Sir John Copland, the perſon who had taken David, King

* Auro et argento et divitiis infinitis, are Fordun's words.

King of Scotland, prisoner at the battle of Durham, secretly resolved to introduce into it a number of men, who should in the night-time endeavour to enter the town through Douglas Tower, and attack the Scottish garrison. The Scots, aware of their critical situation, and eager of maintaining the important post they had so bravely gained, anxious also of reducing the Castle, they were at the utmost pains to discover the intention of their enemies, in which they fortunately succeeded: Upon this, they assaulted and carried Douglas Tower, and defended both it and the town against the English in the Castle and those forces that had come to their aid; all the attempts, however, which the Scots made on the Castle itself were ineffectual. Garentiere, a French Knight, and those who had accompanied him, distinguished themselves in this affair. Robert Stewart the guardan, soon after repairing to Berwick, carried off the Frenchmen; and, after conferring all due honours upon them, sent them to their own country.

We

We have here a ſtrong proof of the great importance in which this town was held in thoſe days; for King Edward, who was yet in France, upon receiving intelligence of the ſucceſsful efforts of his enemies, inſtantly ſet out for his metropolis, where he only ſtaid three days, though his Parliament was then ſitting. Bending his courſe northwards, he arrived before Berwick on the 14th January, A. D. 1356, at the head of a large army, which he had collected together by means of ſummoning all the fighting men of his ſeveral counties to join him. His navy having by this time anchored in the mouth of the Tweed, he beſieged the town both by ſea and land: The Caſtle ſtill holding out for him, he entered it attended by his guards, intending to let down the draw-bridge, and to attack the town in that quarter, while he ſhould direct an aſſault to be made by his army at the ſame time, upon other parts of the walls.

Sir Walter Manny, a brave warrior, was employed in conducting a mine below the wall, by the help of certain miners brought

from

from the foreſt dean. Theſe formidable combinations of force and of art, led the Scottiſh garriſon to determine to offer terms of capitulation, which being agreed on, they were permitted to march out with ſafety. This is the account given of this event by the Engliſh writers. The Scottiſh hiſtorians, on the other hand,* maintain, that the garriſon, on hearing of Edward's approaching them with a numerous army, abandoned the town, after having plundered it, and beaten down the walls.

Some authors are of opinion, that there had been a little treachery practiſed in this enterpriſe favourable to the Scotch †.

The

* Boece, Buchanan.

† Patric of Dunbar Counte of Marche, and Thomas le Seneſchal, that caulled hymſelf Counte of Angus, one and twenty days after thys prepaired themſelf apon a nighte with ſcaling laders cumming to Berwick, and with yn VI dayes after tok be aſſaute one of the ſtronges toures of Berwick, and enterid the town.

This tydinges was brought to King Edwarde at his very landing at Caylays yn to England. Wherfore he taried at his parlament apointed at London but 3 days, and with

al

The King made confiderable additions to the fortifications, and ftrengthened the fortrefs with many new works.

In the year 1377, feven intrepid and valiant Scotch men took poffeffion of Berwick Caftle by ftorm in the night, who continued mafters of it for eight days, although the garrifon was all that time attacked by 7000 Englifh archers and 3000 cavalry, and only loft two of their number, who had increafed to 48 when they were fubdued. Notwithftanding this heroic atchievement, however, which doubtlefs entitled them to a better fate, the Englifh put all of them to the fword.

Upon entering the Caftle, they killed the governor, Sir Robert Boynton, but liberated his lady for a ranfom of 2000 marks.

When the Earl of Northumberland fummoned thefe heroes to furrender, they boldly replied, " That they would not yield it " either

al fpede cam to Berwike, and enterid the caftel, and then the burgefes tretifed with hym, and the toune of Berwick was redelyverid ful fore agayn the Scottes wylle to King Edwarde.—Lel. Col. v. 1. p. 565.

"either to the King of England or Scotland, "but would retain and defend it for the King "of France."

In 1384, the Scotch got poſſeſſion of Berwick by the corruption of the deputy-governor, Henry Earl of Percy. The Duke of Lancaſter at enmity with Henry, and poſſeſſing the King's ear, turned this circumſtance greatly to the Earl's diſadvantage, ſo that he was attainted of high treaſon, and his eſtates forfeited. The Earl, impreſſed with the idea that his immediate preſence, before Berwick, might be of the utmoſt conſequence, beſieged the town with a great army; but the ſecret application of 2000 marks ſpared the effuſion of blood, and the place was regained. This ſucceſs operated ſo powerfully as to procure the King's pardon and the reſtitution of his honours and poſſeſſions.

In the year 1405, a conſpiracy was formed againſt King Henry the IV. in which the Earl of Northumberland and ſeveral others were the principal leaders. The Earl held poſſeſſion of the Caſtle of Berwick. On his hearing, however,

ever, that Henry was bringing againſt him no leſs a force than 37,000 men with engineers and artillery properly fitted for a ſiege, he retired privately into Scotland. The royal army advanced to Berwick, with ſome engines of deſtruction which had never before been brought againſt it, and which Speed, upon the authority of Walſingham, ſays were on this occaſion, for the firſt time, employed in Britain. The firſt diſcharge, from one of theſe cannon of a large bore *, demoliſhing one of their principal towers, the garriſon was thrown into ſuch conſternation that it made an inſtant ſurrender. The Governor, Sir Henry Bolton, and Blinkinſop, underwent immediate decapitation. On the death of King Henry the Vth, in France, and the acceſſion of his infant Son, the Scots, A. D. 1422, invaded England. The Governor of Scotland inveſted Berwick, while Earl Douglas beſieged Roxburgh; but both theſe attempts proved abortive.

In

* The firſt conſtruction of cannon was by iron bars bound together with hoops.—Vide Hutchinſon, p. 80.

In Leland's Collectanea * are the following notes: " Edward Erle of March, becaufe King " Henry had broken convenauntes, was made " King at Weftminfter Anno D. 1459.

" And ftrayte King Edward rode north- " ward, and at Towton, not far from York, " on Palmes Sunday advengid his fathers " deth, and wan the feld, where were flayn " xxM people on both parties. The Erle of " Northumberland, the Lord Clifford, Syr " John Nevil, the Erle of Weft Merlandes " brother, and Andrew Trollop were killid " at this tyme.

" King Henry, the Prince, the Queen, the " Duke of Somerfet, Henry Duke of Excef- " tre, the Lord Roos, Syr John Fortefcue " Chief Judge of England, and Tailbois Erle " of Kyme, being at York, and hering of " this, fled firft to Newcaftelle, and then to " Berwike, delyvering it to the Scottes."

In 1480, the Englifh, during winter, laid fiege to Berwick both by fea and land; the

† P works

* Lel. Col. Vol. I. p. 499.

works being new *, they flattered themſelves they ſhould, with little difficulty, be able to beat down the walls ; but, though ſeveral wide breaches were effected, the garriſon made ſo obſtinate a defence, that, after ſpending moſt part of the winter in carrying on the ſiege, the Engliſh were forced to raiſe it, and with diſgrace retreated from before the town.

King Edward the IVth, A. D. 1482, about the beginning of July, marſhalled his army at Alnwick, which amounted to 22000 men. This formidable force making its appearance ſo unexpectedly in front of Berwick, on the ſouth banks of the Tweed, the garriſon made no reſiſtance, and the town was immediately ſeized. Lord Hailes, who had the command of the caſtle, having anſwered that he had reſolved not to ſurrender it, 4000 men were left to beſiege it, and the main army advanced towards Edinburgh. His Lordſhip diſappointed, however, in receiving ſuccours, loſt hopes, and ſurrendered the caſtle on the 24th day of the ſucceeding

* King James III. of Scotland, after the ſurrender above mentioned, expended a large ſum in re-building the walls, repairing the Caſtle, and furniſhing it with artillery.

ſucceeding Auguſt. A truce was concluded in which Berwick was delivered up to England; and it is ſaid the Scots engaged never in future to attempt the reduction of it. Since which period it has, without interruption, remained in the poſſeſſion of the Crown of England. So overjoyed were the Engliſh nation at this laſt conqueſt of Berwick, that its Parliament, which met in the following January, recommended the Duke of Glouceſter, the Earl of Northumberland, and the Lord Stanley, to the King for their eminent ſervices in the Scottiſh war. The expence of ſupporting the garriſon at Berwick, at this time, amounted to 10,000 merks a year. This may be noticed as an additional proof of the great eſtimation in which Berwick was held by the Engliſh.

In the reigns of Richard the III. of England, and King James the III. of Scotland, commiſſioners were appointed jointly by the two Crowns, to aſcertain the limits of Berwick; on which occaſion, it was agreed the ground in diſpute

dispute should remain uncultivated, unbuilt, and uninhabited.

In a treaty entered into between King Henry the VII. and James the IV. King of Scotland, in the year 1502, it was stipulated, "That "the town and castle of Berwick, with their "ancient bounds and the inhabitants thereof, "should for ever remain and be included in the "present perpetual peace, friendship, league, "and confederacy; so that neither the King of "Scotland, his heirs and successors, nor any "of them, should by themselves, or any of their "subjects, lieges, or vassals, make, or suffer to "be made, war, insult, ambush, or siege, pub-"licly or privately, against the places them-"selves or their inhabitants; nor the King of "England, his heirs, successors, or any of them, "should by themselves, or the inhabitants of "the town and castle, make any war, insult, or "siege, on the King of Scotland or his vassals."

In the month of January, 1502, James IV. King of Scotland, espoused Margaret eldest daughter of King Henry VII. In Leland's Collectanea

* Vide Hutchinson's History, Vol. II. p. 81.

Collectanea is a record, ſtiled "The Fyan-"celles of Margaret eldeſt daughter of King "Henry VII. to James King of Scotland: "Together with her departure from Eng-"land, journey into Scotland, her reception "and marriaged there, and the great feaſts "held on that account. Written by John "Younge, Somerſet Herald, who attended the "Princeſs on her journey." As the ceremonies attending her journey through Northumberland give us a ſtriking repreſentation of the magnificence of thoſe times, they are worthy attention.

"The XXIIIIth day of the ſaid monneth "(June) the Qwene departed from Durham, "accompanyd by hyr noble company, as ſhe "had beene in the dayes paſt, in fayr manere "and good ordre, for to com to the towne of "New Caſtell. Thre mylle fore thens came "to her the Prior of Tynemouth, well a-"poynted, and in hys company xxx horſys. "Hys folks in hys liveray. And ther was in "lyk wys Syr Rawff Harbotelle Knyght, "richly apoynted, well mounted, and hys "folks

" folks in his liveray to the nombre of XL
" horſys.

" At the intrynge of the ſaid towne of New
" Caſtell, the Qwene apoynted hyr, and in-
" tred in noble aſtat. Ich Lord and others
" tuke newe horſys rychly apoynted, in ſpe-
" cial th' Erle of Northumberland, as in the
" manere of the entrynge of York, and hys
" folks in lyk wys.

" Upon the bryge cam in proceſſyon rych-
" ly reveſted the College of the ſaid towne,
" and with them the Freres Carmelets and
" Jacobius with the croſeys, the wich war
" gyffen to the ſayd Qwene to kyſſe, as be-
" fore, by the Archbyſchop.

" After them was the Mayr of the ſayd
" towne, accompayned of the Scheryffes and
" Aldermen, well apoynted, on foot. The
" wich receyved the ſaid Qwene honorably:
" and after the receyvynge the ſaid Mayr
" monted on horſeback, beryng his maſſe be-
" fore hyr.

" At the bryge end, upon the gatt, war
" many children, revſted of ſurpeliz, ſyng-
" yng

" yng mellodiouſly hympnes, and playing on " inſtruments of many ſortes.

" Within the ſaid towne, by ordre, the " bourges and habitants war honneſtly apoynt- " ed. The ſtreytts were hanged, and the " wyndow loups, topps, and ſchipps was ſo " full of people, gentylmen and gentylwo- " men, in ſo great nombre, that it was play- " ſur for to ſee. But they maid non ſound " of artyllery and ordinance.

" In ſuch ſtatt and fayr aray, was the ſaid " Qwene brought and conveyd to the Freres " Auſtyns, wher ſhe was lodged, and honeſt- " ly receyved by thos reveſted with the croſſe, " in the manere as it is reherſed befor. And " when ſhe was brought to hyr lodgyng every " men drew hym to hys awn.

" The next day after, being the xxvth day " of the ſaid monneth, Saunt Jamys day, ſhe " abode all the day in the ſaid towne, and " was at the church maſſe very nobly acom- " payned.

" That ſam day, at even, th' Erle of Nor- " thumbreland made to many Lords, Knights,

" and

" and others, a goodeley baunket, which laſt-
" to mydnyght, for cauſe of the games, daun-
" ces, ſports, and ſongs, with force of ypocras,
" ſuccres, and other metts of many delicy-
" ouſes maners.

" To the ſaid New Caſtell cam the Lord
" Dacre of the North, acompayned of many
" gentylmen, honeſtly apoynted, and hys folks
" arayd in hys liveray.

" The XXVIth day of the ſaid monneth the
" ſaid Qwene departed from the ſaid place,
" after the cuſtome precedent, varey richly
" and in fayr aray. And the ſayd Mayr con-
" veyd hyr out of the ſaid towne, and after
" tuke lyve of her.

" Haff a mylle owt of the ſaid towne was
" Syr Humfrey Lyſle and the Prior of Bryng-
" burn, well apoynted and well horſt, to the
" to the nombre of xx horſys. Their folks
" arayed of their liveray. And a mylle from
" the ſaid towne was in ordre the Scheryffe
" of Northumberland, Syr Rawff Evers, in
" company of many other gentylmen, varey
" well apoynted, their folks clothed in their
" liveray,

" liveray, well monted. And with them " wer many honests folks of the countre, with " spers and bowes, in jackets, to the nombre " of two hondreth horsys.

" With the sam fayr company, was the said " Qwene conveyd to Morpath, and by the " towne passed in fayr ordre, wher ther was " much people; and so she went to the abbay, " wher sche was well receyved by the Abbot " and Religyous revested, at the gatt of the " church, with the crosse. And after the " receyvyng sche was conveyd to hyr lodg- " yngs in the said place for that sam nyght.

" The xxviith day of the said monneth, " the Qwene departed from Morpath, after " the custom before, to goo to Alnewyk, a " place of th' Erle of Northumberlaund. And " in half of the way cam before hyr, Maister " Henry Gray, Esquier, well appointed. In " hys company many other gentilmen, and " hys folks well monted and arayd in his li- " veray, to the nombre of a hundreth horsys.

" Two mylle from the sayd place, the said " Erle cam and mett hyr, well acompanyed, "and brought hyr thorough hys park, where "ſhe kylde a buck with hyr bow. After "which ſhe was conveyde to the ſaid caſtell, "where ſche and hyr company was welcom-"ed by the ſaid Lorde, the wich maid hyr "varey good chere.

"The next day, the xxviiith day of the "ſaid monneth, ſhe was all the holl day in "the ſaid caſtell, and by the Lord well cheryſt "and hyr company.

"The xxixth day of the ſayd monneth the "ſaid Qwene departed from Alnewyk, for to "go for Barrwyk, and at half of the way, "named Belleford, ſhe bayted. For Syr "Thomas Darcy, Capittayne of the ſaid Barr-"wyk, had maid rady hyr dynner at the "ſaid place vary well and honneſtly.

"For that the ſaid Maiſter Henry Gray's "abouffe named is Sheryffe of Ellaund Shyre "and Northumberlaund Shyre, he bore hys "rod before the ſayd Qwene, ſens the en-"trynge of the ſayd Lordſhips to Barrwyk.

"Betwyx Alnewyk and Barrwyk cam to "the Qwene Maiſter Rawff Wodryngton,

"having

" having in his company many gentlmen " well appoynted. Hys folks arayd in liveray, " well horſed, to the nomber of an hundreth " horſys.

" At the comyng ny to Barrwyk was ſhot " ordonnounce, the wiche was fayr for to " here. And ny to the ſayd place, the Qwene " dreſt hyr. And ichon in fair aray, went " the on after the other in fayr ordre.

" At the entrynge of the bryge was the " ſaid capitaine well apoynted, and in hys " company hys gentylmen and men of armes " who receyved the ſaid Qwene into the ſaid " place.

" At the tother end of the bryge toward " the gatt, was the Maiſter Marſhall com- " payned of hys company, ichon bearing a " ſtaffe in his haund.

" After hym was the college reveſted with " the croſſe, the wiche was gyffen hyr for to " kyſſe by th' Archbiſchop as before.

" At the gatt of the ſaid towne was the " Maiſter Porter, with the gard and ſoyars of " the ſaid place, in a row well apoynted.

" Ichon

"Ichon of thoſe had an hallebarde or other "ſtaffe in his haund, as the others. And apon the ſaid gatt war the mynſtraylls of the "ſayd Capitayn, playnge of their inſtruments.

"In the midds of the ſaid town was the "Maiſtre Chamberlayn, and the Mayre, a-"compayned of the bourges and habitaunts "of the ſaid place, in fayre ordre, and well "apoynted.

"In ſuch fayr ordre and company ſhe was "conveyd and brought to the caſtell, wher "ſhe was receyved by the Lady D'Arcy hon-"neſtly accompayned.

"The XXX and XXXIth days of the ſaid "monneth, the Qwene tarried at Barrwyk, "where ſhe had great chere of the ſaid Cap-"pitayne of Barrwyk, and hyr company in "likewys. That ſam day was by the ſaid "Capyiteyne, to the pleaſur of the ſaid "Qwene, gyffen corſes of chaſſe within the "town, with other ſports of bayrs and of "doggs togeder.

"The firſt day of Auguſt the Qwene de-"parted from Barrwyk for to go to Lamberton

"kerke

" kerke in varrey fair company, and well ap-
" poynted.

" First, of the said Archbyschops and Bis-
" chops, the Erles of Surrey and of Northum-
" berlaund, the Lord Dacres, the Lord Scroop
" and his son, the Lord Gray, the Lord La-
" temer, the Lord Chamberlain, Maister Polle,
" and other Nobles and Knyghts. The young
" gentylmen wer well appoynted at their de-
" vises, and ther was sou much of cloth of
" gold, as of other ryche rayments. Their
" horsys frysks in harnays of the selfe: and
" upon thos orfavery, sum others had cam-
" paynes gylt, the others campaynes of Syl-
" ver. Gambads at plasur, that it was fayr
" thyng for to se.

" The sayd Erle of Northumberlaund was
" varey well mounted, hys horse rychly ap-
" poynted, his harnays of gold in brodeux,
" hymselfe in a jakette betten of gold, well
" wrought in goldsmith werke, and brodery,
" and a cloke of porple borded of cloth of
" gold. His Hensmen appoynted as before
" mentioned. Incontinently before hym rode
" the

" the Maiſter of his Horſe, conveying the ſam
" thre Henſmen arayed in jaketts all of orfa-
" very and brodery, and ther harnays of their
" horſys in ſuch wys of orfavery and brodery,
" full of ſmall bells that maid a grett noyſe.
" After thos cam a gentylman ledyng in his
" haund a corſer, covered to the grownde of
" a vary rych trapure betten of gold of orfa-
" very and brodery in oraunge. And ichon
" of the ſam a gren tre in the manere of a
" pyne, and maid the ſaid Lord pannades, and
" they weigited varey honeſtly.

" After cam the ſaid Qwene varey rychly
" arayde and enorned with gold and precyous
" ſtones, ſetting in hyr lytere rychly apoynted.
" Her foteman alwayes ny to hyr well apoynt-
" ed, and monted upon fayr pallefrys, and
" their harnays ryche in appareyll.

" After cam hyr char rychly apoynted,
" fournyſched of ladyes and gentylwomen
" well apoynted, and after that, ſum other
" gentylwomen on horſebak honorably apoyn-
" ted.

" The

"The ſayd Cappitayne of Barrwyk, and "my lady hys wyffe aecompanyed of many "gentylmen and gentylwomen rychly arayd, "and clothed of a liveray, went with the ſayd "Qwene to Edinburghe.

"Before the ſayd Qwene war by ordre Jo-"hannes and hys company, and Henry Glaſce-"bery and hys company, the trompetts, offi-"cers of armes, and ſergeants of maſſe, ſo that "at the departing out of the ſaid Barrwyk and "at hyr Bedward at Lambertonkerke it was a "joy for to ſee and here.

"In ſuch ſtat and aray the ſaid Qwene "cam out of Barrwyk, ichon by ordre, the "Lordes and Nobles thre and thre togeder, "to the ſaid Lambertonkerke, and the com-"pany behind well apoynted and in fair aray, "that it was eſtimed that ther war of the parte "of the ſaid Qwene xviii C or two M horſys "well apoynted."

On the 10th October, in the year 1525, the Commiſſioners of King Henry the VIII. and King James V. met at Berwick, where they concluded a treaty for a three-years peace.

In

In A. D. 1528, the truce was renewed and the peace continued for five years.

In 1547, King Henry the VIII. being dead, and leaving his ſon Edward the VI. then only ten years of age, the Earl of Hertford, then created Duke of Somerſet, in Auguſt marched to Berwick with an army of 18,000, accompanied by a fleet of 34 ſhips of war, 30 tranſports, and a galley. This armament was fitted out on an expedition againſt Scotland. The troops lay encamped without the walls of the town.

Very conſiderable repairs were made in the fortreſs of Berwick in the year 1550, the great expence of which, with thoſe at Calais, are ſtated in the King's journals as the cauſe for debaſing the coin: Alſo, in the year 1552, it is found that great improvements had been made upon the fortifications, in which, by the minutes kept by Secretary Cecil, L.6000 were expended. As no veſtiges of theſe works are now to be ſeen, it is thought they have been raſed by Queen Elizabeth when ſhe put the fortifications upon a modern plan. Edward

ward the VI. and Mary Queen of Scotland, by treaty, made Berwick a county town, and, as Rymer's Fædra notes it, "a free town in-"dependent of both ſtates."

In 1558, there was a hot ſkirmiſh on Halydown Hill, between ſome bands of ſoldiers who were ſtationed there, protecting thoſe employed in mowing hay, and a conſiderable party of French and Scots belonging to the garriſon of Eymouth, who, hearing of their being ſecure and remiſs, ſurpriſed them with a fierce attack. Sir James Croft advancing with a reinforcement from Berwick ended the conteſt, but not before conſiderable loſs on both ſides, the ſkirmiſh having laſted from one till four in the afternoon. In 1566, Queen Mary of Scotland came to view Berwick; when the deputy governor and his train having met her at the extremities of the liberties, conducted her to Hallydown Hill, and from thence to the weſt of the town, where ſhe commanded a perfect view of the place, and was ſaluted by a general diſcharge of cannon.

In 1588, King James the VI. of Scotland did the like, and he received the ſame warlike ſalute. Queen Elizabeth, after having fortified Berwick, inſtituted the following military eſtabliſhments there, in the year 1576, as appears from the archieves of the borough.

The garriſon conſiſted of eight companies of muſqueteers, two of them containing 100, and the reſt 65 men each; the pay of the private men 8d. per day; Captains of larger companies 4s. of leſſer companies 2s. 80 horſemen under command of eight conſtables: the horſemen had 4d. per day added to their former pay of 6l. 13s. 4d. per annum. The gunners were augmented, on account of the great additional number of large ordnance, from 28 to 60, with a Maſter Gunner, a Mate, and four Quarter Maſters: the whole eſtabliſhment for the artillery amounting to about 860l.

The

	£.	s.	d.
The Lord Governor his Salary	133	6	8
A Chaplain - - - - -	13	6	8
A Secretary - - - - -	13	6	8
40 Houſehold Servants, each at	6	13	4
Eſpecial money per annum -	40	0	0
And a reward in conſideration of his Barony.			
The Marſhal, his Salary -	33	6	8
An under Marſhal - -	16	0	0
20 Horſemen, each - -	6	13	4
Two Tipſtaffs, each - -	5	6	8
An increaſe of pay given by her Majeſty - - -	66	13	4
The Treaſurer, his Salary -	20	0	0
Two Clerks, each - -	13	6	8
20 Horſemen, each - -	6	13	4
An increaſe of pay - -	80	0	0
Gentleman Porter, his Salary -	20	0	0
Six Horſemen, each - -	6	13	4
14 Footmen, each - -	5	6	8
An increaſe of pay - -	50	0	0
Chamberlain, his Salary -	20	0	0

12

	£.	s.	d.
12 Soldiers, 4 at - - -	6	13	4
Eight, each - - -	6	0	0
Maſter of the Ordnance per day	0	5	0
One Clerk per day - -	0	1	0
Two Servants - - -	0	0	6
Two Labourers - - -	0	0	6

At the time of this eſtabliſhment, Lord Hunſdon was Governor of *Berwick.* This council was compoſed of Sir Robert Conſtable, Knight, High Marſhall; Sir Francis Ruſſel, Knight, Chamberlain; Robert Bowes, Eſq; Treaſurer; Thomas Sutton, Eſq; Maſter of the Ordnance, and John Selby, Eſq; Chief Porter. The Mayor had an appointment of 10l. per annum, the Cuſtomer 10l. and the Comptroller of the Cuſtoms 5l.

The Maſter of the Ordnance had under his charge upwards of 20 artificers, among theſe was one *Fletcheur*, or arrow maker, one *Bowyer*, and one *Maſter Wheeler*.

The number of men on this eſtabliſhment

was

was 980, and their pay amounted to 12,734l. 19s. 2d. yearly.

In the year 1603, on the death of Queen Elizabeth, King James VI. of Scotland was proclaimed March 26th, at Berwick, King of England, France, and Ireland, by the name of King James I.

There is preſerved in the archives of Berwick, a copy of a letter, written by the Mayor, Aldermen, and Commons, dated on the above day, acquainting the King, that,

"They had, with preſent expedition, and "with what ſolemnity the leiſure of time "would afford, publiſhed and proclaimed his "ſacred Majeſty, King of England, France, "and Ireland; and entreats him to pardon "ſuch defects as by ignorance, omiſſion, or "otherwiſe, by the ſtraitneſs of time had "happened in the performance thereof." To which the King returned the following anſwer:

"To our truſty friends, the Mayor and "Aldermen of the town of Berwick.

"Truſty

"Trusty friends, wee greet you heartily "well. We render you thanks for your so "dutyfull affection, utterit in assisting and "concurring sae willingly with your Gover-"nour, in putting the town of Berwick in our "hands, which we have appointit to be go-"verned in the same form and manner as "heretofore, while we advise otherwise to "dispose upon the same; assuring you al-"ways to find us a gratious and loving Prince, "wha sal be careful to maintaine your wont-"ed liberties and privileges, and to see that "the same be nae ways braugillit, nor other-"waies prejudget. Sua we commit you to "God. From Hallirude house this 27th day "of March 1603."

On the King's arrival at the boundaries of Berwick, he was received with every demonstration of joy and respect by Sir John Carey, then Marshall, accompanied by all the officers of the garrison, at the head of their several bands of horse and foot. While these saluted his Majesty in passing with a discharge of vol-

lies

lies from their muſkets, they were returned by the thunder of cannons from the ramparts, and the air reſounded with acclamations of joy. Upon the King's entering the gate, the keys of the town were delivered to him by William Selby, gentleman Porter, on whom his Majeſty inſtantly conferred the honour of knighthood, and immediately returned him the keys. Having proceeded to the market-place through the armed bands of the garriſon, he was then received by the body corporate of the borough. Hugh Gregſon, the Mayor, preſented him with an offering of gold, and ſurrender of their charter; after which the recorder addreſſed the ſovereign in a ſolemn and pathetic congratulatory ſpeech: all which honours he received moſt graciouſly, and at the ſametime reſtored the charter, aſſuring the town of his royal favour and protection. The King proceeded next to the church to render public thanks to God for granting him ſo peaceable an entrance into his new dominions. Toby Matthew, Biſhop of Durham, preached

an

an eloquent ſermon on the occaſion. From thence the King went to the caſtle; the ordnance were again fired; and the ſtreets reechoed with loud expreſſions of ſatisfaction. On the following day ſeveral nobles from the ſouthern parts of England arrived to offer their obeiſance to their new Sovereign. His Majeſty, accompanied by theſe and the officers of the garriſon, inſpected the fortifications, ports, and magazines; and, in preſence of the officers and ſoldiers who were drawn up in martial array on the ramparts, he diſcharged one of the great guns. The ſame day information being brought that two or three hundred banditti of the weſt march were ravaging the country, and had ſpread as far as Penrith, the King ſent Sir William Selby with two hundred foot and fifty horſe of the garriſon, who being joined by many more in their march, the plunderers abandoned their habitations, many of whom were blown up and burnt, ſome of the offenders were overtaken and ſent to Carliſle caſtle, where they afterwards

afterwards ſuffered the juſt puniſhment of their crimes.

Berwick became the ducal title of James Fitz James, natural ſon of King James the II. of England, whom he created Duke of Berwick, A. D. 1686. The King, with the moſt humane and laudable intention of extinguiſhing for ever all recollection of paſt hoſtilities between his kingdoms, prohibited the name of Borders any longer to be uſed, and to employ as a ſubſtitute that of the *middle ſhires*. He gave orders to demoliſh every place of ſtrength in theſe parts except the habitations of the nobles and barons; their iron gates to be converted into plough ſhares; and recommended the inhabitants to betake themſelves to the culture of the earth and other peaceful occupations. Influenced by the ſame ſpirit, he broke the garriſons of Berwick and Carliſle. The former he reduced at Chriſtmas of this year to a company of 100 men. The day following, he, after having made a preſent to the officers and ſol-

† S dier s

diers of the garriſon, and expreſſing his grateful acceptance of the loyalty and affection of the inhabitants, ſet out from Berwick for London.

From what has been related in the former ſection, it will appear that the Engliſh and Scots, who had for ages harboured an implacable hatred to each other, exaſperated at the right which the Engliſh nation claimed to the crown of Scotland, were almoſt conſtantly engaged in war. Their national antipathies were excited, not only by frequent hoſtilities, and reciprocal injuries, but the Engliſh conſidered the Scotch as vaſſals who had preſumed to rebel, and the Scots, in their turn, looked upon the Engliſh as uſurpers, who aimed at enſlaving their country. Happily, however, upon the union of the two crowns, theſe martial nations, who had long been ſtrangers to the arts of peace, began gradually to enjoy the fruits of that repoſe which had been long and eagerly ſought after by both kingdoms.

To

To this ancient hiſtory of Berwick we judge it proper to ſubjoin a complete liſt of the noblemen and gentlemen who have repreſented the borough *.

Candour

* " Brown Willis ſays, that the burgeſſes were ſummoned to ſend repreſentatives to parliament, in the latter end of the reign of King Edward IV. From the 17th of King Edward IV. to the firſt of King Edward VI. the returns are all loſt, except an imperfect bundle of the 33d of King Edward VIII.

16 Jan.	1542	King Henry VIII.	33 P. at Weſtm.
8 Nov.	1547	King Edward VI.	1 P. at Weſtm.
1 Mar.	1552		7 P. at Weſtm.
		Queen Mary.	
5 Oct.	1553	No return	1 P. at Weſtm.
2 April	1554	George Browne, Odwell Selby, Gentleman.	1 P. at Oxford
		Phillip and Mary.	
12 Nov.	1554	No return	1 & 2 P. at Weſtm.
21 Oct.	1555	John Bredforth, Charles Wharton	2 & 3 P. at Weſtm.
20 Jan.	1557	No return.	4 & 5 P. at Weſtm.
		Queen Elizabeth.	
23 Jan.	1558	No return	1 P. at Weſtm.
23 Jan.	1562	Anthony Temple, Thomas Norton	5 P. at Weſtm.
11 Jan.	1571	Valentine Browne, Knight, Henry Cave, Eſq;	13 P. at Weſtm.
8 May	1572	Martin Garnet, Gentleman, Robert Newdigate, Eſq;	14 P. at Weſtm.
23 Nov.	1585	William Moreton, Thomas Parkinſon, Aldermen	27 P. at Weſtm.
29 Oct.	1586	Valentine Browne, Knight, Thomas Parkinſon, Alderman,	28 P. at Weſtm.
4 Feb.	1588	William Moorton, Mayor, William Selby, Eſq;	31 P. at Weſtm.
19 Nov.	1592	William Moorton, Mayor, William Selby, Eſq;	35 P. at Weſtm.
24 Oct.	1597	William Selby, Thomas Parkinſon	39 P. at Weſtm.
7 Oct.	1601	William Selby, ſenior, Eſq; David Waterhouſe, Eſq;	43 P. at Weſtm.
		King James I.	
19 Mar.	1603	William Selby, Knight, Ch. Parkinſon, Recorder	1 P. at Weſtm.
5 April	1614	William Selby, Knight	12 P. at Weſtm.
30 Jan.	1620	Joh. Selby, Knight, Robſon Jackſon, Knight	18 P. at Weſtm.
19 Feb.	1623	Rob. Jackſon, Knight, Edward Lively, Gentleman	21 P. at Weſtm.

King

Candour oblige us to contradict the following groundless account, to be met with in Hall's New Royal

		King Charles I.	
21 Jan.	1625	John Selby, Knight, Rob. Jackson, Knight	1 P. at Westm.
6 Feb.	1625	Rob. Jackson, Knight, Richard Lowther, Esq;	1 P. at Westm.
16 Mar.	1628	Edward Lawyer, Knight, Edward Lively Gentleman	3 P. at Westm.
13 April	1640	Thomas Widdrington, Knight, Hugh Porter, Esq;	15 P. at Westm.
3 Nov.	1640	Thomas Widdrington, Knight, Rob. Scawin, Esq;	16 P. at Westm.
		Oliver Cromwell	
		Convened an assembly called the Little Parliament, but no representatives for Cities or Boroughs, London excepted, were summoned to it.	
5 July	1654	Geo. Fenwick of Brenkburn, County of Northumland	P. at Westm.
3 Sept.	1656	Colonel George Fenwick, Ob. 15 March (1656)	P. at Westm.
		Richard Cromwell.	
27 Jan.	1658	John Rushworth of Lincolns Inn, Esq; George Payler, Esq; one of the Commissioners of the Navy.	P. at Westm.
		The Convention Parliament.	
25 April	1660	Sir Thomas Widdrington, John Rushworth	P. at Westm.
		King Charles II.	
8 May	1661	Sir Ralph Grey, Sir Thomas Widdrington	13 P. at Westm.
6 Mar.	1678	John Rushworth, Sir Ralph Grey	31 P. at Westm.
21 Mar.	16	John Rushworth, Sir Ralph Grey	P. at Oxford.
		King James II.	
19 May	1685	Philip Bickerstaff, Ralph Widdrington	1 P. at Westm.
		The Convention Parliament.	
22 Jan.	1688	Francis Blake, Esq; Philip Babington, Esq;	P. at Westm.
		King William and Queen Mary.	
20 Mar.	1689	Samuel Ogle [a], and Francis Blake, Esqrs.	P. at Westm.

[a] Samuel Ogle of South Dissington, County of Northumberland, Esq; Commissioner of the Revenue in Ireland, Col. Per. v. III. p. 350.

Royal Encyclopaedia, under the article *election.* " Berwick upon Tweed. A singular election trick " was

		King William III.	
22 Nov.	1695	Ralph Grey, Samuel Ogle, Esq; *Marb 9. 1696. The right of election is stated in the report to be in the freemen.*	7 P. at Westm.
3 Dec.	1698	Sir Francis Blake, Samuel Ogle, Esqr;	10 P. at Westm.
10 Feb.	1700	Jonathan Hutchinson, Samuel Ogle, Esqrs;	12 P. at Westm.
30 Dec.	1701	Samuel Ogle, Jonathan Hutchinson *, Esqrs;	13 P. at Westm.
		Queen Anne.	
20 Oct.	1702	Jonathan Hutchinson, Samuel Ogle, Esqrs;	1 P. at Westm.
25 Oct.	1705	Jonathan Hutchinson, Samuel Ogle, Esqrs;	4 P. at Westm.
8 July	1708	Jonathan Hutchinson, Samuel Ogle, Esqrs;	7 P. at Westm.
25 Nov.	1710	William Kerre, Esq; [b] Richard Hampden, Esq; [c]	9 P. at Westm.
12 Nov.	1713	William Orde, Esq; [d] Richard Hampden, Esq;	12 P. at Westm
		King George I.	
17 Mar.	1714	Grey Neville, Esq; [a] John Shute, Esq; [b]	1 P. at Westm.
10 May	1722	John Lord Viscount Barrington, Grey Neville, Esq; Grey Neville, died 24th April, 1723, a new writ 29th April. William Kerre, Esq; in the room of Grey, and Henry Neville Grey, Esq; in the room of Barrington expelled.	7 P. at Westm.
		King George II.	
28 Nov.	1727	Joseph Sabine, Esq; [c] and George Liddel, Esq;	1 P. at Westm.
13 June	1738	George Liddel, Esq; [d] Hugh Lord Polwarth [e]	P. at Westm.

[b] Brother of John the First Duke of Roxburgh.

[c] Hampden the County of Bucks.

[d] Of Fenham, County of Northumberland.

[a] Neville, one of the commissioners for stating the debts due to the army.

[b] Shute Barrington, created Viscount of Barrington in Ireland, during this Parliament, July 11, 1720, and expelled the house 1723.

[c] A Lieutenant General of his Majesty's forces, Governor of Berwick and Holy Island, and Colonel of the royal regiment of Welch Fuzileers. On his death Hugh Polwarth succeeded to his seat in Parliament.

[d] Ob. Oct 9, 1740.

[e] Hugh Lord Polwarth, on the death of his father in 1740, succeeded to the title of Earl of Marchmont.

" was played off here in 1768: Sir John Delaval
" and R. P. Taylor, Esq; had obtained the promises
" of most of the resident freemen; their oppo-
" nents had secured the non-resident freemen in
" London,

		Thomas Watson, Esq; succeeded to Lord Polwarth's seat, and William Wildman, Barrington Shute, Viscount and Baron Barrington, to Mr Liddel's, by virtue of a writ tested March 6, 1740.	
25 Jan.	1741	Lord Viscount Barrington,[a] Thomas Watson, Esq;	P. at Westm.
* June	1747	Lord Barrington re-elected.—Thomas Watson, Esq; re-elected.	
* April	1754	Thomas Watson, Esq; re-elected.—John Delaval, Esq; elected vice Lord Barrington.	
* April	1761	Thomas Watson, Esq; re-elected.—General John Crawford elected vice J. Delaval, Esq;	
* March	1765	Sir John Hussey Delaval, Bart. elected vice General Crawford who died.	
* March	1766	Lord Viscount Lisburn elected vice J. Watson, Esq; who vacated his seat.	
* April	1768	Sir John H. Delaval re-elected.—Robert Paris Taylor, Esq; elected vice Lord Lisburn.	
* Oct.	1774	Jacob Wilkinson, Esq; and Col. John Vaughan elected vice Sir J. H. Delaval and R. P. Taylor, Esq;	
* Sept.	1780	General Vaughan re-elected.—Lord Delaval elected vice J. Wilkinson, Esq;	
* April	1784	General Vaughan and Lord Delaval re-elected.	
* Sep. 21.	1786	Sir Gilbert Elliot, Bart. elected vice Lord Delaval, created an English Peer.	
* June 22.	1790	General Vaughan re-elected.—Captain Carpenter elected vice Sir Gilbert Elliot.	
* Sep. 28.	1795	Colonel Callander elected vice General Vaughan who died.	
* June 7.	1796	Colonel Callander re-elected.—Earl of Tryconnel elected vice Captain Carpenter.	

*Those marked * are General Elections.*

No. of Burgesses polled 23d April 1754, 476

Watson - - - -	374
Delaval - - - -	307
John Wilkes, Esq; - -	192

[a] Made one of the Lords of the Admiralty, and a new writ being issued 20th February 1746, he was re-elected.

" London, and agreed for their paſſage in " ſome ſhips. Hearing of this, Sir John and " Mr Taylor, by *proper means*, ſecured the " intereſt of the maſters of theſe ſhips, who " took good care to land their cargoes in Nor- " way, by which Sir John and his Colleague " quietly came in and took their ſeats with- " out further expence."

The author grounds his refutation on the following note from an inhabitant of the town of the firſt reſpectability, and which is corroborated by many other perſons of undoubted veracity; beſides, as to this affair, a legal proof could be adduced.

" I have ſeen the ſame ſtory related in ano- " ther work, and it was alſo ſaid to have " been mentioned by Lord Kenyon in a re- " cent caſe in the Court of King's Bench; " but, notwithſtanding, I can aſſure you that " it is a groundleſs falſehood. There was no " conteſt in 1768, and no voters were then " brought from London.

" I well know that burgeſſes have been fre- " quently brought from London to vote at

" the

"the election of members for the borough, "and likewise at mayoralties, but I can "aver, that at no time did they arrive too "late to vote, except in the year 1754, when "some freemen, who were brought by sea, "did not arrive until after the poll was over; "but adverse winds *alone prevented* their ar- "rival. The candidates then were Lord De- "laval, the late Thomas Watson, Esq; and "the celebrated Mr Alderman Wilkes; the "freemen who did not get in time to vote "were in the interest of Mr Wilkes. But "indeed to those who are not at all acquaint- "ed with the spirited proceedings here at an "election, the whole must appear highly ri- "diculous, as there can be no doubt, had such "a transaction taken place, it would imme- "diately have been made a subject of inquiry "in the House of Commons." *

SEC-

* The following quotation taken from Cambden's Britannia, * is inserted as deserving a place here:

"The

* Gibson's Cambden, p. 1100. Folio, London, MDCCXXII.

SECTION III.

Remarkable Occurrences independent of the General Hiſtory.

THE firſt occurrence which ſeems to claim a place here is the following, taken from Sir Frederic Eden on the ſtate of the poor:

" As

" The mathematicians have placed this Town (Berwick) " in 21 degrees and 43 minutes of longitude, and in 55 " and 48 of northern latitude; ſo that the longeſt day " in this climate conſiſts of ſeventeen hours and 22 mi- " nutes, and its night only of ſix hours and 38 *minutes*, " ſo truly has *Servius Honoratus* written of this country: " *Britain* ſays he *has ſuch plenty of day that ſhe has hardly* " *any room for night*. Nor is it a wonder that the ſol- " diers of this garriſon are able to play all night at dice " without a candle, if we conſider their continued twilight " and the truth of *Juvenal's* expreſſion:

—— " *Minima contentos nocte Britannos*.

" Britains with ſhorteſt nights content.

" Take at parting. *J. Johnſton's* verſes upon Berwick."

" Scotorum *extremo ſub limite; meta futoris*
" *Saxonidum gentis par utriuſque labor*,

" *Mille*

† T

"As an inſtance not only of the difficulty "there is to wean men from old habits, but "alſo

"*Mille vices rerum, quae mille eſt paſſa ruinas,*
"*Mirum, qui potuit tot ſupereſſe malis.*
"*Quin ſupereſt, quin extremis exhauſta ruinis;*
"*Funere ſic crevit firmior uſque ſuo:*
"*Opidda ut exaequet jam muntiſſima; Civis*
"*Militis et cenſum, et munia martis obit.*
"*Poſtquam ſervitio duriſque eſt functa periclis,*
"*Effert lætitiæ ſigna ſerena ſua:*
"*Et nunc antiquo faelix ſe jactat honore,*
"*Cum reddit domino debita jura ſuo:*
"*Cujus ab auſpiciis unita Britannia tandem*
"*Excelſum tollit libera in aſtra caput.*

"Bound of the Scottiſh and the Engliſh land,
"Where both their realms and both their labours end;
"After a thouſand turns of doubtful ſtate,
"She yet outbraves the vain aſſaults of fate:
"A happy port in all her ſtorms hath found,
"And ſtill roſe higher as ſhe touched the ground.
"Surpaſſed by none her ſtately forts appear,
"Her ſons at once inur'd to trade and war.
"Now all her ſtorms and all her fears are gone,
"In her glad look returning joys are ſhown.
"Now her old honours are at laſt reſtor'd,
"Securely now ſhe ſerves her ancient lord:

"Bleſs'd

" alſo of the rigour of proprietors of mills in
" ancient times, I tranſcribe the following cu-
" rious

" Bleſs'd with whoſe care united *Britain* rears
" Her lofty head among the rival ſtars."

" It may not be amiſs to add here the account which " Æneas Sylvius, or Pope Pius the Second (who came le- " gate into *Scotland* about the year 1448) gives of the " borderers in this country, in his life written by him- " ſelf."

" *A certain river, namely the Tweed, falling from a high* " *mountain, parts the two kingdoms, over which Æneas fer-* " *ried; and, coming to a large village about ſun-ſet, he alight-* " *ed at a country-man's houſe, where he ſupped with the cu-* " *rate of the place and his hoſt. The table was plentifully* " *furniſhed with pottage, hens, and geeſe; but nothing of either* " *wine or bread appeared. All the men and women of the* " *town flocked in as to ſome ſtrange ſight; and as our coun-* " *trymen uſe to admire the Ethiopians or Indians, ſo theſe peo-* " *ple ſtared at Æneas, aſking the curate what countryman he* " *was? what his errand could be? and whether he were a* " *Chriſtian or no? But Æneas, being aware of the ſcarcity he* " *ſhould meet with on this road, had been accommodated by a* " *monaſtery with a rundlet of red wine and ſome loaves of* " *bread. When theſe were brought to the table, they were* " *more aſtoniſhed than before, having never ſeen either wine* " *or*

" rious law from the statutes of the Guild at
" Berwick, said to have been enacted in 1284."

" Na

" *or white bread. Big-belly'd women with their husbands*
" *came to the table side, and handling the bread and smelling*
" *to the wine, begged a taste: so that there was no avoiding*
" *the dealing of the whole amongst them. After they had*
" *sate at supper till two hours within night, the curate and*
" *the landlord (with the children and all the men) left Æ-*
" *neas and rubb'd off in haste. They said they were going to*
" *shelter themselves in a certain tower at a good distance, for*
" *fear of the Scots who (at low water) used to cross the riv-*
" *er in the night for plunder. They would by no means be*
" *persuaded to take Æneas along with them, though he very*
" *importunately entreated them to do it. Neither carried they*
" *off any of the women, though several of them, both wives*
" *and maids, were very handsome; for they believe the enemy*
" *will not harm them, not looking upon whoredom as any ill*
" *thing. Thus Æneas was left alone (with only two ser-*
" *vants and a guide) amongst a hundred women, who, sitting*
" *in a ring with a fire in the middle of them, spent the night*
" *sleepless in dressing of hemp and chatting with the interpre-*
" *ter. When the night was well advanced, they heard a*
" *mighty noise of dogs barking and geese gagling, whereupon*
" *the women slipped off several ways, and the guide ran away,*
" *and all was in such confusion as if the enemy had been upon*
" *them. But Æneas thought it his wisest course to keep close*

" *in*

" Na man ſall preſume to grind quheit, mai-
" ſeloch, or rye, with hand mylnes, except he
" be

" *in his bed-chamber (which was a ſtable) and their to await the iſſue, leſt running out, and, being unacquainted with the country, he ſhould be robbed by the firſt man he met. Preſently both the women and the guide return, acquainting them that all was well, and that they were friends, and no enemies, who had arrived.*

" But whatever roughneſs might be in the manners of " the people of *Northumberland* at that time, it is certain " that the deſcription which Æneas Silvius gives of them " is not their due at this day. Their tables are as well " ſtocked as ever with hens and geeſe, and they have alſo " plenty of good bread and beer. Strangers and travel- " lers are no novelties to them, the roads betwixt *Edin-* " *burgh* and *Newcaſtle* being as much frequented by ſuch " (of all nations) as almoſt any others in the kingdom. " Wine is a greater rarity in a countryman's houſe in *Mid-* " *dleſex* than on the borders of *Northumberland*, where " you ſhall more commonly meet with greater ſtore of it " than in the villages of any other county in England; " and that wine is not the *conſtant* drink of the country " ought no more to be remarked as a thing extraordinary, " than that *Yorkſhire-ale* is not common in *Italy*. The " Moſs-trooping-trade is now very much laid aſide, and a " ſmall ſum will recompenſe all the robberies that are " yearly

" be in lalk of mylnes quhilk ſould grind the " ſam ine; and in this caſe, gif any man " grindes at hand-mylnes, he ſall give the " threttin meaſure as multer (*i. e.* toll.) And " gif any man contraveins this our prohibi- " tion, he ſall tine (*i. e.* loſe) his hand-mylnes " perpetuallie; and ſall grind his cornes at " mylnes payand the twenty-four meaſure." Regiam Majiſtatem, Statutes of the Guild, c. 19; ſee alſo, c. 42. vol. i. p. 20.

II. Hutchinſon ſtates that the wooden bridge acroſs the Tweed, about an hundred yards above where the preſent ſtone one ſtands,

" yearly committed in this county, where men's perſons " are as ſafe, and their goods as ſecure, as in the moſt ci- " vilized kingdoms of *Europe*. Whoredom is reckoned " as ſcandalous a vice here as elſewhere, and, it may be " truly ſaid, far more ſcandalous than in the ſouthern parts " of the kingdom. In a word, the gentry of *Northum-* " *berland* are generally perſons of addreſs and breeding, " and preſervers of the true old Engliſh hoſpitality in " their houſes; and the peaſants are as knowing a peo- " ple, and as courteous to ſtrangers as a man ſhall readily " meet with in any other parts."

ſtands, was ſwept away by the floods in the reign of King John, and was reſtored by William King of Scotland. In Leland's Collectanea, this event is thus mentioned: "The "bridge of Berwick brake about this tyme "with great force of water, bycauſe the arches "of it were to low, and after the making of "it, as it was then, it durid ſcars ix years." "A. D. 1198, hoc tempore ponte de Berwic "inundatione aſportata, Philippus epiſcopus "prohibuit ne pontem re-edificarent nam al-"tera pars ripæ terra erat Dunelmenſis epiſ-"copi *. Tandem tamen pons refectus ro-"gante Gul. de Stoteville †."

CHARLES

† Lel. Col. v. i. p. 539.
‡ Ibid p. 293.

CHARLES I.

Anno 1633, 2d *June.*

The Speech of the Recorder of Berwick (Mr Widdrington of Gray's-Inn) to the King on his progreſs to Edinburgh to be crowned.

MOST GRACIOUS and DREAD SOVEREIGN,

" WHAT the noiſe of uſeleſs and obſolete cannons! What theſe ſtrong, yet deſolate walls! What the reliques of ſometimes warlike ſoldiers! What the ruins of a poor yet ancient borough; what all theſe would ſay (if they could ſay any thing) and what all your Majeſty's humbleſt and meaneſt ſubjects deſire to expreſs with an unanimous and chearful acclamation, is no more but this, That your Majeſty's preſence doth now bring as much joy and comfort to us all, as ever the loſs of this town of Berwick brought ſorrow to the *Engliſh* or *Scottiſh* nation.

" It were unſeaſonable for us to repreſent to your Majeſty's view the gloomy cloud of our preſſures and wants: No, I need not do it. The mite we are to caſt into your Majeſty's ty's treasury will quickly tell you them. We cannot do it, for that cloud is suddenly vanished by the radiant beams of your sun-like appearance, by whose approach these rusty ordnances, these solitary walls, these soldiers, this now despicable town, have all instantly received their former life, lustre, and vigour; and hence we are induced to think that this year (being the year of your Majesty's most royal progress) is likewise the year dreamed on by Plato, wherein all things were to return to their former life, splendor, and excellency.

"You have in your Majesty's eye the representative body of the poor Town of Berwick, yet a Town for (*fuimus Troes*) that hath been the delight, nay the ransom of kings; a true *Helena*, for which many bloody battles have been fought, lost, and regained, several times within the compass of one century of years. A Town the strongest fortress of both of your Majesty's flourishing kingdoms; yet, upon each discord and dissension, banded as a ball between them; if held in the hands of one, then tossed by the other kingdom, a ball that never found reſt until the happy Union.

"A Town at this day as uſeleſs as arms in time of peace, yet may ſerve for your Majeſty to caſt your eye upon as a little map of both your kingdoms, as participating of the nature of both, yet doubtful whether moſt beyond the ordinary limits of the one and without the juriſdiction of the other kingdom, but conſpicuous in the eye of both.

"A Town neither wholly regulated by *Engliſh* or *Scottiſh* laws, but by cuſtoms and uſages in ſome things different from both, yet rather inclined to *Engliſh* laws, and more affecting *Scottiſh* faſhions and language, as being oftener ſaluted by the reſcripts of the one, and ſeeing and hearing of the other.

"Although it is now Engliſh, and ſo hath continued ſince the time of King Edward IV. yet ſuch is our diſtance from the centre of the kingdom, that the lines of thoſe felicities now enjoyed by that kingdom, by your Majeſty's happy Government and reſidence there, do

not

not ſo happily concentre in us, and your own right have long ſince given into your hands.

"Our humble prayers are, that not only that, but all your other crowns, may be unto your Majeſty crowns of roſes without the mixture of any thorns.

"And we moſt affectionately wiſh that the throne of King *Charles*, the great and wiſe ſon of our *Britiſh Solomon*, may be like that of King *David* the Father of *Solomon*, eſtabliſhed before the Lord for ever."

Guild Hall Books from 1643 *to* 1651, *folio* 134.

Barwick upon Tweed.

"Att a private Guild there, holden the 30th day of July, Anno Domini 1649, before the Right Worſhipful Andrew Criſpe, Eſq; Maior, Mr Stephen Jackſon, Alderman, and the reſt of the Guild-brothren. Ordered, that, according to the Guild's deſire, the man which tryeth the witches in Scotland ſhall be ſent for, and ſatisfaction to be given him by the Towne

in

in defraying his charges, and in coming hither, and that the town ſhall engage that no violence be offered him by any perſons within this Towne."

What a humiliating picture of our race does not the above exhibit when contraſted with the preſent enlightened ſtate of the human mind; and what an incitement does it not hold forth to man to exert every power and faculty of his ſoul to acquire true knowledge in what relates to his preſent and future happineſs.

Our limits forbid us from deſcanting farther on this moſt intereſting topic, the contemplation of which muſt impreſs the mind of every good man with true ſentiments of benevolence and piety.

The following are extracts from the Pariſh Regiſters.

June 1659.

THE tenth of June, in the year above mentioned, there was deſtroyed by a fire that aroſe firſt from Rich Winloc houſe, the

the number of thirty-ſeven houſes, ſome houſe or tenement, containing ſeveral two, ſome four families. Being on a Wedneſday, it beginning about ſeven o'clock in the morning and continued till the houre of four in the afternoon, the wind being in the weſt was very tempeſtuous, ſo that all was very ſoon deſtroyed.

Ra Crawforth, Clerk Regiſter.

JANUARII the 19th 1673, being Munday morning, was then by the ſtorm on the Sunday in the afternoon, and Sunday night, before the Munday morning, by the force of weather, ſix ſhips were caſt away betwixt the Holy Iſland and Lamerton Point, belonging to the coal fleet of Newcaſtle. Fifty ſale weighed up there ankers at London times, and very few its thought eſcaped of them. All this is writ for a memoriall, by Ra Crawforth Clerc and Regiſter.

It will appear that in theſe days the pariſh clerk kept the regiſter.

In the year 1745, the Dutch troops, that were then landed here, brought a diſeaſe with them

them reſembling a jail fever. The infections were communicated to the inhabitants, and ſwept off numbers, ſo that in the two months of November and December, 109 funerals appear in the regiſter.

The ſame year during the rebellion in Scotland, the inhabitants of Berwick manifeſted an uncommon degree of zeal, and diſplayed a ſpirit of loyalty ſo diſtinguiſhed in ſupporting the cauſe of their king and country againſt the rebels, as reflects the greateſt honour upon the hiſtory of the Town.

As ſoon as the kingdom became alarmed, upon the breaking out of the rebellion, moſt of the principal inhabitants here were unanimous in uniting to defend their town and protect the crown of their benign ſovereign againſt the ambition and hoſtile deſigns of the *Pretender*.

Accordingly they tendered their ſervices to Government; which being accepted, they formed themſelves into companies, choſe their own officers; and, like men linked in a common cauſe, much to their honour, without pay, did

did the duty of the garrifon, and inftantly threw afide all perfonal or political animofities. Their number amounted to 15 companies, which were raifed in one day. They did not put themfelves to the expence of regimentals. In confideration of ther prompt loyalty, however, government fupplied them with arms and ammunition.

Such unanimity is but feldom to be met with in a borough town. It does great credit to Berwick, and is highly deferving of commendation.

About thirty-one years ago, there was a violent ftorm of thunder and lightening, which, however, did no other damage but fhivering the gallows to a thoufand pieces. But fuch have been the exemplary morals of the inhabitants of Berwick, that fince that period there has been no occafion for the erection of a new one.

It ftood on an eminence clofe by the fide of the road leading to Fowlden, near to the old caftle.

In

In the year 1771, 12th August, his late Royal Highneſs Henry Duke of Cumberland, brother to his preſent Majeſty, viſited Berwick, and was entertained by the Mayor, William Balderſton, Eſq; and corporation, and at the ſame time preſented with the freedom of the town; as were alſo Earl Percy, and Lord Algernon Percy who accompanied him—the Duke of Northumberland and Sir John Huſſey Delaval, who had formerly been preſented with the freedom of the corporation, alſo accompanied his Royal Highneſs—the Earl and Counteſs of Hume, and moſt of the neighbouring gentry, waited on him at the Governor's houſe where he ſtaid while in town. In the evening, there was a ſplendid ball and ſupper given by his Grace the Duke of Northumberland.

His *Royal Highneſs* choſe for his partner the then *celebrated beauty*, *Miſs Johnſton of Hilton.*

In the year 1773, the corporation of Berwick brought an action in the Court of King's Bench againſt James Johnſon, a non-freeman, for

for keeping an open ſhop and ſelling linen-diaper goods by retail. The cauſe was tried at Northumberland aſſizes the ſame year, and a verdict was given for Johnſon ſubject to the opinion of the Court.

In Michaelmas term following, after the cauſe was argued, the Court gave judgment in favour of Johnſon, by which deciſion non-freemen are at liberty to follow their trades in that town, but are ſubject to the payment of higher tolls or duties, at the quay and gates, than freemen of the corporation, which tolls the corporation have immemorially had a right to.

Anno 1786, a puerperal or child-bed fever made its appearance in Berwick, which ſoon became very general, and of which twenty-eight women died in a ſhort time.

A practitioner of the town attended in ſix caſes where the ſymptoms were ſtrongly marked, and all the women recovered. He attributed his ſucceſs chiefly to the following cauſes:

1. To ordering the fires in his patients bed-rooms to be extinguiſhed.
2. To the admiſſion of a free-circulation of air, not only in the apartments where they lay, but alſo as far as could be done in all the adjoining rooms and paſſages.
3. To a liberal uſe of cold drink.
4. To few bed clothes.
5. To a frequent change of bed and body linen.
6. To the excluſion of light.
7. To quietneſs and reſtriction in converſation.

We beg leave to remark that this diſeaſe is but of very rare occurrence when women in this critical ſtate are properly managed. But it is not eaſy to impreſs the minds of mid-wives and nurſes, who in general have but an extremely limited knowledge of the ſtructure of the human body, and animal economy, with the great impropriety and danger that there is in keeping women in the child bed ſtate ſhut up in a hot room, and living on

(as

(as is too generally the caſe) nouriſhing articles of food; and, together with it, permitting them the uſe of wine, ale, caudles, &c. particularly young women of a plethoric habit and ſanguine temperament.

The writer preſumes that a fact, which he ſhall immediately ſtate, will be admitted by the unprejudiced reader to afford a ſtriking proof, that the practice of treating lying-in-women in general on what phyſicians term the antiphlogiſtic courſe, or cool regimen, is more conſiſtent with and better adapted to that ſituation than the diet above-mentioned; and it is, that the practitioner above alluded to, during twenty-four years practice in the obſtetric art, has been ſo fortunate as not to have loſt one patient in any caſe when timely employed, and where the ſole direction was entruſted to himſelf.

It is apprehended, that in thus adverting to a profeſſion, which of all others is moſt intimately connected with the deareſt intereſts of humanity, the withholding from the public any peculiar circumſtances which might tend

tend to the elucidation and improvement of this ſcience, if not criminal, would be at leaſt inconſiſtent with that liberality and candour which the world is entitled to expect from an author. This impreſſion of duty is, therefore, the only apology that he ſhall offer for having introduced this ſubject.

The preſent bloody conteſt in which this country has for theſe ſeveral years paſt been engaged with France, gave riſe to an occurrence in this place, in the year 1794, which, both from its ſingularity and importance, we preſume deſerves to be here narrated

Before the approach of the winter of that year, a ſubſcription was opened at Edinburgh for raiſing a fund for ſupplying our brave troops on the Continent with flannel waiſtcoats. Impreſſed with the idea that no article of clothing might more eſſentially contribute to the health of the ſoldiers, who were to be encamped in a wet and marſhy country during winter, than ſhoes that would powerfully reſiſt wet and moiſture, the author of this

publication

publication caused a pair to be made with thick wooden soles and heels, in imitation of what are called cloggs but lighter, and the edges of the soles and heels rounded in the form of channel pumps and blackened.

These, with a letter accompanying them, he transmitted to the Right Honourable Thomas Elder, then Lord Provost of the City of Edinburgh. His Lordship laid the shoes, together with the letter, before a general meeting of the subscribers to this benevolent institution, who unanimously approving of them, the author hereof was immediately honoured with a polite letter from the Lord Provost, requesting that he would purchase 2000 pairs for the purpose recommended. Having by letter convened at Wooler most of the principal clogg makers in Northumberland, they agreed to furnish the shoes at 2s. 9d. per pair, to be delivered in Berwick free of any expence of carriage. This they accomplished in three weeks from the time of the agreement, with 40 additional pair of shoes.

They

They were all immediately ſent to Edinburgh, and from thence they were tranſported to the Continent in the Oſnaburgh cutter.

We have been informed by an officer who was encamped along with the troops, that, ſo effectually did theſe ſhoes anſwer the purpoſe of keeping the feet dry and comfortable, the right of wearing them frequently became a ſubject of diſpute and contention.

This ſort of ſhoes is univerſally worn all over Northumberland, Cumberland, and ſeveral other counties by labourers; even gentlemen wear them in wet weather.

It would be improper to take leave of this ſubject without obſerving, that the ſubſcription above-mentioned was principally ſet on foot by that moſt active, judicious, and intrepid Magiſtrate, Colonel Elder, the Lord Provoſt, to whom, and his colleagues in office, this country ſtands highly indebted for the preſent public tranquillity it ſo happily enjoys. From this well founded aſſertion none ſurely will withhold their aſſent but ſuch as would

would glory in the violation of every principle of honour, virtue, and humanity, and in the introduction of anarchy, rebellion, rapine, and plunder. Such barbarous innovations and atrocities as these miscreants would wish to introduce, when perpetrated even in the ages of ignorance and superstition, have ever been branded by the virtuous and civilized part of mankind with being disgraceful to the human character. But if such is the epithet bestowed on the untutored, and who had, alas! but seldom or never tasted of the inestimable blessings of national peace and domestic happiness; of the pleasures of an unreserved, confidential, social intercourse, and enjoyed the balmy and soothing sensations, resulting from the study and exercise of a refined taste, in what language is to be found words adequate to depict that degree of turpitude, of those men who, in these enlightened times, and with the advantages of a finished education and a thorough knowledge of the world suffer themselves to

be

be led, by diſappointment or caprice, deliberately to deviſe and attempt the ruin of their native country, and together with it ſacrifice the lives and happineſs, not only of thouſands of its preſent inhabitants, but of ten thouſands yet unborn!

Upon the 20th October 1797, a pilot boat accompanying a ſmack ſailing down the Tweed in a violent wind and ſtormy ſea, was overſet near the mouth of the harbour, by which the rowers, conſiſting of four men, were precipitated into the mercileſs billows. One of theſe waves, however, providentially rolled againſt the bodies of three of the men, in ſuch a direction, and with ſuch force, as inſtantly landed them on the dry beach; and not being ſtunned, and enjoying a free reſpiration, they eagerly took to their heels and eſcaped unhurt; the fourth man, leſs fortunate, after having for a conſiderable time moſt ſtrenuouſly braved the waves, was picked up by a part of the crew belonging to the ſmack.

About

About a year ago a gentleman, a ſtranger to Berwick, inſtead of riding down the high-ſtreet of Caſtlegate in his way to the town in a dark night, and there then being no lamps lighted in that quarter, rode down that part of this ſuburb called Wind Mill-hole. After having paſſed all the buildings to the right, the lights in the windows of Tweedmouth came in view, which he, unfortunately miſtaking for thoſe of Berwick, puſhed his horſe forward to the edge of the bank of the Tweed, and, ſtill urging the animal on, both were precipitated to the bottom, a deſcent upwards of 150 feet; two thirds of which is a perpendicular; and wonderful to relate, although the horſe's brains were daſhed out, yet the rider eſcaped unhurt and climbed up another part of the aſcent carrying his ſaddle and bridle along with him.

The bridge over *Whitadder*, called *Gainſlaw Bridge*, ſituated within the liberties of Berwick, three miles diſtant from the town, was almoſt entirely carried off by a flood on the 21ſt October 1797. The ſame devaſtation happened here to a bridge about twenty years ago.

Since writing the above the following have come to hand:

"Samuel Wilſon's book of extracts now "in the town clerks office."

Folio 106. "No Mayor to brew or bake."

—— 113. "The fairs altered."

—— 114. "None to take Scotch apprentices."

—— 121. "A burgeſs disfranchiſed for "enliſting."

—— 135. "The inhabitants taxed for lead "pipes to the town."

CHAP.

CHAP. III.

Public Buildings.

I. *Governor's Houſe.*

THIS houſe and offices conſtitute the north eaſt ſide of that imperfect ſquare called the palace adjoining to the ſaluting battery. It is a pretty large ſtone building, three ſtories in height. It fronts two ways, one towards the ſea, and the other towards the bridge. The view in both theſe directions is much obſcured by the walls; they, however, ſcreen it greatly from the eaſt and northerly winds.

It commands a very beautiful and extenſive proſpect of the bay from the upper ſtorey. Holy iſland and Bamborough Caſtle are alſo ſeen

ſeen from it. It enjoys a very free circulation of air: and what ſtill farther enhances its value, a neat garden of the richeſt ſoil belongs to it, which lies behind it. Cloſe by the outſide of the garden wall there is a rookery.

This edifice was built about the ſame time with the barracks.

II. *The Barracks.*

THESE buildings are very ſtrong. They are two ſtories in height, of free ſtone, and ſtand on high ground eaſt north eaſt of the town.

The ſituation is healthy and well aired. They compoſe a ſquare of 217 by 121 feet inſide, excluſive of which they have two back yards, with reſervoirs in each for aſhes and other conveniences. There are twenty-four rooms for officers, and ſeventy-two for privates; the latter contain 576 men. There is an ordnance ſtore, which forms the ſouth

face

Engraved For Dr. Fuller's History of Berwick.

Drawn by Joseph Alexander, Berwick. *Engraved by R. Scott.*

VIEW *of the* BARRACKS *and* PARADE *from the* WALLS *above the* COW PORT.

face of the ſquare. The north face of it conſiſts of a guard-houſe, a black-hole, and a gate-way, over which, on the outſide, the King's coat of arms are exquiſitely carved in ſtone: and in the middle of the ſquare there is a fountain that ſupplies the barracks with water. There alſo, and in the adjoining parade, young troops are drilled; but the puniſhment of *flagellation* is only inflicted within the ſquare.

Since writing the above, a thorough repair of theſe barracks has commenced. Every apartment is to have a new floor and new windows. The windows in the upper ſtorey are to be enlarged and made ſquare, inſtead of being ſemicircular at the top as before. A large kitchen at the back of the building, upon the north-eaſt ſide, is already built, for cooking the men's victuals in. This will be a great convenience, as formerly each ſoldier had to prepare his victuals in his own room. There is alſo a large apartment where the troops may dreſs themſelves.

Theſe

These repairs will soon be completed, as a great number of men are employed in carrying on this useful and necessary work.

These barracks were finished 1719.

III. *The Hospital.*

THIS building is situated on the west side of the back way, near the barracks. It is two stories in height and tolerably well aired.

The house contains twenty-four beds for the sick, and is provided with a surgery, but which is by far too small for holding the medicines that are requisite for a complete regiment.

Were the high wall taken down which incloses this building in front, and a railing put in its place, it would render the ventilation of the house still more complete.

IV. *Ordnance Houſe.*

THIS building, which is appropriated for the dwelling houſe of the commanding royal engineer, ſtands cloſe to the artillery ground, on the ſouth ſide of the barracks, about 100 yards from them. It is two ſtories high, and very commodious. Beſides, it is walled in and furniſhed with a good garden and ſuitable offices.

V. *The Main Guard.*

IT is moſt incommodiouſly placed in the high ſtreet, 100 yards diſtant from the Scotch Gate, the ſpot where it ſhould have ſtood. It meaſures 65 feet in length.

It conſiſts of a room for the officer of the guard, a large apartment in the middle of the houſe for the ſoldiers, with benches for them to lye upon it. There is likewiſe a large fire place in it. Beſides it has an apartment call-ed the black-hole.

In

In front there is a piazza too, which ſcreens the men on guard.

VI. *The Town Hall.*

By attending to the plate repreſenting the ground plan of the Town, this building will be found to ſtand longitudinally, and nearly in the middle of the high ſtreet at its lower end.

It is a ſtately pile of modern architecture, conſiſting of fine hewn ſtone, three ſtories high, a handſome ſpire, and a beautiful pediment or frontiſpiece ſupported by four graceful circular columns of the Tuſcan order, being 32 feet in height and nine feet and a half in circumference. Were this elegant piece of architecture placed in a ſituation where it might appear to advantage, it would vie with almoſt any other in the kingdom. The ſteeple is compoſed, firſt, of the Tuſcan, ſecond, Doric, and, third, Ionic order; and is one hundred and fifty feet in height. It is furniſhed

Engraved for Dr. Fuller's History of Berwick.

Drawn by A. Carse. Engraved by R. Scott.

Drawn by Joseph Alexander, Berwick. Engraved by R. Scott.

EAST VIEW *of the* GOVERNOR'S HOUSE &c *of* BERWICK.

niſhed with an excellent pail of bells, eight in number. It has alſo a fine clock which exhibits the hours in all directions. The roof is made of ſtrong timber, and is covered with lead and ſlate; the engraving will ſhow that the roof is embelliſhed with ſurrounding balluſtrades, and further ornamented by vaſes, &c. Part of the ground floor conſiſts of cells for confining perſons apprehended for capital crimes, or ſuch as are under ſentence of death; ſome other apartments of it are let out by the corporation to tradeſmen. The eaſtern part of the above floor is formed into a piazza, which is allotted for the poultry, meal, egg, and butter markets, and alſo for the hiring of ſervants. It is called the Exchange; and meaſures 46 feet 9 inches in length, 38 feet 8 inches in width, and 13 feet in height.

The middle ſtorey conſiſts of two halls, a committee room, two ſmaller apartments, and a large ſtair-caſe leading to the uppermoſt floor.

The firſt or outer hall is ſixty feet long, thirty-one and a half broad, and ſeventeen feet high. In this hall the mayor and members of parliament are elected, and the courts, both civil and criminal, are held here, as are alſo the guilds. It has four large windows in the ſouth ſide of it, in front of which are the erections where the courts ſit. On the wainſcoting above the mayor's chair (as it may be called) there is a drawing of juſtice reſting her feet on a figure of the terreſtrial globe.

The King's coat of arms, repreſented on a ſquare piece of canvas, project from the top of the wainſcoting immediately above the middle of the Mayor and Juſtices bench.

Over the great door of this hall in the inſide the arms of the corporation, on a ſmall ſcale, are emboſſed. In the north corner of the hall there is a hewn ſtone building with an iron door for holding the archives of the corporation.

The inner hall is forty-ſeven feet four inches in length, twenty-three feet eight inches in breadth, and ſixteen feet in height. It is exceedingly well lighted, having four windows

dows fronting the ſouth, and a large Venetian one in the eaſt end of the hall. The aſſemblies were formerly held here, and the Mayor's dinners and other great entertainments were alſo given in it. Over the chimney-piece is another repreſentation of the blind goddeſs done upon a large ſcale in ſtucco, A. D. 1770.

The arms of the corporation are beautifully emboſſed in the front of the pediment, and are much admired for their exquiſite workmanſhip. The date of their erection we learn from the following inſcription in carved letters on the baſe of the pediment.

" MDCCLVII. Samuel Burn, Eſq; Mayor."

On the entablature is the following inſcription in raiſed capitals, ornamented with gold leaf, all capitals :

" FINISHED A. D. MDCCLIV.

" WILLIAM TEMPLE, Eſq; MAYOR."

Over the outer door is another inſcription, viz.

" Joſeph Dodds, architect, 1754."

The

The whole of this building was not erected at the ſame period. That part conſtituting the outer hall or Town houſe, as it is commonly called, was finiſhed agreeable to the inſcription 1754. The other part, conſiſting of the inner hall, was finiſhed 1761, as appears by the following inſcription on a belt, near the top of the eaſter gable.

"William Hall, Eſq; Mayor, 1761."

Beneath the Venetian window, on another belt, there is another inſcription, viz.

"Henry Hodſon, Eſq; Mayor, 1760."

The laſt built part is ſeven feet nine inches wider than the firſt. The projection thus formed is on the back part of the building. The whole length of the edifice, including the thickneſs of the walls, is 136 feet three inches. We aſcend to the portico by thirteen ſteps. It meaſures twenty-ſix feet ſix inches in length, and eleven feet three inches in breadth.

The upper flat is occupied as a common goal, and is perhaps the moſt healthy and pleaſant one in the kingdom. This is owing to its many large windows, from which the priſoners

ſoners enjoy ſeveral excellent views of the Town, the German Ocean, Bambro' Caſtle, and Holy Iſland.

There is a long gallery which they are allowed to perambulate. Tradeſmen when confined have a liberty to work in this goal. We have even heard of ſome who retrieved their fortunes in it.

Perſons laid up for debt or petty offences are permitted to walk on the roof of the building to enjoy the free air. This circumſtance, together with the extenſive and beautiful ſurrounding proſpects already noticed, muſt both be a pleaſant and ſalutary indulgence to the priſoners. Add to this, whilſt theſe captivating objects tend to ſoothe the mind, and to alleviate the ſufferings of confinement, they, at the ſame time, hold out the ineſtimable bleſſings of unreſtrained liberty—the birth right, and generally the reward of virtue, induſtry, and honeſty; but the indolent, the fraudulent, the robber, and the murderer are not entitled to this heaven-born enjoyment.

The

The Town-houſe is built of ſtone, which was quarried at Edrington caſtle, the property of Joſeph Marſhall, Eſq; and is ſaid to be by far the fineſt in this neighbourhood.

The eaſt end or Exchange, as it is commonly termed, was built of ſtone procured at New-mills within the liberties, and which belong to the corporation.

VII. *Reſervoir of Water.*

THIS reſervoir ſtands about half way between the foot of Caſtlegate and Scotch gate, on the north ſide of the pavement. It meaſures ſixty feet in length, ſixteen feet in width, and eight feet in depth. The quantity of water which it is capable of holding is 200 tons. Nothing of the building is ſeen but its front, which is of fine hewn ſtone; the other parts of it are covered with earth.

Over the door in hewn letters are,

"Begun to be built 1789. G. Forſter, Eſq; "Mayor."

"Finiſhed 1790. David Stow, Eſq; Mayor."

The

Engraved for Dr. Fuller's History of Berwick.

Drawn by A. Cooper

Drawn by A. Carse

Engraved by R. Scott

VIEW of BERWICK CHURCH

The Church.

In A. D. 1641, the Mayor and burgeſſes petitioned Charles the I. to grant them a patent or brief in order to collect money to build a church, as the old one, which is ſaid to have ſtood at the head of Mary-Gate, and to have been called St Mary's Church, had been taken down in the reign of Queen Mary, and appropriated for building walls and other fortifications.

The brief, which is here annexed, was granted, but the work did not commence until 1648. It was finiſhed 1652, under the direction of Colonel George Fenwicke * of Brenkburne,

* He lies buried in the church, nearly oppoſite the pulpit, with the following epitaph over him:

Col. Geo.
Fenwicke of
Brenkburne, Eſq;
Governor of Berwick,
In the year 1652 was

A

Brenkburne, during the time of the Rebel Parliament. The expence of it amounted to fourteen hundred pounds, as appears in the archives of the corporation.

This handſome edifice, conſiſting of two ſtories in height, ſtands a little to the north of that area termed Parade: The intervening ſpace is occupied as the church-yard.

The ſecond ſtorey does not ſtand on the walls of the firſt, but is ſupported by two rows of pillars in the church, joined together by arches. The pillars are three on either ſide, placed 15 feet diſtant from the walls of the ground ſtorey. A ſtranger viewing the outſide of this church might ſuppoſe he ſaw one church ſtanding on the top of another.

It is not ſtrictly built according to any of the orders of architecture. The windows, which are

A principal inſtru-
ment of cauſing this
Church to be built;
And died March 15th
1656.
A good man is a public good.

are large and elegant, approach nearer that of the Venetian than to any other kind of window. There are ten in number facing the ſouth, five in the under and five in the upper ſtorey. There are the ſame number in the back part of the building.

It has a large Gothic window in the eaſt end, with one on both ſides of it ſimilar to thoſe in front. Theſe, with two windows in the weſt end, light the church uncommonly well.

It has ſeveral beautiful lofts or galleries, and is upon the whole moſt handſomely ſeated. The principal ſtair-caſe is ſpacious and elegant. It has alſo an excellent organ placed in the weſt end of it. The altar piece, in the oppoſite end, is exquiſite workmanſhip.

By the engraving it will be ſeen to have no ſpire, which is ſaid to be characteriſtic of Cromwell the uſurper, in whoſe reign it was built. The bells in the Town-houſe ſerve for aſſembling the congregation.

The building meaſures ninety feet eight inches in length, within the walls, and fifty two feet and a half in width.

It is ſaid that Divine ſervice was firſt performed in it by a Presbyterian minister during Cromwell's usurpation.

The church-yard, including the church, consists of two acres and twelve perches of ground. The south side of the church-yard is the principal burying ground. The grave stones are so very numerous as to surprise strangers, and excite unpleasant emotions. It is accounted for in this way, *1st*, From there being no other place in all the parish appropriated for interment; *2dly*, From no money being exacted, as in many other towns, for the liberty of erecting monuments.

At the back of the church we discovered a monument with the inscription upon it almost totally obliterated. What is legible is here stated as a matter of some curiosity.

"——Hill. De. Departed this
"Lyfe—IE. of——yeare 1577."

This date is 125 years prior to the building of the present church*.

Vicar's

* *The Brief by the King for Building a Church.*

CHARLES, by the grace of God, King of England, Scotland, France, and Ireland, Defender of the Faith, &c.

Vicar's House

STANDS on the weſt ſide of the Parade. It is a handſome building of brick, two ſtories

&c. To all and ſingular Archbiſhops, Biſhops, Archdeacons, Deans, and their officials, Parſons, Vicars, Curats, and to all ſpiritual perſons; and alſo to all Juſtices of Peace, Mayors, Sheriffs, Bailiffes, Conſtables, Churchwardens and Headboroughs, and to all Officers of Cities, Boroughs, and Towns Corporate; and to all other our Officers, Miniſters, and ſubjects whatſoever they be, as well within liberties as without, to whom theſe preſents ſhall come, greeting.

WHEREAS, by a petition to ourſelfe exhibited, bearing date the ninth day of July 1641, we are credibly given to underſtand by our truſty and well beloved ſubjects the Mayor, Bayliffes, and Burgeſſes of Barwick upon Tweed, in our kingdome of England, neer adjacent to our kingdome of Scotland, humble ſhewing; and to our knowledge, that our towne of Barwicke, being an antient and great towne, and many inhabitants there reſiding; there was formerly a very faire and ſpacious church, which church, in Queene Maries raigne, was pulled downe and utterly demoliſhed, and the ſtones and other materials thereof were employed for the erecting of a new wall and fortification, in or neer the place where the ſaid church then ſtood, with an intention to have built another church inſtead thereof, in a more convenient place of the ſaid towne ſtories in height, with a coach roof. It has nine windows in front, with a double gate and

towne of Barwicke; but the alteration of time being and continuing very troubleſome, and no ſettled peace betwixt the two kingdoms; the ſaid inhabitants were neceſſitated to make uſe of a very little church, meanly built, and not room enough to contain half ſo many people as inhabit in the ſaid towne; and then our Royal Father, after the happy and bleſſed union between the two kingdoms, ſeriouſly taking the premiſſes into his princely conſideration, did purpoſe and reſolve (after the finiſhing of the bridge at Barwicke over the river of Tweed) to erect and build a new church in the ſaid towne: But it pleaſed God that our ſaid late deare Father departed this life before that great work of the bridge was finiſhed, or the other pious work of the church taken in hand; and now ourſelfe have finiſhed to our great charge the work of the ſaid bridge; and do reſolve to fulfill, according to our ſaid deare Father's intention, the humble ſupplication and petition of our true and loyal ſubjects aforeſaid, in granting them our gracious letter patents of collection, (according to their deſire), whereby they may be enabled to aſke, gather, receive, and take the charities of all our pious and well diſpoſed ſubjects towards the furtherance of the new building of the houſe of God, in ſo great and populous a town. Now we, in our princely compaſſion to works of this nature, and according to our wonted clemency, have therefore thought good to recommend the ſaid work unto all and railing. It has excellent offices and a good garden behind the houſe.

The

all our loving ſubjects whatſoever, within our realme of England. Not doubting but that they will freely and liberally (and the rather for our recommendation hereof) extend their charitable benevolence for the erecting and new building of the ſaid church in our town of Barwick aforeſaid.

Know yee therefore, that of our eſpeciall grace and princely compaſſion, we have given and granted, and by theſe letters patent under our Great Seale of England, do give and grant unto our ſaid ſubjects, the Mayor, Bailiffes, and Burgeſſes in our town of Barwick aforeſaid, and to their deputy and deputies, the bearer or bearers hereof, full power, licence and authority, to aſke, gather, receive, and take the alms and charitable benevolence of all our loving ſubjects whatſoever, inhabiting within all our counties, cities, boroughs, and towns corporate, pariſhes, villages, and in all other privileged places whatſoever, within our kingdome of England, and not elſewhere, for and towards the effecting of ſo good, ſo neceſſary, and pious a work, and to no other uſe, intent, or purpoſe whatſoever.

Wherefore we will and command you, and every of you, that at ſuch time and times as the ſaid Mayor, Bailiffes, and Burgeſſes in our town of Barwick aforeſaid, their deputy or deputies, the bearer or bearers hereof, ſhall come and repaire to any of your Churches, Chappels, or

other

The Bridge.

THIS beautiful bridge is ſituated cloſe by the *quay*, nearly in a line with the weſtern lane,

other places, to aſke and receive the gratuities and charitable benevolence of our ſaid ſubjects, quietly to permit and ſuffer them ſo to doe, without any manner your lets or contradictions. And you, the ſaid Parſons, Vicars, and Curates, for the better ſtirring up of a charitable benevolence, deliberately to publiſh and declare the tenor of theſe our letters patents, or the copy or briefe hereof, unto our ſaid ſubjects, upon ſome Sunday ſhortly after the ſame ſhall be tendered unto you, and before the expiration of the date hereof, earneſtly exhorting and perſuading them to extend their liberall contributions in ſo good and charitable a work.

And you, the Churchwardens of every pariſh where ſuch collection is to be made (as aforeſaid), to collect and gather the almes, and charitable benevolence, of all our loving ſubjects, as well ſtrangers as others; and what ſhall be by you ſo gathered, to be by the miniſter and yourſelves endorced on the backſide of theſe our letters patents, or the copy or briefe hereof, in words at length, and not in figures; and the ſumme and ſummes of mony ſo gathered and endorced, our will and pleaſure is, ſhall be delivered to the bearer or bearers of theſe our letters patents, warranted and allowed to receive the ſame, and to no other perſon, when as thereunto you ſhall be required.

And,

lane, and 50 or 60 yards below the site of the old timber bridge. It is built of fine hewn stone, and has 15 spacious and elegant arches. It measures 1164 feet in length, including the land-

And, *lastly*, whereas we are informed of the great abuse which is now crept in amongst these poore people who sell their licences unto some other person, whereby mens charity goeth not the right way, but unto such as deserve it least, that from henceforth our will and pleasure is, that if it may appear unto you, or any of you, that the Mayor, Bailiffes, and Burgesses in our town of Barwick aforesaid, have contracted any bargain, or made, or shall make, sale of these our letters patents, whereby the benefit shall passe from them to any other person, that thereupon these our letters patents to be voyd and to none effect, any statute, law, ordinance, or provision heretofore made to the contrary in any wise notwithstanding.

In witness whereof, we have caused these our letters to be made patents, to continue for the space of one whole yeare next after the date hereof, and no longer. Witness ourselfe, at Westminstre, the one-and-twentieth day of July, in the seventeenth year of our raign. DAWE.

GOD SAVE THE KING.

Printed by T. Badger, for J. Bodington.

Endorsed.—Collected at Thornhill the seaven-and-twentith of March, the summe of tenne shilling and tenne pence, by William Mountain, Costin Currant, Thomas Annislay, and John Clayton, church-wardens.

land-ſtalls. Its width is 17 feet. At each of the pillars, which are 14 in number, there is an out-let to both ſides; without theſe there would be much greater danger either in walking or riding along the bridge than there is at preſent. The ſixth pillar ſeparates Berwick from the county Palatine of Durham. The battlements at the out-lets at this pillar are always covered with ſods as a guide to conſtables and others in the execution of warrants for the apprehenſion of delinquents.

The ſouth gate of the town, together with the adjoining guard-houſe, ſhut up the bridge at its northern extremity. Towards the middle of it there are two ſtrong wooden barriers 148 feet diſtant from each other. In order to give additional ſecurity to this mode of defence, they are made to project conſiderably beyond the battlements.

After long reſearch, we fortunately hit upon a bundle of parchments, and three large books; all of them are in manuſcript, and contain every tranſaction reſpecting the building of this celebrated bridge.

As a matter of curioſity, and even of utility,

lity, we have given a place here to the foling ſtatements extracted from theſe old records above-mentioned, which form part of the archives of the corporation. They are tranſcribed as accurately as the obliterated ſtate of the manuſcript would admit of.

" 20th July 1637, Duplicament of the Account of the Mayor and Burgeſſes of Berwick upon Tweed for new building a Stone Bridge and a Church*,

" Stating, That King James, by indenture under the Great Seal of England, bearing date the 23d of May, in the 6th year of our reign of England, France, and Ireland, and of Scotland the 41ſt, did grant to James Bailyf, burgeſs of the town of Berwick, for new building a ſtone bridge over the river of Tweed, as well 10,000l. of debt and arrearages of rents, being of record, or not of record, concealed and unjuſtly detained goods, or the value of them due in right of the Crown of our England and dutchy of Lancaſter, in any year or years, from the 1ſt year of the reign of King Henry the 7th, until the end of the 42d year of the

* N. B. There does not appear to have been any of this money applied to the building of a church.

reign of the late Queen Elizabeth, for the which no eſtabliſhment, compoſition, extent, or ſeizure of record hath already been had or made: As alſo, one moiety of 18,000l. of debts remaining due and anſwerable in the right of our Crown of England or dutchy of Lancaſter, in any year or years ſince the 1ſt year of the reign of King Henry the 7th, until the end of the year of the 30th year of the late Queen Elizabeth, the ſame debts as well of 10,000l. as the moiety of 18,000l. to be levied, recovered, and enjoyed to the only uſe and behoof of the ſaid James Bailyf and his aſſigns, for and towards the building of the ſaid ſtone bridge at Berwick aforeſaid, as by the ſame indenture amongſt other things may appear; which ſaid grant of debts, as aforeſaid, ſo paſſed in the name of the ſaid James Bailyf, was nevertheleſs granted by us at the humble petition and ſuit of our right truſty and right well beloved *Couſin and Counſellor George*, *Earl of Downebarr*, deceaſed; and the moneys thereupon received for the moſt part was paid for the uſe of the ſaid Earl towards the building of the ſaid bridge,

part

part whereof, the heirs, executors, or administrators of the ſaid Earl, ſtands anſwerable unto us upon the account of the ſaid James Bailyf. Now, for as much as the ſaid James Bailyf having, by our order, ſurrendered the ſaid grant of debts to be cancelled, and thereby all the remainder of ſaid debts not formerly levied by him, and for that we are not willing that a work of ſo much good conſequence as the building of the ſaid bridge, tending ſo much to the benefit of the ſubjects of England and of Scotland, to have the ſame rely upon uncertainty of monies to be levied out of old debts which are ſlowly recovered, do grant 8,000l. at the time hereafter mentioned, viz. 2000l. for the works to be done this year, and afterwards 1000l. yearly, or more, at the diſcretion of our Treaſurer of England and the Chancellor of our Exchequer; until the ſaid ſum of 8000l. be fully ſatisfied, our will and pleaſure is, that our Treaſurer of England do ſet down orders in writing, as you ſhall think meet to be obſerved by the Mayor, Bailiffs, and Burgeſſes, for their better proceedings of the ſaid work, which ſhall be your ſufficient warrant

and

and diſcharge in this behalf." It then proceeds with the following orders to the Mayor:

"Two honeſt and diſcreet burgeſſes to have the daily overſeeing of the workmen and labourers, and one to have the cuſtody and charge of the materials, and delivery of the ſame out to the workmen as the ſervice ſhall daily require.

"The Mayor, and ſix of the beſt and moſt ſufficient Aldermen and Burgeſſes of the town, to ſubſcribe their names to the weekly books of the charges paid to the different workmen: That at the ſame time George Nichollſon, Eſq; now paymaſter, be alſo preſent at the ſaid weekly payments, and ſubſcribe to the ſame, and to be made acquainted with all other proceedings of the ſaid works for his Majeſty's better ſatisfaction therein.

"That he certify once in three months, the ſtate of the ſame works, and how they forward them, to the end his Majeſty may be acquainted therewith, and alſo how far you proceed every year. That James Burrell, maſter maſon, be allowed 2s. 6d. *per* day for overſeeing and directing the ſaid work during the con-

continuance thereof, in like ſort as he received in the time of the late Earl of Dunbar; and alſo allow the wages of 16d. a-day for a clerk to keep the books of payment.

" The whole of the accounts following, on ending the ſaid bridge in 1634, were declared before the Right Honourable and Right Reverend Father in God, William, Lord Biſhop of London, Lord High Treaſurer of England and France, Lord Cottington, Chancellor, the 20th July 1637, in the 13th year of the reign of our Lord Charles, by the grace of God, King of England, France, Scotland, and Ireland, defender of the faith. Given under our Privy Seal, at our Palace of Weſtminſter, the 21ſt of May, in the 9th year of our reign of England, and of Scotland the 44th.

Caſh iſſued from the treaſury to Sir Robert Jackſon, Knight, occaſionally from the 26th May 1611, to the 23d November 1635, -	L. 15,000	0	0
Sum total of payments and allowances made yearly, from			
Carry over	L. 15,000	0	0

Carried over	L. 15,000	0	0
the 20th June 1611, to the 6th September 1634,	14,396	13	6
	L. 603	6	6

Whereof allowed to the ſaid accountant by warrant of the Right Honourable William, Lord Biſhop of London, Lord High Treaſurer of England, dated the 7th day of July 1637, grounded upon his Majeſty's pleaſure, ſignified by Sir Sidney Montague, Knight, one of the maſters of the requeſts, dated the 23d day of June 1637, as well for the riding charges of divers perſons to London and back again ſundry times by the ſpace of * 23 years, 4 months, and 4 days, ended the 24th of October 1634, with other neceſſary charges and expence at the receipt ſignet and Privy Seal, procuring money and warrants for building the ſaid ſtone bridge, and in certifying from time to time the Lords of the Privy Counſel how thoſe works proceeded and went forward, as by the two books of accounts, delivered

* The period of commencing and ending of the Mayor and Bailiffs accounts paſſed in the Exchequer. The account previous thereto having been kept and paſſed at the Exchequer by the Earl of Dunbar, for about a twelvemonth before, will complete the period of building the bridge, viz. 24 years, 4 months, and 4 days.

livered to the auditors, particularly appeareth 499l. 10s. 10d as alſo for ſundry charges by them diſburſed ſince the ſaid 24th October 1634 in repairing of the ſaid bridge, until, and for the 9th of February 1636, viz. for emptions and for proviſions of ſtones, deals, clay, chingles, ropes, tar, and other neceſſaries, 31l. 8d. wages of maſons, carpenters, labourers, and others, 11l. 13s. 4d.; and for taſk work done in and about eleven of the aforeſaid 14 pillars, 21l. 3s. 8d. in all, as by a third book lately delivered to the auditors upon oath of Sir Robert Jackſon, Knight, one of theſe accountants, and ſubſcribed by the Mayor, Aldermen, and Burgeſſes of the town of Berwick, appeareth 63l. 17s. 2d. Which ſums, conjoined together, and allowed, amount unto - - - L. 563 8 0

And then the ſaid accountants will remain indebted upon this their account, the ſum of - 39 18 6

L. 603 6 6

GUIL. LONDON *.

Geo. Cottington,

Examinat per nos { Joſ. Worfield. Geo. Bingley, } Auditores.

The

* For Gulielmus Londinenſis.

The length of the bridge 388 yards, and 17 feet broad. Built in the ſpace of twenty-four years four months and four days, ended the 24th day of October 1634, in the tenth year of the reign of King Charles.

Workmen employed occaſionally every year:

Surveyor 18d. per day.

Clerk 16d. per day

Two Maſter Maſons 20d. per day

From 22 to 51 other Maſons, ſome 13d.—12d.—10d. and 9d. per day.—10d.—6d. and 4d. a tide.

Two Maſter Carpenters 20d. per day.

From 15 to 23 other Carpenters 10d. per day. Apprentices 7d. and 6d. per day.—6d. for night tide, and 4d. per day.

11 Smiths, ſome 12d.—10d.—9d. and 8d. per day.

From 8 to 10 Quarrymen, ſome 10d.—9d. and 8d. per day.—4d. night tide, 3d. the day.

From 33 to 80 Labouring Men, ſome 7d. 6d.—5d. and 4d. per day.—2d. per tide.

From

From 23 to 42 Labouring Women, 4d. per day.

From 2 to 7 Labouring Boys, 4d. per day.

From 6 to 8 Lightermen, ſome 10d.—8d. and 7d. per day.—4d. per tide.

2 Sawyers 8d. per day.

4 Ship-wrights and boat-wrights 30d.—24d. and 18d. per day.

2 Slaters 12d. ſome 7d. a day.

2 Wheel wrights 10d. per day.

The particular payments for ſix days work, begun the 17th June, and ended the 23d.

2*s*. 6*d*. *per diem*.—15*d*. *per tide*.

			£.	s.	d.
James Burrell, ſurveyor	6	days	0	15	0
Water-work -	5	tides	0	6	3

16*d*. *per diem*.

John Shell, clerk	6	days	0	8	0

MASONS.—20*d*. *per diem*.—10*d*. *per tide*.

Lancelot Branxton, maſter-maſon - -	6	days	0	10	0
Water works -	5	tides	0	4	2

14d. per diem.—4d. per tide.

				£.	s.	d.
Bartie Cotes	-	8	days	0	7	0
Water works	-	1	tide	0	0	4

14d. per diem.—4d. per tide.

				£.	s.	d.
Clement Brocket		5¼	days	0	5	8½
Water works	-	1	tide	0	0	4
Thomas Blythe	-	4½	days	0	4	10½
Water works	-	1	tide	0	0	4
Andrew Forefter		5	days	0	5	5
Stephen Sym	-	4¾	days	0	5	1½
Water works	-	1	tide	0	0	4
John Nealfon	-	5½	days	0	5	11
Water works	-	4	tides	0	1	4
William Crow	-	3½	days	0	3	9½
Water works	-	1	tide	0	0	4
Edward Winley		3¾	days	0	4	1½
John Alexander		6	days	0	6	6

12d. per diem.—4d. per tide.

				£.	s.	d.
Sanyell Burrell	-	6	days	0	6	0
Michael Millner		1	day	0	1	0
Chriftopher Sanderfon		6	days	0	6	0
Water works	-	1	tide	0	0	4
James Cawart	-	likewife		0	6	4

10*d.*

10d. per diem.—4d. per tide.

			£.	s.	d.
Jeſper Jackſon	-	6 days	0	5	0
Water works	-	1 tide	0	0	4
William Rogers		likewiſe	0	5	4
Charles Robſon		likewiſe	0	5	4
John Butler	-	5½ days	0	4	7
Water work	-	1 tide	0	0	4
Thomas Craie	-	5¼ days	0	4	4½

10d. per diem.—3d. per tide.

Thomas Roſe	-	6 days	0	5	0
Water works	-	1 tide	0	0	3

9d. per diem.

Henry Jackſon		6 days	0	4	6
George Coxſon		6 days	0	4	6

8d. per diem.

Clement Ramſhaw		6 days	0	4	0

7d. per diem.

Tobias Colledg		6 days	0	3	6
Raphe Moors	-	6 days	0	3	6

6d. per day.—2d. per tide.

Mark Horſley	-	6 days	0	3	0
John Cawart	-	6 days	0	3	0
Water works	-	2 tides	0	0	4

4*d.*

4d. per diem.

				£.	s.	d.
Robert Preſton	-	6	days	0	2	0

CARPENTERS.—16*d. per diem*—6*d. day-tide*—8*d. night tide.*

				£.	s.	d.
Ralph Fairley	-	6	days	0	8	0
Water works	by day	3	tides	0	1	6
	by night	1	tide	0	0	8

13*d. per diem.*—6½*d. per tide.*

				£.	s.	d.
Clyver Givon	-	6	days	0	6	6
Water works by night		1	tide	0	0	6½

12*d. per diem.*—6*d. per tide.*

				£.	s.	d.
Raph Garnett	-	6	days	0	6	0
Water works	-	1	tide	0	0	6

10*d. per diem.*—4*d. day-tide.*—5*d. night-tide.*

				£.	s.	d.
James Anderſon		5	days	0	4	2
Water works	-	1	tide	0	0	5
Robert Atkinſon		6	days	0	5	0
Water works	-	1	tide	0	0	5
John Dinnes	-	6	days	0	5	0
Water works	by day	1	tide	0	0	4
	by night	1	tide	0	0	5

9*d. per diem.*—4½*d. per tide.*

				£.	s.	d.
Robert Givon	-	6	days	0	4	6

John

				£.	s.	d.
John White	-	6	days	o	4	6
Water works	-	1	tide	o	o	4½
8d. per diem.—4d. per tide.						
Edward Catterell		6	days	o	4	o
Water works	-	1	tide	o	o	4
Robert Rofe	-	6	days	o	4	o
James Waddie	-	6	days	o	4	o

SHIPWRIGHTS.—2*s.* 6*d. per diem.*—6*d. per tide.*

William Burden		5	days	o	12	6
Work by night		4	tides	o	2	o
2s. per day.—6d. per tide.						
Arthur Browell		5	days	o	10	o
Work by night		4	tides	o	2	o
Stephen Riveley		5	days	o	10	o
Work by night		4	tides	o	2	o
18d. per diem.—6d. per tide.						
Henry Burrell	-	5	days	o	7	6
Work by night	-	4	tides	o	2	o
Robert Burrell	-	5	days	o	7	6
Work by night		4	tides	o	2	o

SMITHS.

SMITHS.—8*d.* *per diem.*

			£.	s.	d.
John Prefton -	6	days	0	4	0

LEIGHTNERMEN.—8*d.* *per diem.*

William Mowdie	6	days	0	4	0
Edward Crawforth	6	days	0	4	0
5d. per diem.—2½d. per tide.					
John Nicholfon	6	days	0	2	6
Water works -	1	tide	0	0	2½

QUARRYMEN.—9*d.* *per diem.*—3*d.* *per tide.*

Thomas Wetherburn	3	days	0	2	3
Water works -	4	tides	0	1	0
8d. per diem.—3d. per tide.					
Thomas Law -	5½	days	0	3	8
Water works -	4	tides	0	1	0
Thomas Bankes	5½	days	0	3	8
7d. per diem.—2d. per tide.					
Ofwole Walker	6	days	0	3	6
Water works -	4	tides	0	0	8
6d. per diem.					
Thomas Armour	6	days	0	3	0

LA-

LABOURERS.—*6d. per diem.—3d. and 2d. per tide.*

			£.	s.	d.
Lancelot Selbie	6	days	0	3	0
John Crawforth, junior	6	days	0	3	0
John Crawforth, ſenior	6	days	0	3	0
Water works -	5	tides	0	1	3
George Law -	6	days	0	3	0
Water works -	4	tides	0	0	8
Edmond Thurburn	likewiſe		0	3	8
Thomas Daies -	likewiſe		0	3	8
Chriſtopher Purvis	likewiſe		0	3	8
Francis Spencer	likewiſe		0	3	8
Stephen Nicolſon	likewiſe		0	3	8
William Mayne	5½	days	0	2	9
Water works -	2	tides	0	0	4
Robert Lattie -	5¾	days	0	2	10½
Water works -	2	tides	0	0	4
John Branxton	likewiſe		0	3	2½
Leonard Brown	likewiſe		0	3	2½
Patrick Read -	5¾	days	0	2	10½
Water works -	3	tides	0	0	6
William Humble	6	days	0	3	0
Water works -	3	tides	0	0	6
Charles Haule -	likewiſe		0	3	6

LA-

LABOURERS.—*6d. per diem.—3d. and 2d. per tide.*

		£.	s.	d.
James Singleton	likewise	0	3	6
Alexander Maxwell	likewise	0	3	6
Andrew Storie	likewise	0	3	6
Thomas Bell -	$5\frac{3}{4}$ days	0	2	$10\frac{1}{2}$
Water works -	4 tides	0	0	8
Thomas Monkaster	6 days	0	3	0
Water works -	4 tides	0	0	8
William Camell	likewise	0	3	8
Richard Kendrow	likewise	0	3	8
Robert Maine -	likewise	0	3	8
George Shanks	likewise	0	3	8
Thomas Wood	$5\frac{3}{4}$ days	0	2	$10\frac{1}{2}$
Water works -	2 tides	0	0	4
Nicholas Alexander	6 days	0	3	0
Barwick Carston	6 days	0	3	0
Thomas Robinson	6 days	0	3	0
Richard Lewes	6 days	0	3	0

5d. per diem.

Thomas Shole -	6 days	0	2	6
Bartic Smith -	$5\frac{3}{4}$ days	0	2	$4\frac{3}{4}$
Edward Lee -	$5\frac{3}{4}$ days	0	2	$4\frac{3}{4}$

4*d.*

4d. per diem.

			£.	s.	d.
Gyles Hill	-	6 days	0	2	0

WORK by the Great.—*Smith work.*

Gilbert Hunt, ſmith, for making of a new dregg and mending one old dregg, as alſo for ſetting three iron hoops on a lime buſhell - - - -	0	3	0

PROVISIONS.

Hather 7 turſes 2s. 4d.—oyſter ſhells one buſhell 6d.—one ſmall lime riddell 5d. - -	0	3	3
Sum of the payments the 23d of June 1615, twenty-two pounds three ſhillings and eleven-pence three-farthings - -	22	3	11¾

Michael Sanderſon, Mayor.
John Orde.
Mark Saltonſtall.
James Burrel.
Stephen Jackſon.
John Shell, Clerk.
Hn. Grigſon.

† Dd In

In Auguſt 1620, the Biſhop of Durham repairing to Berwick to ſee how his Majeſty's bridge work there went forward, and to view the accompt, and finding that the charge of that work was ſpun out at length and grew great by day-work of all hands, beſides a daily charge to his Majeſty for entertainment of a ſurveyor, a maſter maſon, and a clerk of the work, and having had ſome conference that year before his going to the north into that effect, with the Right Honourable Fulke Grevell, the chancellor of the exchequer and commiſſioner for his Majeſty's treaſury, thought it fit, upon advice with others his Majeſty's commiſſioners there for that work, to bring the whole buſineſs to a certaintie upon articles both for the charge and the time of finiſhing the whole work; to which effect, after deliberation at Berwick, the ſaid Lord Biſhop addreſſed his letters to the Right Honourable the ſaid Chancellor of the Exchequer in manner and form following:

May it pleaſe your honour, I have, according to your directions, been at Berwick, and ſpent

ſpent ſome time in a careful ſurvey of that work, where, I confeſs, I received leſs contentment than I expected, finding that the expences of his Majeſty's monies riſe apace, but the bridge riſeth ſlowly; I do not find but that the Mayor and his brethren are careful and faithful, but partly through want of timber in due time, which came not to Berwick till the end of July, partly by the hurt done with the great water that happened the laſt year, the expences are more than I expected, and the main work leſs forwarded: At this my being there I fell into compounding for the whole work to be well and ſubſtantially performed by a ſet time for a certain ſum of money, and for much more timber as neceſſarily muſt be had for the perfecting and finiſhing of the whole work; and if ſuch a courſe may ſtand with his Majeſty and your honour's good liking, I will proceed in it. I do utterly diſlike the ſpining of it out either by days work, or parcelling it to taſk, for ſo the overſeers of the work and the workmen will delay and gain time of us do we what we can.

His

His Majeſty hath been pleaſed to impart 1000l. for this year's work, and your honour hath given us warrant for 200 tons of timber, whereof 100 is already conveyed to Berwick, and the other 100 will be there, God willing, very ſhortly, ſo that hereafter I hope there ſhall be no delay for want of timber, for that I preſume we ſhall obtain more ſpeedy warrant of your honour for ſuch timber as muſt neceſſarily be had for the full perfecting of the work; the ſafety and preſervation of the bridge, when it is done, will much conſiſt in the well timbering of the pillars upon which the arches are turned. There were finiſhed, the laſt year, ſeven of fourteen; I hope there will be done this year, before they give over work, the landſtall on the ſouth ſide, with a pillar and arch next adjoining, and the eighth pillar and arch to the work where they left the laſt year, ſo that afterwards there will remain to be done five arches with ſo many pillars, and all the carpenters and ſmiths work thereto belonging. The preſent project that I have in hand is for the finiſhing of the whole,

whole, which if I can obtain to be done with a perpine wall throughout the whole bridge, on both ſides, and the caping ſtones and the paving of the bridge throughout, and all the iron work belonging to it, 1200l. more than is already paid, and 200 tons of timber; which good ſecurity to his Majeſty's uſe to have it well and ſubſtantially done, the bridge to be made paſſable, with all kinds of carriages, by midſummer-day next; and the perpine wall, caping, and paving, to be performed and finiſhed within a convenient time; after, I think, it will be the beſt way that can be taken both for the thrifty and expedite performance thereof. If your honour like well of this courſe, and wiſh me to proceed in it, I pray you to ſignify your mind ſo ſoon as conveniently you may; and, God willing, by then, that I ſhall receive your letter, ſend you an exact particular of the whole work, and the prices whereupon we agree wherewith before my coming from London; I in a ſort acquainted Maſter Surveyor of his Majeſty's works, and which he ſo ſaid he held to be be far more reaſonable and cheap than could have expected, as to wit, for a foot of aſhler, the wining at the quarry, the carrying it to the place where it is to be wrought, and the working of it, at 5d. the foot; the ſmooth pens for the arches to be meaſured on the ſuperficies of the bow; the getting of the ſtone at the quarry, the carrying of it, and the working of it on all the ſides, every ſtone containing 2 feet 2 inches in depth, at 9d. the foot; rough pens for the falſe arch over the arch of ſmooth pens, getting, carrying, and working at 3d. the foot; burs or rough ſtones for filling work, 4d. the load; for getting and carrying lime, at 5d. the boll, every boll containing more than five buſhels of London meaſure; ſand at 12d. the lighter. I ſhould be tedious and troubleſome to your honour to ſet down the particulars of the ſetting of all this ſtone, with other materials concurring to this work, and of ſcaffolding, which, notwithſtanding, if it pleaſe you ſhall be ſet down exactly in every particular, for every particular arch and pillar, that your honour may ſee

a

a juſt reaſon of the ſum we agree upon. There hath not been that uſe made of his Majeſty's commiſſion for eaſe of his Majeſty's charge for the carriage of the ſaid timber by land and by water which I expected, and which I would have done had I been here in the country when the firſt uſe was made thereof; but the gentlemen of the country being unacquainted with that kind of his Majeſty's right and ſervice, and willing to ſerve their neighbours and tenants, took hold of the words of the commiſſion, at reaſonable prices, and by that means the carriage of this 200 tons of timber hath coſt his Majeſty 40l. more than I expected ſhould have done, which I cannot now redreſs.

I fear I am too bold with your honour, conſidering how precious time is with you in regard of your many and great occaſions; and therefore, with remembrance of my love and ſervice, and prayers for your health and happineſs, commit you to God, and reſts

Your Honour's loving poor friend.

To Mr Chancellor of the Exchequer, the 22*d Aug.* 1620.

The

The Inventory of ſuch neceſſaries as are remaining in the cuſtody of Mr James Burrell and Lancelot Branxton, which they are to deliver into his Majeſty's ſtore at the finiſhing of his Highneſs's ſtone Bridge of Berwick upon Tweed.

Iron crows, great and ſmall,	13
Iron pinches	12
Setting pinches	9
Screws of iron	3
Sledges	12
Stone axes	17
Earth picks	6
Quarry picks	8
Scapling hammers	4
Walling hammers	3
Trowells	5
Formers	6
Square augur	1
Drift pin	1
Small wood rammers, with iron ends, for raming burrs in the branders	5
Iron rams for beating burrs	3
Drift bolts	2
Five men beatles	3
Wood cow with ſwapp	1
Huds	4
Mortar tubs	3
Water caſks	2
Wheell barrows	2

Raige

Raige bolts	4
Iron wedges	57
Timber hooks	2
Grapples	3
Sarcher	1
Marking iron	1
Pieces of iron work for the ſcaffold	2
Mandrell	1
Carpenters adze	4
Ditto wedges of iron	2
Long ſaw	1
Thwart ſaw	1
Stone carts	2
Braſs ſhieves	8
Wood ſhieves	3
Great and ſmall blocks	5
Gyns	6
Gyn ropes	2
Bellows (pair)	2
Studies or anvils	2
Beckhorne	1
Tongs	5
Conter frames for arches	3
Ladders	3
Leightners	4
Ropes for them, of ſorts	7
Anckers	5
Dregg	2
Small boats	3
Creeper	1
Levels	3
Long rules	3
Cadges	4
Boat hook & poles	5
Beam and ſcales (pair)	1
Lead weights	300
Grind ſtones	2
Bowlſter	2
Ax mandrell	1
Fore hammer	1
Hand hammer	1
Strake nail tool	1
Spike nail tool	1

Braſs ram	1	Fir ſlice	1
Rams armed with iron	2	Six men barrows	3
Ram unarmed	1	Hand barrows	4

James Burrel, Lancelot Branxton.

The particular payments for ſix days, begun the 22d June and ended the 28th thereof.

2*s. per diem.*

	Days	L.	s.	d.
James Burrell ſurveyor	6	0	12	0
John Farqarſon ditto	6	0	12	0
MASONS.—18*d. per diem.*				
Lancelot Branxton maſter maſon -	6	0	9	0
12*d. per diem.*				
John Nealſon	$5\frac{3}{4}$	0	5	9
William Crowe	$5\frac{3}{4}$	0	5	9
William Ward	6	0	6	0
Thomas Sadler	6	0	6	0

11*d.*

11d. per diem.	Days	L.	s.	d.
Michaell Millner	5¾	0	5	3½
10d. per diem.				
Robert Robſon	5¾	0	4	9½
James Pedden	5¾	0	4	9½
9d. per diem.				
Richard Forſter	5¾	0	4	3½
William Bowle	5¾	0	4	3½
7d. per diem.				
Thomas Alliſon	5¾	0	3	4½

CARPENTERS.

Raphe Garnett	6	0	6	0
Thomas Atcheſon	6	0	6	0
Robert Atcheſon	6	0	6	0
John Whitt	6	0	6	0
John Dinnis	6	0	5	6
James Anderſon	6	0	5	0
Thomas Steel	6	0	5	0
Leonard Bradforth	6	0	5	0
8d. per diem.				
Nicholas Ogle	6	0	4	0
Michael Lyall	6	0	4	0

7d.

7d. per diem.	Days.	L.	s.	d.
John Smith	6	0	3	6
LIGHTERMEN.—8*d. per diem.*				
Edward Crawforth	6	0	4	0
6d. per diem.				
John Ferrer	6	0	3	0
QUARRYMEN.—9*d. per diem.*				
Thomas Law	6	0	4	6
Thomas Bank	6	0	4	6
LABOURERS.—6*d. per diem.*				
Thomas Armourer	6	0	3	0
Edward Thurborn	6	0	3	0
William Main	6	0	3	0
Thomas Bell	6	0	3	0
Francis Spencer	6	0	3	0
William Humble	6	0	3	0
Thomas Wood	6	0	3	0
Charles Ferrer	6	0	3	0
Charles Lyall	6	0	3	0
Barwick Carſton	6	0	3	0
Alexander Maxwell	6	0	3	0

6d.

6d. per diem.	Days.	L.	s.	d.
Steven Nicolſon	6	0	3	0
Andrew Story	6	0	3	0
Richard Dawglas	6	0	3	0
Robert Young	6	0	3	0
Archibald Thomſon	6	0	3	0
Edward Grinley	6	0	3	0
Edward Thomſon	6	0	3	0
George Thomſon	6	0	3	0
Robert Camell	6	0	3	0
John Nielſon	6	0	3	0
John Bell	6	0	3	0
James Ferrer	6	0	3	0
John Forreſt	6	0	3	0
John Hugh	6	0	3	0
William Camell	6	0	3	0
Glendeny	6	0	3	0
Daniel Bowmaker	6	0	3	0
Patrick Read	6	0	3	0
George Shank	6	0	3	0
Michael Paxton	6	0	3	0
Thomas Burris	6	0	3	0
Leonard Brown	6	0	3	0
Edward Alexander	6	0	3	0

6d. per diem.	Days.	L.	s.	d.
Oswald Batiman	6	0	3	0
Robert Lattie	6	0	3	0
Ralph Gilchrist	6	0	3	0
John Branxton	6	0	3	0
Thomas Read	6	0	3	0
John Petterew	6	0	3	0
Sandy Mennon	6	0	3	0
William Baker	6	0	3	0
John Trumble	6	0	3	0
George Cromwell	6	0	3	0
William Robson	6	0	3	0
John Willoby	6	0	3	0
Michael Purvis	4½	0	2	3
Thomas Mitton	5	0	2	6
Thomas Catterthwaite	6	0	3	0
BOYS.—*4d. per diem.*				
Thomas Cowper	6	0	2	0
Gawen Dennis	6	0	2	0
Paid 31 women labourers, for tides work wrought this week, at 2d. per tide, amounting to		2	11	0

PRO-

PROVISIONS.

	£.	s.	d.
Paid unto Elias Pratt, ſmith, for 10 pile-howes with the nails, at 11d. *per* howe, -	0	9	2
For working and making 1 ring and 1 check for the ram, weighing 1 ſt. 5 lb. and a-half, at 6d. *per* ſtone, - -	0	0	9
For making of 4 ſmall crows, weighing 8 ſt. 6 lb. at 6d. *per* ſtone, - - -	0	4	3½
For mending 2 great crows, 1 pinch, and laying a ſtone pick,	0	1	4½
Paid to Edward Dawglas, cooper, for 6 ſowes, at 16d. *per* ſowe,	0	8	0
Paid to George Todd for mending a long whip-ſaw, -	0	0	4
One quire of paper, -	0	0	4
Paid David Shell for 7 ſcoops, at 14d. *per* piece, -	0	8	2
Paid Thomas Cleghorn for ſharping of tools, - -	0	2	4

More

	£.	s.	d.
More for making a plate to a barrow, the mending of a great crow, - -	0	0	5
Paid to Edward Crawforth, leighterman, for carrying of the lighter up to Ethermouth for ſtones, 3 tides, - - -	0	1	0
And to Edward Grinley and John Ferrer for helping of him to the ſame tides, - -	0	1	6
Paid unto Thomas Beadnell, carter, for carriage of 12 cart load of ſtones from the quarry,	1	1	0
Paid unto Roger Driver for 30 ſacks of burnt lime-ſtone, at 9d. *per* ſack, - -	1	2	6
Paid more to him in full of lime,	0	13	3
From Newcaſtle.—Paid to John Catterill for half a ton and 24lb. of iron, -	7	6	4
More paid to him for freight of the iron and ropes, -	0	6	8

Sum

	£.	s.	d.
Sum total of this week's reckoning paid, -	30	3	2½

William Bowyer, Mayor.
Robert Jackſon.
Mark Saltonſtale.
John Orde.
Henry Grigſon.
Michuell Sanderſon.
James Burrell.

The particular payments of work begun the 18th of September, and ended the 24th thereof.

Paid unto Mr James Burrell and Lancelet Branxton in part of payment of 350l. for the finiſhing of the new bridge according to their covenant as by their bill appeared the ſum of -	L. 5	0	0

CARPENTERS employed to take down the old bridge.—12*d.* *per diem.*

	Days	L.	s.	d.
Thomas Atchefon	6	o	6	o
Robert Atchefon	6	o	6	o
9*d.* *per diem.*				
John Smyth	6	o	4	6

QUARRYMEN employed to win ftones to lay about the branders.—9*d.* *per diem.*

Thomas Law -	6	o	4	6
6*d.* *per diem.*				
Thomas Armorer	6	o	3	o

LIGHTERMEN.

Ed. Crawforth	6 days 4 tides	o	5	4
John Brown	6 days 4 tides	o	4	o

LABOURERS employed about the boats to fetch great ftones to fill the deep and fortify the branders.—6*d.* *per day.*

Edmond Thurburne	6	o	3	o
Thomas Bell	6	o	3	o

William

	Days	L.	s.	d.
William Humble	6	0	3	0
William Mayne	6	0	3	0
Francis Spencer	6	0	3	0
Roger Driver	6	0	3	0
William Camell	6	0	3	0
Thomas Camell	6	0	3	0
Thomas Tuder	6	0	3	0
Thomas Mitten	6	0	3	0

WOMEN employed for ſanding the new bridge.—3*d.* *per diem.*

Mary Cowper	6	0	1	6
Mariery Harrett	6	0	1	6
Elizabeth Dent	6	0	1	6
Alice Thompſon	6	0	1	6
Margaret Thurborne	6	0	1	6
Annes Dennis	6	0	1	6
Elizabeth Cocke	6	0	1	6
Jane Smyth	6	0	1	6
Ann Robinſon	6	0	1	6
Margaret Johnſon	6	0	1	6
Katherine Mark	6	0	1	6

PRO-

PROVISIONS.

Paid to John Nealſon, and the reſt of the maſons, for wining, ſtaving, and leading of 68 1-half feet of plain aſhler, at 4d. *per* foot, for the making up of the ſcaffold gapp - - L.	1	2	10
Paid unto Elias Pratt, ſmith, for ſtraighting and peicing of broken crows - -	0	2	4
For making of 2 new crows for weighing piles of the old bridge, 5 ſtone 9lb. at 6d. *per* ſtone	0	2	9
Paid to Mrs Walker 20 bolls of lime	0	6	8
Sum total of this week's account paid amounts to - L.	10	14	5

William Bowyer, Mayor.
John Orde.
M. Sanderſon.
James Burrell.
Robert Jackſon.
Mark Saltonſtall.
Hn. Grigſon.

"Whereas

"Whereas there was a letter directed to Sir Robert Jackſon, knight, dated at Durham-houſe the 26th of April 1627, from Mr Edward Linels ſecretary to the Right Honourable Reverend Father in God, Richard Lord Biſhop of Durham, which appears by the ſaid letter was written by direction from the ſaid Lord Biſhop, wherein was a note of hand of a warrant incloſed, importing the ſaid Lord Biſhop's pleaſure concerning the allowance of 100l. to Sir William Bowyer, knight, out of the monies received towards the finiſhing of his Majeſty's ſtone bridge of Berwick aforeſaid, and thereby deſiring that the ſame note might be ingroſſed in the ledger book, and to paſs as the common weekly bills; but ſince the ſaid Lord Biſhop hath been pleaſed to write unto the ſaid Sir Robert Jackſon, knight, Mayor of Berwick, from Auckland, bearing date the 14th of July 1627, therewith incloſing another warrant ſigned under his Lordſhip's hand, ſignifying his Majeſty's pleaſure for the confirmation and allowance of the ſaid 100l. unto Sir William Bowyer, knight; and as by the

the ſaid letter appeareth, his Lordſhip deſired that the ſame warrant ſhould be ingroſſed in the ledger book of accompts of the ſaid bridge work, which ſaid hereafter appeareth is accordingly done.

"His Majeſty of his princely goodneſs hath been pleaſed to be informed by me, the Biſhop of Durham, that his humble ſervant, Sir William Bowyer of Berwick, knight, hath done to his father of bleſſed memory, King James and himſelf, good and faithful ſervice divers years paſt about the work of Berwick bridge; and that for his better attendance and care-taking of that work, through my perſuaſions with the ſaid corporation of Berwick and himſelf, he, by ſundry elections, was continued Mayor of that corporation divers years, to his great trouble, extraordinary charge and pains; and, in demonſtration of his Majeſty's gracious acceptance of his the ſaid Sir William Bowyer's good ſervice, his Majeſty is well pleaſed, that upon the account of the monies paid to that corporation for the ſaid work, in the time of his the ſaid Sir William Bowyer

yer being mayor there, be allowed unto him, the ſaid Sir William Bowyer, the ſum of one hundred pounds, after the rate of twenty pounds per annum, for five years: Hereof I hold it fit to advertiſe you, that both the ſaid allowance of 100l. may be made unto him, and alſo that an entry hereof may be made in your books of accounts for that work, that the ſame be well accepted and allowed of by all ſuch as ſhall hereafter have the examination or peruſal of the ſaid accounts."

Robert Jackſon, Mayor.
William Bowyer.
John Orde.
Mark Saltonſtall.
H. Cryton.
Michael Sanderſon.
James Burrell.

"The Biſhop of Durham, in his care to have this work ſubſtantially and faithfully performed, cauſed one John Johnſton ſurveyor of the bridge-work of Newcaſtle, a man there reputed

ted ſkilful in thoſe works and honeſt in his actions, to be preſent at the whole tranſaction of the ſaid articles and agreement, and was afterwards at the charge of his own purſe of giving the ſaid Johnſton 2s. per diem during the time of Mr Burrell and Lancelot Branxton working the ſame, to reſide at Berwick to ſee that the work ſhould be done truly, faithfully, and ſubſtantially, according to the articles in all point.

"After which, the work was ſo wrought that by Michaelmas after, the pillars and arches, with the filling of the courſe thereof, were finiſhed; but there coming in October an extraordinary time of abundance of rain and ſtorms, that made ſuch flood all throughout the north part as the like thereof hath been known in any man's memory, and the river of Tweed bringing down with it ſtrange abundance of ſtacks of hay, corn, and timber, bore down a great part of the old timber bridge there, which, together with the violence of waters and abundance of ſtuff that came down therewith, falling upon the ſtone bridge,

bridge, being yet green, and the lime not dried and knit, and the centers of ſome of the arches being not ſtricken but ſtanding, overthrew all the work done that year. After which fall of the bridge, his late Majeſty, King James, was graciouſly pleaſed, out of his princely care to have that work finiſhed, to grant his privy ſeal, dated the 24th day of June, in the 20th year of his reign, for 3000l. more, for the readyfying and finiſhing of the bridge; and whatſoever ſhould remain thereof (the bridge being finiſhed) the ſame to be employed towards the building of a *Church there at Berwick.*" The expending of 3000l. appeareth in the account following:

"*23d Nov.* 1635. All monies received out of his Majeſty's treaſury, including the 3000l. towards building the bridge *and a church*, if a ſurplus remained, amounted to -	15000l.
On ſettling accounts before the auditors, when the bridge was finiſhed, there only remained a balance of 39l. 18s. 6d. out of - -	15000l."

" *The Stone Bridge upon the River of Tweed at Berwick, containing fourteen arches and as many pillars, with their branderths of wood about them.*"

" The length of the landfall, next Berwick, is about 65 yards.

" The wideneſs of the *firſt* arch is 19 yards 4 inches.—The thickneſs of the *firſt* pillar is 8 yards.—The length of the ſaid pillar from peak to peak is 17 yards and 9 inches.

" The wideneſs of the *ſecond* arch is 24 yards 29 inches.—The thickneſs of the *ſecond* pillar is 7 yards; and the length of the ſaid pillar is 15 yards 9 inches.

" The wideneſs of the *third* arch is 19 yards 3 inches.—The thickneſs of the pillar is 6 yards; and the length thereof is 14 yards 9 inches.

" The wideneſs of the *fourth* arch is 19 yards 21 inches.—The thickneſs of the pillar is 5 yards 21 inches; and the length is 13 yards 3 inches.

" The

" The wideneſs of the *fifth* arch is 16 yards 2 feet.—The thickneſs of the pillar is 5 yards 21 inches; and the length thereof 13 yards 3 inches.

" The wideneſs of the *ſixth* arch is 14 yards 6 inches.—The thickneſs of the pillar is 9 yards; and the length thereof is 17 yards 3 inches.

" The wideneſs of the *ſeventh* arch is 14 yards.—The thickneſs of the pillar is 5 yards; and the length thereof is 12 yards 1 foot.

" The wideneſs of the *eighth* arch is 13 yards.—The thickneſs of the pillar is 4 yards; and the length thereof 12 yards 1 foot.

" The wideneſs of the *ninth* arch is 12 yards.—The thickneſs of the pillar is 4 yards; and the length thereof 12 yards 1 foot.

" The wideneſs of the *tenth*, *eleventh*, *twelfth*, *thirteenth*, *and fourteenth* arches as the *ninth*. —The thickneſs of theſe five pillars as the *ninth*; and the length of them as the *ninth*.

" The length of the landfall next Tweedmouth 36 yards.

" The

"The breadth of the paſſage between the two vamours of the bridge is 17 feet.

"The height of the work from the foundation to the ſetting of the vamours about 15 yards high."

The ſtones for building this bridge were procured in a quarry at the eaſt end of Tweedmouth.

CHAP. IV.

Conſtitution and Government.

SECTION I.

Conſtitution of Berwick, Laws, and Courts.

BERWICK was originally a Scotch Town. It appears, however, to have been erected into an Engliſh borough at a very early period from its having had ſeveral charters granted by the kings of that nation. The laſt of which was granted by James the Firſt, and ſanctioned by an Act of Parliament paſſed in the firſt year of his reign in England. Under this Act the burgeſſes now claim their various privileges, immunities, and exemptions, as well as very large territorial domains and poſſeſſions. The liberties are co-extenſive with the

the pariſh itſelf. Within theſe, however, as particularly ſtated above, a number of private gentlemen are alſo poſſeſſed of eſtates. The landed property of the corporation, if let, would amount to a very conſiderable yearly rent. Great part thereof is let out upon leaſes, and part of it is parcelled out into ſeparate allotments poſſeſſed by the freemen. Theſe are called burgeſſes meadows and ſtints. There may be about 300 or 400 of ſuch meadows and ſtints, which are occupied by the ſenior burgeſſes and their widows: As they drop, the next in ſeniority have a right of chooſing into their allotments, by which means an opportunity is annually afforded of ſo many of the junior freemen coming into poſſeſſion of meadows or ſtints.

The yearly value of a meadow and ſtint may run from 5l. to 15l. per annum; but this depends upon the nature and cultivation of the ſoil; ſometimes too from peculiar circumſtances they exceed that amount.

Since its conqueſt by the Engliſh, Berwick has been governed by their laws, except in one

one or two inſtances, ſuch as the mode of paſſing a fine of lands within the borough and liberties thereof, which is peculiar to itſelf. It has alſo an exempt juriſdiction, not being within either of the next adjoining counties of Durham or Northumberland. But though it is poſſeſſed of an exempt juriſdiction within itſelf, yet it is not a county.

It has a Mayor and four bailiffs, however, who all in a body (or a majority of whom) act as ſheriff in the execution of all writs and mandates from the King's Courts at Weſtminſter. For though they hold a Court of record within the borough for the deciſion of all cauſes, both real and perſonal, to any amount, yet the King's writ runs into the borough, and ſuitors have it in their option to commence their ſuits either in the ſuperior courts or the court of the borough. The latter, however, are ſubject to be removed into the ſuperior courts by *certiorari* writ of *error*, bill of injunction, &c.* For which reaſon

* Vide Burrow's Reports, Rex vers. Cowle, Vol. ii. p. 834.

ſon matters of conſequence are commonly tried on actions brought into the courts at Weſtminſter; thoſe of inferior moment being tried in the Borough-Court on account of the ſmall expence attending ſuch trials.

The judges of this borough-court are the Mayor and Bailiffs, with a jury of twelve men.

The Mayor, Recorder, and Juſtices, have, by their charter, a power to hold general and quarter-ſeſſions of the peace within the borough, for the trial of petty felonies, treſpaſſes, and other miſdemeanours. They have alſo a power of holding a general goal delivery for the trial of capital felonies; and ſuch as are capitally convicted at theſe trials are executed within the borough, it having a gallows for the purpoſe. The ſeſſions, or court of goal delivery, cannot be held without the Mayor and Recorder, who, when elected into office, continue Juſtices of the Peace for life within the borough. Gentlemen who have ſerved the office of Mayor are likewiſe denominated Aldermen.

The

The conſtitution of the borough, or corporation in *guild*, is a mixed or popular one. The Guild is compoſed of the Mayor, the Juſtices, an Alderman for the year, four Bailiffs, and the reſt of the Guild brethren. Every queſtion in Guild, with regard to the affairs of the corporation, is decided by a majority of the burgeſſes; the Mayor not having a caſting vote as formerly.

The employment of *Alderman, for the year*, conſiſts in doing little offices for the Mayor, receiving and preſenting petitions to the Guild, &c.; but the office is not appointed by charter.

The Mayor *, as alſo the Alderman for the year, and four Bailiffs, are choſen annually at Michaelmas, when the Mayor is inveſted with the inſignia of office which is a white rod. He likewiſe wears a gown, as do alſo the other Magiſtrates, the Alderman for the year, the Bailiffs, Coroner, and Town-Clerk.

Four ſerjeants at mace are appointed to at-

* The preſent Mayor is Samuel Burn, Eſq. The ſalary is 100l. a-year, for which the Mayor gives a public dinner at each of the four quarter-ſeſſions.

tend the Mayor and Bailiffs who have ſalaries allowed them, and are clothed at the expence of the corporation. This is alſo the caſe with regard to the jailors, waits, bellmen, beadles, &c.

For theſe many years no *private* Guilds have been held; committees being now appointed to carry the orders of the Guild into effect: To one of which has lately been given the power of obtaining an act of Parliament for lighting, paving, and cleaning the ſtreets. Theſe committees give orders on the Treaſurer for moſt of the payments. The ordinary ſalaries, which amount to nearly 1000l. *per annum*, are likewiſe paid by the Treaſurer.

Four head Guilds are held in the year at ſtated periods, reſerving to themſelves the power of adjournment. The Mayor likewiſe has power to call a Guild; and muſt do ſo if it is required by twelve of the burgeſſes.

The ſons of burgeſſes are admitted to the freedom at the age of twenty-one. Others, again, obtain it only by becoming apprentices to burgeſſes whom they muſt ſerve for ſeven years,

years. At the commencement of their apprenticeſhip, too, they muſt be preſented to the Guild for its approbation. If approved of, they are immediately enrolled, and pay the uſual fee, which, for theſe few years, has been 30l. Beſides theſe means of obtaining the freedom of this borough, it is ſometimes conferred as a mark of the higheſt diſtinction upon illuſtrious characters. Theſe, too, upon taking the oath of a burgeſs, are admitted to all the privileges of the corporation. It is ſingular, that an order of Guild ſhould have once exiſted againſt Scotchmen enjoying the freedom; which order, however, was moſt likely reſcinded ſoon after the union.

The number of burgeſſes reſident within the borough is about 500, and there may be about as many more ſtanding upon the Guild-roll, who are diſperſed over the kingdom and throughout the different parts of the world*.

This

* Since writing the above, we have been favoured with a Guild-roll, and find that the number of burgeſſes at preſent amount to 980.

This ſtatement of the number of burgeſſes belonging to the borough refutes a ſtatement given of them in Hall's New Royal Encyclopœdia: It is there ſaid, that 'The right of 'election is in the freemen reſident and non-'reſident to the amount of 600.'

Although it appears by the roll that the number of burgeſſes is nearly one thouſand, yet no ſuch number has ever been brought forward to vote at the election of members of Parliament. It may likewiſe be noticed, however, that about forty are diſqualified from voting, by their holding employments in the cuſtoms, exciſe, &c. At the conteſt in 1786, when Sir Gilbert Elliot, now Lord Minto, was elected, the total number who voted was 677*.

A canvas has frequently been ſet on foot in the borough three or four years before the diſſolution of Parliament having taken place; and, as a Berwick burgeſs was never known to break his promiſe, the candidates, who are fortunate

* The numbers being, for Sir Gilbert Elliot 361, John Hiley Addington, 316.

fortunate enough to obtain it, can have no doubt of its being fulfilled.

A canvas, which took place before the laſt general election, is ſaid to have coſt the three candidates 5000l.; but the death of Sir John Vaughan put an end to the conteſt; and Sir John Callander, who had been brought forward by the gentlemen who had ſupported Lord Minto, was elected without oppoſition, and was re-elected at the general election *.

The Mayor, Bailiffs, and Burgeſſes of Berwick are alſo Lords of the Manor of Tweedmouth and Spittal, in the county Palatine of Durham, having purchaſed the Royalties of the Earl of Suffolk in the year 1657 for 570l. They hold a Court-leet and Court-baron at Tweedmouth twice a-year, viz. at Eaſter and Michaelmas, for the trial of debts and treſpaſſes under 40 ſhillings. The tenants of the manor alſo do ſuit and ſervice at theſe courts; and are admitted by the Lords, upon deaths or alienation, to the copy-hold lands and tene-

ments

* Berwick ſends two members to Parliament. The preſent members are Lord Tyrconnel and Sir John Callander, Bart.

ments holden of them as Lords of the manor on payment of ſmall fines. There is a pretty large common belonging to the manor, which is a great nuiſance in harbouring vagrants, but it is ſoon to be divided in conſequence of an act of Parliament having lately been obtained for that purpoſe.

It is by the corporation right to theſe Royalties that wharfage, and ſhipping of all goods, is prevented at Tweedmouth, and confined to the harbour at Berwick.

Candour and *truth*, as well as a juſt tribute to true patriotiſm, oblige us here to obſerve, that this ancient borough has ever ſhone conſpicuous in ſupporting the dignity of the Crown and maintaining the independence of the State.

As a proof of the loyalty of the corporation, we beg leave to ſtate, that laſt year it frankly gave 1000l. towards carrying on the preſent war. Add to this, individual burgeſſes contributed liberally towards a general ſubſcription of the inhabitants at large upon that memorable occaſion.

The

The corporation has alſo in many other caſes of public ſubſcriptions highly diſtinguiſhed itſelf.

SECTION II.

Armorial Bearings.

THE Arms of the Corporation were originally a Bear ſtanding cloſe by the trunk of a tree in luxuriant foliage.

Rapin, in his Hiſtory of England, ſays, "November 1422.—Henry the VI. being "only a few months old when proclaimed "king, John Duke of Bedford, uncle to "Henry, was appointed regent: He broke "the great ſeal, and cauſed a new one to be "made with the arms of *France and Eng-* "*land, and the effigies of the young king hold-* "*ing a ſceptre in each hand.*"

This

This deſcription perfectly accords with the ſeal of the corporation, with this difference only, that they have added the Bear and Tree, which it is underſtood is all they ſhould bear in their *eſcutcheon*; for in a very large ſeal, and alſo in a ſmall one which we have ſeen, neither the effigies of the king nor the national arms are repreſented.

The Town's arms, placed both in the outſide and inſide of the Town-houſe, have, in addition to the armorial bearings above deſcribed, a Bear and Tree in foliage on each ſide as ſupporters, with chains about their necks. The following is the inſcription around the ſeal, in the old type, *Sigillu maioratus villæ Berwici ſuper Twedam.*

SEC-

SECTION III.

Grand Farm and other Revenues of the Town.

THE duties taken at the *Quay* and *Gates* conſtitute the *Grand Farm*, which, for ſeveral

* *A* TABLE *of the Town's* DUTIES *to be taken at the Key by the Grand Farmers for all Manner of Goods, according to ancient Cuſtom.*

	£.	s.	d.
Firſt, EVERY Ship that comes to the Town, being ſtrangers, and making uſe of the bell to call her corn, ſalt, apples, or onions, if ſhe have in her the quantity of ſix ſcore quarters of corn or ſalt, to pay two bolls, and if twenty quarters, three Wincheſter buſhels, and ſo proportionably; and if an hundred barrels of apples or onions, two barrels, and if twenty barrels, then but one, and ſo proportionably.			
For every hundred firkins of carrots or turnips, one, and ſo proportionably.			
To anchorage of each ſhip with a boat	0	2	4

ſeveral years paſt, has varied conſiderably. In

	£.	s.	d.
Every veſſel that comes in without a boat or wherry - -	0	1	0
Every open boat, of ſtrangers, coming in with cod, herring, &c. and ſold in the market			
If not ſold in the market -	0	0	6
Every barrel of ſalmon, cod, or herring, of burgeſſes, outwards -	0	0	2
Every barrel of ſalmon, of ſtrangers, outwards	0	0	4
Every barrel of cod or herring, of ſtrangers, outwards - -	0	0	4
Every laſt of flax, of ſtrangers, inwards	0	2	0
Every ton of iron, of ſtrangers, inwards	0	2	0
Every ton of iron, of burgeſſes, outwards	0	1	0
Every ton of iron, of ſtrangers, outwards	0	2	0
Every barrel, of ſtrangers, inwards	0	0	4
Every hogſhead of tobacco, landed from any of his Majeſty's plantations, and ſo proportionably - -	0	0	4
Every hogſhead of tobacco, of ſtrangers, outwards - - -	0	0	8
Every barrel of tar imported or exported by ſtrangers only - -	0	0	4
Every ton of braſſes, of ſtrangers, ſhipped at the Key, as wharfage -	0	0	2

Every

In the year 1794 it let at 655l.—in 1795 it rose

	£.	s.	d.
Every barrel of goods, of ſtrangers, outwards, not before mentioned, and ſo proportionably - - -	0	0	8
Every ton of wine, brandy, or geneva, of ſtrangers, inwards, and ſo proportionably	0	10	0
Every ton of wine or brandy, of burgeſſes, imported from any foreign country, and ſo proportionably - -	0	3	4
Every ton of wine or brandy, of burgeſſes, and ſo proportionably, outwards	0	1	8
Every ton of wine or brandy, of ſtrangers, outwards - -	0	5	0
Every chaldron of coals, of burgeſſes, outwards	0	0	2
Every chaldron of coals, of ſtrangers, inwards	0	0	4
Every chaldron of coals, of ſtrangers, outwards	0	0	8
Every hundred ſpars, of ſtrangers, inwards	0	0	4
Outwards, pro ditto, by ſea -	0	0	2
Deals and nine ells, of ſtrangers, inwards, the hundred - -	0	0	6
Outwards, pro ditto, by ſea -	0	0	3
Twelve ells, of ſtrangers, inwards, the hundred	0	1	0
Outwards, pro ditto, by ſea -	0	0	6
Double trees, of ſtrangers, inwards	0	2	0
Outwards, pro ditto, by ſea	0	1	0

Every

rose to 810l.—in 1796 it let at 620l.—in 1797

	£.	s.	d.
Every pack or horse-load of goods, of any sort whatever, that belong to a stranger, coming into Town, and sold, or going through the Town - -	0	0	4
Every horse-load of earthen ware, glasses, &c. of strangers, exposed to sale in the market, over and above the stallage -	0	0	4
Every pack, fardel, or bundle of bale goods, &c. sixteen stone to the pack, of strangers, coming in by sea - -	0	0	8
Every such pack, &c. outwards -	0	0	8
Every pack of wool, of strangers, outwards, by sea - - -	0	0	2
Every thousand pantiles, of strangers, and so proportionably, inwards -	0	0	6
Outwards, pro ditto - -	0	0	3
Every quarter of corn shipped by a burgess	0	0	1
Every quarter of corn shipped by a stranger	0	0	2
Every thousand bricks, of strangers, inwards	0	0	2
Every thousand slates, of strangers, inwards	0	0	6
Outwards, of strangers -	0	0	3
Every boll of corn, of strangers, brought in at the gates, and shipped off by the town's permission,			

1797 at 425l. and laſt year it fell ſo low as 420l.

There

	£.	s.	d.
permiſſion, no burgeſs being employed therein by commiſſion	0	0	3
Every boll of ſalt ſhipped for a ſtranger, outwards - -	0	0	2
Every bag of hops, of ſtrangers, coming in by ſea, and ſo proportionably -	0	2	0
Every hundred weight of madder, fuſtic, and ſuch commodities, of ſtrangers, inwards	0	0	4
Every quarter of bark imported by ſea by a ſtranger, to the farmer -	0	0	2
Every dicker of hides, of burgeſſes, outwards by ſea, and ſo proportionably -	0	0	2
Every dicker of hides, of ſtrangers, outwards by ſea, and ſo proportionably -	0	0	4
Calf-ſkins, ſalt and dried, of ſtrangers, outwards, by the great hundred -	0	0	6
Ditto of burgeſſes - -	0	0	3
Every hundred ſkins of white leather, dreſſed or undreſſed, - -	0	0	2
Every cheſt of lemons or oranges, of a ſtranger, inwards, and ſo proportionably	0	1	0
Every quarter of clover or rye graſs, of ſtrangers - - -	0	0	8

Every

There is a ſimilar ſpecies of revenue to the above,

	£.	s.	d.
Every ton of tallow, of burgeſſes, outwards	0	2	0
Ditto of ſtrangers, outwards -	0	4	0
Every twelve dozen of candles of burgeſſes, outwards - - -	0	0	3
Of ſtrangers - - -	0	0	6
Every thouſand eggs, of a burgeſs, outwards	0	0	6
Every thouſand eggs, of a ſtranger, outwards	0	1	0
Every ten dozen of ſtockings, of burgeſſes, outwards by ſea - -	0	0	2
Ditto of ſtrangers, outwards by ſea	0	1	4
Every kit of ſalmon, of burgeſſes -	0	0	0½
Every kit of ſalmon, of ſtrangers -	0	0	1
Every groſs of bottles, of ſtrangers, and ſo proportionably - -	0	0	4

Meal ſhipped at this port ſhall pay the ſame fees as are paid for ſhipping of corn, and no more; and four hundred weight of meal ſhall be equal to a quarter of corn.

All other goods not mentioned here, to pay by way of hundred, barrel, pack, or by weight, as goods of that value do; and if any diſpute ariſes that way, to be determined by the Mayor for the time being.

Printed by order of Guild. *A true Copy*,

EDWARD WILLOBY, Town-Clerk.

A

above, viz. the ballaſt quay duties: This is alſo let yearly in Guild.

The

A Table or Schedule of the Tolls or Duties to be taken at the Gates by the Tollers.

	£.	s.	d.
Every boll of corn or ſalt ſent out at either gate - - -	0	0	1
Half a boll - -	0	0	0½
Leſs, nothing			
Every boll of corn ſold to a burgeſs, though after it comes from the place of growth, to pay nothing at the gates			
Every bar of iron carried out at either gate	0	0	0½
Leſs, nothing.			
All iron wrought in town, for the encouragement of trade, nothing.			
Every horſe-load of deals not exceeding ſix	0	0	0½
If eight - -	0	0	0¾
Every two deals - -	0	0	0¼
Every cart-load, not exceeding thirty deals	0	0	1
Every wain-load of deals or timber	0	0	2
Every horſe-load of allum, coperas, oil, and other merchantable goods bought of a burgeſs, and going out of town -	0	0	1
If ſuch commodities be bought of a ſtranger	0	0	8
Every boll of corn ſold to a ſtranger coming in at the gates -	0	0	1

Every

The other ſources of revenue are the lands and

	£.	s.	d.
Every boll of corn of ſtrangers coming into town, and lofted or ſhipped	o	o	1
Every boll of corn ſold in the market, to pay a Wincheſter quarter.			
Every hundred weight of madder, fuſtic, and ſuch like commodities, of ſtrangers (including clover and all other graſs ſeeds ſold by weight) coming in by ſea, and going out at the gates - -	o	o	4
Every dicker of hides of burgeſſes	o	o	2
Ditto of ſtrangers - -	o	o	4
Every ten dozen of ſtockings of burgeſſes, and ſo proportionably -	o	o	2
Of ſtrangers - -	o	1	4
Every pack of wool of burgeſſes going out at the gates			
Of ſtrangers - -	o	1	o
Every pack of wool of ſtrangers coming to be ſhipped off - -	o	o	2
Of burgeſſes - -	o	o	1
All wool coming into the market, or going from thence, to pay only the uſual toll of one halfpenny the ſtone in the market, and at the gates nothing			

Every

and fishing waters belonging to the corporation,

	£.	s.	d.
Every gross of bottles and so proportionably	0	0	4
Every pedlar's stall set up in the market	0	0	1
All others that sell cloth without stall	0	0	0½
On the fair each pedlar -	0	0	4
Otherwise without stall -	0	0	1
Every ox or cow sold in the market	0	0	2
Every horse sold in the market -	0	0	4
Every horse-load of onions, or other fruit, coming in at the gates -	0	0	1½
Every huckster or other person, selling apples, carrots, &c. in the market, to pay to the tollers for each stand -	0	0	0½
Every horse-load of cod, herring or other fish sold in the market (salmon excepted, and burgesses exempted for cod-fish) to pay nothing at the gates			
If not sold in the market -	0	0	1½
Every horse-load of cheese of strangers	0	0	1½
Every firkin of butter of strangers	0	0	1
Every hogshead of brandy, rum, &c. bought of a burgess, and going out at the gates, and so proportionably -	0	0	9

tion, as are alſo the grand tythes—a coalliery

	£.	s.	d.
Every anker of brandy or wine of ſtrangers coming in or going out of the gates	0	0	3
A half anker - -	0	0	1½
Leſs, nothing			
Every half anchor of Geneva or Engliſh Spirits, bought of a burgeſs, and ſo proportionably - - -	0	0	1
If imported by a ſtranger, or ſold by an unfreeman - -	0	0	3
Every horſe load of ale, bought of a burgeſs	0	0	1
If bought of a Stallinger, double -	0	0	2
Every anker of ale, bought of a burgeſs	0	0	0½
If bought of a ſtallinger -	0	0	1
Every barrel of tar -	0	0	1
Every cart-load of bark -	0	0	3
Every horſe-load -	0	0	1
Every hogſhead of lintſeed -	0	0	3
Every hundred weight of clover, and other graſs ſeeds ſold by Weight bought of a burgeſs, and ſo proportionably	0	0	2
Every boll of Rye graſs, bought of a burgeſs, and going out at the gates -	0	0	1
Every boll of ditto, bought of a ſtranger, and going out at the gates -	0	0	2

Every

llery in Tweedmouth Moor—quarries, &c.

The

	£.	s.	d.
Every horſe-load of houſhold-furniture, coming in by ſea, and going out at the gates	0	0	0½
Every cart-load ditto -	0	0	1
Every Wain-load - -	0	0	2
Every wain-load of pantiles or ſlates	0	0	2
Every cart-load ditto -	0	0	1
Every twelve dozen pound of candles coming in at the gates -	0	0	2
Every horſe-load of tallow of ſtrangers coming into town to be ſhipped off -	0	0	2
Every horſe-load of eggs coming in at the gates	0	0	1½
Beſides one egg in every creel paid in the market to the tollers who clean the market, but no leſs number than thirty to pay an egg to the tollers			
Every horſe-load of hoops and ſtaves	0	0	1
An hundred ditto - -	0	0	0½
Half an hundred - -	0	0	0¼
Leſs, nothing			
Every wain-load - -	0	0	4
Every cart-load - -	0	0	2
Every boll of meal belonging to ſtrangers ſold in the market, or offering to ſell in town			

(wheat

The aggregate of the whole revenues is esti-
mated

	£.	s.	d.
(wheat meal excepted) the ancient toll-dish, heaped, containing five Winchester pints			
Half the boll to be tolled with the half-dish, and the quarter, or fourth part of the boll with a quarter-dish			
Every boll of wheat meal, belonging to strangers, coming in at the gates -	0	0	1
All corn and grain going to the corporation's mills, called the New Mill and Grange-burn Mill, to be grinded, to pay no toll at the gates, when the corn and grain is carried by the horses belonging to the said mills			
Every baker selling bread in the market, to pay towards the cleaning the market, per quarter - -	0	0	2
All lead manufactured in town, and going out at the gates, to pay per hundred weight	0	0	$0\frac{1}{2}$
Half an hundred -	0	0	$0\frac{1}{4}$
Less, nothing			

Be it remembered, that the tollers are to clean the market weekly, on Monday morning, and no dirt to lie there. No toll to be paid at the gates for bread or butcher-

meat,

mated at between 6000l. and 7000l. yearly.

SEC-

	£.	s.	d.
meat, except a whole veal, with the ſkin	0	0	2

N. B. If the toller at either gate impoſe upon any perſon, either going out or coming into town with goods, upon conviction before Mr Mayor, or any of the juſtices, the toller ſhall pay ſixpence; and any perſon that ſhall attempt to defraud the toller of his dues, upon ſuch conviction, ſhall pay ſixpence.

Printed by Order of Guild. *A true Copy.*

EDWARD WILLOBY, Town-Clerk.

All corn belonging to ſtrangers, when the ſame comes to town, is to pay toll at the gates, and if the ſame be grinded at the New Mills the toll is to be refunded by the tollers, on producing a ticket from the tenant of the ſaid mills, certifying that the corn is grinded there. Alſo that no toll ſhall be taken for meal of any ſort grinded at the ſaid mills, ſold in town, either in the houſe or market.

SECTION IV.

Taxes.

THE Taxes are the ſame in Berwick with thoſe in other parts of England, except in a few trifling ones, ſuch as borough meal, rent, &c.

CHAP. V.

Population.

SECTION I.

Former State of Population.

FROM the above-mentioned account of Berwick, by M. Jorvin, it may be thought to have been more populous a century ago than at preſent. The contrary, however, we believe to have been the caſe. Our concluſion is founded on the following well authenticated ſtatement, and other circumſtances communicated by the Reverend Joſeph Rumney, the preſent vicar of the pariſh.

" The annual average of funerals for 12 " years, from 1733 to 1744, both incluſive, " appears,

"appears, from this pariſh regiſter, to have "been 106, which, multiplied by 36, makes "the population, 50 years ago, to have been "3816." But according to Mr Rumney's account, who has lately examined the regiſter of chriſtenings and funerals for a century and upwards, the population at that time would not exceed one half of the preſent. Add to this, many of the oldeſt inhabitants both in Berwick and Caſtlegate aver that the preſent population in Caſtlegate greatly exceeds that of any former period within their recollection. Beſides, much leſs than a century ago, all Bridge Street, Sandgate, Palace Street, Palace, houſes on the Ramparts, part of the Back-way, Fool-Ford, Neſt, &c. &c, have been built; moreover all the old houſes were in general greatly ſmaller than thoſe of modern erection.

SEC-

SECTION II.

Present State.

THOUGH the Author regrets that various professional avocations have hitherto put it out of his power to number the inhabitants as he intended, by going from house to house, yet he flatters himself, that from the registers of funerals and baptisms communicated by Mr Rumney, and the dissenting ministers, upon an average, for five years preceding 1796, and from other sources of information, yet he will be enabled nearly to ascertain the real population of the town.

By multiplying the funerals by 36, and the baptisms by 26, the population amounts to 7930 in the year 1796.

The population of Berwick has increased rapidly within these 20 years, particularly the last ten or twelve, and it is still increasing..

For some years past the rents of houses have advanced greatly. In that period many houses have been built, but now there is very little room for erecting more within the walls.

In 1796, the houses which paid church-rate were 1300: Last year 1500 paid it; and the collector of the tax assures us that there are some hundreds of houses occupied by poor people that do not pay the rate. If this information is correct, the population at present, (February 1799) may be stated at 10000 contained within the walls and liberties of the borough; and if to that number we add the inhabitants of Tweedmouth and Spittal, which are considered as appendages to Berwick, the whole population may be estimated at nearly fourteen thousand. Many persons of observation agree with us in opinion, that the above statement may be looked upon as just.

Berwick furnishes 14 men to the militia, and 24 to the supplementary militia.

Under the last act for raising a certain number of men for the navy, the proportion for this place was fifteen.

Mr.

Mr Rumney eſtimates, "that the propor-"tion of Epiſcopalians to Preſbyterians, in the "pariſh of Berwick, is as one to two and an "half."

SECTION III.

DISEASES.

General Obſervations.

CONSISTENT with the import of the word *Statiſtic*, every one who has hitherto drawn up the ſtatiſtical account of a city, town, or pariſh, has at leaſt enumerated the diſeaſes to which theſe places are ſubject: The object of which is doubtleſs the prevention of diſeaſe.

The Board of Agriculture, impreſſed with a conviction that the ſubject of diſeaſe is more intimately

intimately connected with the intereſts of humanity, and with the proſperity of a nation, than any other, have ſuggeſted to the writers in ſtatiſtics, that they ſhould not only point out "the diſeaſes to which the people are "ſubject," but alſo "their cauſes and their "cure." This will be found ſtated under the head, "Plan for eſtabliſhing a Board of Ag-"riculture," Appendix, B. contained in a publication in 1797, intituled, "Communica-"tions to the Board of Agriculture on ſub-"jects relative to the Huſbandry and Internal "Improvement of the Country," Vol. I.

Sir John Sinclair, in his Addreſs, in the above work, to the clergy of England on his intended plan, that they ſhould draw up the ſtatiſtical account of that part of the kingdom, has inſerted the ſame words.

Barely to ſtate the diſeaſes incident to a place cannot be attended with any other effect than to put perſons on their guard againſt them. This of itſelf is a matter of great conſequence:—But when the importance of ſtrict-

ly

ly attending to the means of preferving health in general is confidered;—When the danger confequent upon the neglect or mifmanagement of acute or inflammatory difeafes, to which many thoufands in Great Britain annually fall victims, is duly attended to, every man of knowledge and candour will coincide in opinion, that the objects of the Board of Agriculture, in this refpect, are highly proper, and that fuch true philanthropy well entitles this moft patriotic inftitution to the gratitude of their native country.

The Board has it by no means in contemplation, that the efforts of ftatiftical writers will enable perfons, not poffeffed of a regular medical education, either to practife medicine, or even to prefcribe to themfelves or families. Notwithftanding this, however, mankind in general, by attention and application, may have it much in their power to prevent difeafes, and, if not to cure them, at leaft, in particular cafes, to check their progrefs until medical aid can be procured.

In

In making our obſervations on this important ſubject, our chief aim will be to excite a due obſervance of the rules neceſſary for the preſervation of health in general, and to arouſe the early attention of mankind to the occurrence of acute or inflammatory diſeaſes in particular, that no time may be put off in calling in the moſt ſkilful practitioner, as the delay of one hour is but too often the loſs of life. This alone conſtitutes a great national object, and is well entitled to the attention of the Board of Agriculture.

Were the ſubject of diſeaſe to be treated of on the plan here propoſed, throughout every pariſh in the united kingdom, this kind of medical knowledge would thereby be much more generally diffuſed than probably could ariſe from ſingle publications, even though written by authors of the firſt celebrity. Beſides, the Board of Agriculture, by ſanctioning them, and afterwards reprinting them in their works in a condenſed form, would in all likelihood excite a ſtill more univerſal attention

tion to them, which in time might be productive of the most essential advantages.

In a subsequent part of this work we shall have occasion to enter more fully into the merits of this subject.

The *diseases* incident to Berwick are such as generally occur in places of a similar situation and climate; nor is it subject to any that can be said to be strictly peculiar to itself.

We formerly observed, that this town had generally obtained the character of being healthy. This, however, does not arise from our own observation alone, but also from that of others.

It is not in the recollection of the oldest practitioner here, nor of the most aged inhabitant, that an epidemic fever ever appeared in any of the principal streets of the town, which is chiefly to be ascribed to the free ventilation they so fully enjoy.

That disease by physicians termed *typhus*, or what is commonly understood by a slow

nervous

nervous fever, is ſometimes to be met with among the lower claſſes of the people living in the confined lanes. When caſes of this kind occur in hot weather, or in the latter end of autumn, they frequently aſſume ſymptoms of putridity, that ſometimes terminate fatally.

On the approach of, and during winter, eſpecially if the ſeaſon is uncommonly ſevere, very old perſons, by expoſing themſelves without doors, are ſometimes ſuddenly carried off by *peripneumonia notha*, or baſtard *peripneumony*, a ſpecies of inflammation peculiar to the *lungs*. This diſeaſe, however, prevails in all northerly climates.

Dyſpeptic or ſtomach complaints, and connecting with them that long train of ſymptoms uſually called *nervous*, are not ſo general in Berwick as in many other places. This is a ſtrong proof of the *ſalubrity* and *tonic* powers of its ſurrounding atmoſphere.

All towns, ſuch as Berwick, ſituated on a riſing ground, cloſe by the ſea and the banks of a large river, where, in cold, wet, and tem-

peſtuous

peſtuous weather, the wind ruſhes with violence through the ſtreets and lanes, perſons going abroad on thoſe occaſions, lightly clothed, will be liable to be ſeized with one or other of the following diſeaſes, eſpecially if their bodies are at the time in a very perſpirable ſtate.

1. A common *catarrh* or *cold*, which, when neglected or improperly treated, and the ſymptoms thereby conſiderably increaſed, conſtitute *catarrhal fever*, vulgarly called a *fever of cold*.

2. *Angina*, that is *quinſey* or inflammatory ſore throat, ſometimes conjoined with cough and pain at the breaſt.

3. *Peripneumony* or inflammation of the lungs.

4. Inflammation of *tubercles* or ſmall knots in the lungs previouſly formed, which when terminating in ſuppuration, or formation of matter, and the ſores do not afterwards heal, conſtitute the *proximate* cauſe of *phthiſis pulmonalis*, commonly termed *conſumption*.

5. Inflammation of the abdominal *viſcera*, or what is generally denominated inflammation of the *bowels*.

6. *Acute* rheumatiſm or rheumatic fever, and many other dangerous affections of an inflammatory nature.

Agreeably to what has been ſtated under *General Obſervations*, we have, 1. To point out ſuch rules as are neceſſary to be obſerved, and which appear to be moſt effectual in conducing to the preſervation of health in general. 2. Curſorily to point out thoſe general means which appear to be moſt effectual in removing complaints of an inflammatory nature.

3. To conclude with a few obſervations on the importance of perſpiration, together with the pernicious effects which generally reſult from its obſtruction, with the means of removing them.

Health may be defined a right diſpoſition of the body, and of all its parts, conſiſting in a due *temperature*, a *complete* conformation,

juſt

just connection, a *ready* and *perfect* exercise of all the *vital functions*.

In directing our attention to the means of preserving health, the following subjects claim our chief consideration:

1. Aliment.
2. Air.
3. Exercise.
4. Sleep.
5. Clothing.
6. Cleanliness.
7. Tranquillity of mind.

Of Aliment.—Wholesome food and regular diet constitute two of the most important points to be attended to in order to preserve a due balance of health; as irregularity in diet, and living on unwholesome aliments, are often productive of dangerous diseases.

As the body by means of certain diets may be brought to undergo great changes, it becomes an object of moment to make choice of that kind of food which we find to be most

suitable

ſuitable to our individual conſtitutions; the want of proper attention to this rule frequently gives riſe to many ſerious complaints. It is mentioned above that nature ſeems to have intended that the food of man ſhould conſiſt partly of an animal, and partly of a vegetable nature. This diet, we are clearly of opinion, is the beſt in general; for it is found, that in thoſe countries where rich animal food conſtitutes the principal nouriſhment of the inhabitants, inflammatory and ſcorbutic diſeaſes generally prevail. On the contrary, it is well known, that thoſe who live moderately on butcher meat, and, along with it, take plenty of vegetables, are not ſo liable to ſuch diſeaſes.

To lay down fixed rules with regard to diet is impracticable, on account of the different conſtitutions of mankind. The great rule is ſurely to ſtudy ſimplicity. We ſee that all nature delights in the moſt plain and ſimple nouriſhment; and every animal, except the *lord* of the *creation*, follows her dictates. *Man*

alone

alone riots at large, and ranſacks every corner of the earth in queſt of luxuries to pamper his appetites, while he remains indifferent as to their poiſonous and deſtructive tendency.

All thoſe who put that value on health which they owe to themſelves, ſhould be content with one meal of animal food in the twenty-four hours, and if it is of one kind only ſo much the better. A full meal at ſupper, conſiſting either of animal food or ſuch things as are difficult of digeſtion, has, in too many inſtances, been found the ſource of fatal diſeaſes.

Both exceſs in eating and faſting, by weakening the powers of digeſtion, impair the appetite, eſpecially in the old and the young. Hence the propriety of regular meals, taken ſo as to gratify, not to ſatiate, the natural cravings of the ſtomach.

According to ſome phyſicians, many of the ſudden deaths which happen to perſons far advanced in life, are occaſioned by long faſting or a too rigid abſtemiouſneſs. Under a ſtate of inanition, the functions of the vital organs

are

are greatly impaired, which appears from the ſymptoms of faintneſs, giddineſs, the pale *cheek* and *ghaſtly* look.

A ſolid breakfaſt is, for obvious reaſons, of great conſequence, not only to the feeble but alſo to the vigorous: experience, however, has taught every one that neither of the two can enjoy this morning repaſt ſufficiently unleſs they eat a light ſupper and go early to bed.

The following quotations from the author of Medical Extracts, we hope will not be deemed unentertaining to our readers:

" *Of Breakfaſt.*

" As our anceſtors breakfaſted early, they " dined alſo early, and had at leaſt two meals " after this, as appears from the allowance " appointed for a *Lady Lucy*, who ſeems to have " been one of the maids of honour in the " Court of *Henry* the VIII. I may be allowed " to mention their articles of food, as a mat- " ter of curioſity, to ſhow in what manner the " *fine ladies* lived in thoſe days."

" This

" This lady was allowed for *breakfaſt*,—*a*
" *chine of beef—a loaf*, and a gallon of ale."

" *Of Dinner*."

The ſame lady, who had ſo *ſolid* a *breakfaſt*, had for dinner,—" *A piece of boiled beef—a*
" *ſlice of roaſted meat*, and a gallon of ale."

" *For Supper*.

" *A meſs of porridge—a piece of mutton—*
" *a cheat* (or finer loaf,) *and a gallon of ale*.
" To be ſociable after ſupper, there was left
" on the table—*A manchette loaf—a gallon of*
" *ale, and half a gallon of wine*."

" We have an account alſo of the *breakfaſt*
" of an *Earl* and *Counteſs* in the lent ſeaſon,"
" viz.—A loaf of bread—*two manchettes*
" (which ſeems to have been loaves of a
" coarſer bread,)—*a quart of beer—a quart of*
" *wine—two pieces of ſalt fiſh—ſix baconed*
" *herrings—four white herrings, and a diſh*
" *of ſprats*."

We are taught, by the aſtoniſhing multiplicity of different kinds of aliments which na-

ture

ture has furniſhed for the food of man, that his diet ſhould not be too uniform. At the ſame time, it appears proper to remark, that all ſudden changes and great deviations are improper and even dangerous.

Perſons of a plethoric habit and ſanguine temperament ought to avoid food highly nouriſhing, or that is ſtrongly ſtimulating, as well as to be abſtemious in the uſe of wine, ſpirits, ſtrong ales, &c. A free indulgence in which are but too often, it is to be lamented, productive of the moſt fatal diſeaſes, ſuch as *palſy*, *apoplexy*, inflammation of the *brain*, &c.

That elegant and enlightened writer, Addiſon, remarks on intemperance thus:

"For my part when I behold a faſhionable "table ſet out in all its magnificence, I fancy "that I ſee *gouts*, and *dropſies*, and *fevers*, "and *lethargies*, with other *innumerable* diſ-"tempers, lying in *ambuſcade* among the "diſhes."

It has juſtly been obſerved by phyſicians, that temperance may be called the *parent* of health; equally well may it be ſaid, that intemperance

temperance is the ſource of diſeaſe. A ſlight attention to the ſtructure and nature of the human frame clearly points out the great danger of intemperance, both with regard to eating and drinking. Fortunate it is for man, however, that exceſs in the latter, generally by depraving the appetite, puts it out of his power to indulge in the former. Hence that *verſatility* or accommodating principle of our conſtitution, which conſtitutes one of the moſt wonderful *phenomena* of the animal economy, is put leſs on the ſtretch, which otherwiſe might be overcome and *death* enſue.

What! is it poſſible to conceive that man, whoſe whole nature revolts at the proſpect of diſſolution—who is endowed by his Creator with a principle of ſelf-preſervation, which forms the ſtrongeſt paſſion of his ſoul, ſhould yield ſo readily to thoſe vile impulſes of his mind, which ſubject him to *diſeaſe*, *miſery*, and *death*.—How *ignoble* the idea.—How *baſe* the *adoption* of ſuch a *ſyſtem*—a *ſyſtem* founded in *ſenſuality*, and whoſe ultimate *for-*

feitures are, *alas!* no lefs than lofs of *charac-ter*, and, what is *worft* of *all*, the *difpleafure* of *that Being* who called *him* into *exiftence* for the *nobleft* purpofes!

Of Air.—In a note to the preliminaries to this work, we obferved, that the atmofphere confifts of two diftinct airs or gafes, the one vital, and the other azotic. The former is abfolutely neceffary to the prefervation of life, whereas the other is altogether unfit either for the maintenance of animal life or flame. This is proved by experiment; for it has been found, that by fubjecting animals to infpire pure azotic air, they almoft inftantly died; and, on the contrary, animals of the fame fpecies acquired more livelinefs and activity when made to inhale oxygen or pure vital air.

It is fuppofed that in this climate, the proportion in general between thefe two airs is three of azotic to one of oxygen or vital air. It is wonderful, that though the vital air is fpecifically heavier than the azotic, yet they are never found ſeparate neither in the atmoſphere nor in jars. It is no leſs ſurprizing, that the upper regions of the atmoſphere contain a greater proportion of vital air than thoſe nearer the earth. This is confirmed by experiments made by an *eudiometer*. As far as we know, theſe ſingular and ſeemingly incredible *phenomena* have not as yet been accounted for either by philoſophers or chemiſts.

We are, as the learned and ingenious Mr Boyle ſays, to conſider the atmoſphere as one large chemical veſſel, in which an infinite number of various operations are conſtantly going on. It is continually receiving a part of the ſubſtance of all the bodies of the earth, by evaporation, to mix in this *truly great alembic*, and to float for a while in common *.

Any

* The bounty of the Governor of the univerſe to his creatures is, perhaps, in no inſtance more eminently diſplayed than in making even the vegetable world ſubſervient to man. About twenty-one years ago, the celebrated Dr Prieſtly, in the progreſs of his philoſophical purſuits on air,

Any change made in the atmoſphere, which leſſens the proportion of vital to azotic air, renders it more or leſs unfit for the great and important purpoſes of reſpiration. The more pure and dry, therefore, the atmoſphere of a place is the more healthy will it be found.

All kinds of putrid effluvia, as well as all ſulphureous acid and metalline exhalations, contaminate the atmoſphere and render it very unhealthy.

From the foregoing obſervations, it will appear of what vaſt conſequence it is to breathe freſh air. Perſons in general are, however, more intereſted in what they eat or drink than in what kind of air they draw into their lungs.

air, diſcovered that plants of all kinds abſorbed a very conſiderable quantity of azotic or mephitic air for their nouriſhment, which, in the note at p. 6. we have ſtated to be highly deleterious to animal life; but the matter does not reſt here—the Almighty has alſo fitted living vegetables to throw out the other ſalutary portion of the air, viz the vital part, thereby keeping up in a perpetual circle a copious ſupply of good air for the various uſes of *reſpiration* and *combuſtion.*

lungs. The ſtrongeſt proof we have of the ſalubrity of reſpiring pure air freely, is in the ſmall pox, and its ſalutary effects in all kinds of fevers are alſo well known.

The writer, many years ago, was told by a gentleman of the firſt reſpectability, that an intimate acquaintance of his, while under the ſmall pox from inoculation, experienced excruciating pain in his forehead whenever he approached the fire, or when the room became much heated; but the moment he pulled up the window and breathed freſh air the pain abated, and in a few minutes went off altogether.

If ſuch were the feelings of a full grown perſon, what tortures muſt not young children in the ſmall pox ſuffer, who are ſhut up in a ſmall apartment from which the freſh air is excluded, and the room overheated by a large fire while the helpleſs infant lies in a bed or cradle half ſmothered with blankets?

Having now ſeen that priſtine health and long life moſt eſſentially depend on freſh and wholeſome air; and, on the contrary, that a contaminated

contaminated atmoſphere is inimical to the human conſtitution, it will appear evident, 1. That all buildings ſhould ſtand on dry ground and an airy ſituation, unencumbered with plantings, in order that the circulation of air may be as free as poſſible.

2. That the apartments of houſes ought to be lofty and roomy, particularly the bed chambers; and that the doors and windows ſhould be occaſionally thrown open to promote a free ventilation all over the houſe.

3. That, where it can be done, all bed clothes ought to be expoſed every day to the open air for a conſiderable time before the bed is made up, taking care, however, to remove any dampneſs which they may have imbibed from the atmoſphere.

4. That all churches, courts of law, &c. ought to be frequently ventilated and freed of dampneſs, by warm ſtoves and other means.

5. That the ſtreets of all conſiderable towns ought to be regularly laid out, ſpacious and kept thoroughly clean.

6.

6. That the health muſt always be more or leſs endangered by going into great crowds for any length of time.

7. That living in the country is, in point of health, to be preferred to living in large cities or towns, eſpecially in thoſe where great manufactures are ſituated.

8. That no manufactures, brewing, &c. ought to be carried on in cities or towns, but ſome where disjoined from them.

It is to be hoped that what we have here ſtated on this moſt important ſubject will be deemed ſufficient by the candid reader, and we ſhall therefore next proceed to inveſtigate the ſubject.

Of Exerciſe.—*Rouſſeau* juſtly obſerves, that temperance and exerciſe are the two beſt phyſicians in the world. It may with truth be added, that whoever has the wiſdom to pay a proper regard to them will but ſeldom have occaſion to employ any other. The proof of this reſts with every man's own experience.

One

One of the greateſt gifts which man has received from his Maker is, that latitude or accommodating power given to his conſtitution, which, in our obſervations on aliment, we ſtated as conſtituting one of the moſt wonderful phenomena in the animal economy. By this verſatile principle the human frame may be gradually brought to endure incredible degrees of fatigue, cold, and wet.—Hence the man who earns his bread by the ſweat of his brow can remain in the open fields the whole day with impunity, though ſupported on no better fare than bread and milk.—The active ſoldier comes in time to be ſo inured to fatigue and faſting, that it is no great hardſhip for him to lie in the open fields for nights ſucceſſively upon a morſel of bread and a drink of water.—The hardened *ſailor*, with his muſcles braced like *ſtrong elaſtic cords*, can, though *icicles* hang from every hair, mount to the top-maſt regardleſs of the fury of the elements, and he continues to enjoy unimpaired health.—But, alas! ſhould the pampered *beau* of the *city*, who *ſtruts* along with *mighty ſtride*,

ſtride, be overtaken with a ſhower of rain, ten to one but he will afterwards be ſeized either with a *rheumatic fever*, *ſore throat*, or ſome other *acute* diſeaſe.

The conſtruction and nature of the human body clearly evince, that a conſiderable ſhare of exerciſe is abſolutely neceſſary for the preſervation of pure health and athletic vigour. The infinite ſeries, convolutions, and ramifications of veſſels, ſo ſmall that they elude the reſearches of even the fineſt microſcope, and in which fluids eſſential to animal exiſtence circulate, require a great degree of regular exerciſe of the body in order to promote a free circulation, and a due ſecretion from every organ. Hence obſtruction, and the veſſels, as a conſequence of it, becoming altogether impervious, may be prevented; which effects, when produced by indolence, inactivity, or any other cauſe, lay the foundation of many obſtinate, painful, and dangerous diſeaſes: Hereby the *wrinkled brow*, attendant on *old age*, may be accounted for.

Without the aid of medical knowledge, every

† O o man

man of common obſervation muſt know, that perſons following employments which lead them daily to take much exerciſe in the open air, are in general far more healthy, active, and robuſt, than others whoſe profeſſions confine them to the houſe. The former includes all who are employed in agricultural and other rural affairs, and the latter implies certain kinds of manufacturers, tradeſmen, &c. &c.

It is worthy of remark, that moſt men who lead a ſedentary life become ſooner or later affected with a long train of complaints, to which the vulgar, and even phyſicians, have affixed the common term *nervous*, (a moſt uſeful *reſource* in *practice*.) When theſe arrive at ſuch a pitch as to conſtitute the diſeaſe called *hypochondriaſm*, the ſubject of it is truly pitiable. For the prevention of this, of all others the moſt whimſical and unhappy diſeaſe, *exerciſe* has been found to be the chief remedy, as well as for curing it, eſpecially when accompanied with a ſucceſſive change of new objects, and the faſcinating enjoyments of well timed amuſements, and of agreeable company.

This

This diſeaſe ſeldom or never invades the man of active exertion without doors, unleſs he meet with ſome diſaſtrous event that ſuperinduces dejection of ſpirits, and confines him at home. Farther, regular and moderate exerciſe, joined to temperance, by preſerving the natural tone of the ſtomach and every other organ of the body—health in this caſe has been found to prevail in a pre-eminent degree.—On the contrary, indolence, inaction, conjoined with intemperance, by producing a languid circulation, (excepting under a ſtate of inebriety when it is pernicioully quick), general relaxation and debility of the whole ſyſtem is brought on.—Hence want of appetite, indigeſtion, crudities, dropſies, rupture of the blood veſſels, &c. &c. often ſupervene.

Having now repeatedly ſtated, that, to aſſiſt nature in performing the various and important functions neceſſary to preſerve animal life and good health, exerciſe is eſſentially requiſite, three things next preſent themſelves on this ſubject as worthy of conſideration.

1. What is the beſt mode of exerciſe in general?

2. What is the fitteſt time to take it, and to what degree ſhould it be carried?

As to the firſt, it is preſumed it will appear evident, from the foregoing obſervations, that thoſe kinds of exerciſe which will likely conduce the moſt to preſerve health will be ſuch as communicate *action* to all the bodily organs, as walking, riding, digging, &c. and that kind of exerciſe which can be longeſt continued, and, at the ſame time, give the leaſt fatigue, muſt be preferable to that which ſoon over-heats the body and occaſions languor. The former has been denominated the exerciſe of *geſtation*: The latter implies that of running, jumping, throwing heavy weights, hand-ball, cricket, ſwiming, and ſome others.

Moſt authors are of opinion, that riding on horſeback is the moſt healthy of all kinds of exerciſe. In this we agree with them. Sailing ſtands highly recommended alſo. Walking is the moſt natural of all exerciſes, and, when properly and regularly taken, contributes powerfully to health. The ſalutary effects of bodily exerciſe are greatly heightened by thoſe pleaſures of the mind which in general

neral are enjoyed in hunting, ſhooting, playing at golf, dancing, and the like. The freſh air can never, upon any occaſion, be fully enjoyed in carriages.

With regard to the fitteſt time for uſing exerciſe; experience has taught the ſenſible and attentive part of mankind, that a conſiderable degree of it while the body is in a debilitated ſtate, as well as the taking of exerciſe immediately after a full meal, are both hoſtile to health, and, in either caſe, when carried to great exceſs, occaſionally produces ſudden death. This is well known to the medical reader. The importance of this fact ſeems to demand that we ſhould endeavour to account for it, with a view to excite that degree of caution which mankind ought at all times to beſtow on their health in the ardour of every purſuit requiring great bodily fatigue.

As the tone of the ſyſtem and ſtrength of the body depend on a well regulated ſupply of wholeſome food, ſo, on the contrary, a degree of relaxation and debility will always be found to accompany the want of it in proportion to the extent of that want. That as exercise increases the secretions from the blood, or, in other words, the waste of the body, and as it is carried on by muscular exertion, the continuation of it, while the stomach is empty and the vessels more or less in a state of depletion, the vital organs must suffer a diminution of their powers in proportion thereto, which if carried to a certain length, death will inevitably ensue. On the other hand, as a full meal of solid nourishing food produces a plethoric state of the vessels more or less, and is accompanied with temporary fever, especially if much wine, spirits, or strong malt liquors are taken along with it; exercise, employed under such circumstances, by farther increasing the velocity of the blood in the *brain*, as well as thereby distending its vessels to a degree still more preternatural, a rupture of them, or a compression of that vital organ, arising from the accumulated distention, may take place. The occurrence of the first is almost, in all cases, suddenly fatal, and the

other

other is frequently ſo, if the compreſſion is very conſiderable.

Beſides, the preſſure of the ſtomach, when full, againſt the lungs impedes, in ſome degree, the circulation of blood through them, as well as the free expanſion of them in reſpiration; and, as a conſequence, may produce an afflux or accumulation of blood in the head.

The agitation of the ſtomach *alone*, when *full*, for obvious cauſes, may be attended with conſequences which forbid the uſe of exerciſe while in that ſtate,—ſuch as headach, ſickneſs, nauſea, and other unpleaſant effects.

If the above concluſions are admitted to be juſt, it will thence follow, that the moſt proper times for uſing exerciſe will be the morning, forenoon, and afternoon. Healthy perſons, who live regular, will be able to take from one to two hours exerciſe before breakfaſt with great advantage; and the hearty repaſt which it will diſpoſe them to make will enable them to reſume their exerciſe with pleaſure and alacrity an hour or two afterwards. The forenoon's exerciſe ſhould cloſe an hour or two before dinner, ſo that time may be given for the temperature of the body to return to its natural ſtandard. The afternoon's exerciſe ſhould not commence until the proceſs of digeſtion is pretty far advanced, and it ought to ceaſe before the air acquires much humidity.

Exerciſe is either active or paſſive; the former includes walking, running, hunting, dancing, &c.—The latter, riding ſlowly on horſeback, in a carriage, or ſailing in a ſhip.

The effects of laſſitude and langour, accompanied with thirſt and a dryneſs of the mouth, attendant on violent exerciſe, indicates the impropriety of carrying it ſo far. It has been already obſerved, that perſons accuſtomed to labour daily in the open air acquire the power of bearing incredible degrees of fatigue, cold, and wet, without ſuffering in their health. It is alſo known, that men may bring themſelves, by degrees, to walk almoſt as far in one day as an ordinary horſe can do. This is ſtrongly exemplified in the Edinburgh chairmen and cadies. Some of

theſe

theſe would think it no difficulty to walk 40 or 50 miles into the country in one day, and to return the following, though only living on bread and ſmall beer.

From the preceding obſervations, it would appear that the following inferences may be juſtly drawn.

1. That perſons beginning to take exerciſe ſhould uſe it ſparingly, and increaſe it gradually as they find they can bear it without producing much fatigue.

2. That every ſort of violent exerciſe muſt have a pernicious tendency.

3. That perſons long inured to great bodily exertion may uſe violent exerciſe with a greater chance of impunity than a perſon not accuſtomed to take it, or one of a weak conſtitution.

4. That when a perſon under exerciſe begins to feel tired and languid he ſhould deſiſt from it, and not reſume the uſe of it until he has recovered his ſtrength by reſt.

5. That the weak and valetudinary ought

to be cautious in uſing exerciſe before breakfaſt.

In again contemplating that original verſatility of the human frame, by which, and by the additional powers that it acquires from habit, the conſtitutions of men in general will be found to admit of their pulſe being increaſed by high living, and the uſe of ſtrong inebriating liquors. Theſe, when taken to exceſs, will raiſe the pulſe from 60 or 70, in a ſtate of health, to 120 ſtrokes and upwards in the minute without extinguiſhing the vital flame; even though, in many inſtances, this courſe, accompanied by every other irregularity, ſhould be continued with but ſhort intervals of ſobriety for weeks, months, nay for a ſeries of years ſucceſſively. Hence it is aſtoniſhing, that men of enlightened minds could ever doubt of their having been formed by real deſign.

The Omnipotent, in his bounty to his creatures, has in no inſtance more eminently diſplayed infinite wiſdom and goodneſs than in this; for how extremely miſerable would the

ſtate

ſtate of man have been had no latitude or verſatility of conſtitution whatever been thus beſtowed upon him, while, at the ſame time, he were poſſeſſed of the ſame deſires and propenſities which are congenial to his preſent nature.

Had this really been the caſe, the total extinction of human exiſtence would ſoon have taken place, had it been poſſible for an animal body, ſo conſtituted, to have arrived at maturity: For in proportion to the magnitude of every deviation from that diet and temperature of body, under which alone, in this caſe, health could poſſibly have been preſerved, diſtempers of courſe would have enſued of greater or leſſer malignity, which, in their numerous obvious conſequences, would in a ſhort time have depopulated the globe.

We conclude theſe digreſſive remarks by obſerving, that in proportion to the greatneſs of thoſe reſources provided by nature for the preſervation of man, ſo much the more content and happy ought he to be with his preſent condition of life. At the ſame time, it

is

is proper to remark, that as an accountable being, a greater degree of reſponſibility attaches to him for his conduct in this world than would have done had the human frame been ſo conſtructed, that every blaſt of wind, the ſlighteſt deviation in diet, made either by choice or neceſſity, the moſt trifling commotion of mind, ariſing from misfortune or any other cauſe, ſhould have been followed by pain and diſeaſe.

Of Sleep.—Sleep may be defined a certain ſtate of the human body, which though the *vital organs* continue to perform their reſpective functions, yet the organs of the ſenſes ſuffer a temporary ſuſpenſion of their powers, by which they are inſenſible to the ordinary impreſſions of external objects.

Sleep being rather a peculiar affection of mind than any particular property belonging to the body, it has, therefore, been conſidered as ſtanding more immediately connected with metaphyſics than with the ſubject of phyſiology or knowledge of the human body. However

ever that may be, one thing is certain, ſleep is eſſential to the preſervation of health: for in all living bodies there are two different proceſſes continually going on, the one of waſte, the other of repair, or, in other words, there is one proceſs of aſſimilation, and another of diſſolution. The former, in a ſtate of health, predominates in youth; but the latter prevails in old age. Each of theſe ſtates ſubſiſt nearly on a par in the vigour and meridian of life. It is a well known fact, that a moderate degree of exerciſe of the body as well as of the mind will promote both; and, on the contrary, it is indiſputable, that the immoderate exertion of either, or that exertion which is not properly adapted to our ſtrength, habits, or period of life, weakens the aſſimilating or nouriſhing powers, while they increaſe thoſe of diſſolution; and it has likewiſe been found, that the means which nature commonly calls to her aſſiſtance to reſtore the equilibrium, is that moſt powerful *agent* ſleep.

Having pointed out that ſleep is an important means of promoting nutrition, thereby tending

tending to preserve a due balance of health; it is neceſſary to add, that it is of the utmoſt conſequence to regulate the hours of ſleep conſiſtent with nature's plan. Of this, every perſon who has beſtowed the leaſt attention to thoſe ſenſations which he has experienced, muſt be enabled to judge for himſelf, whether he adheres to or deviates from her *unerring* dictates.

To enter into a diſcuſſion on that part of the ſubject would far exceed the limits aſſigned to this part of the work. We, ſhall, however, barely notice, that the practice of ſitting late at night and lying long in the morning are both of them ruinous to the conſtitution.

The practice of forcing nature, as it were, by means of that power of the mind, called *volition* or the *will*, to indulge in repeated ſlumbers, after that a ſufficient quantity of ſleep has been taken, is not only prejudicial to the conſtitution in general, but in the plethoric and the enfeebled it is attended with immediate danger,

danger, arifing from caufes which are known to the faculty.

The luxuries of the moft fumptuous tables, and beds of the fineft down, when exercife and retiring early to reft are neglected, cannot vie with that luxury which the labouring man enjoys from a plain diet and found fleep.

This is a fubject worthy the contemplation of the higheft ranks, as well as the attention of the inferior orders of mankind, the natural tendency of which would be to incline the more opulent to ufe greater reftraint in their purfuits after gratification, and to teach the middling and lower claffes, that though they do not *abound* in riches, or *ftrut* in vain fhow, yet that they enjoy more real happinefs than if they were to drive to Court in the moft fplendid carriage.

Here is a *fpecies* of equality which, in the mind of every good man, muft excite inexpreffible admiration and gratitude. As it flows from a fountain out of which no ftream can iffue but what is perfectly pure, fo it is founded-

ed

ed in true and univerſal benevolence. It would be the height of *impiety* to compare this *beaven-born ſyſtem of equality* with that *viſionary* and *prepoſterous* ſort of equality which lately has been held out to mankind by the *baſeſt* of the human race, from the impureſt motives and for the moſt deteſtable purpoſes—purpoſes directly leading to complete anarchy and the commiſſion of every crime that can reflect diſgrace on the human character.—This *baſeleſs fabric*—this *diabolical phantom*, has but too generally, it is to be lamented, perverted the minds of the lower orders of ſociety, and thereby diſturbed the national as well as the domeſtic peace and happineſs of this and every other civilized country in the world, threatening in its conſequences the overthrow of *all* inſtitutions, *human* and *divine*, and ſweeping before it, with an *irreſiſtible torrent*, every *trace* of whatever raiſes man *ſuperior* to the ſtate of *ſavage* nature!

Of

Of Clothing.—In the preliminary obſervations, we ſtated, that clothing has for its objects:

1. The protection of our bodies from the inclemency of the atmoſphere.

2. The ornamenting of our frame.

As the effect intended to be produced by clothing is to preſerve the body in a due temperature of heat, ſo that perſpiration may not be obſtructed, the nature and extent of our clothing muſt be directed by the climate we live in as well as by the different ſeaſons of the year.

Perſons in the prime of life will require leſs clothing than perſons far advanced in years, becauſe in the former the circulation of blood is more equal and vigorous, and of courſe the generation of heat in the body is quicker and of greater extent than is the caſe in old age.

That kind of clothing worn next the ſkin, which is the leaſt conductor of heat or that moſt powerfully retains it, is to be preferred to all others, and this has long been found to be flannel and lately fleecy hoſiery.

The pride of man often leads him to commit many errors in the decking out of his body, which are productive of diſeaſes that frequently have a fatal termination. Every one knows the tragical effects which often occur from perſons throwing off a warm dreſs, and in its place ſubſtituting ſome ſlight gaudy one, and this only for the purpoſe of attracting the attention of the multitude for the night.

Inſtances might be adduced to prove, that too tight boots have occaſioned death. The ſame fatal conſequences have, on ſome occaſions, ariſen from the pairing of corns, the growth of which are never produced but by ſtrait ſhoes.

The greateſt perfection in dreſs, doubtleſs, conſiſts in *warmth*, *thorough cleanlineſs*, and *eaſe*. Yet it too often happens, that in attempting to *attire* with ſuperior elegance, and to exhibit a fine ſhape, recourſe is had to ſuch methods as in their conſequences occaſion difficulty of breathing, fainting fits, and violent headachs.

headachs. Befides this, they fometimes lay the foundation of dangerous difeafes, fuch as fpitting of blood and confumption of the lungs. Diftortion too is not unfrequently an effect of this practice *.

Of Cleanlinefs.—The want of cleanlinefs, confidered in its full extent, is the fource of more mifery to mankind than arifes from any other caufe, the ravages of civil war only excepted.

We confider cleanlinefs to be of fo much importance, as not only to intereft individuals, but alfo to become an object of the firft moment in a national point of view. From that impreffion, in our opinion, there ought to be a code of laws inftituted to enforce univerfal cleanlinefs.

To inveftigate this fubject as fully as it is entitled to, would afford matter for a volume; it would, therefore, not accord with our prefent limits to enter upon its merits here.

* The above refers to the fafhion which prevailed fome years ago; but, in juftice to the good fenfe of the prefent tafte, whatever bad confequences might have refulted from it, are now completely obviated.

here. We ſhall only add, that the health—happineſs—honour—and the pride not only of the individual is involved in it, but alſo the intereſt—the happineſs—the ſecurity—the honour—pride—and independence of a nation.

Of Tranquillity of Mind.—That tranquillity of mind which ariſes from a conſciouſneſs of having faithfully diſcharged every duty incumbent on an accountable being, is one of the higheſt attainments and gratifications of which human nature is ſuſceptible.

Beſides this ineſtimable reward, ſpontaneouſly reſulting from the performance of actions founded upon the pureſt motives, the author of our exiſtence has ſo conſtituted the mind of man, and connected it with his corporeal ſyſtem, that whatever conveys hilarity and joy to the ſoul, imparts additional health to the body; whereas, on the contrary, from whatever cauſe the mind is ruffled, and its tranquillity leſſened, or its powers and faculties impaired, the health of the body becomes more or leſs affected.

Experience

Experience has ſhown, that perſons of chearful diſpoſitions, and all thoſe who partake moderately of the comforts of life, and who by a virtuous conduct do not not ſubject their minds to be tortured by ſelf-accuſation, are, comparatively ſpeaking, much more healthy and vigorous than the naturally chagrined—the voluptuous—the diſappointed, &c. Hilarity of ſpirits quickens both the circulation of blood and the appetite, and thereby gives additional tone and invigoration to the whole animal machine. From all which it may be deduced, that the ſoul and the body thus act and react on each other reciprocally, in order to preſerve their original union pure and perfect, that no interruption may be given to a full and free performance of their reſpective functions; and this affords one of the ſtrongeſt proofs that can be adduced in favour of the exiſtence of a Supreme Intelligence, who is perfection itſelf; and who, in all his works, has manifeſted a clear deſign of ultimately bringing man to happineſs. For we ſee, that temperance, regularity, and virtue are re-

rewarded with good health and the approbation of a good confcience, while vice and immorality are accompanied by difeafe, anguifh, and contempt from the world. What a fource of hope and joy does not all this prefent to the difconfolate of every defcription, and what an incitement does it not hold out to mankind, to lead a life of virtue and morality?—a farther corroboration of what we have advanced on the original defign of providence.

We have next curforily to point out thofe general means which appear to be the moft effectual in removing complaints of an inflammatory nature, or of arrefting their progrefs until medical aid can be obtained.

But that we may the more readily be underftood by the general run of readers, we beg leave to premife,

1. That from whatever caufe local inflammation is either externally or internally excited, the blood is propelled in greater quantity than is natural into the veffels of the part affected. Hence an unufual diftention of them

them takes place; and, as a direct conſequence thereof, an overſtretching of the nerves as well as of the muſcular fibres connected with theſe veſſels. When the ſtretching force is conſiderable, it is neceſſarily accompanied with pain, and this acting as a ſtimulant to the brain and nervous ſyſtem, the energy of both is preternaturally increaſed as well as the irritability of the whole vaſcular and muſcular ſyſtems, which of courſe accelerates the circulation of the blood, thereby conſtituting what has been termed general or ſymptomatic fever.

2. That whatever contributes to augment the quantity of the blood in the body, increaſes the energy of the brain and nervous ſyſtem, which conſequently adds to the force of the circulation *.

3.

* Here, however, it may be remarked, that the quantity of blood may be morbidly increaſed, that is, the blood veſſels within the head may be ſo diſtended by a general plethoric ſtate of the body, induced by a highly nouriſhing diet, as not only to impair the energy of the brain, but to deſtroy it altogether.--Hence, as one cauſe, we account for the occurrence of lethargy, palſy, apoplexy, &c.

3. That by whatever means the quantity of blood is ſuddenly diminiſhed, the nervous energy is leſſened in proportion, and conſequently the circulation becomes more languid. This is confirmed by blood-letting, and it is the moſt powerful agent in nature for diminiſhing the impetus of the blood in inflammatory diſeaſes *.

4. That hitherto no practice has been diſcovered by which it is poſſible to preſerve life in caſes of fever where the velocity of the blood increaſes to a certain pitch, perhaps, to 200 pulſations or more in the minute. Hence in caſes of inflammation ariſing to a certain degree, it is impoſſible to avert a fatal termination of it.

From theſe axioms or ſelf-evident facts it will be obvious that, in all caſes of inflammation, every application that is ſtimulating muſt aggravate

* As a ſort of exception to this general law of the ſyſtem, we have to ſtate, that on the commencement of inflammation of the inteſtines, the pulſe commonly feels low and creeping, but, on taking away blood by the lancet, the pulſe riſes and beats firmer. This is a moſt important matter, and demands the ſtricteſt attention.

aggravate the fymptoms; whereas, on the contrary, whatever is cooling and weakens the powers of the body, muft have a direct tendency to mitigate every inflammatory affection.

The intelligent and judicious phyfician, well aware of the truth of all thefe circumftances, will be directed, in a cafe of inflammation accompanied with acute pain and general fever,

1. To direct a quantity of blood to be abftracted from the fyftem from time to time in proportion to the violence of the fymptoms and ftrength of his patient.

2. He will order cooling and relaxing medicines to be adminiftered occafionally.

3. Will enjoin his patient to live on a low diet, and to abftain from all vinous, fpirituous, and fermented liquors.

4. Will permit thirft to be fully gratified.

5. To prevent mufcular exertion as much as poffible; and to promote perfpiration will confine his patient to bed.

6. With a view to determine the blood as much as poſſible to the lower extremities, as well as to promote univerſal and copious perſpiration, thereby to leſſen the quantity of blood tranſmitted to the ſeat of inflammation, (ſuppoſing it in the trunk of the body or bowels) will recommend the frequent fomentation of the lower extremities with tepid decoctions of emollient herbs or warm water, meanwhile taking care that the heat applied be not ſo great as to raiſe the pulſe.

7. Will cauſe the light to be ſhut out and reſtrict his patient in converſation.

8. The breathing of a pure and cool air will be ſtrongly enforced.

9. The ſoothing of the mind by every means will be particularly adviſed, and he will ſupport his patient's hopes by holding out the proſpect of a ſpeedy recovery.

All internal inflammatory diſeaſes ought to be attempted to be cured by *reſolution*, that is by diſperſing the inflammation; for when they proceed to ſuppuration the conſequence

is

is always fatal, unlefs the matter formed be difcharged by fome external opening either made by nature or art. All internal cafes terminating in mortification muft be fatal.

In cafes of external inflammation, not affecting the fyftem in general, the repeated application of leeches to the part affected, together with reft, a low diet, cooling medicine, and the frequent renewal of cloths dipt in a folution of fugar of lead, and fometimes poultices will be all that is requifite to remove the difeafe or palliate the fymptoms. Let it always be remembered, however, that the difcuffion of external inflammation, which may occur in fevers, being generally critical, is often productive of fatal confequences; the promoting of their fuppuration, therefore, will always be recommended by the intelligent and attentive practitioner.

The general plan of treatment juft now pointed out, is that which the moft eminent phyficians purfue in fuch cafes of inflammation.

Upon

Upon the whole, it will appear of what great importance it is early to attend to inflammatory attacks; for ſhould inflammation in ſome particular affections increaſe to a certain degree, either in conſequence of neglect or improper treatment, the moſt powerful remedies, which probably in the beginning would have effected a cure, cannot prevent a fatal termination to it.

From the hints we have communicated, a perſon ſituated at a great diſtance from medical advice, and who may be attacked with acute pain in any part of the body that excites heat, thirſt, &c. will readily perceive the propriety of reſtricting himſelf to reſt and a low diet, while, at the ſame time, he has recourſe to drink freely of diluting liquors, ſuch as barley water, thin gruel, and the like. Upon the ſame principle he will naturally be led to take cooling medicine occaſionally, and finally, too, to loſe blood by the lancet proportioned to the degree of pain and ſtrength of his body. This laſt remedy, in all violent caſes, ought, as already noticed, to be the firſt put in practice. Becauſe the ſlighteſt inflammatory affection, which is either neglected or injudiciouſly treated, ſuddenly aſſuming a formidable aſpect, frequently ends in death; and numerous inſtances could be adduced of external contuſions, ſcarcely perceptible, being followed by an extinction of the vital principle ſo quickly as to exceed credibility.

We ſhall here glance at the ſubject of perſpiration as propoſed.

It is well known to every perſon, who is in the leaſt converſant with the animal economy, that the diſcharge through the pores of the ſkin, called *perſpiration*, is by far the moſt conſiderable, and among the moſt important that occurs in the ſyſtem. Of courſe it follows, that from whatever cauſe perſpiration is obſtructed the human frame muſt be ſubjected to diſeaſe.

Moreover, it is well known that the general cauſes of diminiſhed perſpiration are cold and wet, particularly wet feet and ſitting with wet or damp clothes. Experience has taught mankind,

mankind, that though the body be well cloth-ed in general, yet the influence of this does not extend to the lower extremities in ſuch force as to maintain a ſufficient proportion of heat in them, unleſs they are, at the ſame time, well guarded with ſtockings and ſhoes ſuited to the weather and ſeaſon of the year.

The celebrated *Sanctorius* was the firſt who beſtowed particular attention upon the ſubject of inſenſible perſpiration. This great phyſician and philoſopher carried on a courſe of experiments, with aſtoniſhing aſſiduity and ſucceſs, for thirty years, by which he opened a new ſcene in medicine, to which former phyſicians and philoſophers had been almoſt total ſtrangers.

M'Kenzie on Health tranſcribes from Sanctorius thus,

" Inſenſible perſpiration, by the pores of the
" ſkin and by the breath, is greater than all
" the ſenſible evacuations joined together; for
" if a ſtrong man, who uſes moderate exer-
" ciſe in good weather, eats and drinks eight
" pound weight a day, he will diſcharge five
" of

"of them by inſenſible perſpiration, and we "are more relieved by a free inſenſible per-"ſpiration than by all the ſenſible evacuations "united."

Authors of the firſt celebrity might be adduced to prove that ſuppreſſed perſpiration is the general ſource of moſt internal inflammatory diſeaſes; and many inſtances could be ſtated to ſhow that the ſudden ſtoppage of the cutaneous diſcharge has been quickly followed by death.

The moſt powerful ſecurities againſt obſtructed perſpiration are a flannel ſhirt and foot ſocks. This ariſes from flannel abſorbing the perſpirable matter, and, by being a ſlow conductor of heat, it retains longer than any other ſubſtance yet known, except fleecy hoſiery, which, by ſome late authors, has been ſaid to poſſeſs ſuperior powers to flannel, and to be a more pleaſant wear.

The celebrated *Dr Black* obſerves, that flannel and other ſubſtances which keep our bodies warm are compoſed of a rare and a ſpongy maſs, the fibres of which ſo ſlightly touch

each

each other, that the heat moves ſlowly through the interſtices, which being replete with air only, and that in a ſtagnant ſtate, affords but little aſſiſtance in conducting the heat.

Count Rumford has carried his inquiries on this important ſubject ſtill farther; and, by means of ſeveral ingenious experiments, is of opinion, that there is a relation betwixt the power which the ſubſtances uſually worn, as clothing, have of abſorbing moiſture, and that of keeping our bodies warm. He expreſſes much ſurpriſe, that the cuſtom of wearing flannel next the ſkin ſhould not have prevailed more univerſally. He is decidedly of opinion, that its uſe would prevent many diſeaſes; and, he ſays, there is no greater luxury than the comfortable ſenſation ariſing from wearing it, eſpecially after one has been accuſtomed to it.

" It is a miſtaken notion, (he obſerves), that " it is too warm a clothing for ſummer. I " have worn it in the hotteſt climates, and at " all ſeaſons of the year, and never found the " leaſt inconvenience from it. It is the warm

" bath

" bath of a perſpiration, confined by a linen " ſhirt wet with ſweat, which renders the " ſummer heats of ſouthern climates ſo inſup- " portable, but flannel promotes perſpiration " and favours its evaporation, and evapora- " tion, as is well known, produces poſitive " cold."

It has been obſerved, that new flannel, after having been worn ſome time, acquires the property of ſhinning in the dark, but loſes it on being waſhed.—Philoſ. Tranſ. No. 483. § 7.

From theſe, and preceding obſervations, it will, in the firſt place, be evident, that the moſt powerful preventative to obſtructed perſpiration will be a warm and ſufficient clothing of the whole body, particularly the lower extremities.

2. In caſes where the body has been long expoſed to cold and wet, and a perſon feels chilly and has ſlight ſhiverings accompanied with langour, and a dull heavy pain in the forehead, &c. indicating diminiſhed perſpiration, immediate recourſe ought to be had to warm bathing, general as well as partial, af-

terwards going to bed and drinking very liberally of warm diluting liquids until a copious perſpiration comes out, and has been kept up for a length of time, properly ſuited to the circumſtances of the caſe.

3. That all wet and damp clothes ſhould be changed the moment that dry and warm ones can be procured.

We are convinced, that moſt of the ladies, who die of conſumptions in Great Britain, owe their premature deaths to neglected or ill managed colds, brought on either by going into the air in bad weather lightly clothed, and getting their feet wet, or by catching a cough at ſome public place, or in coming home from it while over-heated, and exhauſted from having been out of bed moſt part of the night. It ſhould be remembered, that the human frame, as already obſerved, is in no ſtate whatever ſo ſuſceptible of diſeaſe as when it is relaxed and worn out by exceſs of any kind, eſpecially if the body is at the time perſpiring freely and expoſed to cold or wet.

Numbers, both of ladies and gentlemen, break

break their conſtitutions, and ſome ſuddenly loſe their lives, from the preſent prevailing faſhion, of inverting the order of nature, by keeping it up almoſt whole nights ſucceſſively. Viewing man as an accountable being, this mode of life is criminal. But while human nature remains the ſame, the mind of man, in the ardor of purſuit for pleaſure, is not to be reſtrained, eſpecially in what is ſanctioned by the example of the great.

That man who has the wiſdom, prudence, and reſolution, to controul his paſſions, to avoid intemperance, and to go to bed regularly before midnight, and riſe early in the morning, will but very ſeldom have occaſion to conſult a phyſician. Theſe are truths of the greateſt importance, and highly merit the attention of all who wiſh to enjoy good health —a chearful, happy, and long life.

It is told of the *illuſtrious Boerhaave*, that after his death his books were ſold by auction. The laſt brought to the hammer was a large thick folio, moſt elegantly bound in red Morocco, and ſuperbly ornamented with gold leaf, and

and the book was fealed. The impatient curiofity excited in every mind, and manifefted in every countenance, upon this magnificent folio, fealed with the feal of the great *Boerhaave*, being produced, was inconceivable. Not doubting but it contained the whole *arcana* of the healing art, as well as a fpecific for all difeafes, a competition for it took place among gentlemen of fortune. At laft the book was knocked down for feveral hundred pounds, (a prodigious fum in thofe days); yet, when this fuppofed *invaluable treafure* was opened, to the aftonifhment of the purchafer, he found all the leaves a total blank. After having turned them over and over again he at laft difcovered fome words written on the infide of one of the boards,

"*Keep your feet warm,*
"*Your body open, and*
"*Your head cool.*"

SEC-

SECTION IV.

Longevity.

IT is presumed that the subjoined communications, with which we have been favoured from two respectable sources, will be deemed ample information on this subject.

1. The Reverend Joseph Rumney, the present Vicar, states, "The longest life upon record is 105, one 100, some few 90, many 80 and upwards."

2. Communicated in a letter from the Reverend Mr Andrew Thomson minister of the Relief Congregation here, dated, Berwick, February 1. 1797. "I am favoured with your card, and am sorry it is not in my power to give you a more particular answer than the following, because I did not take a memorandum of the numerous instances of longevity which have fallen out since my settlement in Berwick. Joseph Cheeseman,

"a

"a native of Hexham, in the county of Nor-"thumberland, enlisted for a soldier when "he was twenty years of age nearly: He "served in the army forty-one years, when he "obtained his discharge, and was put on the "pension list: He continued either as an out "pensioner or in garrison duty during the "space of forty-nine years, and died in the "beginning of the year 1794, aged 110: He "retained all his faculties; and could read "without the use of spectacles till the day of "his death: He got a new fore tooth about "three weeks before he died. His widow, a "woman upwards of 70, is still living in "Castlegate, and is ready to attest the above "facts.

"Thomas Morrison, a gardener and mem-"ber of my congregation, died some years "ago at the age of 104, if my memory serve "me right. William Addison, a gardener, a "native of Old Hamstocks in Scotland, and a "member of my congregation, died in 1789, "aged 101. Ann Hood, in 1784, aged 92. "There is at present living in Shaw's Lane

"a

" a woman of the name of Mary Gardiner, " who was born March 1696: She retains her " intellectual powers, but has been confined " to her room for these eighteen months. " Previous to that time she attended regularly " every Sabbath at my meeting-house. She is " a woman singularly acquainted with divine " things. There are at present living in Castle-" gate, High Greens, and Wind Mill-hole, " more than a dozen of people who are be-" tween eighty and ninety; among these, Mar-" jory Elliot, a native of Wooler, born in the " year 1710, is at present living and enjoying " the use of her mental powers; Mary Hume, " aged about 86; a man of the name of James " Widderburn, the father of the corporation " of Berwick, who was admitted a freeman " in the year 1731, and who consequently " was born in or before the 1710, &c. &c. " In Berwick there are many that I know " upwards of 80; James Stewart, living in " Shaw's Lane, and an old dragoon, was born " in the year 1709; Serjeant King of the in-" valids; Mr Steavenson a late bailiff, born

" 1713,

" 1713, and many others that I could name.
" I have known many people who have died
" within these few years upwards of 90, nay
" of an hundred. I should apprehend that I
" would not exceed the truth if I should state
" that there are at present an hundred people
" living in the parish of Berwick upwards of
" 80. It would require more time than I can
" afford to ascertain this matter. If the num-
" ber of inhabitants in the parish be 10,000,
" the aged people above 80, according to this
" conjecture, will be to the number of inha-
" bitants as one to 100." Since the above was written many persons have died in the town considerably above 80 years of age, and one woman died lately upwards of an hundred.

CHAP.

CHAP. VI.

Ecclefiaftical State.

SECTION I.

State of the Eftablifhed Church.

A Better account of the Church here cannot be given than the following, by its prefent incumbent, the Reverend Jofeph Rumney, which he has moft obligingly communicated to us.

" We have the parifh regifters of marriages, chriftenings, and burials, in tolerable good prefervation from the year 1574, and, by examining thofe more minutely, I have found out the following particulars.

" Before the year 1657 no name of any clergyman is recorded. From 1653 to 1657 marriages were performed by Juſtices of the Peace. During theſe years Elias Pratt, Stephen Jackſon, Andrew Criſpe, John Sleigh, juſtices and mayors, make conſpicuous figures in that line.

" In the year 1657, for the firſt time, a marriage appears to be ſolemnized before a clergyman, whoſe name is Nicholas Wriſſell; whether Epiſcopalian or Preſbyterian does not appear from the regiſter, but moſt probably the latter, as he is called our miniſter; and this was before the reſtoration. It appears that this Nicholas Wriſſell was alſo the ſchoolmaſter, as there is a receipt in his hand writing now extant, in which he acknowledges to have received from the Mayor fifteen pounds for a quarter's ſalary for teaching ſchool. Mr Wriſſell continued to officiate till 1661."

Mr Rumney, after having given as complete an account of the vicarage of Berwick as the pariſh regiſter admits, concludes thus:

" Mr

"Mr Thorp died December 1767, and was ſucceeded by the preſent incumbent Joſeph Rumney, who has alſo been maſter of the grammar ſchool for teaching the Greek and Latin languages ſince the year 1750—a married man with a ſon and two daughters.

"The living is in the patronage of the Dean and Chapter of Durham. The ſtipend 80l. *per annum*, paid by the Corporation of Berwick out of tythes which they rent of the Dean and Chapter. No glebe but the church yard and the garden belonging to the vicarage houſe.

"The Corporation give 30l. a year for a Sunday afternoons ſermon, which the vicar at preſent enjoys.

"Beſides the vicarage, there is a Thurſday's lecture in the patronage of the Mercer's Company, London, founded by a Mr Fiſhborne many years ago, paid from the corn tythes of Chollerton and Barrisford, near Hexham, in Northumberland. The preſent lecturer is William Rumney, the vicar's ſon. The tythes

are

are variable. They have been at 60l. *per annum*, and they have been at 120l *."

It

* In Hutchinson's History of Northumberland we have a complete statement of the vicarage of Berwick since 1299, and is as follows.

"BERWICK VICARAGE.—Dedication, Holy Trinity.

"Priory and Conv. Durham propr.—Dean and Cha. Durham patr.

"King's B.	Yearly T.	Proc. Epic.	Real Val.
20l.	2l.	10s.	110l. *

Vicars.—Will. de Angerham.—Joh. de Bambrough 1299, p. mort. Angerham.—John de Tarent, 6. Jan. 1330.—Rob de Gamelton 1340.—Rob. de Wollestorp 1356, p. ref. Gamelton.—Tho. de Kellaw 1358.—Joh. de Insulasacra 1360, p. ref. Kellaw. —Will. de Sherborne 1374, p. mort. de Insula, —Joh. Pays 1390, p. ref. Sherborne.—Will. de Werdal 1398, p. mort. Pays.—Will de Durham

1401,

* Anthony Beck, Bishop of Durham, is reported to have built a large church at Berwick.—Kenet's Par. Antiq. p. 347. An. 1301. 29. 30. Edw. I.

Upon inquiry on a writ called ad quod Damnum, the jurors found it would not be a loss or prejudice to the King, if Alice de Lacy, the wife of Thomas Earl of Lancaster, daughter of Hen. Lacy Earl of Lincoln and heir to the manors of Burcester and Midlington, should grant one messuage and four acres of land in Poterington (Dioc. Oxon.) to a Chaplain that should celebrate divine service in the church of Berwick, for the soul of the said Alice and Adam de Poterington.

It would be inconsistent in a publication of this kind, and incompatible with the respect

1401, p. mort. Werdal.—Will. Castell 1446, p. mort. Durham.—Alan Hindmerse 1484, p. mort. Castell.—Will. Marshall in decr. Bac. 1507.—Tho. Thompson, Cl. 2. May, 1536, p. mort. Marshall. Pr. Pri. & Conv. Durham.—Rob. Selby Cap. 23. Nov. 1541, p. ref. Thompson. Pr. Dean and Cha. Durham.—John Blackhall, Cl. 24. May, 1565, p. mort. Selby, Pr. Ep. Dun. h. v jure devoluto.—Tho. Clerke sacri verb. dei Min. 18. Dec. 1567, p. depr. Blackhall. Pr. Ep. Dun. h. v. jure devol.—Rich. Clerke, A. B. 26. Feb. 1589, p. mort. Clerke.—Will. Selbye, A. M. 22. July, 1607, p. mort. Clerke.—Leo. Rountree, Cl. 16. May, 1607, p. ref. Selbye.—Richard Smith 1610, p. ref. Rountree.—Gilb. Durie, A. M. 22. July, 1613, p. mort. Smith.—Nich. Wressel and Luke Ogle intruders, depr. for non-conformity.—Will. Coxe, A. M. 29 July, 1662, Pr. D. and Cha. Durham.—John Smithson, A. B. 22 July, 1664, p. ref. Coxe.—Will. Mitford, A. M. 2. Jan. 1672, p. mort. Smithson. —Pr. D. and Cha. D. sede vac.—Tho. Bourne, A. M. 13. June, 1674, p. ref. Mitford. Pr. D. and Ch. D. sede vac.—John Harper, A.M. 1680, p.

respect due to the church to pass over the gentleman who has the pastoral charge of this parish.

In

p. cess. Bourne.—Patr. Robertson, A. M. 29. July, 1686, p. res. Harper.—Rob. Blakiston, A. M. 1700, p. mort. Robertson.—Tho. Cooper, A. M. 21. Nov. 1726, p. cess. Blakiston.—Tho. Thorp, A. M. 13. Jan. 1747, p. mort. Cooper*. Joseph Rumney, Cl. 20. July, 1768, p. mort. Thorp.

A Lectureship was founded by the Mercer's Company in London.

Lecturers.—John Smithson 1664.—Geo. Greenaway 1740. —Will. Wollfall, A. M. 14. Feb. 1745.—Tho. Wrangham, Cl. 1754.

A Benedictine Nunnery, said to be founded by King David of Scotland, A. D. 1153.

A Monastery of Grey Friars, founded by Sir John Grey; it was one of the Convents of the custody of Newcastle. King Edward III. by charter, in the 13th year of his reign, confirmed to it an allowance of 20 merks yearly, settled on the Friars of this Convent by the Kings of Scotland.

* He served an apprenticeship of seven years to a grocer at York, and was after that a year at a Scotch University, and then took his B. A. degree at Queen's Col. Oxon. and his M. A. at Cambridge. He died at Berwick, 12. Dec. 1767, aged 71.

In *justice* then to our present vicar, he has uniformly distinguished himself as an excellent *teacher* of the *classics*, and a most eminent *preacher* of the *gospel*.—That tribute of praise which is ever due to unassuming manners—exemplary morals—liberality of sentiment,—and to unremitting attention to the sacred functions of office, cannct be better bestowed than

Scotland. This gift is declared to be bestowed as a free charity and pure alms for the support of these poor Friars. v. Stephens Mon. p. 25 of the App. vol. 2.

A Monastery of Friars Preachers.

Hospital of St Mary Magdalen.

John de Cerve was Custos of this H. 13. Edw. III. A. D. 1319.

Segedon or Segden Hospital or Hermitage.

Frere Will. Mestre de la Meson de St Austyn de Seggeden 1296.

Nich. Neuton Custos of the free Chapel of St Mary Magdalen near Berwick, and of the hermitage of Segeden annext to it. Pat. 16. H. 6.

Monastery near the Bridge. Dedicated to the Holy Trinity.

It is mentioned 2d Edward III. founded, Pro Ministro & Fratribus Sanctae Trinitatis Pontis Berwici.

Capella de Ravensdale prope portam ad Pontem Berwici.

than upon Mr Rumney: In ſhort, ſuch ſhining abilities and endearing qualities have long ſecured him the higheſt eſteem of this whole town and neighbourhood.

SECTION II.

Diſſenters.

THERE are four different *Sects* of diſſenters in Berwick, viz.

1. There are two meeting houſes which differ but little from the eſtabliſhed Church of Scotland. The oldeſt of which is called the *Low*, and the other the *High Meeting*.

2. A place of worſhip upon the *Relief* eſtabliſhment, known by the name of the Middle Meeting.

3. A Burgher Congregation.

4. A Methodiſt Meeting Houſe.

The *Low Meeting Houſe* was built 1719. It is in an area on the north-eaſt ſide of Hidehill.

It

It is a good building, and is upon the whole commodiously seated. It has a clock in the front gallery, the gift of Mr William Landells.

The house itself was built from contributions chiefly procured in London by the Reverend John Turner its first minister.

The present incumbent is the Reverend James Smith.

In 1729, the late Joseph Watson, Esq; of Berwick, bequeathed 20l. a year to this meeting house and the high one: Of this each minister is to have 5l. The remaining 10l. to be distributed among 20 poor women, housekeepers, and inhabitants in Berwick, to be named by the said ministers.

The *High Meeting House* was built by subscription 1724. It is a large building, elegantly seated, and has an excellent clock. It is situated a little below the Main Guard, in an area about 30 yards back from the High Street, on its north side. The present incumbent is the Reverend John Kellock.

The *Relief Meeting Houſe* is ſituated between the High Street and Shaw's Lane, near the eaſtern extremity of the latter. It was built by ſubſcription 1756, and was for ſeveral years afterwards on the ſame footing with the high and low meetings. It is moſt beautifully ſeated, and has a clock, the gift of the late Samuel Burn, Eſq; Mayor.

The amount of the miniſter's ſalary depends on the number of ſeats rented.

The preſent incumbent is the Reverend Andrew Thompſon.

The *Burgher Meeting Houſe* is ſituated in Golden Square, cloſe by the Bank Hill. It was built 1770; but owing to the vaſt increaſe of hearers it had to be greatly enlarged in 1796. The preſent incumbent is the Reverend John Blackhall.

The *Methodiſt Meeting Houſe* was built 1797. It ſtands on the north ſide of Walker Gate Lane. Its architecture is in the Gothic ſtile. The building is neat, well lighted, and it has a gallery in the eaſt end of it.

CHAP.

CHAP. VII.

Charitable Inſtitutions.

SECTION I.

State of the Poor.

THE houſe appropriated for the reception of the poor of this pariſh is ſituated near the upper part of Church-ſtreet. It conſiſts of ten apartments, a kitchen, pantrys, beſides a kitchen and room for the keeper and his family. There is a room within the premiſſes for the overſeers to hold their meetings in.

Humanity and candour oblige us to confeſs that theſe lodgings are but ill adapted to the ſeveral conditions of the aged and infirm, as they are extremely cold in winter. This

is

is owing to the buildings having ſuffered much from the ravages of time.

The beds are chaff laid on boards, with two or three pairs of blankets, and moſt of them are ſupplied with a coverlet. They have no curtains or other defence againſt the cold.

The regulations with regard to diet are as follow:

Beef or mutton and broth together with potatoe or cabbage pudding, and half a pound of wheaten bread for dinner two days a week. —Two days, potatoe broth made with ſuet, onions, &c. with bread, for dinner.—For two days, a pint of table beer, with bread and a halfpenny worth of cheeſe or butter for dinner is each man's allowance a day. One day, new milk and barley boiled for dinner..

Pottage for breakfaſt with milk or ſmall beer. Two days, bread and broth for ſupper, and the other five days pottage.

Clothing.—The men and boys are clothed in thick blue woollen cloth, manufactured at Gallaſhiels

Gallaſhiels in Scotland, and purchaſed in a ſhop in the town at 2s. 6d. per yard.

The women's gowns are made of a coarſe cotton, called French Drogget, purchaſed at 1s. 6d. per yard. Suitable aprons are purchaſed at the ſame price per yard.

The boys and girls are educated in reading and writing.

The women who chuſe to ſpin are allowed one half of the profit. What is ſpun is wrought into coarſe linen for ſhirts for the poor houſe.

There are at preſent 300 who receive charity from this inſtitution. Forty-three are in the houſe; the remaining 257 live in the town and adjacent country; and are paid from one ſhilling and ſixpence to two ſhillings, once a week.

The keeper of the houſe furniſhes the poor lodged in it with victuals, coals, and waſhing, for 2s. 4d. weekly, young and old. Beſides he and his family have their lodgings free.

There is a ſurgeon to attend both the houſe and ſuch of the poor as are ſick in the town.

SEC-

SECTION II.

Poor Rates.

THE present poor rate is two ſhillings in the pound, which, if continued for one year, raiſes the ſum of 1600l. When to this is added the rent of Grange Burn Mill, (45l.) the total is 1645l.

Liſt of Rates for the following Years:

Years.	s.	d.	Years.	s.	d.
In 1753	1	0	In 1757	0	10
—54	1	0	—58	1	0
—55	0	11	—60	0	8
—56	0	10	—62	0	9
—64	0	10	—85	1	6
—65	0	11	—87	1	2
—66	0	8	—88	1	4
—67	0	7	—89	1	2
—68	0	8	—91	1	4
—69	0	10	—92	1	4
—70	0	9	—94	2	0

In

Years.	s.	d.	Years.	s.	d.
In 1771	0	9	In 1795	2	0
—77	1	0	—96	2	0
—78	1	0	—97	2	0
—79	1	3	—98	2	0
—80	1	6	—99	2	0
—84	1	6			

SECTION III.

Donations, &c.

1632. "VALENTINE MORE, Efq; of " London fecured a fum of " money upon Cock Law, a farm belonging " to the Corporation of Berwick, for which " they were annually to pay ten pounds to " ten poor men or ten poor women. Twenty " fhillings a year each at quarterly payments; " which poor people were to be appointed by " truftees named in the deed of truft by their " heirs

"heirs and affignees." The prefent truftee is Mrs Afkew of Pallinfburn.

1652. "Roger Tweedy of Stepney, Efq; "by will fecured in the hands of the Corpor-"ation of Berwick, a fum of money, from the "intereft of which, twelve two penny loaves "fhould every Sunday be diftributed in the "church by the minifter and church wardens, "to twelve of the pooreft of the congrega-"tion." Two more loaves were afterwards added upon the fame fecurity. We cannot at prefent afcertain the donor.

In 1758, March 20. "John Brown of "Berwick, gentleman, by will bequeathed "a thoufand pounds to five truftees who "were empowered and enjoined by the faid "will to fill up their number whenever they "fhould be reduced by death to three, upon "this truft, that they fhould pay the intereft "thereof at quarterly payments, to ten poor "men and ten poor women living in the town, "and proteftants." The prefent truftees are William Greive, Efq; of Eaft Ord, Burnet Roger Greive, Efq; of Sanfon Seal, the vicar of Berwick,

wick, William Jeffrey's, Efq; of Sunwick, and James Bell, Efq; late Mayor of Berwick."

20th Guild Book, folio 286, May 19th 1676. "This day Mr Mayor, viz. Thomas "Watfon, Efq; Mr Pratt, Alderman, furviv-"ing *feoffees* in truft for difpofing of ten "pounds per annum, which one Mr Mortoff "gave to ten poor people within this borough "as appears by his grant; and for that, you "feoffees are to be nominated at the next "Guild, that a new deed be made to them "from the faid feoffees, according to the in-"tent of the faid Mr Mortoff's grant."

20th Guild Book, folio 349. "In the "year 1680, new truftees were appointed for "the diftribution of Mr Mortoff's monies."

Charity School.

As far as we can judge from the records of this inftitution, it owes its rife to the humane and benevolent exertions of the late Capt. Bolton of Berwick.

The houfe was built in the year 1725, and coft 149l. 19s. 3¼d. It ftands in the weft fide of the back way. It has a handfome front, and a fmall garden behind it. The fituation is dry and airy.

We find that Capt. Bolton was the firft treafurer appointed to this inftitution. In the courfe of building the fchool, his contributions at different times amounted to 77l. 11s. 8d.

Donations left to the above Charity School extracted from the records of the Inftitution.

"Percival Clennel, late of *Lilburn* in the "County of *Northumberland*, Efq; Fifty "pounds, by his will bearing date 2d July "1743."

"John Brown late of this borough, gentle-"man, one hundred pounds, by his will bear-"ing date 20th March 1758."

"Capt. James Bolton late of this borough, "eight hundred pounds, by his will bearing "date 28th November 1765."

"The late Robert Edmonfton, Efq; 91l. "2s. 3d. being two tenths of his perfonal ef-"tate, 1778."

"31ft

" 31ſt Auguſt 1792, Mr John Bell cooper,
" 20l.

" George Reid, Eſq; 5l."

In addition to theſe, 100l. was lately given by a gentleman who would not allow his donation to be made public.

There are ſome other gifts, the value of which we could not exactly aſcertain.

The number of children admitted to this charity to be educated and clothed, is 20 boys and 6 girls.

They are taught reading, writing, arithmetic, navigation, and church-muſic.

The preſent teacher, Mr George Patterſon, has 40l. of ſalary a year. We are happy to learn that the funds of this inſtitution are in a thriving condition.

CHAP.

CHAP. VIII.

Education.

SECTION I.

Public Schools.

THERE are ſix free ſchools belonging to the corporation.

1. The grammar ſchool in which the Latin and Greek claſſics are taught by the Rev. Joſeph Rumney.

The ſalary is 40l. yearly, together with a dwelling-houſe and garden. Beſides, Mr Rumney teaches non-freemen's children in the public ſchool, who pay fees. He is allowed an uſher, who receives from the corporation a ſalary of 40l. a year.

2.

2. A mathematical ſchool taught by Mr Thomas Rae. The ſalary is 40l. yearly, and 2l. for coals. Arithmetic, land-meaſuring, and navigation are alſo taught in this ſchool. The number of ſcholars has increaſed much of late years. The preſent number is about ſixty. The maſter is allowed to teach non-freemen's children at bye hours.

3. A writing ſchool taught by Mr James Renwick. The ſalary is 50l. a year. The maſter to furniſh pens and ink. Two pounds is allowed yearly for coals.

4. Three reading ſchools taught by Meſſrs John Sharp, William Paulin, and Andrew Thomſon. Their reſpective ſalaries 35l. each, and two pounds for coals.

There are alſo ſeveral private ſchools of conſiderable reputation where moſt of the non-freemen's children are taught.*

SEC-

* Since the above was written, the corporation has built a large and elegant ſchool-houſe. It conſiſts of five ſpacious rooms, with ſuitable offices, which are to be appropriated for the mathematical ſchool, the writing, and the three reading ſchools. It is moſt delightfully ſituated on

the

SECTION III.

Female Education.

TWO or three attempts have been made by different perſons to eſtabliſh a boarding-ſchool here for young ladies, but hitherto without ſucceſs.

About 11 years ago, a Mrs Davidſon opened a ſchool here, and has met with good encouragement. The following is the account which we have received of this ſchool from herſelf.

" Mrs Davidſon teaches reading, ſpelling, and plain needle-work, at five ſhillings *per* quarter, and two ſhillings and ſixpence entrance. She likewiſe teaches flowering; when that is included, ſhe charges ſeven ſhillings and ſixpence *per* quarter.

" Mrs

the Bank-hill adjoining to the grammar ſchool. Four of the rooms fully face the Tweed, and command a complete view of the bridge. The ſituation is dry, and it enjoys a very free ventilation, which muſt contribute highly to the health of the ſcholars.

"Mrs D. takes young ladies to board and educate at twenty pounds *per annum*.

"Mr Davidſon teaches writing at five ſhillings *per* quarter, and two ſhillings and ſixpence entrance."

Mrs Rudd, in the high-ſtreet, has taught reading and ſpelling with approbation, for ſome years paſt. Fees five ſhillings *per* quarter, and two ſhillings and ſixpence at entry. There are ſeveral other female teachers of reading.

Within theſe few years three ſchools have been opened for teaching various branches of needle-work, which conſiſt of white-ſeam, coloured work, Dryſden, filigree, and child-bed linen, alſo the faſhionable kinds of leather, paper, cloth, and groteſque works.

CHAP.

CHAP. IX.

Revenue Department.

SECTION I.

Cuſtom Houſe.

THIS eſtabliſhment conſiſts of the following places or appointments, viz.

1. A Collector.
2. A Comptroller.
3. A Searcher.
4. A Depute Comptroller, paid by the patent Comptroller.
5. A Surveyor.
6. Two Land Waiters.
7. Two Riding Officers.
8. Six Tide Waiters.

9.

9. One Weighing Porter.
10. A Riding Surveyor.
11. Twelve Coaſt Waiters and preventive Officers along the coaſt.
12. One Depute Searcher at Alemouth.
13. One principal Coaſt Officer.

The revenue ariſing from the cuſtoms for the year 1798 amounted to 6000l. In the year 1782 it was only about 1000l.

SECTION II.

Poſt Office

Conſiſts of

1. A Poſt Maſter.
2. A Clerk.
3. A Letter Carrier.

The revenue of this office is generally from ſixteen to ſeventeen hundred pounds a-year. The preſent poſt maſter is James Forſter, Eſq.

SECTION III.

Excise Office

Consists of

1. A Supervisor.
2. Three Officers.

The revenue arising from the Excise in Berwick amounts to about L. 6690 yearly.

And that of Tweedmouth, including Spittal, is about 2390

L. 9080

CHAP. X.

Military Department.

SECTION I.

The Ramparts.

THE town is completely ſurrounded with a rampart of reſpectable ſtrength, but without out-works, having four principal gates, as may be ſeen by looking at the ground plan. It has been mentioned above that the fortifications underwent great repairs in the reign of Queen Elizabeth. From the year 1761, until about 1770, the walls were almoſt completely rebuilt in many parts, particularly the quay-walls and gates, together with the ſaluting battery.

In the year 1782, ſome repairs were began to be made on the walls from time to time, until

until 1786, which were completely finiſhed four years afterwards. We ſubjoin the following account with which we have been favoured reſpecting the fortifications. The ground plan will ſhow the reſpective ſituations of the different places to be deſcribed.

"Meg's Mount, Demi Baſtion, with a double flank on the right.

"Cumberland Baſtion, with upper and retired flanks to ſcour the ditch, &c.

"Braſs Mount Baſtion.—Under the cavalier are two caſemated powder magazines, covered by the retired flanks on the right and left.

"Wind-mill Mount, with double flanks.

"A very reſpectable powder magazine between the Wind-mill Mount and King's Baſtion.

"King's Demi Baſtion, without a cavalier, has a flag-ſtaff and retired flank on the left.

"Fiſher's Fort, or Six-Gun Battery, near the Governor's houſe.

"Bramham's, or Four-Gun Battery. Theſe two batteries preſent a fire of heavy artillery upon

upon the Bar and entrance of the harbour, under which it would be a hazardous enterprize to attempt entering it.

" Coxton's Tower near it on the right for holding powder made up, ammunition, &c.

" Saluting Battery, on which are mounted 22 four pounders, near the Governor's houſe.

" The maſter gunner's magazine on Palace-green, formerly a reſervoir for water for the uſe of the Governor's houſe, brought acroſs the Tweed in lead pipes from St Cuthbert's well in Tweed-mouth.

" Flank battery foot of Bank-hill.

" Iron ordnance mounted,	24 pounders	8
	12 ditto	6
	9 ditto	16
	4 ditto	22
" Ditto mortars, -	13 inches	2
		54

SEC-

SECTION II.

The Garrifon.

THE garrifon of Berwick confifts of

A Governor.

A Deputy Governor.

A Town Major.

A Town Adjutant.

A Chaplain who does not refide.

A Surgeon who does not refide.

A Mafter Gunner and 6 invalid gunners. Alfo 3 companies of invalids, of 1 Captain, 1 Lieutenant, 1 Enfign, 4 Serjeants, 4 Corporals, 2 Drummers, and 66 privates each. There is likewife a Surgeon appointed to attend the invalids. In the laft war, an adjutant was appointed for the invalids who continues to receive the pay, but does not attend. There is alfo an Ordnance Store-keeper who conftantly refides here. There is likewife a Barrack-mafter refiding, and the commanding Engineer of the northern diftrict of England has a reſidence and his eſtabliſhment in this garriſon.

Holy Iſland is an appendage to the garriſon of Berwick. The eſtabliſhment there conſiſts of a maſter gunner and two invalid gunners. In time of war, as at preſent, an officer's guard, from the troops laying in Berwick, are ſtationed at the iſland in addition to the gunners.

The preſent Governor of Berwick is General Sir William Howe, Bart.

Deputy Governor Major General Ludlow.

SECTION III.

Volunteer Corps.

THERE are two volunteer corps in Berwick; the Berwick Loyal Volunteers; and the Gentlemen Independent Volunteers.

The former was raiſed ſoon after the beginning of the preſent war, by Lieut. Col. Hall, commandant of the corps. It then con-

consisted of two companies; but, in June 1797, it was augmented to four. They receive pay two days in the week.

The latter was formed in the year 1797, and serve without pay. The commandant is Burnet Greive, Esquire.

CHAP.

CHAP. XI.

Manufactures and Trade.

SECTION I.

MANUFACTURES.

Linen.—Spinning.—Linen for private Consumption.—Damask.—Diaper.—Sacking.—Sail-Cloth.

AS our various manufactures are ftill in their infancy, it may be thought unneceffary to give a detailed account of them; neverthelefs, for reafons which will appear in a fubfequent part of this work, we deem it confiftent with our duty to do fo.

Linen, &c.

There is no eftablifhed linen manufacturing

company in Berwick, which may be chiefly owing to the want of ſpinners, and this again may be accounted for from the great wages now given to women employed in agriculture. There are a few weavers who manufacture linen for home conſumption, but for ſome period back they have not carried on buſineſs to the extent they did formerly.

Damaſk and Diaper Manufacture.

Mr William Scott in Caſtlegate commenced buſineſs in theſe two branches in the year 1784. He generally keeps ſeven or eight looms employed, two of which are for weaving linens and dimity. One of the looms is ſo large as to admit of working table-cloths ten quarters wide. This manufacture employs from twenty to forty ſpinners and winders. The weavers earn from 6s. to 14s. weekly. He alſo weaves damaſk and diaper without ſeams.

Mr M'Cay, muſlin manufacturer, ſometimes employs

employs a loom or two in working damaſk and diaper.

Sacking Manufacture.

This manufacture was eſtabliſhed by Mr Thomas Cockburn in 1793.

The building conſiſts of four floors in height, and is 100 feet in length, and 20 feet in breadth. It ſtands in the Greenſes, Caſtlegate, near the Bell Tower, on a dry bottom, where there is a free circulation of air. It faces the weſt; and has a beautiful area in front. This building, with its area, makes a very handſome appearance. The ground floor will hold 24 looms; twelve are employed in the manufacture of ſacks, and require from 80 to 100 men, women, and children. There are, upon an average, manufactured from 50,000 to 60,000 yards of ſacking cloth. This cloth is ſold from 8d. to 1s. a yard. It is made of hemp imported from the Baltic. The men earn from 6s. to 15s. weekly, women from 2s. 6d. to 4s. and children from 1s. to 2s. 6d. It was with

great

great difficulty that Mr Cockburn could bring the men, women, and children to labour this kind of work. But now that they are accuſtomed to it they work with more alacrity.

Sail Cloth Manufacture.

This manufacture was eſtabliſhed by James Clunie and Co. in January 1793. It is the firſt of the kind that has been in Berwick. Since its commencement, it has given daily employment to 150 ſpinners at their own homes, and 25 workmen in different branches within doors. Theſe men make, on an average, twelve ſhillings weekly, which is paid to them every Saturday morning, that they may take advantage of the market. During harveſt they are allowed to employ themſelves in the healthful and invigorating exerciſe of reaping. The wages of the ſpinners vary according to their induſtry; and may be computed at from 1s. 6d. to 3s. 6d. per week. They are paid on the delivery of their work after it has been inſpected by the foreman. The raw materials of this manufacture are flax and hemp,

hemp, imported from Peterſburgh and Riga; which being heckled is given out to ſpin into different grifts according to quality, and it is bleached before it is made into cloth. The ſale of the manufactured article is moſtly confined to the Tyne and Thames. During this war ſome ſails have been made to Government by contract.

2. *Cotton and Muſlins.*

A manufacture of this ſort was eſtabliſhed by Mr M'Cay in the year 1788. As no ſuch branch of manufacture had ever been before attempted in this part of the country, Mr M'Cay had to encounter thoſe difficulties peculiar to manufactures. He began his buſineſs by erecting four looms, and he gradually increaſed their number to the end of the year 1792, when they amounted to twenty-ſix. Theſe looms employed twenty journeymen and ſix apprentices. The goods manufactured were chiefly checks and ſtripes for ſailors ſhirts. They were ſold from one to two ſhillings a yard.

yard. The muſlins brought into the market, when ornamented, ſold from 1s. 6d. to 10s. 6d. The quantity of cloth which each loom produced, on an average, was 40 yards weekly. The number of yards wrought that year were 54,080. Soon after the commencement of the preſent war, he found it adviſable to contract his buſineſs in this line.

In the beginning of the year 1793, though he had diminiſhed the number of his looms, he extended his buſineſs by engaging in the tambouring of muſlins. The number of perſons he employed in this branch was thirty-four during that year. The number of perſons in his employment, including weavers, winders, tambourers, &c. were ninety-one.

3. *Bleachfields.*

A bleachfield was erected by James Clunie and Co. ſail cloth manufacturers, anno 1793.

The field is moſt pleaſantly ſituated on the north banks of the Tweed, about a mile above the town and in the immediate vicinity of Spring Gardens.

This

This bleachfield was principally ſet on foot for bleaching yarn for ſail cloth. Yarn, however, is alſo taken in at this field for checks and white thread. They are all dry bleached.

This bleachfield is completely provided with every neceſſary apparatus.

The leys, ariſing from the pot aſhes made uſe of at this manufacture, are preſerved until the liquor amounts to a certain quantity. It is then made to undergo a particular proceſs, by which, without the addition of any ingredient whatever, a reproduction of pot aſhes takes place, which is of a ſuperior quality to the firſt. We regret, however, that we are not at liberty to ſtate the mode of conducting this proceſs. At the ſame time it may be proper to remark, that the perſon who made this valuable diſcovery was a common bleacher in Lancaſhire, who, in conſequence of it, realized a conſiderable fortune.

4. *Woollen.—Stockings.—Carpets.—Felts.—Hats.—Dyers.*

Mr Cockburn sack cloth manufacturer began in the year 1795 to manufacture several kinds of woollen stuffs, such as felts for paper mills, waggon covers, Scotch and English flannels, besides men's broad cloths of an inferior quality.

Mr C. observes in writing, "That there is "every reason to think a woollen manufac-"ture may be carried on in Berwick to a great "extent, and to very great advantage, hav-"ing such a great choice of wool in the neigh-"bouring country, which can be brought "home at a small expence. It only wants "(he says) people of property to enter into "the spirit of carrying on manufactories in "Berwick. Indeed a great national benefit "might in a few years be derived from the "port of Berwick. Its situation is excellent "for either foreign or inland trade; and there "is not a better navigation from any port in "Great Britain to London than from Ber-"wick upon Tweed."

Stockings.

Worfted and thread ftockings have been manufactured in Berwick for many years. At prefent there are three manufacturers in this branch.

Mr Edward Gray too, who has three ftocking looms, carrys on the bufinefs of wool combing, and manufactures about thirty packs of wool every year. He conftantly keeps about forty fpinners employed on the flab and long wheel. Lamb wool ftockings of thefe manufactures fell from 2s. 3d. to 4s. per pair, and in general give great fatisfaction.

The other manufacturers are Mr Archibald Inglis, Mr Roger Struther, each of whom employ two looms.

Carpets.

Mr William Graham has carried on a manufacture of carpets in Caftlegate for about 21 years. He generally employs five looms, and, upon an average, has made 5000 yards of carpeting yearly. The only difficulty he has experienced in carrying on this trade, is the neceſſity he has always been under of ſending moſt of his wool to be ſpun in the country. This extraordinary expence might be ſaved, provided he could prevail on the people of this place to ſpin it.

It may here be obſerved, that an averſion to labour of this kind prevails in all towns where manufactures have not been long eſtabliſhed on a large ſcale.—This is chiefly to be aſcribed to the lower orders of the people not introducing their ſons and daughters to early habits of active employment, and frugal œconomy, and in not diſcharging theſe moſt important of all parental duties, the due cultivation of their minds by a ſuitable education, and the example of an upright and virtuous conduct.

Felt Manufacture.

Mr Mark Young in Tweedmouth commenced this buſineſs of manufacturing ſheep's ſkins into leather, in the year 1795. He alſo manufactures the wool; that is, he ſorts it according to its different qualities preparatory

tory to its being manufactured into cloth. Mr Young ſells his wool to the manufacturers at Wooler, Kelſo, Jedburgh, Selkirk, Galaſhiels, Dalkeith, &c. He ſays an oil mill is much wanted here for making ſhamoy leather.

Hats.

Mr Hubback commenced a manufacture of hats in June 1789. At firſt he only employed a few men; but finding, on trial, that the opinion he had formed of Berwick reſpecting its ſituation being favourable to commercial and manufacturing exertions, he increaſed their number, and now carries on a pretty extenſive buſineſs. His journeymen earn from 21 to 25s. weekly.

Dyers.

Mr Porteous, dyer of ſilk, cotton, and all kinds of ſtuffs, reſides in Caſtlegate, where he has carried on buſineſs in the above branches for four years paſt. He ſays he can (by a cheap proceſs) make cloths generally uſed for great coats reſiſt a heavy fall of rain completely

completely for 12 ſucceſſive hours, and without changing the colour. He can obliterate all ſpots of greaſe, &c. from cloth. There are three dyers in Tweedmouth who alſo ſcour cloths.

5. *Leather.—Tanneries.—Boot and Shoe Manufactures.—Shoes with Wooden Soles and Heels.—White Skinners.—Gloves.*

There are two curriers of leather in this town.

1. Mr John Morriſon commenced the manufacture of leather in the year 1784, which he has been gradually increaſing ever ſince. At preſent, he employs four men, who are paid according to the work they perform. On the average of a year they make 18s. a week.

Mr Morriſon deals to the amount of nearly 8000l. yearly—that is the ſum paid for goods bought in. He manufactures calves ſkins, cordovan, neats leather, cordovan and calves legs for boots, ſaddlers and coach makers leather, and alſo leather for army work. He ſupplies a great part of the ſurrounding country

try with leather. He has at preſent an order from a houſe in Glaſgow for 500 pairs of cordovan legs for boots.

2. Meſſrs George and William Thompkins, ſhoe and boot manufacturers, curry leather, but not to ſuch an extent as even to anſwer their own demand *.

Tanneries.

There are two tanneries belonging to Berwick; one ſituated in the borough, and the other in Tweedmouth.

The Berwick tannage employs ſix men and a clerk. The men make from 12s. to 14s. per week. They have a horſe mill for grinding the bark. They boil the bark after it has undergone the former common practice of infuſing it in cold water. This is for the purpoſe of extracting the aſtringency completely, and is found to be a profitable practice. There are about 100 pits in theſe works. The firm of the Company is Knowles, Marſhall, & Co.

A

* Since the above was written, Mr Thompſon has commenced the currier trade in the High Street.

A tannery in Tweedmouth has been carried on for a great number of years. The yard was purchaſed by Mr William Walker in 1787. Next year, a mill was erected for grinding oak bark, making it paſs through what are called cutters on a new conſtruction. No machine of this kind was in this part of the country at that time. In 1790, as an improvement to this mill, a pair of grinding ſtones were added, which are turned round horizontally by means of one horſe. This is for the purpoſe of grinding the bark more quickly than formerly into ſmall pieces, or even into duſt if required. This mill will now grind one ton of bark in a day. About three years ago, Mr Walker increaſed the buſineſs of this tannery to double of that done in it in 1787. In 1796, it was diſcovered at this tannery, that by infuſing oak bark in boiling water the whole remaining aſtringent quality of the bark was extracted, after it had undergone the uſual method of doing it. This is found to be a great ſaving in the uſe of bark, as a given quantity will now, by this new proceſs, afford a much greater quantity

tity of aſtringent liquor than it would do by the old method.

The various kinds of leather manufactured at this tannery are backs, bends, crop, dintles, light hides, horſe hides, calf ſkins, ſeal ſkins, hog ſkins, and ſheep ſkins. This work at preſent is carried on by five men and two apprentices, and pays an yearly duty to government of from 300l. to 350l. It is carried on under the firm of William Walker & Co.

Boot and Shoe Manufactures.

Meſſrs George and William Thompkins leather dealers, curriers, and manufacturers of boots and ſhoes, inform us that they, on an average, employ 100 men conſtantly through the year.

Mr Brown boot and ſhoemaker employs a conſiderable number of men.

Manufacture of Shoes having Wooden Heels and Soles.

Mr Thomſon and Mr Scott in Tweedmouth manufacture ſhoes of the above deſcription. As this article is cheap and conducive

cive to health it deſerves our attention. At preſent we cannot aſcertain the exact time when theſe ſhoes began firſt to be worn. It is, however, a great many years ſince they were introduced into Northumberland. Mr Thompſon has in ſome ſeaſons ſold 2000 pairs. A pair for a man coſts 4s. and for a woman 2s. 8d. The ſole is an inch and a quarter, the heel one inch and a half thick. The upper leathers are nailed with ſmall broad headed nails to the edges of the ſoles and heels.

Thus a perſon wearing theſe ſhoes is carried much farther from the ground than with common ones: Add to this the wood reſiſting dampneſs, the feet of courſe retain their natural heat, by which means the active labourer can remain with impunity a whole day in deep and wet ground. They are now made in all the conſiderable towns in Northumberland, Cumberland, and ſome other counties in England. There is a houſe in London where they are alſo manufactured.

Skinners.

Skinners.

Formerly a ſkinnery was carried on in Berwick with conſiderable ſucceſs, but nothing of the kind has been attempted in it for ſome time paſt *.

Mr Mathew Weatherhead and Son carry on the buſineſs of a white ſkinnery in Tweedmouth.

Gloves

Are manufactured in Berwick by Mr George Palmer. He alſo makes leather breeches. He wrought as a journeyman for many years with a Mr Ford of Berwick, who generally kept ſixteen journeymen and apprentices conſtantly employed in making gloves and leather breeches. The manufacture proved very lucrative. Mr Palmer laments that he could never raiſe a capital ſufficient to enable him to carry on theſe branches of trade to any great extent himſelf. He is clearly of opinion, that there is at this time a tempting

* Since writing the above a ſkinnery has been eſtabliſhed under the firm of Marſhall & Co.

opening here for a man, with a little money, to eſtabliſh a manufacture of gloves and leather breeches. It is ſurely very ſingular, that in ſuch a town as Berwick, and ſituated in a rich and populous country, there ſhould not be a tradeſman who can make either a pair of gloves or leather breeches but this old man.

6. SHIPPING.

Ship Building.

There are two ſhip builders in this place.

Mr Gowans, on the Berwick ſide, employs from 20 to 25 journeymen and apprentices. The pay of a journeyman at preſent is 15s. weekly; four veſſels upon an average are built here yearly.

Mr Bruce in Tweedmouth generally employs about the ſame number of hands as Mr Gowans, and builds about the ſame number of veſſels. The largeſt veſſel ever built in Berwick was launched on the Tweedmouth ſide, on the 15th March laſt. It is a handſome brig of 375 tons burthen. On the ſame

day

day there was launched, on the Berwick ſide of the water, a moſt beautiful brig, belonging to Meſſrs Burnett and Thomas Greive, burden 300 tons.

The juſtly celebrated character that the Berwick built veſſels or ſmacks have acquired is ſo well and univerſally known in all commercial countries as to render an account of them here altogether unneceſſary. There is one boat builder in Berwick and another in Tweedmouth *.

Sail Manufacture.

This branch of trade is carried on by Mr John Miller Dickſon, one of the partners of the roperie company. He began buſineſs in September 1793. He employs one man and three apprentices. The journeyman makes about 12s. weekly. The apprentices are bound for ſeven years,—the firſt year they receive 2s. 6d. a week, which is gradually raiſed to 6s. In a ſhort time they can work as well as journeymen. When Mr Dickſon firſt began this

* There is alſo now a third company of ſhip builders, under the firm of Joſeph Todd and Company.

this manufacture he used to purchase Hollands duck for making sails.—It cannot now be procured on account of the present war. But, as a substitute, he has been employing a cloth manufactured at East *Cocoa*, in Sommersetshire. He now finds that a very strong *cloth* of this kind, which Mr James Clunie of this town has been at great pains to manufacture, affords him strong hopes that it will answer even better than the East Cocoa cloth. Mr Dickson is now making it into sails.

7. *Roperies.*

There is a Berwick Roperie Company, consisting of Messrs Richard Todd, Ferrow Marshall, John Robertson, junior, and John Miller Dickson. This Company was instituted in April 1794. The articles manufactured here are from small ropes to cables. The journeymen earn about 12s. weekly. The rise that has for some time past taken place in the price of hemp has been discouraging to the views of this infant Company in extending their

their ſcale of trade; however finding, on trial, that their ſpeculations have turned out very much to their expectations, they are determined to perſevere, and will probably puſh their operations to a greater extent.

Mr Samuel Fenton has carried on the buſineſs of a rope-maker in Berwick for theſe 24 years paſt. He employs ſix men, who earn from 12s. to 14s. weekly.

The manufacturing of cord and ſmall ropes, for the fiſheries, is carried on in Berwick by Meſſrs Berry, Gilly, &c. It employs two men and three apprentices.

The Meſſrs Drydens, in Tweedmouth, have had a roperie eſtabliſhed there for 16 years paſt, and carry on a conſiderable buſineſs.

8. *Nets.*

Nets for catching ſalmon are made by the fiſhers themſelves.

The Meſſrs Drydens, already mentioned, manufacture nets for confining ſheep on turnip-fields. They make about 140 of theſe

nets

nets upon an average yearly; each net consists of 50 yards in length and four in breadth.

9. *Naileries.*

There is no manufacture for making of iron in Berwick. There are two manufactories in the nail way carried on here, one by Mrs Wilson of Bridge Street, who generally keeps 18 men constantly employed in making nails, and one man for making spikes. The nailors commonly earn 20s. per week, and the spiker 30s. although perhaps he does not work more than four days in the week.

Another manufactory of the same kind is carried on by a clerk to one of the timber merchants who keeps four nailors constantly employed.

10. *Breweries.*

There are two breweries in Berwick conducted on a large scale, and one has lately been erected in Tweedmouth. The firms of the respective houses are,

1. Burnet

1. Burnet Roger Greive and Sons, Berwick. This brewery is upwards of 60 years ſtanding, and employs from 12 to 14 men beſides clerks. As well as ſtrong and ſmall beer, the Meſſrs Greives brew excellent porter. They make their own malt.

2. Gregſon and Pratt, Berwick. This brewery is upwards of 22 years ſtanding, and employs 13 men and two clerks. They alſo make their own malt.

3. Meſſrs Sibbit, Dickſon, and Co. Tweedmouth. This brewery employs ſix men, in which ſtrong, table, and ſmall beer are manufactured. There is an excellent ſet of machinery attached to this brewery, drove by water, for grinding the malt, raiſing the water from the well to a ciſtern on the top of the houſe, and for pumping the wort from the lower backs up to the kettles.

11. *Snuff Manufacture.*

A manufacture of ſnuff and tobacco is carried on by the above mentioned Mr Thomas

Cockburn.

Cockburn. Theſe manufactures were eſtabliſhed anno 1778.

The mill where the ſnuff is manufactured is at New Water Haugh, about two miles diſtant from Berwick.

12. *Horn Spoons.*

The making of horn ſpoons is carried on in Tweedmouth by James Tait. The common kinds are ſold from 2s. to 6s.; beſt kinds from 8s. to 24s. per dozen. What are not ſold at home and in Berwick market on the Saturdays are diſpoſed of at the neighbouring fairs. On an average there is manufactured at this houſe 624 dozens of ſpoons annually. This manufacture is upwards of 12 years ſtanding.

Horn ſpoons have, within theſe 15 years, doubled their price: This is principally owing to the great dearth of horns.

Ma-

Manufactures of Tyles and of Bricks.

There is one carried on by Mr John Forſter. The works are within the liberties of Berwick, at a place called Cocklaw, three miles weſt from town. Mr Forſter's father, who farmed Cocklaw, accidentally diſcovered this ſtratum of clay. He then took a leaſe of the farm, and eſtabliſhed a manufacture of tyles and of bricks, which he carried on for 25 years. His ſon ſucceeded him in the year 1787. Mr Forſter employs eight on an average through the whole year; they are paid 11s. 3d. weekly in ſummer, and 7s. or 8s. weekly in winter. There are in general not leſs than from 150,000 to 180,000 tyles manufactured here yearly. The manufacturing of bricks requiring a much greater proportion of coal than that of tyles, and the fuel being at a conſiderable diſtance, Mr Forſter finds that the former is by no means an object ſo deſerving of his attention as the latter. Prices of tyles 6s. 6d. *per* hundred, or 3l. 5s. *per* thouſand; bricks 2s. *per* hundred, or 1l. *per* thouſand. As a proof of Mr Forſter's manufacturing his tyles of the beſt quality, he makes it an invariable condition with purchaſers to uphold their ſtanding the weather for 6 years; that is to ſay, whatever number of tyles may happen to fail in the courſe of that time from the effects of the weather, he re-places them, by new ones, without making any additional charge. The bed of clay lies in the form of a circular baſon. The ſtratum is about twelve feet thick in the middle of the baſon, and thinner as it approaches the outer circle. Mr Forſter calculates that this body of clay may laſt for 100 years, upon the ſuppoſition of making the ſame quantity of tyles and bricks yearly that he has done for ſome years paſt. The ſuperincumbent ſoil is about one foot thick, and it is cold and wettiſh. In dry ſeaſons, however, it bears good crops. Laſt year it produced nine Berwick bolls *per* acre. There is a ſimilar manufacture carried on in Tweedmouth by Mr Selby Murton. He commenced buſineſs in 1788. The manufacture had formerly been carried on by another perſon, but had acquired no celebrity. From this Mr Murton, at his firſt outſet, met with little encouragement as he did not uſe to ſell more than about 7000 tyles in a ſeaſon. However, from paying an unremitting attention to his buſineſs, and improving the articles of his manufacture, his demand at laſt began daily to increaſe. He has, for ſome years paſt, ſold upwards of 170,000 tyles and 200,000 bricks. He employs 7 men. The tyle-makers earn from 12s. to 14s. weekly; brick-makers from 10s. to 12s. There are two *ſtrata* of clay ſeparated by a thin *ſtratum* of ſand. The thickneſs of the two beds of clay put together is 16 feet. The extent of theſe ſtrata is exceedingly great.

14. *Blue Manufacture.*

A manufacture of this ſort is carried on at Spittal by Mr Davidſon. At preſent Pruſſian, Mecklenburgh, and Fig blues are manufactured here. Some years ago, there were alſo Glauber ſalts, aqua-fortis, and oil of vitriol

vitriol made at these works. At one time yellow-ochre was prepared at this village. The ingredients are to be found within half a mile of the buildings. A spring of water runs through the premisses sufficient to drive machinery of considerable extent.

15. *Coach Making.*

Mr Joseph Brown commenced this business twelve years ago.

He generally employs six men in chaise work, and four in iron work. The former are paid 15s. and the latter 12s. weekly.

Mr Brown is the first of his profession that ever settled in Berwick.

16. *Printing.*

This profession has been carried on in Berwick for upwards of 60 years.

There are at present three printers in it.

17. *Making of Kelp.*

The manufacture of this article is carried on in Lord Lisburn's premisses near the Mag-

dalane-

dalane-fields. It is at prefent rented by Mr Smith. He generally makes about 20 tons of kelp yearly.

18. *Manufacture of Red-Herring.*

This took place in 1797. The buildings are fituated on the fouth fide of the Tweed, at the eaft end of Tweedmouth, and are very commodious.

19. *Starch.*

A manufacture of this fort has lately been fet on foot at Tweedmouth by Mr Selby Murton.

SECTION II.

Coafting Trade.

BEFORE furnifhing our readers with an account of the trade of this port, we fhall make no apology for tracing it as far back as can be done with certainty.

It

It cannot be precifely afcertained when falmon, or any kind of goods, were firft fent in veffels from Berwick to London. Previous to that period, however, we find that falmon ufed to be fent from the Tweed to Newcaftle by land. They were cured there, and conveyed by fea to London, where they paffed for Newcaftle falmon.

The veffels employed to carry falmon to the Capital, generally took feveral weeks in performing a voyage. This induced one Marfhall to make a trial of carrying falmon on horfe back to London. He hired one Home, who, along with him, fet out from this for the capital with fix horfes loaded with falmon newly haled from the Tweed. They reached London; and fold their fifh to fuch advantage, that, after paying all expences, they cleared 20l. more than if they had fold them in Berwick. This may have happened upwards of 60 years ago. Home is ftill living, but fo much fuperannuated that he can give but a very inaccurate account of the matter himfelf. Only one of the horfes tired on the road in

going

going to town. The hiring another in its place conſtituted the principal expence on the journey. It is ſaid that Marſhall made a practice of carrying ſalmon in this manner to Billingſgate, where he obtained the name of *London John*.

We have been favoured with the following from reſpectable authority:

" When I had the pleaſure of ſeeing you laſt, I mentioned that, about fifty years ſince, two well veſſels, of fifty tons each, were then found ſufficient to carry the whole of the coaſting trade between this place and the port of London. I ſhould, however, at the ſame time, have obſerved, that this was only the caſe in the winter months, as there were always a good many more well veſſels employed in the ſummer for the purpoſe of carrying the produce of the London market. Theſe veſſels in general were about forty tons burden each, and for the moſt part belonged to Harwich and Graveſend; and, as they came here ſolely on account of the ſalmon trade, they always went away again at the

the close of the fishing season, and two of the largest remained all the winter for the purpose already mentioned."

Hence it would appear, that fifty years ago there were no vessels belonging to Berwick for carrying salmon to London.

There are at present 21 smacks employed by the two Shipping Companies of this place in that trade, and in carrying other goods to and from London and Leith. The Leith trade was first entered into by the Union Company in June 1796. The Old Company followed the example in February 1797.

Formerly all goods sent by the smacks, with goods from London for Edinburgh, Glasgow, &c. were landed at Berwick, and afterwards sent by land carriage to their respective destinations; and all goods from the above places for London, by the smacks, were conveyed hither by land. It is here proper to remark, that the Glasgow, Edinburgh, &c. merchants, some years ago, finding that, by the expeditious navigation of the smacks, they received their goods much sooner by the

above

above method than they uſed to do by the Leith traders, ſent very large quantities of them to be ſhipped at Berwick for London, and at the ſame time ordered moſt of their goods from thence by the ſame mode of conveyance. This gave riſe not only to a keen competition between the ordinary carriers, but was alſo the means of two companies eſtabliſhing themſelves for the purpoſe of conveying goods land-wiſe. One of theſe conſiſted of the Union Company, with a view principally of carrying their own goods. The other Company was eſtabliſhed on a very large ſcale, and carried goods to Edinburgh, Glaſgow, and Newcaſtle.

The great expence, however, attending the carrying on this extenſive buſineſs, together with the reduced prices of carriage, would not ſupport the trade, and therefore the Company relinquiſhed the enterpriſe.

The Union Company, upon commencing the Leith ſhipping trade, gave up their land-carriage between this and Edinburgh; they ſtill, however, carry goods by land from Leith to Glaſgow, and from Glaſgow to Leith.

The following is from the beſt authorities. "The coaſting trade of this port has been increaſing for a conſiderable number of years paſt, and is now of very conſiderable extent; the principal part of which reſults from the famous ſalmon fiſhery of the river Tweed, and the ſurplus produce of the neighbouring country, ſince the great improvements and increaſe of cultivation. There is a very extenſive and regular coaſting trade now carried on between this port and London; and, without contradiction, there is not ſuch a regular and ready communication between any two places of equal diſtance in the whole kingdom, nor perhaps in the whole world: This is principally owing to the particular conſtruction of the veſſels employed in this trade, their being well found and manned, and managed by experienced and active coaſting ſeamen. There are now 13 or 14 veſſels, of from 70 to 120 tons burden, carrying 10 or 12 men each, conſtantly employed between Berwick and

and London, each of which perform, upon an average, 14 voyages in the year. There are four, five, or ſix ſail regularly every week, and frequently perform the voyage in three or four days; and ſeveral have gone from, and returned to, Berwick with cargoes within a fortnight. This regular trade was at firſt erected for the ready conveyance of ſalmon fiſh, manufactured here for the London market, and ſtill is and muſt remain its principal ſupport. The conſequence of the ſalmon fiſhing here may appear from the following tolerable exact ſtatement. The yearly rentals of the fiſheries in the Tweed, for the courſe of a few miles, amounts to between 7000l. and 8000l. in which between 75 and 80 boats, with about 300 men, are conſtantly employed during the ſalmon fiſhery, between the 10th of January and the 10th of October. There has been known to have been 40,000 kits, or upwards, ſent from this town in the courſe of the ſeaſon, beſides a vaſt quantity of ſalmon trouts ſent alive to London; the number of kits has not been ſo great for a few years paſt, owing

owing to a method of fending great quantities of falmon frefh to London during all the fummer feafon, packed in ice, collected in the winter feafon, and preferved through the whole fummer for that purpofe. A general view of the extent of the coafting trade from this port will appear from an average."

Quantities of goods fhipped, taken on an average for the four preceding years, viz. 1791, 1792, 1793, *and* 1794.

Goods fhipped coaft-wife from this port.	WOOL. No. of packs.	WOOL. Hundred weights.	Quarters of corn, Winchefter meafure.	Sacks of hulled barley, oatmeal, and wheat flour.	Tons of potatoes.	Kits of pickled falmon.	Tubs of falted pork.	Chefts of eggs.	Firkins of butter.	Boxes of candles.	Barrels of herrings.	Bales of paper & Count books.	Tanned leather, hundred weights.	Tallow, hundred weights.	Blue, hundred weights.	Bolls of canvas and facking.
	1700	5300	26,887	7277	850	28,100	3500	4000	210	110	400	2000	140	150	350	250

" This is a tolerably correct account of the goods generally fhipped coaftwife, which conftitute the principal coaft trade of this port outwards, though there are many other articles of merchandize frequently fhipped; but they are fo multifarious that it is almoft impoffible to give any ftatement or claffification thereof.

The goods brought into this port coaftwife are alfo very confiderable; but it is almoft impracticable to give any account or ftatement thereof, as they confift of all the various articles of Englifh manufactory and general merchandize required for the ufe and confumption of the neighbouring country."

The

The advantages resulting from the trade of this port are numerous and important.

The article of eggs is a curious and lucrative branch of trade here. They are brought from all parts of the country on both sides of the Tweed in carts and in panniers. Great numbers are brought from about Hawick, Selkirk, and all the adjacent country.

Most of the money received by egglers is spent in the town for groceries and other articles. The grocer who deals in eggs has often a double advantage by this traffic; for, *1st*, he has a profit on his groceries, and *2dly*, on his eggs. He no sooner ships his eggs, and writes to his merchant in London, than he draws upon him, and receives his cash at the bank.

The sum paid yearly for eggs in this town may, on an average, be estimated at 20,000l. The number of chests of eggs sent from this to London, from 10th October 1797 to 10th of October 1798, is 5254 chests, and 58,396 quarters of corn.

We are much disappointed that we have not obtained an account of the quantity of grain

grain exported coaſtwiſe from this port in the courſe of laſt winter, as it is ſaid to exceed by far that of any former period.

There were, about two months ago, fifteen large veſſels laying together in the harbour waiting for cargoes of corn.

The increaſe of the trade of Berwick may be judged of from this, that in 16 years the Revenue of the Cuſtom Houſe has riſen from 1000l. to ſix thouſand pounds a year.

SECTION III.

Foreign Commerce.

WE ſubjoin the following, with which we have been favoured from indiſputable authority, as it is the beſt account we are enabled to give reſpecting the foreign commerce of this place.

" The port of Berwick, lying in a centrical ſituation between the great ports of Leith and Newcaſtle, and at nearly equal diſtances from each, ſurrounded by a populous and well cultivated

tivated country, to which it is the quay for trade, might naturally be ſuppoſed to command a very conſiderable import and export trade; but, notwithſtanding the advantages of ſituation, having no manufactories of conſequence, its foreign commerce is not ſo conſiderable as might be expected, and conſiſts chiefly of the raff and iron trade from *Norway* and the *Baltic*. The foreign trade of the port was probably checked from extending, as might have been expected, by the exclusive privilege and right to trade formerly claimed by the freemen, as burgeſſes of this town, under the charter granted to it as a corporation, which exclusive right being very ſtrictly and tenaciouſly adhered to when trade and commerce were eſtabliſhing themſelves by manufactories, to the evident advantages of every town and neighbourhood where they were permitted and encouraged. Adventurers were prevented, by that preſcriptive right or claim, from ſettling in the town or eſtabliſhing manufactories, which has undoubtedly been detrimental to the trade of the place, and

and prejudicial to the intereſt of the adjacent country. However, the improving ſtate of the country, both in building and cultivation, for upwards of 30 years paſt, has conſiderably increaſed the conſumption and demand of the articles of general importation at this port, and conſequently has encouraged and increaſed the exportation alſo. A general account whereof, upon an average of four years, viz. 1791, 1792, 1793, 1794, is ſubjoined.

An average account of the number of ſhips, with the account of their tonnage, importing cargoes at this port, diſtinguiſhing each country.

Countries.	No of Ships.	Tonnage.
Denmark	2	150
Holland	4	340
Pruſſia	6	960
Ruſſia	5	650
Sweden	10	785
Norway	13	1260
	40 Ships	4145 Tons."

" *An*

" An Average Account of the Kinds and Quantities of Goods Imported from Foreign Countries, distinguishing each Country."

Countries.	Loads of Timber.	Hundred Deals	Hundred Battins.	Tons of Iron.	Cwts. Hemp.	Cwts. Flax.	Bushels of Lint seed.	Cwts. of Cloverseed.	Cwts. of Tallow.	Barrels of Tar.	Quarters of Wheat.	Quarters of Barley.	Quarters of Oats.
Norway,	1080	60½	5										
Sweden,		203½	33½	250									
Prussia,	840	6½			2						574	196	519
Russia,	242½	40	24½	15½	735	445	200		137½	56			
Holland,				5		1622	1012	432½					82½
Denmark,													520
Average totals,	2162½	310½	63	270½	737	2067	1212	432½	137½	56	574	196	1121½

" There was, during the period before averaged, a cargo of 60 tons of oak bark imported from Germany, and a part of a cargo of 80 pipes of wine, with a few boxes of lemons, imported from Portugal; but theſe, with other trifling articles imported from other countries, being accidental, can ſcarcely be conſidered as forming any part of the general trade of the port, and therefore are not included in the foregoing average account of imports.

There was formerly a conſiderable export trade to foreign countries from this port of ſalted fiſh and corn, but for ſeveral years paſt that traffic has been declining; and from the great demand and conſumption of fiſh in the London market, and the prohibitory regulations againſt exporting corn, there has been nothing of export trade at this port during the period referred to in the above account, which can be conſidered as conſtituting any part of the trade of the port, and therefore no account is ſtated thereof."

We

We are informed, from another reſpectable quarter, that the exportation of grain from this port, about 50 years ago, to foreign countries, was immenſe. Some idea of it may be formed from this, that, at that time, one of our principal corn merchants loſt 10,000l. in one ſeaſon upon grain. And it may be added, that this gentleman had acquired ſo much wealth in that branch as not to have ſuffered the ſmalleſt pecuniary embarraſſment from the misfortune.

SEC-

SECTION IV.

Navigation and Shipping.

THE navigation between this port and London by the Berwick ſmacks for ſafety and expedition is univerſally admitted to exceed that of any other in the known world. See coaſting trade.

There are at preſent two Commercial Shipping Companies belonging to Berwick. The Old Shipping Company, and the Union Shipping Company. The firſt was inſtituted in the year 1764; and commenced trade with four veſſels.

The following is a liſt of ſmacks at preſent belonging to this Company:

1. Britannia Packet.
2. Commercial ditto.
3. London ditto.
4. Berwick Merchant.
5. Berwick Packet.
6. Neptune.

7.

7. Ceres.
8. Tweed Packet.
9. Addiſon.
10. London and Berwick Packet.

One is building.

The Union Shipping Company was inſtituted in the year 1794.

Liſt of ſmacks belonging to it.

1. Berwickſhire Packet.
2. Glaſgow ditto.
3. Edinburgh and Berwick ditto.
4. Kelſo ditto.
5. Coldſtream ditto.
6. Roxburgh ditto.
7. Ceres.
8. Hazard.
9. Leith ditto.
10. Eliza ditto.
11. Sprightly ditto.

One is building.

Theſe ſmacks carry from between 60 and 70 to 140 tons burthen; ſome of them have wells for carrying trouts alive to London.

The

The number of veſſels belonging to Berwick including the ſmacks amount to about forty.

SECTION V.

Harbour and Quay.

THE ſea coaſt within the liberties of Berwick commences at the mouth of the river, and extends in the direction of N. W. upwards of three miles. On the Spittal ſide of the river, the ſhore is quite a ſandy beach for more than half a mile in length. The river ſtrikes the bar or entrance into the harbour.

From the mouth of the harbour a range of low rocks run up the north ſide of the river 1278 feet. They then change their courſe, and run 798 feet in a ſtraight line towards the land on the ſame ſide.

A capacious baſon called the *Meadow Haven* lies behind theſe rocks. It is formed by them and two other ridges in the N.N.W. and N.E.

N.E. of the bafon. This haven has a level fandy bottom, and is quite dry at low water. In the north fide of it, there is an opening into the fea between a fmall pointed rock ftanding by itfelf and the range of rocks on the eaft of it, wide enough to admit a fmack to pafs.

There is a fimilar outlet in the E. corner of this haven fufficiently wide to let large fized veffels out to fea. The white fifhermen have made a *gut* or opening from the river into the haven near that corner where the rocks formerly mentioned bend towards the land. When the weather is unfavourable for them to put to fea by the river mouth, they row their boats through the *gut* into the haven above mentioned, and proceed by the north or eaft paffage formerly pointed out.

From this account of the harbour, ftrangers may conclude that it is formed entirely by the rocks juft now defcribed; but it may be obferved that this is not altogether the cafe: for the remains of a *pier* are ftill to be feen upon them, part of which meafures 10 or 12 feet in height. That part of the foundation which lies along the ſide of the river meaſures 926 feet in length, and in ſome parts 35 feet in breadth. There are two beacons placed in the ſite of this ſide of the pier, 492 feet diſtant from each other. In ordinary tides, the water riſes from 15 to 16 feet on the lower beacon, and 10 feet on the upper one.

The ſide of the pier that runs towards the land meaſures 632 feet in length, and it is 48 feet in breadth at the ſide of the river. From this point, however, the pier becomes gradually narrower as it approaches the ſhore; and where it terminates on the land ſide it is only 28 feet broad. There are a great many of the ſtones of which the pier had been built ſtill to be ſeen in confuſed heaps, and great numbers quite detached from one another. It may be remarked that a practice has long exiſted of carrying away ſtones from this pier for building bats or fiſhing places and for other purpoſes; the bad effects of which will be pointed out in a ſubſequent part of this work. The breadth of water at ſpring tides oppoſite

oppoſite the *gut*, by which the fiſhermen go into the meadow haven, is generally about 180 feet; but the channel where ſhips of any conſiderable burden can be navigated is in general only 30 feet broad.

We beg leave to refer the reader to the ground plan of the town for the different turns the river makes in its courſe from the bridge to the bar. We can find no account of the building of this pier in hiſtory. All we know of it is from *oral tradition*, and that it has always been called *Queen Elizabeth's Pier*.

The diſtance between this pier and the ſhore gate, where the quay is ſituated, is about 850 yards. The quay or key is divided into the old and new keys. The former is 302 feet in length, and the latter is 326.

There is alſo a ballaſt key or a place appropriated to keeping ballaſt.

We have a dry dock here which will hold five ſmacks. That part of the river oppoſite the ballaſt key is called the *Ford*, from ſtones uſually collected there by floods. Owing to thoſe ſtones and other rubbiſh the river is ſhallower here than in any other part of it below the bridge.

On the quay, the different offices and warehouſes belonging to the two trading Companies are ſituated. Part of it is likewiſe let out at yearly rents by the corporation to tradeſmen and to timber merchants.

Soundings of the Harbour.

In December 1796 we received the following from reſpectable authority: "The depth "of water on the bar or entrance into the har-"bour of Berwick at the top of high water, "in ſtream tides, is about twenty feet, and at "the ſame time there is fourteen feet water "on the ford; and at the top of high water "in the neap tides, there is fourteen feet water "on the bar, and ten feet water on the ford." This, however, is to be conſidered as an average ſtatement; for when it is raging weather either at the ſtream or neaps, the tides will be higher, and, when the weather is very moderate, they will be lower than what I have mentioned.

In

In April 1797, we took the ſoundings of the harbour, and found that they correſponded with the above ſtatement.

In March 1799, the ſoundings are much as in 1797; but the ſand bank at Spittal Point is increaſed.

SECTION VI.

Harbour Dues.

IT is enacted among the regulations of the Borough, "That every ſhipmaſter of any "ſhip or veſſel ſhall pay three ſhillings and "fourpence to the water Bailiff, at his office "on the quay, for harbour dues and plank-"age."

"To pay one ſhilling for every ton of bal-"laſt inwards, and fourpence for every ton "outwards."

SEC-

SECTION VII.

State of Freights.

WE have been favoured with the following table of the present State of Freights from London to Berwick, viz.

	£.	s.	d.
A Puncheon or Pipe of Rum, Wine or Foreign Spirits, of any kind -	0	8	0
A Hogſhead of ditto -	0	5	0
A half Hogſhead of ditto -	0	2	6
A Hogſhead ſolid Sugar -	0	7	6
A ditto packed ditto -	0	7	6
A Tearce ditto ditto -	0	3	9
A Cheſt ditto ditto -	0	2	6
A large Hogſhead Dye Stuff -	0	7	6
A common Bag Dye Stuff -	0	1	3
A Hogſhead Treacle -	0	6	3
A half Hogſhead ditto -	0	3	6
A Hogſhead of Porter, Oil, or Cyder	0	5	0
A Barrel of Porter or Cyder -	0	3	4
A Kilderkin ditto ditto -	0	1	8
A Bag Hops - -	0	6	3
A Packet ditto - -	0	3	9
A Cheſt of Lemons - -	0	2	6

A

	£.	s.	d.
A Bag Clover or Rye Grafs -	0	2	6
A fmall Bag Nuts - -	0	1	6
A Hogfhead Earthen Ware -	0	7	6
A Crate Earthen Ware -	0	5	0
A Barrel Soap - -	0	2	6
A Cheft Hard Soap -	0	2	6
A Box Tea - -	0	1	3
A Candy Box - -	0	0	9
Cheefe, Allum, and Iron *per* cwt.	0	0	9
Tanned Leather *per* ditto -	0	1	0
Hemp and Flax *per* ton -	1	0	0
Bark *per* ditto -	0	15	0
A Barrel Bulk of Furniture or Wearing Apparel	0	2	6
A four wheeled Chaife -	4	7	6
A Single Horfe ditto -	1	11	6
Carriage by Land			
Goods from Newcaftle *per* Stone -	0	0	6
Ditto from Edinburgh			

Rates of Freights from Newcaftle to Berwick, by Sloops Induftry and Betfy.

	£.	s.	d.
A CRATE Earthenware, full Size	0	4	0
A ditto ditto a Size lefs	0	3	6
Loofe Mugs, *per* dozen -	0	1	6
Cheefe, *per* ton -	1	0	0
Soap, *per* ditto -	0	15	0

Iron,

			£.	s.	d.
Iron,	*per* ditto	-	0	10	0
Metal,	*per* ditto	-	0	15	0
Tanned Leather,	*per* ditto	-	1	0	0
Hemp and Flax,	*per* ditto	-	1	0	0
Whitening,	*per* ditto	-	0	8	0
New Rope,	*per* ditto	-	0	15	0
Old ditto,	*per* ditto	-	0	14	0
Old Rags,	*per* ditto	-	0	15	0
Oil Cake,	*per* ditto	-	0	15	0
Lead,	*per* ditto	-	0	9	0
Pipe Clay,	*per* ditto	-	0	10	0
Copperas,	*per* ditto	-	0	10	0
Alum,	*per* ditto	-	0	10	0
Salt,	*per* ditto	-	0	12	0
A Crate of Glaſs, No. 18.		-	0	3	9
A ditto ditto, No. 15.		-	0	3	0
A ditto ditto, No. 0.		-	0	2	6
A Puncheon, or Pipe of Liquor		-	0	8	0
A Hogſhead of ditto		-	0	4	0
A Half Hogſhead ditto		-	0	2	0
Small caſks, ditto, in proportion					
A Leaguer Oil	-	-	0	8	6
A Pipe or Puncheon ditto		-	0	7	6
A Hogſhead ditto		-	0	4	0
A Half Hogſhead ditto		-	0	2	0
A Hogſhead Glaſs, full Size		-	0	7	6
A Tierce ditto		-	0	3	6
A Cheſt ditto	-	-	0	2	0

A

	£.	s.	d.
A Hogſhead of Lintſeed -	0	4	0
A Bag of Clover, or Turnip Seed -	0	2	6
Dye Stuff, *per* cwt. -	0	1	0
A Hogſhead Treacle -	0	6	0
A Half Hogſhead ditto -	0	3	0
A Barrel Porter or Beer -	0	2	0
A Bag of Hops - -	0	5	0
A Pocket ditto - -	0	2	6
A Cheſt Lemons or Oranges -	0	2	0
A Cheſt of Tea - -	0	1	3
A Barrel Pitch, Tar, or Roſin -	0	1	6
A Bundle Paper, 1ſt Size, 3d. 2d do. 4d. 3d do. 6d.			
Wool Cards, *per* dozen -	0	0	6
Bottles *per* groſs -	0	2	0
A large Millſtone - -	0	18	0
A Five Foot Grindſtone -	0	1	9
and in proportion upwards			
Timber, *per* load -	0	12	0
Plank, *per* ditto -	0	14	0
Oakum, *per* cwt. -	0	0	9
Chimney Tops, *per* dozen -	0	8	0
Chaiſe Wheels, *per* ſet -	0	5	0
Shot in Bags, *per* ton -	0	10	0
Iron Shovels, *per* dozen -	0	0	6
Spades, *per* ditto - -	0	1	0
Cinders, *per* chaldron -	0	9	0
Ship Anchors, *per* cwt. -	0	0	9
Mops and Bruſhes, *per* dozen -	0	0	9

A

	£.	s.	d.
A Cag of Lead of two cwt. -	0	1	0
Hamper Wine or Spirits -	0	1	6
Malt, *per* bag - -	0	1	3
A cheſt of Pipes -	0	1	6
A Bottle in a Hamper -	0	1	6
Nails, *per* cwt. -	0	0	6
Fire Bricks, *per* 1000 -	1	0	0

SECTION VIII.

Banks.

THERE is one bank in Berwick, and an agent for the Britiſh Linen Company.

The bank was eſtabliſhed on the 10th day of March 1788. The firm of the houſe is Burdon, Surtees, Embleton, and Company.

Buſineſs is tranſacted here to a great amount; and, in juſtice to the inſtitution, it is but fair to ſtate, that its matters are conducted in ſuch a liberal and accommodating manner as reflects great honour on the bank in general, but

but in particular upon Mr Embleton one of the partners, who has the immediate direction and management of it.

The advantages which reſult to this town, and the neighbouring country, from this inſtitution, are exceedingly great; and they are ſo univerſally known as renders it unneceſſary to expatiate upon them here.

The agency of the Britiſh Linen Company is of long ſtanding, and has been conducted with great propriety, which reflects much honour upon the agent, James Bell, Eſq; late Mayor.

CHAP. XII.

Fisheries.

SECTION I.

The River Tweed, its Origin and Termination.

RIVERS constitute one of the principal features of the surface of the earth; and few subjects afford greater scope to the contemplative powers of the philosopher, the patriot, the virtuous, and the good.

Pliny emphatically compares the origin and progress of rivers to the life of man. How captivating to the eye of the attentive observer, how grand and impressive is the idea which is formed in the mind in contemplating a mighty river at its source, bubbling

bling out from beneath the lifeleſs clod, or burſting forth from the chinks of a rock, and ſetting out on its journey with a ſtream ſo ſmooth and gentle as only to overcome the ſmalleſt reſiſtance, and, in its progreſs, tendering its ſervices on all ſides, and at once becoming both the ſupport and ornament of the country.

The noble river Tweed iſſues from a mountain in the county of Tweedale in Scotland, at a place called Tweed's Croſs, cloſe by the ſide of the road leading to the town of Moffat.

"Both Annan and Clyde," ſays Pennycuick in the Hiſtory of Tweedale, "have their firſt riſe from the ſame height, about half a mile from one another, where Clyde runneth weſt, Annan to the ſouth, and Tweed to the eaſt."

This ſtream, at its origin, is ſometimes ſo ſmall in ſummer, that a tube of an inch diameter would be ſufficient to convey all the water, and it runs for about a quarter of a mile before it begins to increaſe, when it is called Tweedſhaws. Beyond this a rivulet

joins

joins the Tweed ; it then changes its easterly course, and, running north by west, returns to its native hill as if it had lost its proper course. It here forms a semicircle with the hill, and on that account is called Tweed-hoop. It then crosses the Moffat road a second time at the inn called Tweed-hoop-foot. At this place it again changes its course, and, running south-east, is, about three miles from its source, joined by the water Core.

In the course of six or seven miles, 19 or 20 rivulets run into the Tweed. After Tweedale, it meanders through Selkirkshire, and the county of Roxburgh, receiving, in its progress, several small rivers, such as Ettrick, Leader, Tiviot, besides a great number of smaller streams. Soon after leaving Kelso, it falls into Berwickshire ; and, in its course through that county, the Eden and Till empty themselves into it.

This stream, which has now acquired great powers, enters the liberties of Berwick at Gainslaw, and, about a mile below, it is joined by the Whittadder.

This

This is the laſt of the numerous alliances formed by the Tweed, which now being greatly increaſed, and far advanced in its career, exhibits additional beauties. It becomes more grave and dignified in its motions; is fond of peace and quiet; and, in all the ſolemnity of majeſtic ſilence, rolls on its mighty waters till it is loſt in the unfathomable depth.

SECTION II.

Salmon Fiſhery.—Mode of Fiſhing and Sale.

THE ſalmon fiſhery conſtitutes the moſt intereſting branch of trade carried on in Berwick.

It has been ſtated, that there are about 300 men employed in the fiſheries.

We have already mentioned, that the Tweed ſalmon is of the very beſt quality. The fiſhing commences on the 10th day of January, and continues till the 10th of October.

Some

Some ſeaſons ſalmon are very plenty, and others very ſcarce. We have ſeen from one to 100 of them taken at a draught: But we are aſſured, that there have been many inſtances of from 200 to 500 taken at one hawl; and, if report is to be credited, 700 have been brought on ſhore at one draught.

"The capture of ſalmon in the Tweed," ſays Mr Pennant, "about the month of July, is prodigious. In a good fiſhery, often a boat load, and ſometimes near two, are taken in a tide: Some few years ago, there were above 700 fiſh taken at one hawl; but from 50 to 100 is very frequent."

Beſides ſalmon, there are gilſes and trouts caught in the Tweed.

The preſent rental of all the fiſhing waters together, from the mouth of the river to Norham, which is ſeven miles from Berwick, is about 10,000l. yearly, excluſive of the tithes.

All the ſalmon, ſent to London from this place, were, till of late, boiled and put into kits; but that practice has, for ſome years paſt, been

been laid aside. The whole of the salmon are now sent in ice, which has been discovered to preserve the fish fresh for a long time. How this came to be first known in Berwick was owing to the following circumstance: Mr Dempster, a member of Parliament, about 12 years ago, calling on Mr John Richardson of Perth, at his fishery, told him, it was a practice on the continent to pack salmon in ice, as it had been found to preserve them so fresh that they might be sent many hundred miles without spoiling. This induced Mr Richardson to make the trial; the result of which not only corroborated the fact, but also proved to be very lucrative to Mr Richardson.

The same experiment was made here, and with success, in the year 1788. Since that period several ice houses* have been built in

* The aspect of ice houses should be towards the east, or south-east, for the advantage of the morning sun to expel the damp air, as that is more pernicious than warmth, for which reason trees, in the vicinity of an ice house, tend to its disadvantage. The best soil for an ice house to be made in is chalk, as it conveys away the waste water

in this plan; and the quantity of ice put into them yearly is aſtoniſhing. The two Companies laid in 7600 cart loads between them laſt winter; expence about 450l. for ice. There are 32 ſalmon coopers in Berwick.

There are four different modes of catching ſalmon uſually employed at preſent, viz. the ſweep, the ſtell, the bobb, and the hanging nets.

The ſale of ſalmon is entirely confined to the coopers; none are brought to public market. The coopers, however, are always ready to oblige any perſon with a ſalmon at market price.

When the gilſes become plenty, which generally happens about the latter end of July, the women call them through the ſtreets.

Ever ſince the introduction of ice in preſerving ſalmon, their price has greatly riſen.

For ſeveral years paſt, ſalmon has ſold from 3s. to 35s. per ſtone. They have been known to

ter without any artificial drain; next to that, looſe ſtony, earth, or gravelly ſoil. Its ſituation ſhould be on the ſide of a hill, for the advantage of entering the cell upon a level.

to have been ſold as low as 6d. and 7d. per ſtone.

SECTION III.

White Fiſhery.—Lobſter Catching and Sale.

THESE kinds of fiſhing are carried on by three boats belonging to the fiſhermen of Greenſes, Caſtlegate, and by five boats belonging to Spittal. Each boat pays a *modus* of a few ſhillings yearly in name of tythe.

When the herring fiſhing commences upon this coaſt, or up the Frith of Forth, all our white fiſhermen reſort to it, and often with great advantage.

Five men are employed to each boat.

Lobſters are in general to be found on this coaſt in great plenty. The Old Shipping Company here have had them taken by contract for ſeven years.

They pay ſeven ſhillings a ſcore for all lobſters, which are $4\frac{1}{2}$ inches in the barrel, but only 3s. 6d. per ſcore for all under that dimenſion. They are caught in what are called cruives, 3 feet in length and $1\frac{1}{2}$ foot in height. There is a hole in each end of the cruive into which the lobſters enter to take the bait within it. The bait is a piece of haddock, cod, &c.

They are ſometimes ſold in the market place, and frequently carried from houſe to houſe. Some years ago, a good lobſter might have been purchaſed for 3d. now 6d. and 8d. are given for them.

The circumſtance of lobſters throwing off their ſhells once a year (about the month of June) and reproducing them, as well as the reproduction of a claw when loſt by accident, conſtitutes two phenomena in nature truly wonderful, and not unworthy of the contemplation of the philoſophic mind.

CHAP.

CHAP. XIII.

Police.

SECTION I.

Fairs and Market Days.

THE Corporation, as will appear by their charter, have a right to hold two markets weekly, viz. on the Wednefdays and on the Saturdays. They have alfo a power to hold one fair in the year, to continue from the Feaft of the invention of the Holy Crofs until the Feaft of St John Baptift.

There is no weekly market held but on the Saturdays, and the fair only lafts one day.

Several years ago the corporation eftablifhed three markets, called High Markets, to be held

held yearly for the hiring of ſervants and the ſelling of horſes and cattle.

The *1ſt* is held on the ſecond Wedneſday of May.—*2d*, On the Wedneſday preceding the 26th Auguſt.—*3d*, On the firſt Wedneſday of November.

Theſe markets are the ſame as fairs.

SECTION II.

Markets.—Butcher Market.

THIS market place, which forms an irregular ſquare, is ſituated near the foot of Church Street.

In juſtice to the corporation, we muſt ſtate that, within theſe few years, they have made a great improvement in this market, by paving it neatly. It is ſupplied with two gates, which, when ſhut, prevent attempts to it. When they are open, it is a great thorough fare betwixt the High Street and Church Street.

There

There are ſhambles ſituated on the outſide of the market place facing Church Street.

The prices of all kinds of butcher meats here have been gradually riſing for ſome years paſt. The current prices two years were,

Beef from 4½d. to 6d.
Mutton from 5d. to 6d.
Lamb 6d.
Veal from 5d. to 8d.
Pork from 4½d. to 6d.

The preſent prices are,

Beef from 4d. to 6d.
Mutton from 5d. to 6d.
Veal from 5d. to 7d.
Lamb from 3s. 6d. to 4s. 6d. per qr.
Pork from 3d. to 4d.

Twelve years ago the prices were,

Beef from ½d. to 4d.
Mutton from 3d. to 4d.
Lamb from 2½d. to 3d.
Veal from 2½d. to 3½d.
Pork in proportion.

Berwick being ſituated in the immediate neighbourhood of two rich and populous counties,

counties, (Northumberland and Berwickſhire), the butcher market is conſtantly ſupplied with every kind of meat of the beſt quality.

Moſt of the black cattle killed here are oxen, weighing from 60 to 120 ſtones.

The market is occaſionally accommodated with fine kyloes. There is no market in the kingdom better ſupplied with mutton than this.

Berwick has been long famous for good veal. The beſt fed calves come at preſent from Haggerſton, in Northumberland, and Chirnſide, in the county of Berwick. Veal was formerly often ſent from this to Edinburgh, and ſometimes to Newcaſtle.

Within theſe few years ſeveral remarkable large fat oxen and cows have been killed in Berwick market.

As a matter of curioſity, and even importance, we do not conſider it improper to ſtate the following inſtances.

1. An ox, five years old, belonging to James Wilkie, Eſq; of Fowlden, in the coun-

ty of Berwick, was killed in the year 1793, and weighed as follows:

	ſtones.	lb.
Four quarters	120	0
Tallow -	29	7
Hide -	10	0
	159	7

2. A cow, the property of Mr Wilkie of Broomhouſe, was killed in 1796, and its four quarters weighed 102 ſtones.

3. Weight and dimenſion of an ox bred at Ladykirk, county of Berwick, by William Robertſon, Eſq; and which was killed at Berwick in March 1797.

He was a moſt beautiful well proportioned animal, and weighed, with rough fat left in him, one hundred and fifty ſtone twelve pounds, fourteen pounds to the ſtone; and his tallow weighed ſixteen ſtone.—The above was the weight of his four quarters as ſold by the butcher.

His

His age was four years eleven months, and his dimenſions as follow:

	Ft.	In.
Length from head to rump -	8	5
Length of neck - -	2	1
Girt before the ſhoulder -	9	4
Girt behind the ſhoulder -	9	3
Girt at middle - -	10	10
Girt before the flank - -	10	3
Girt behind the flank and over the hips	9	9½
Girt of bone below the knee -	0	9¾
Girt of bone below the neck -	0	11
Breadth at hips - -	3	0
Breadth at ſhoulders -	3	0
Breadth from hind rib to hind rib over the chine - - -	3	11½
Breadth over the loins to the outſide of the falſe ribs of fat - -	2	8
Breadth from ground -	1	9
Height at crop - -	5	8
Height at ſhoulders - -	5	7½

It may be obſerved that this ox was a year younger than the Blackwell ox bred by Mr Hill,

Hill, and two years younger than the Howick oxen bred by Sir Henry Grey, and nearly about the ſame weight; and was allowed, by every perſon who ſaw him, to be the fatteſt animal of his kind which was ever ſlaughtered in the north of England, if not in the whole kingdom. And, what is wonderful, he had nothing better than the common fare of young ſtock on the farm where he was bred (viz. Upſetlington, Berwickſhire) until he was three years old.

The gentleman that bred this ox has had a great many oxen, from three to five years old, exceedingly fat, and weighing from 95 to 120 ſtone the four quarters.—His cows generally weigh from 70 to 90 ſtone.

Impartiality, and that praiſe which is due to every one who forwards the improvement of his country, oblige us here to ſay, that few characters in this kingdom, of independent fortune, ſuch as Mr Robertſon is, are ſo well entitled to the thanks of his country in that reſpect than this gentleman. It ſhould be added, that Mr Robertſon has paid equal attention to the improving the breed of ſheep, by means of procuring rams from Mr Stones of Leiceſterſhire.

Some years ago, Lieutenant Colonel Renton of Lamberton had alſo a beautiful fat ox killed in Berwick market which was of an extraordinary weight.

Fiſh Market.

This market is held in the high-ſtreet. White fiſh are commonly to be had here in great abundance. They were formerly ſold very cheap; but, ſince the butcher market has got ſo high, the prices of fiſh have alſo riſen in proportion. The variety conſiſt of cod, codlings, ling, haddocks, turbot, ſoles, whitings, ſkate, flounders, lobſters, crabs, &c. The quantity taken here is ſeldom ſufficient for the demand of the market, but the deficiency is made up from the fiſheries of Eyemouth, Northfield, and Burnmouth in Scotland, and from Holy Iſland.

Muſſels and cockles are brought from Budle in Northumberland, and Holy Iſland. They are

are not ſold in the market, but are moſtly carried about the town in creels. Oyſters are ſold in different houſes in the town from 1s. 6d. to 2s. 6d. the hundred. They are brought from Newhaven and Preſton-pans, in the neighbourhood of Edinburgh.

Haddocks might have been got ſome years ago for 6d. a ſcore; now they would coſt from 1s. 6d. to 2s. 6d. unleſs the market were overſtocked. Cod, turbot, and ling rate in the ſame proportion.

This day, May 20. 1799, the Author bought a cod, newly haled from the ſea, for 10d. which weighed 20lb. He alſo purchaſed an excellent ſkate for twopence. The quantity of fiſh in the market is this day prodigious. Our white fiſh here is perhaps not excelled in any part of the iſland, and is a great bleſſing to the poor of this town and neighbourhood. About two years ago, a haddock, meaſuring 32 inches in length, and weighing 11¾lb. was bought in this market for one ſhilling and ſixpence.

Poultry

Poultry Market.

This market is held in the Exchange every Saturday. The price of fowls, geeſe, ducks, turkies, pigeons, &c. have riſen in proportion to other articles of food.

Fifteen years ago the average prices were

A gooſe from 1s. to 1s. 6d.

A turkey from 1s. 8d. to 2s.

A pair of fowls from 1s. to 1s. 3d.

A pair of ducks from 1s. 2d. to 1s. 3d.

A pair of chickens from 5d. to 6d.

A pair of pigeons from 4d. to 5d.

At preſent,

A gooſe from 2s. 6d. to 3s.

A turkey from 3s. 6d. to 4s.

A pair of fowls from 2s 6d. to 3s.

A pair of ducks from 2s. to 2s. 2d.

A pair of chickens from 1s. 4d. to 1s. 6d.

A pair of pigeons 6d.

Green Market.

The green market is held in the middle of the high-ſtreet, at the weſt end of the town-hall. It joins with the fiſh market. On the

Satur-

Saturdays, all the ſouth front of the town-hall is occupied with gardeners ſtalls. The culinary articles ſold, are cabbages, greens, potatoes, onions, leeks, peaſe, beans, carrots, turnips, radiſhes, artichokes, cellery, lettuces, &c. and a few cucumbers.

Fruits are ſold in the ſame ſtreet, and in various parts of the town. Few ſtrawberries are cultivated in Berwick or its vicinity. Theſe garden ſtuffs, above enumerated, are all good of their kind and cheap.

There are about 20 acres of ground occupied in gardens in Berwick and Tweedmouth.

Corn Market.

This market has been held at the head of Hidehill, and foot of the High-ſtreet, from time immemorial. Corn is ſold here by ſample; and ſuch is the probity of both ſeller and buyer, that few or no diſputes ever ariſe between them. The punctuality, as to payment, obſerved by the corn merchants, has long and juſtly entitled them to the higheſt confidence.

Eggs

Eggs and Butter Markets.

Eggs and butter are ſold on the Saturdays in the Exchange.

The prices of eggs vary from 5d. to 1s. a dozen; and butter from 8d. to 1s. 1d. *per* pound.

Market for Woolen Cloth.

The great demand there is in Berwick for coarſe woolen cloths and flannels have, for ſeveral years, induced many of the weavers and ſome of the ſhop-keepers, both in Berwick and Tweedmouth, to purchaſe thoſe articles from Morpeth, Jedburgh, Galaſhiels, Dalkeith, &c. which they again ſell in the high ſtreet upon the market day.

Beſides theſe markets, there is one held in the high ſtreet on the Saturday, for the ſale of Wooden utenſils, and one for new made cloths, &c. Hardware and old books are alſo expoſed to ſale on the High Street.

Wool uſed to be regularly ſold in the wool market at the proper ſeaſon of the year, but it is now moſtly given up.

SECTION III.

Average number of Cattle, &c. killed annually.

THE average calculation of the number of the different kinds of animals killed yearly in Berwick, is as follows:

Black cattle	830
Sheep	8320
Calves	500
Lambs	3200
Hogs	50

Swine ſent by the coopers from the port of Berwick to London, amount to about 4000 yearly.

CHAP.

CHAP. XIV.

Manners, &c.

SECTION I.

Manners and Cuſtoms.

IN genuine politeneſs and eaſy manners, Berwick is not inferior to any borough in the *Iſland* of the ſame ſize and extent. The more faſhionable part of the inhabitants are hoſpitable, without profuſion, and charitable, without oſtentation. This alſo applies in general to the other claſſes.

It may be obſerved that the young ladies of Berwick are entitled to the character of being graceful and affable in their manners, as alſo of being remarkable for humane and generous diſpoſitions.—Communicated by the Reverend Mr Rumney.

" Beſides

" Besides, I must do justice to the inhabi-
" tants. The lowest and poorest of the people
" are kindly treated by their superiors. The
" inhabitants of Berwick are not unfeeling
" churls, but may justly lay claim to the vir-
" tues of humanity as theirs. Fairly represent
" to them any case of distress, and convince
" them of the reality of it, I will undertake
" for them they will open their hearts and
" purses liberally to relieve it. I am fully
" authorised to assert this from my own ex-
" perience, in the numerous collections and
" subscriptions I have been concerned in for
" several years past, in times of dearth and
" scarcity, and occasions of sickness and dis-
" tress. Nay, our ladies too on many occa-
" sions dance to relieve the distrest; and tax
" their own pleasures to supply the poor with
" necessaries; many reduced families having
" been timely relieved by charity."

At balls and assemblies the ladies dress elegantly and in the fashion.

The burgesses were accused of having been

formerly ſhy to ſtrangers, but that is now no longer the caſe.

Candour requires we ſhould here ſtate, that the inhabitants of Berwick have generally obtained the character of being honourable in their tranſactions.

Both the church and meeting houſes are in general well attended; and few people are to be ſeen in the ſtreets during divine ſervice. Some of the unprincipled and diſſipated, however, frequent the ale houſes even on the Sundays.

Tradeſmen and artificers here are generally as ſober and induſtrious as in moſt other places. At the ſame time it muſt be confeſſed, that ſome of the operative burgeſſes, truſting in a great meaſure for the ſubſiſtence of their families to the gains ariſing from their meadows, ſtints, &c. but too often neglect their occupations by going from one ale houſe to another, without reflecting that they are taking the moſt effectual means to entail diſtreſs and miſery on themſelves and families; and this at no leſs an expence (independent

of

of pecuniary matters) than the violation of the ſacred duties of, perhaps, a huſband, a parent, and a member of ſociety.

The labouring poor are, upon the whole, very economic and frugal, and in general neatly dreſſed on Sunday.

In this, as well as in other boroughs, conteſts will ariſe, which, it were to be wiſhed, could be avoided, as it would tend to promote and inſure the pleaſures of an harmonious and enlivening ſociety. Such jarring intereſts, independent of their tendency to render the mind callous to the finer feelings, have been found in other places an unſurmountable obſtacle to improvement. Happy is it for a people where no grounds for ſuch diſcord exiſt. Thus unbiaſſed by oppoſite or political views, they would more naturally unite in opinion, and direct their combined efforts to ſuch objects of improvement as their local advantages would admit.

There is no claſs of people in domeſtic ſociety ſo eſſentially uſeful as ſervant-women; and when they diſcharge their duty faithfully,

fully, they are highly deſerving of encouragement. That there are many ſuch in Berwick we entertain no doubt; but, on the contrary, where ſervant girls, though conſcious of thoſe duties which they owe to their maſters and miſtreſſes, prove unjuſt or idle away their time, there is no character more contemptible. Theſe obſervations equally apply to men ſervants. Man or woman, who ape their ſuperiors in dreſs or expenſive living, never fail to excite the indignation and contempt not only of thoſe they imitate, but alſo of thoſe in ſituations below them.

Every man who is endowed with virtuous principles, and poſſeſſed of amiable diſpoſitions, will be ſolicitous to obtain and preſerve that character by which he may ſecure to himſelf the approbation of all good men. A man of this deſcription will be ſcrupulouſly anxious to obſerve, in his manner of living, ſuch a line of conduct as to entitle it to be viewed by mankind in the light of a meritorious mediocrity.

Were

Were men ſo prudent as rigidly to adopt this maxim, that train of innumerable evils which attends an oppoſite courſe of conduct might be prevented; and inſtead of ſuch perſons ſubjecting themſelves to the cenſure of the world, they would infallibly command the eſteem of all men of real worth.

Cuſtoms.

The ancient cuſtoms of *Eaſter* are ſtill obſerved here. They conſiſt of three ſucceſſive days of public diverſion and amuſement on the ramparts, and afford much entertainment to the children, ſervant girls, and young lads. They are alſo a ſource of amuſement to the parents and inhabitants at large, as well as to the people in the neighbourhood.

The firſt day (Eaſter Monday) is called the Children's Day. It is pleaſurable to ſee what a great number of lovely and finely dreſſed children make their appearance on this day. Being attended by a multitude of ſervants, they parade and run about for many hours,

hours, amufing themfelves in a variety of ways.

This charming groupe is joined more or lefs by the parents of the children, who, together with fuch as are attracted by curiofity, form, on fome occafions, a company of a great many hundreds. They affemble in greateft numbers behind the barracks, where the rampart is broadeft. The fruiterers attend in full difplay, as well as many itinerants in various purfuits. The whole together may be called a *fportive fair*.

A bell rings every morning at 5 o'clock (Sundays excepted) to warn tradefmen and labourers to prepare for work. One rings at nine in the morning and eight at night.

There is a common cryer who goes through the ftreets; his ordinary fee is 6d. for each cry.

There are four men, called *town waits*, who belong to the Borough. Their bufinefs is to walk before the Mayor, Recorder, and Juftices, playing on violins all the way to and from the church on Chriftmas day, the day of the

election

election of a Mayor, and on the 5th of November. They are alſo obliged to attend theſe gentlemen at their four public dinners. They have a very large blue cloak, faced with *gold lace*, and a big cocked hat, alſo laced with gold, which they wear on theſe occaſions. Theſe waits have a cuſtom of ſerenading the town. This nocturnal excurſion commences in November, and is continued till Candlemas. Theſe men are allowed to follow other occupations. Their fixed ſalary is 6l. among them yearly. There are two beadles belonging to the corporation, whoſe buſineſs is to attend the town-hall at the aſſizes, and to walk before the Mayor and Juſtices when the fair is proclaimed.

It is ſtill cuſtomary for the Corporation to ride the liberties of the borough.

The aſſociation of gardeners, which took place in 1796, have a proceſſion through the ſtreets yearly. It is accompanied with muſic; and, in the middle of the proceſſion, a number of men carry a large wreath of flowers. The different officers belonging to this inſtitution

tution wear their reſpective inſignia; and the whole ſociety dine together.

There are in Tweedmouth and Spittal annual feaſts celebrated among the inhabitants. Theſe feaſts conſiſt in each family entertaining their friends who aſſemble from all quarters.

SECTION II.

Public Amuſements.

THE public amuſements of this place are chiefly the aſſemblies and theatre.

The aſſemblies in honour of the King and Queen's birth days, and thoſe during Lamberton race week, are generally well attended by the more faſhionable part of our inhabitants, and are often crowded by ladies and gentlemen from the country.

The reſt of our aſſemblies are, upon the whole, but thinly attended, which, we preſume, may be chiefly aſcribed to that bane of concord, *political contention.*

' *Music has charms to soothe the savage breast,* ' *to soften rocks and bend the knotted oak.*' But alas! how unavailing would even the masterly strokes of a Handel, nay, even the inimitable melody of the nightingale, be in cheering up the countenances of rival politicians, whether they meet in the convivial circle, or in the enlivening dance; and, though in the midst of female beauty and elegance, the *zest* of such enjoyments: The uninterruption of whose happiness has ever been held sacred by all men who have justly laid claim to the envied accomplishments of genuine politeness.

That dæmon of discord, *political contention*, but too often extends to kingdoms and to empires, and, in its destructive consequences, kindles the flames of war, nation against nation; and, when occurring in a single state, excites intestine commotions, which, if not wisely and timely suppressed, plunges its heedless inhabitants into all the horrors of civil war; sweeping before it, with irresistable fury, every trace of virtue and humanity, and threatening the extirpation of the human race.

Theatrical performances have occaſionally been exhibited in Berwick for a great number of years paſt, ſometimes in the Town Hall, and ſometimes in a houſe in Golden Square. To remedy this inconvenience, however, about five years ago an elegant Theatre was erected in Hidehill, by Mr Kemble, manager of the Theatre Royal, Edinburgh,

SEC.

SECTION III.

Societies and Clubs.

THERE are nine or ten aſſociations in Berwick, called *Benefit Societies*. As the nature of theſe inſtitutions is generally known, it is unneceſſary to give a minute deſcription of them here. It is worthy of remark, however, that in ſome of theſe ſocieties, no converſation or diſpute, regarding the conſtitution of Great Britain, is allówed; and that whoever ſpeaks diſreſpectfully of his country is liable to a fine.

They have alſo ſeveral clauſes enjoining, under certain pecuniary fines, a regular attendance on public worſhip.

There are two maſon lodges in Berwick, and one in Tweedmouth.

SECTION IV.

Inns.

THERE are 59 public houſes in Berwick. The number of principal inns is three, viz. the *Red Lion*, the *King's Arms*, and the *Hen* and *Chickens*.

The Red Lion is ſituated near the Main Guard, in the north ſide of the High Street. It is a very large and commodious inn, and at preſent is occupied by Mr William Denovan. It had ſeveral great additions made to it ſome years ago by the proprietor, the late Mr George Hall. The principal of which are, 13 bed-rooms, a coffee and aſſembly room. Theſe bed-rooms are well aired and lighted.

The coffee room is 49 feet in length, 16 in breadth, and 11 feet in height.

The aſſembly room is very elegant. It meaſures 55 feet in length, 25 in breadth, and 20 feet in height. It is furniſhed with three large cryſtal chandeliers and ſix ſmaller ones.

Two

Two daily London papers, an Edinburgh paper three times a week, and the Newcaſtle Weekly Hue and Cry, are taken in at the coffee room, the expence of which is defrayed by an yearly ſubſcription.

There are ſtabling at this inn for 66 horſes, and moſt of the ſtables are ſupplied with water pipes.

A daily coach runs from this inn in its turn, called the High Flyer.—Has four horſes, and goes between London and Edinburgh. It ſtarted in March 1798.

Poſt chaiſes are kept at this inn.

The King's Arms inn is ſituated about the middle of Hidehill. The buildings are of hewn ſtone, and very ſtrong. The inn is commodious; and, from its being built on the top of a bank, enjoys a free circulation of air. The mail coach has always ſtopped here; and it is one of the ſtages where a ſpare coach is kept in readineſs. This houſe is alſo connected with the *High Flyer*. The preſent land-

lord

lord of the King's Arms is Mr George Dixon. Chaises are kept at this inn.

The Hen and Chickens is at the foot of Sandgate, near the Shore Gate. It is a very substantial stone building, consisting of three stories in height, and has many commodious apartments. It has a coffee room upon a similar plan with that of the Red Lion.

The present landlord is Mr Robert Johnson.

A coach called the Telegraph ran from this house from March 1798 to March 1799. The proprietors of this coach, however, and those of the High Flyer joined together in carrying on the latter, but dropped the former.

CHAP.

CHAP. XV.

Country part of the Diſtrict.

SECTION I.

Preſent Agricultural State of the Country Diſtrict.

IN Chapter I. Section V. it was ſtated, that ſeveral ſmall eſtates lie within the liberties of the Borough. The lands belonging to the corporation, however, are of great extent, as noticed in Chap. IV. Sect. I. It was alſo there ſtated, that the greater part of them were let upon leaſes, and part of the grounds were parcelled out into ſeparate allotments poſſeſſed by the freemen.

Little

Little attention was beſtowed upon the landed property of the Borough till about 30 years ago, when moſt of the grounds were incloſed and ſubdivided. Before that period, the number of meadows and ſtints were ſo great, and the culture of the ſoil ſo much neglected, that their value was very inconſiderable, and, on ſome occaſions, might have been purchaſed for a mere trifle. The modes of management, which of late years have been followed by thoſe who have the farms in leaſe, deſerve attention.

The following courſes conſtitute the general ſyſtem of huſbandry practiſed in the pariſh:

1. Graſs land or Lee.	4. Wheat.
2. Oats.	5. Turnip.
3. Potatoes.	6. Barley & graſs ſeed.

OR

1. Lee.	5. Clover, once, ſometimes twice, cut.
2. Oats.	
3. Turnip or potatoes.	6. Wheat.
4. Wheat or barley & graſs ſeeds.	7. Beans.
	8. Barley & graſs ſeeds.

OR

OR

1. Lee.	4. Wheat.
2. Oats.	5. Beans or peafe, or barley with grafs feeds.
3. Potatoes or turnip.	

The fubjoined courfe is propofed to be made trial of by one farmer in the Borough.

1. Fallow.	5. Wheat.
2. Wheat, with grafs feeds.	6. Turnip or potatoes.
3. Clover.	7. Barley & grafs feeds, or Wheat and grafs feeds.
4. Drilled Beans.	

We only know of one farmer who takes two white crops after grafs. This perfon keeps one third of his farm in grafs and two thirds in tillage.

SECTION II.

Nature of the Soil.

EXCEPTING a few ſmall farms of muiry ground, which, notwithſtanding, are very improveable, all the lands are fertile. Some of them are of a very ſtrong rich deep loam. Upon the whole, the greater part of the lands of the pariſh are of a fine light loam, well adapted to the cultivation of grain, graſs, and turnip.

SECTION III.

Manures.

THE manures generally employed here, are ſtable, cow, and ſtreet dung, together with lime. Soot is alſo uſed, and is very effective.

SEC-

SECTION IV.

Produce.

THE produce of the lands within this parifh is wheat, barley, oats, beans, and peafe, together with potatoes, hay, and clover.

There are great quantities of potatoes raifed here. In the year 1796 about 780 acres were planted. A perfon, who has paid great attention to this branch of hufbandry, calculated, that each acre, on an average, would produce about 120 heaped Winchefter bufhels, or five tons, of 20 cwt. each ton: So that the whole would amount to about 93,600 bufhels, or 3900 tons. The quantity fent from this port annually to London and Yorkfhire, for feed, is very great. Eleven veffels, loaded with potatoes, have been known to have failed in one tide.

Seven or eight different kinds of this invaluable root are reared in this diftrict.—

From

From 22 to 25 bolls per acre is the average produce; but there have been inſtances of 40 and 50 having been produced per acre.

SECTION V.

Rent.

THE grounds vary in rent from 20s. to 4l. 10s. per acre.

An incloſure, called the Cow Cloſe, conſiſting of an 103 acres, was lately let out into four parcels. The rent of the whole amounts to 442l. yearly. Adjoining to this field, there is a ſmall incloſure of about five acres let at 42l. yearly.

SECTION VI.

Mills.

THERE are ſeven flour mills, four gray ſtone mills, and four mills for making barley in the pariſh.

SECTION VII.

Townſhip of Tweedmouth, including Spittal, ſouth of Tweed.

THE lands of the Townſhip of Tweedmouth, which includes Spittal, are divided into in-field and out-field. The in-field amounts to 450, and the out-field, or common, nearly to 800, acres.

The

The in-field lands are at preſent occupied by eight tenants and four other perſons who have from two to four acres each.

The mode of agriculture adopted here by the farmers is as follows:

They generally keep one-third of their farms in fallow, or rather in turnips or potatoes. After potatoes they ſow wheat in autumn, and after turnips wheat in ſpring. After wheat, if the ground is in good condition, they plant beans in drills without manure. After beans they manure and ſow wheat again, after which, without manure, barley is ſown along with graſs ſeeds.

Tweedmouth, ſituated at the ſouth end of Berwick Bridge, is a large irregular built village. It is famous for the aſſembly of Barons held in it in the fourth year of the reign of King Edward I. Hutchinſon ſays, an ancient hoſpital, dedicated to St Bartholomew, ſtood here. It has a neat church, pleaſantly ſituated on the ſide of the Tweed.

It has alſo a meeting houſe on the ſame footing as the High and Low Meeting Houſes of

Berwick.

Berwick. The preſent incumbent is the Reverend William Hall.

A Sunday's ſchool was eſtabliſhed here ſome years ago, to which great attention has been given. Tweedmouth does not appear to be ſo healthy as Berwick. This may be aſcribed to its great expoſure to the northerly and north-eaſt winds, together with the want of a ſtrict police, by which the ſtreets, lanes, and front of the houſes, are not kept dry and clean. Were proper attention beſtowed upon ſuch an important matter as this, Tweedmouth would be a very pleaſant and a much more healthy place to live in than it is at preſent.

Several houſes have, of late years, been built, which gives the village a greater degree of neatneſs than it had before, and ſhows its improving ſtate. There are ſeveral ſprings in the lands of this townſhip, ſome of which are capable of driving machinery; one of theſe is St Cuthbert's well, ſituated a little beyond the eaſt end of the village.

Spittal is ſituated about a mile eaſt from Tweedmouth, cloſe by the ſea and the mouth

of

of the river. It has a very wide ſtreet and a very narrow one. Excepting ſome houſes which have been built of late years, the buildings of this populous village are intolerably bad, which frequently muſt become a ſource of many diſeaſes to its inhabitants; and which is but ill ſuited to the great number of people who reſort to it in ſummer for the mineral water * as well as for ſea bathing.

Spittal has one meeting houſe on the ſame footing as the meeting houſe of Tweedmouth.

The preſent incumbent is the Reverend Henry Cant.

SEC-

* The properties of this mineral water will be deſcribed below.

SECTION VIII.

Soil, Manures, Produce, Rent.

THE ſoil of the in-field land of the townſhip is a deep rich loam.

Barley lands get three ploughings, and, if very foul, four, but this is ſeldom requiſite.

The manures moſtly employed are horſe and cow dung.

The lands produce very weighty crops, eſpecially the fields which lie along the ſide of the river, and the grain is of an exceedingly good quality.

Potatoes are raiſed here in great quantities. The cottagers pay from 5l. 10s. to 6l. 10s. per acre beſides tythe.

The rent of the lands is about two guineas an acre beſides tythe.

The Common being now divided, that perplexing, unnatural, and oppreſſive privilege or inter-common is annihilated; and every perſon who is intereſted in the inſtitution of equable laws and the cauſe of virtue—in perſonal ſafety and ſecurity of property, muſt rejoice, that, by the diviſion of this Common, a lurking place is cut off from the profligate and abandoned.

CHAP.

CHAP. XVI.

Miſcellaneous Obſervations.

1. *Antiquities.*

THE remains of the Old Caſtle conſtitute a very ſtriking piece of antiquity. They are ſituated about 400 yards north by weſt from the Scotch Gate, on the north banks of the Tweed.

We can find no account in hiſtory of this ancient fortreſs which points out the time of its building. As it would appear to have been almoſt inacceſſible, it muſt have been nearly impregnable. Its ſurrounding ſcenery has already been deſcribed: Few of its buildings remain. The ſcattered fragments of them, and

and confuſed heaps of ſtones which are every where to be ſeen, evince the high antiquity of this once important fortreſs, which, for upwards of a century, has been mouldering under the wrath of time.

The Bell Tower, which ſtands about 400 yards north by eaſt from the Caſtle, is another monument of antiquity, and may be conſidered as having been coeval with the Caſtle, as the uſe of the Tower was for diſcovering an enemy either at ſea or land. The ringing of the bell was the ſignal given at the Tower on the approach of an enemy. What remains of this ruin is four ſtories in height. The ground where it is ſituated is a great deal higher than the town; and it is built on the old wall, commanding a moſt extenſive proſpect of the German Ocean and adjacent country.

Its figure is a pentagon. According to tradition, there was a covered way between the Tower and the Caſtle.

There are the remains of a ſquare fort or out-work in the Magdalane Fields, upon the top of the ſea banks, which communicated

with

with the north eaſt gate of the town by a covered way. The excavation is ſtill to be ſeen.

There are diſtinct traces of camps on the top of Hallydown Hill.

Queen Elizabeth's Pier, which is deſcribed above, conſtitutes an antiquity of great importance, and which will be noticed again in a ſubſequent part of this work.

Some years ago, in digging for a foundation for a reſervoir of water, lately built between Scotch Gate and the foot of Caſtle Gate, a number of human ſkeletons were found; accordingly it is ſuppoſed to have been the burying ground belonging to the church which Queen Mary ordered to be taken down for the repairing of the walls.

About 32 years ago, in digging at the foot of the Weſtern Lane, ſome remains of Gothic windows and arches were found.

2. *Antiques found.*

In digging into the banks at Weſtern Lane, about 32 years ago, a gold coin, of one of the Edwards

Edwards (ſuppoſed to be Edward the third) was found there; it was about the breadth of half-a-crown, but thin, the gold ſoft and pliant.

A gentleman in this town has in his poſſeſſion two balls, about the ſize of a five or ſix pounder. The one was dug out of the bank of the Caſtle Hill, about half-a-mile above the Old Caſtle, and has probably been ſhot from it; the other was dug out of the north bank of the Tweed, oppoſite to Norham Caſtle. They are both of ſtone, caſed with lead, the lead worn off on one part. This gentleman has alſo a coin of Henry the VIII. found in the Old Caſtle, about the ſize of a ſhilling.

There is in the poſſeſſion of Mr Brown, coach-maker here, three pieces of timber work, which, when joined together, repreſent a *hero* holding a ſcepter in his right hand, with his left arm hanging over the neck of the figure of a horſe, whoſe head projects from below that arm. They were found among

ſome

ſome lumber in the Old Town-Houſe, about the time it was taken down; and are ſuppoſed to have been affixed to the ſtern of one of the veſſels compoſing the Spaniſh Armada, and which had been driven aſhore at that ever memorable epoch.

3. *Natural Curioſities.*

THE natural curioſities of Berwick are but few; one of them however is of importance; and it is, that quickſilver, in a pure ſtate, has been found at two different periods in digging for a cellar and the foundation of a houſe in Hide Hill. It will be more particularly deſcribed under the article *mines*.

About two miles to the north of Berwick, under a very ſteep and tremenduous rocky ſhore, there is a large cave, opening to the ſea, acceſſible at low water or half ebb, called the Pigeons Cave. It has been excavated by the waves of the ſea, and appears capable of holding 1000 men.

There

There are other two caves nearer the town; one of them is called the Burgeſſes Cove; and the other the Singing Cove.

4. *Quarries.*

THERE are ſeven free ſtone quarries at Newmills, within the liberties, belonging to the Corporation, five of which are at preſent let for 6l. 16s. 6d. And ſix at Tweedmouth, let for 60l. 10s.

Rough ſtones ſell at theſe quarries for 8d. the double cart load.

5. *Mines and Minerals.*

THOUGH there are no working mines, yet there is one metal and three minerals within the liberties of Berwick.

1. Pure quickſilver has been repeatedly found in conſiderable quantities in Hidehill.

We ſubjoin the following communication from The Reverend Mr Rumney on that ſubject.

" About

" About 30 years ago, in digging for a foundation and a cellar within a few yards of the Cat Well in Hidehill, great quantities of quickſilver were found mixed with the ſtiff earth or clay which was dug out. Several cart loads of this clay were carried to the ſhore before it was known to be ſo mixed with the quickſilver; and this ſtratum of clay and quickſilver extended for ſome yards, as far as the proprietor had occaſion to dig. And four or five years ago, the proprietor of the houſe adjoining up the hill found the ſame ſtratum, I am credibly informed. I myſelf took up a piece of the clay, about the ſize of an egg, and, upon breaking it in two, the quickſilver ſparkled and rolled out in little globules; and that ſmall piece of clay produced as much pure quickſilver, to the beſt of my recollection, as would have filled a tea ſpoon. The query is, How came it there? I cannot conceive that any perſon could have had ſuch a quantity in his poſſeſſion, and that it had been ſpilled; nor, if it had been ſpilled, that it could have inſinuated itſelf ſo equally in ſuch ſmall globules throughout an extent, and to ſuch depth, of a ſtiff earth or clay; but am inclined to believe, as many others do, that there is ſome ſort of mine of that metal in that neighbourhood."

Several perſons who gathered ſome of the quickſilver have informed us that the metal was very uniformly mixed with the clay, and in great abundance.

Iron ſtone has been found in different parts of the coaſt, within the liberties of Berwick, and ſome of it is to be ſeen in the vicinity of the Old Caſtle. This ore, however, is not in ſuch abundance here as to render it an object of attention.

A mineral has been lately diſcovered in the banks ſituated near the Old Caſtle, the property of Mrs Aſkew of Goſwick.

Profeſſor Hope, of the Univerſity of Edinburgh, has had the goodneſs to analyze this mineral; the reſult of which was, that it contained $\frac{45}{100}$ of the oxyde of iron, and $\frac{55}{100}$ of quartſy particle. The latter, being of a ſilicious nature, might be uſeful in the making of glaſs,

glaſs, but unleſs the mineral could be eaſily procured, in great quantities, it would not be valuable. The ſtratum is about nine inches thick.

Very lately a mineral was diſcovered upon the ſea ſhore, at the Magdalen Fields, the property of Lord Liſburn. Upon analyzing this, the above mentioned Profeſſor Hope found that it contained nothing but iron and ſulphur.

It is ſuppoſed that copper may be found in the Bank Alley. Three years ago, in the making of an excavation in this bank for the building an ice houſe, a ſtratum of earth was found which appeared to contain a great deal of copper. A large lump of the earthy clay was ſhown to a perſon who had ſeen copper ore; and, upon examining it, he was of opinion that it contained a conſiderable quantity of that metal. What corroborates this is, that there is a ſpring in the neighbourhood of the Bank Alley known by the name of the Cat Well, and which, as will be ſeen in the ſubſequent article, is ſtrongly impregnated with copper.

6. *Mineral*

6. *Mineral Springs.*

THERE is one mineral ſpring in Berwick and another at Spittal.

The former is ſituated near to the middle of Hidehill. It is called the *Cat Well.*

We lately analyzed this water, and found it contained fixed air, calcareous earth, ſulphuric acid combined with lime, and, laſtly, a conſiderable proportion of copper. It is much reſorted to by people with tender eyes; and, as we are informed, it has been found uſeful in ſcorbutic and ſtomach complaints.

Spittal mineral well, about half a mile from the village of that name, is a very ſtrong ſpring, iſſuing from the face of a riſing piece of mooriſh ground.

Upon analyſing this water, it contained fixed air, iron, and a ſmall proportion of ſulphuric acid. It has been found particularly beneficial in all thoſe complaints where chalybeates and other tonics are proper to be taken. It has for many years been greatly reſorted to by perſons of various deſcriptions from all parts of the country, particu-

larly

larly from the neighbourhood of Hawick. The opportunity of fea bathing at Spittal is another great inducement to perfons to refort to the well.

No doubt can be entertained of the medicinal virtues of this mineral water. There are a great many well attefted cafes where it has effected a complete recovery. In fuch requeft, indeed, is this water held, that, in the fummer feafon, many who have come to drink it have been obliged to go home again for want of lodgings.

7. *Water.*

BERWICK is very amply fupplied with water of an excellent quality.

It has two fources. The one in the New Clofe, near Letham-fhank; the other in Newfarm Moor, weft by north. After being joined by fmaller fprings, they meet at the fouth end of the Cow Clofe, and run in a ftone conduit for about a quarter of a mile, when they enter wooden pipes, and difcharge themfelves into the refervoir at the foot of Caftlegate. The length of the wooden pipes is about half a mile.

8. *Fuel.*

FEW towns are fo well fupplied with this moft ufeful article as Berwick.

There is one coal-hill which belongs to the Corporation, fituated on Sunnyfide Hill, only about a mile fouth from Tweedmouth.

There are three pits at Coldfide, about two miles fouth from Tweedmouth; three pits at Morton, three miles diftant from Berwick; and one at a place called the Corner, about half a mile farther from the town than Morton colliery is. Some people, however, occafionally purchafe coals from *Lucker*, eight miles from Berwick. Thefe are fine fplint ones and burn with a vivid light.

It is curious, that while the prices of coals have been rifing for fome years paft here, their meafure has in proportion decreafed, that is, the meafure is not heaped as formerly. The prefent prices are, great coal 4d. per boll,

great

great and ſmall mixed 3d. per boll. The ſplint coal, at Morton, $4\frac{1}{2}$d. per boll, ſmall 2d. per boll, and great and ſmall mixed 3d. per boll.

A boll of theſe coals, upon an average, is ſuppoſed to weigh 10 ſtones; five bolls then, which is the uſual quantity of a one horſe cart load, will weigh about ſix cwt. The price's now paid for ſuch a load is 2s. 9d. and 3s. formerly 2s. and 2s. 6d. were the prices.

Except the ſplint coal at Morton and Lucker, all the other ſeams of coal are of that kind called *culm*.

It would be fortunate for the town were the farmers in the neighbourhood of theſe coal-hills, like the farmers in the vicinity of Edinburgh, to drive coals to Berwick. The farmers would derive a double advantage by it, as their carts might return loaded with dung, which is the practice in the place above alluded to; and the inhabitants of the borough, who keep no carts, would not be ſo liable to peculation in this coſtly article as they are

are at present. The observation would not have been made, were we not assured, from undoubted authority, that this practice is but too generally followed.

9. *Price of Labour.*

ABOUT twelve years ago labouring men were paid one shilling per day.

At present one shilling and sixpence is paid both in summer and winter.

Ditches five feet wide and three feet deep 10d. per rood.

Dyke and batter 2s. per rood.

Drains three feet wide and two and a half deep 8d. per rood.

Women reapers in 1797 2s. *per diem.*

Men ditto in ditto 2s. 8d. some 3s.

Potatoe hoers 1s. per day.

Mowing hay 2s. 6d. per day, or 3s. and 3s. 6d. per acre.

A single horse cart, leading stones, 3s. per day. Double ditto 7s. Summer and winter the yoking generally eight hours.

The

The wages of mechanics have riſen greatly within theſe few years. For inſtance, journeymen cabinet-makers, carpenters, and maſons, are paid twelve ſhillings weekly.

CHAP. XVII.

A Diſſertation on thoſe Sciences and particular Subjects which appear to be moſt intimately connected with the improvement and growing riches of a Country, and the advancement of the human mind.

THIS work having for its object the promoting and enſuring the general and permanent good of man, it is apprehended that a ſlight diſcuſſion of thoſe branches of knowledge with which his happineſs and proſperity are more materially connected, will not be deemed improper here.

General Obſervations.

It will readily be admitted, that the whole of the arts and ſciences, are more or leſs connected with the improvement and increaſing proſperity of a country. That ſome of the arts

arts and ſciences are more immediately connected with them than others; and that whatever can promote and advance their improvement muſt tend to meliorate the condition of man. Hence he will be enabled to conduct himſelf through life with additional eaſe, comfort, and reſpectability, and will have it more in his power to proſecute the ſtudy of general ſcience. This may heighten the chance of diſcovery, and finally afford him a fairer opportunity of gratifying every humane and virtuous feeling that can enoble and dignify the human character.

The inveſtigation of the following ſubjects appear to be thoſe moſt compatible with the objects had in view, viz.

1. Culture of the earth.
2. Commerce and manufactures.
3. Philoſophy.
4. Law.
5. Medicine.
6. Theology.

Culture

Culture of the Earth.

The obſervations which have been made on agriculture under the head of preliminaries, renders it unneceſſary to add much more here on that ſubject.

It is univerſally acknowledged, that of all the arts which have excited the attention or called forth the exertions of mankind, none have hitherto been diſcovered which are ſo truly valuable, and ſo generally uſeful as agriculture. This appears not only from its rewarding the ſkill and induſtry of the individual, but from its being the ſureſt means of exalting the proſperity of a nation.

As the arts of cultivation increaſed among the Athenians, which are ſaid to have been firſt taught them by *Triptolemus*, and the bleſſings they yielded became generally experienced, the maſs of the people ſoon preferred them to the ravages of war or the cruel depredations of ſavage life. Accordingly we find, that the Athenian kings, conſidering it more glorious to govern a ſmall kingdom by wiſe laws than to extend their dominions by foreign

foreign conquests, withdrew their subjects from the field of battle, and chiefly employed them in cultivating the soil. Thus, by unremitted application, in a short time they reduced agriculture to an art.

In the empire of *China*, agriculture is considered as the most honourable of all professions. Hence the husbandman enjoys many distinguished privileges over the merchant and mechanic.

In that most populous empire *, the tillage of the earth is not only encouraged by law, but also by the example of the emperor, who annually tills the earth with his own hands. The sovereign names 12 of the most illustrious persons in his court to accompany him, and to hold

* M. Grosier, from an accurate investigation of some Chinese records respecting the number of persons liable to taxation throughout the empire, has showed that it cannot be less than 200 millions; but in Sir George Staunton's account of the late embassy to China, the population of the empire is stated to be three hundred and thirty-three millions of persons.

hold the plough after he has performed his part of the ceremony. Among theſe are always three princes of the blood. When the ploughing is finiſhed, the emperor throws the ſeeds into the furrows.

Previous to this ſolemnity, a grand feſtival is celebrated, and a ſacrifice offered up to Chang-ti; (the ſupreme God) after which the emperor and his attendants prepare themſelves by three days faſting and continence. The whole is conducted with the greateſt pomp and magnificence.

Xenophon obſerves that agriculture is the nurſing mother of the arts: For, ſays he, "Where agriculture ſucceeds proſperouſly, "there the arts thrive; but where the earth "neceſſarily lies uncultivated, there the other "arts are deſtroyed."

The ancient Romans eſteemed agriculture ſo honourable an employment, that the moſt illuſtrious ſenators of the empire, in the interval of public concerns, applied themſelves to this profeſſion; and ſuch was the ſimplicity of thoſe ages, that they aſſumed no appearance of of magnificence and ſplendor, or of majeſty, but when they appeared in public. At their return from the toils of war, the taking of cities and the ſubduing of hoſtile nations, their greateſt generals were impatient till they were again employed in the cultivation of the fields.

The enriching effects of agricultural purſuits were never ſo eminently diſplayed in Great Britain as they are at this eventful æra. A modern farmer of abilities, and who gives proper attention to his profeſſion, lives, at preſent, much better than gentlemen of fortune did fifty years ago. If he conducts himſelf with propriety in private life, his company is courted by his landlord as well as by the neighbouring gentry. He not only enjoys the conveniencies, but even the luxuries of life. He can afford to partake of the ſports of the field as well as the amuſements of the town; and when his country is threatened to be invaded by a foreign foe, he and his ſons, at their own expence, voluntarily equip themſelves in military array, and mounting their

trusty

trusty steeds, fully caparisoned, sally forth in defence of their native land.

Besides, there are many parishes in Great Britain in which one or more farmers of landed property are to be found, some of them to a very considerable extent. It is no uncommon thing to meet with farmers possessing from ten to thirty thousand pounds and upwards; some of whom keep their carriage, and live in a stile of magnificence when compared to that in which their fathers lived, even though the necessaries of life are at present treble to what they were in those times.

Having, in the preliminaries to this work, recommended the study of chemistry as essential to the formation of a scientific system of agriculture, we conceive it behoves us here more fully to point out the great importance of that branch of science; and this, it is presumed, will appear evident from the following facts:

1. Every kind of soil is a chemical composition.

2. That there are four primitive earths, each of which have distinct chemical properties, and

and every ſoil conſiſts of two or more of theſe elementary parts combined in different proportions.

3. That a certain proportion of theſe primitive earths combined together conſtitutes the richeſt of all ſoils.

4. That every ſoil poſſeſſes more or leſs a native food for the growth of plants.

5. That the native nouriſhment of a ſoil may be augmented by proper manure unleſs it be ſaturated.

6. That the growth of every kind of grain diminiſhes more or leſs the food contained in any ſoil—the extent of which may be aſcertained by a chemical proceſs.

7. That the putrefactive proceſs in a great quantity of manure may be ſo powerful as to overcome the vital powers or deſtroy the organization of plants. Hence the danger of ſaturation.

8. By the powers of chemiſtry, it has been diſcovered, that water and air impregnated with putrid effluvia from animal and vegetable

organized ſubſtances, conſtitutes the principal nouriſhment of plants.

The farmer who is maſter of this part of chemiſtry will, 1ſt, be enabled to aſcertain the compoſition of the various ſoils, as well as the different kinds of manures which are beſt adapted to particular ſoils, and in what proportions they ſhould be employed, as has been obſerved above.

2. He will be able to diſcriminate the primitive earths and their chemical properties, &c.

3. He will have it in his power to determine what ſoils are beſt adapted to particular kinds of grain, as noticed elſewhere.

4. He will diſcover the degree of nouriſhment contained in a given quantity of ſoil before ſowing.

5. By analyſing the different ſoils, after the crops are removed from the ground, he will aſcertain the quantity of manure that will be requiſite to make up the deficiency.

6. He will be aware not to ſaturate the ſoil, while, on the other hand, he will perceive the impropriety of impoveriſhing his lands by ex-

hauſting

hausting crops or the want of a sufficicncy of suitable manure.

Were gentlemen of landed property and farmers to conduct experiments of this nature with accuracy, they might, independent of those advantages already enumerated, derive many others. There are two for instance which merit attention. The first is, gentlemen, in offering their farms in lease, would, by analysing the soils, be better enabled to judge of their value; and, on the other hand, were farmers permitted to have recourse to the same source of ascertaining the nature and richness of the soils, they would know what rent they might offer with safety.

The 2d. is, a great many controversies and law suits might often be prevented between landlords and tenants, especially at the latter end of leases: Moreover, were such a system adopted, it would not only render gentlemen and farmers expert chemists, but, by enriching both, it might be productive of great national advantages. For whatever may be said of this scheme, it will be admitted, by the candid

did and intelligent reader, that the ſcience of farming is ſtill in its infancy.

In addition to chemiſtry, a knowledge of botany and meteorology would, for obvious cauſes, be highly advantageous to the practical farmer.

To obviate the inconveniency of the preſent farmers of Great Britain attending a college, we would propoſe that they ſhould invite perſons, properly qualified, to go from one diſtrict to another, to teach thoſe doctrines of chemiſtry which chiefly relate to agriculture; and the lecturer ſhould not only deliver the theory, but ought alſo to ſhow the method of analyſing the various ſoils and manures.

It would be a wiſe inſtitution were chemiſtry to be taught in this manner in every conſiderable inland town.

The analyſing of the ſoils, manures, &c. might be a profitable branch to the apothecary or druggiſt.

What a pity that the unbounded ambition and pride of man ſhould ſquander away upon

war,

war, that national wealth which might be appropriated to the cultivation of the arts and ſciences!

After having ſaid ſo much of the ſchools, which relate to agriculture, we ſubjoin the following quotation to ſhow the great advantages to be derived from the field. It is extracted from Mr John Johnſton's Communications to the Board of Agriculture reſpecting the celebrated Mr Elkington's moſt approved mode of draining land.

" In the year 1763, Mr Elkington was left by his father the poſſeſſion of a farm called Princethorp, in the pariſh of Stretton upon Dunſmore and county of Warwick. The ſoil of this farm was very poor, and in many places ſo extremely wet, that it had been the cauſe of rotting ſeveral hundred ſheep, which was the firſt means that determined him, if poſſible, to drain it, which he began to do in 1764. The field in which he began was of a wet clay ſoil, rendered almoſt a ſwamp (and indeed in ſome places a ſhaking bog) by the ſprings iſſuing from a bank of gravel and ſand adjoining it, and overflowing the ſurface of the clay.

clay. In order to drain this field, he cut a trench about four or five feet deep, a little below the upper ſide of the bog, or where the wetneſs began to make its appearance; and after proceeding with it ſo far in this direction and its depth, he found it did not reach THE MAIN BODY OF SUBJACENT WATER, from whence the evil proceeded. On diſcovering this, Mr Elkington was at a loſs how to proceed. At this time, while he was conſidering what was next to be done, one of his ſervants accidentally came to the field where the drain was making with an iron crow or bar, which the farmers in that country uſe in making holes for fixing their ſheep hurdles. Mr Elkington having a ſuſpicion that his drain was not deep enough, and a deſire to know what kind of ſtrata lay under the bottom of it, took the iron bar from the ſervant, and after having forced it down about four feet below the bottom of the trench, on pulling it out, to his aſtoniſhment, a great quantity of water burſt up through the hole he had thus made and ran down the drain. This at once led him

to

to the knowledge of wetneſs being often produced by water confined farther below the ſurface of the ground than it was poſſible for the uſual depth of drains to reach, and induced him to apply an auger as a proper inſtrument in ſuch caſes. Thus did the diſcovery originate from chance, the parent of many other uſeful arts! In this manner he not only accompliſhed the drainage of this field, which ſoon rendered it completely ſound, but likewiſe all the other wet ground on his farm."

Commerce and Manufactures.

In this æra, when philoſophy has reared its head and diſpelled thoſe clouds of ignorance which for ages had obſcured the eye of reaſon, man, in contemplating the univerſe, finds himſelf ſurrounded with objects of admiration and grandeur, which irreſiſtibly impreſs him with a ſenſe of the infinite wiſdom and beneficence of the Supreme Intelligence.

Among the innumerable beauties ſcattered over the face of nature, that of the earths being divided into ſea and land, and into conti-

nents

nents and iſlands, conſtitutes one of the firſt magnitude, and is of the utmoſt conſequence to mankind in reſpect to their happineſs, power, and grandeur.

Had the whole of the habitable globe been formed into one continent, the miſeries incident to the human race would have been infinitely greater than in its preſent interſected ſtate. For, in the firſt place, all the interior parts, eſpecially thoſe ſituatted in the hotter regions, would ſeldom or never have been free from contagions and other diſtempers, whereby the cultivation of the ſoil, and the carrying on of manufactures and other employments, would have been attended with the greateſt diſadvantages, and often abandoned altogether.

2. That jealouſy which naturally would have ſubſiſted between the different kingdoms compoſing this vaſt continent, together with many other cauſes, would have rendered it abſolutely neceſſary for each ſeparate ſtate to keep a large military force in continual pay.

Alliances

Alliances muſt have been frequently formed and as often violated, and as there could not have been any foreign nation to preſerve the equilibrium of power, the flames of war would frequently have burſt forth in all quarters, carrying in its train, miſery, devaſtation, and death.

The numerous and important advantages of an inſular ſituation compared with thoſe of a continent are obvious. The following ſeem to claim ſome notice here.

1. The vapours from the ſea which ſurround iſlands, by abating the violence of heat and moderating the rigour of cold, render them in general much more healthy, and conſequently much more favourable to vegetation than any diſtrict of a large continent in the ſame degree of latitude. There is a remarkable inſtance of this in the three iſlands of *Hieres* oppoſite to Toulon. Here the fruits of France and Italy arrive at the greateſt perfection, and, what is ſtill more curious, all the medicinal herbs of Italy, Greece, and Egypt, grow wild. The climate too is

ſingularly temperate and exquiſitely pleaſant in all ſeaſons.

2. It is likewiſe obſervable that there is a greater variety of ſoil, and a greater degree of fertility in iſlands in general than on continents. This is ſuppoſed to ariſe principally from the mildneſs of the atmoſphere, from frequent ſhowers, and by both being conſtantly impregnated with the food of plants.

3. The acceſſibility of an iſland is peculiarly advantageous; for, by its being open all around, it receives ſupplies from all quarters, whilſt, at the ſame time, it eaſily admits of exporting from every point its manufactures and other articles of trade.

4. Thoſe parts of an iſland ſituated on oppoſite ſides of it may be conſidered as two diſtinct countries, each deriving reciprocal advantages from one another by commerce and manufactures, whilſt the intermediate country, or at leaſt a great part of it, is much benefited by both.

5. That active and enterpriſing ſpirit which characteriſes iſlanders, chiefly flows from this, that if the winds are contrary on one ſide they

are favourable on the other; and the ſea being the common track to both coaſts, the ocean is continually ploughed by veſſels, ſome outward and others homeward bound.

6. One of the moſt ſtriking and important features of an iſland is that frontier which it preſents all around it, and which ſubſiſts for ever without repair. And whilſt it preſents the moſt effectual barrier to the invading foe, it alſo, from its fiſheries, contributes moſt eſſentially to the ſubſiſtence of its inhabitants as well as to the promotion of its commerce.

7. The ſurrounding fiſheries of an iſland are not only a mine of riches of themſelves, but by giving conſtant employment to a ſtout robuſt laborious race of men, conſtitutes, together with an extenſive commerce, a never failing ſource for keeping up a powerful navy, which the comparative ſmallneſs of an iſland to a continent renders indiſpenſably neceſſary, in order to ſecure to its inhabitants the undiſturbed enjoyment of their local advantages.

An iſland may be conſidered as a world of itſelf; and if its inhabitants have the wiſdom

to

to improve thoſe advantages which nature generally, with a laviſh hand, beſtows upon them, and, at the ſame time, firmly coaleſce together for their common ſupport and protection, they may, in moſt caſes, bid defiance to all other nations.

To prove this, we have only to contemplate Great Britain, which, by the attention it has given to the culture of the ſoil—to its manufactures and commerce—to its fiſheries—to its laws, religion, and government—and, finally, to its fleets and armies, ſtands unrivalled in the annals of fame. What a ſublime ſubject for the powers of the fineſt genius!

Philoſophy.

Philoſophy, in its utmoſt extent, embraces for its objects whatever relates to Man, to Nature, and to God *.

As it relates to the wants of the human ſpecies, it is of greater importance, and of more

* The illuſtrious Lord *Verulam* defines it, "*Interpretatio naturae.*" And the immortal *Cicero*, "*Scientia rerum divinarum et humanarum cum cauſis.*"

more immediate and general uſe to mankind than all the other branches of knowledge, the cultivation of the ſoil only excepted.

In the full contemplation of this ſublime ſcience, man riſes ſuperior to himſelf, and in a manner forgets that he is mortal. The diſcovery of thoſe truths on which the happineſs, the power, the grandeur, and the glory of the human race depend, fill the ſoul with emotions ſo exquiſitely ſoothing, that he irreſtibly fixes his eye on heaven, anticipating, in ſome degree, thoſe joys which are the reward of virtue.

That the unwearied reſearches of philoſophers, many of them of exalted genius, ſhould have been unſucceſsful, till within theſe two centuries paſt, in eſtabliſhing a ſyſtem of philoſophy on the baſis of demonſtration, conſtitutes a phenomenon in ſcience truly wonderful. What particularly leads us to form this concluſion is, that all the actions of children are completely illuſtrative of the preſent ſyſtem of philoſophy, the foundation of which

muſt

muſt ever remain unſhaken while truth itſelf exiſts, and human nature the ſame.

Thoſe propenſities which, for the wiſeſt purpoſes, are implanted in the mind of man, and which ſtimulate him to exert every power and faculty of his ſoul to acquire a knowledge of the univerſe, appear in children at a period which, while it excites our aſtoniſhment, it alſo proves the ultimate deſign of creation. The infant babe, while yet it ſuckles its fond mother, and after having, from a repetition of every act of tenderneſs and care towards it, acquired confidence, moſt beautifully betrays the ſtrongeſt affection, and exhibits rapturous proofs of giving her a decided preference to all its other keepers; thus rivetting for ever in the boſom of the parent her natural love and attachment to her offspring. How inimitable the contrivance! how beneficent the deſign!

About the time a child arrives at two years of age, the native curioſity of his mind impels him to run about, not only to review ſurrounding objects, but alſo to handle and tumble

tumble then in every poſſible direction. This love of novelty keeps him conſtantly flying from object to object, and from one ſpecies of diverſion to another. When worn out with fatigue, however, he is carried to bed to enjoy that balmy repoſe which moſt effectually renovates the powers of nature, ſo that the little hero is enabled next morning to reſume his moſt enchanting and arduous career. Theſe occupations of children are generally called childiſh or innocent amuſements, whereas in fact they proceed on the ſame principles as thoſe which gave birth to the ſublime theories and immortal diſcoveries of a Locke and a Newton.

The indulgence of this undetermined curioſity in children, though not accompanied with an abſtract contemplation of any of the objects which excite their attention, is the real beginnings of the grand ſtudy of nature. Every new object has its peculiar attractions. Every incidental experiment which pleaſes is eagerly repeated, ſhowing a confidence in the conſtancy of natural operations. He ſoon becomes

comes fond of ſimilitudes and a recurrence of the ſame events. As the powers of his mind continue to unfold themſelves, queſtions are ſtarted and concluſions drawn, which, when examined, are found to reſt upon the true and unerring principles of that *induction* which is the baſis of modern philoſophy, and which ſtands in direct oppoſition to that ſyllogiſtic wrangling which for thouſands of years kept philoſophers conſtantly diſputing and raiſing one falſe hypotheſis on the ruins of another.

> With thee, ſerene Philoſophy, with thee,
> And thy bright garland, let me crown my ſong!
> Effuſive ſource of evidence, and truth!
> A luſtre ſhedding o'er the ennobled mind,
> Stronger than ſummer noon; and pure as that,
> Whoſe wild vibrations ſooth the parted ſoul,
> New to the dawning of celeſtial day.
>
> *Thomſon's Seaſons.*

In thus contemplating the education of kind nature, it is beautiful to ſee her make the play of her ſcholars, from the beginning to the end of their lives, their moſt inſtructive leſſons, while, at the ſame time, ſuch purſuits;

eſpecially

eſpecially in infancy and youth, both promote the growth and ſtrength of the body. It is farther to be obſerved, that without this principle of curioſity and inductive propenſity, man muſt have lived in a ſtate of almoſt total ignorance. Nothing but the impulſe of hunger and cold would have forced him to exert himſelf to procure ſuſtenance and clothing. Independently of the above, his great native indolence and inaction would have retarded the growth of his body, ſo that, if in ſuch a ſtate of exiſtence, were it poſſible for man to arrive at maturity, his frame would be ſo feeble, and his body ſo ſuſceptible of diſeaſe, that he would be unfit for every kind of laborious exertion.

By philoſophic reſearches, man has been enabled not only to aſcertain the ſtation which that glorious luminary the *Sun* occupies in the heavens, but alſo its magnitude and diſtance from our earth, together with many of its moſt important uſes.

From no part of nature's unlimited and ſtupendous works can the contemplative mind derive ſuch ſoothing and rapturous emotions as in beholding this immenſe orb of fire, with inconceivable luſtre and majeſty, apparently riſing out of the ocean to diffuſe life, joy, and ſupport to every province of animated nature.

How truly captivating is it to contemplate the ſun in the centre of the planetary ſyſtem, poſſeſſed of a power of attracting the earth and the other planets towards him, with a force exactly counterbalancing their centrifugal force; or that tendency which the planets have of flying off in a tangent to the circle they perform in their revolutions around this luminary, whoſe vital luſtre overcomes the powers of viſion.

Let us here pauſe for a moment, and conſider what would be the conſequences were the Creator of the univerſe either greatly to increaſe the ſun's attraction or to ſuſpend it altogether? In the former caſe, the earth, together with all the planets, would inſtantly be deſtroyed in one general conflagration. And, in the latter, they would be hurled with incredible velocity through unknown

regions,

regions, to be daſhed to pieces againſt other worlds, or to terminate their exiſtence in a manner which eludes human comprehenſion. How dependant man! How humble and ever grateful to heaven!

The ſtarry firmament exhibits an unbounded ſcene of contemplation. In attempting to conceive, that not only all the ſtars which are viſible to the naked eye, but alſo all thoſe brought into view by microſcopes, are more than probable *ſuns*, or *centers* of diſtinct *ſyſtems* regulated by the laws of gravitation, each communicating heat and light to animate as many inhabitated worlds as our ſun does, the mind is loſt in the immenſity of the idea.

Without philoſophy, the globe muſt have continued a deſart; and man, expoſed to the inclemencies of the ſeaſons and the fury of wild beaſts, would have remained an object of commiſeration. To his mental powers the riſe of the arts muſt be aſcribed. Aſſiſted by the ſciences, what was formerly a wilderneſs now teems with plenty. Populous cities, magnificent villas, ſuperb temples, and gild-

ed

ed palaces, every where decorate the face of the earth. All civilized nature is glad, and he who is not happy muſt look to himſelf for the cauſe of it.

Without thee, what were unenlighten'd Man!
A ſavage roaming thro' the woods and wilds,
In queſt of prey; and with th' unfaſhion'd fur
Rough clad; devoid of every finer art,
And elegance of life. Nor happineſs
Domeſtic, mix'd with tenderneſs and care,
Nor moral excellence, nor ſocial bliſs,
Nor guardian law were his; nor various ſkill
To turn the furrow, or to guide the tool
Mechanic; nor the heaven-conducted prow
Of navigation bold, that fearleſs braves
The burning line, or dares the wint'ry pole;
Mother ſevere of infinite delights!
Nothing ſave rapine, indolence, and guile.
And woes on woes, a ſtill-revolving train!
Whoſe horrid circle had made human life
Than non exiſtence worſe: but, taught by thee,
Ours are the plans of policy, and peace;
To live like brothers, and conjunctive all
Embelliſh life. While thus laborious crowds
Ply the tough oar, *Philoſophy* directs
The ruling helm; or like the liberal breath
Of potent Heaven, inviſible, the ſail
Swells out, and bears th' inferior world along.

Thomſon's Seaſons.

All

All the aſtronomical, optical, mechanical, hydroſtatical, and chemical diſcoveries, as well as thoſe in all the other arts and ſciences, have been effected by means of philoſophical purſuits, the important uſes of which our limits do not here permit to point out. We ſhall, however, remark that, by philoſophy, the ſtateſman, acquiring a knowledge of the different motives which influence the human mind, is enabled to govern kingdoms; and the pilot, knowing the powers of the magnet, navigates a ſhip through the trackleſs ocean. Yet, notwithſtanding all the boaſted knowledge of man, he ſhould think modeſtly of his rational powers. It is to that principle of curioſity implanted in the human breaſt, that God has chiefly entruſted his nobleſt work, the improvement of man's intellectual powers and faculties.

Independent of thoſe advantages which the arts and ſciences have derived from philoſophy, there are ſtill others of the utmoſt importance, and which here claim our attention. It is eaſy to conceive, that ſuch diſcoveries may

yet

yet be made in philoſophy by which nations as well as individuals may greatly add to their riches. Were it that the ſcale of human happineſs extended in proportion to the increaſe of riches, their acquiſition would be the moſt deſirable thing in nature: But alas! the many inſtances of the downfal of empires, originating in luxury and diſſipation, ſhould teach men to look on wealth and extent of dominion with a jealous eye. Men abounding in riches by pampering their bodies and whetting their appetites, are ever in danger of falling victims to ſenſuality and other crimes.

The vices of a nation, as well as of individuals, have beginnings which are imperceptible, but the allurements of gratification often lead both to the brink of the precipice before they are aware of the danger. Hardened in folly and criminality, they, ſooner or later, are precipitated into the abyſs of deſtruction.

Philoſophy being the hand maid to the arts and duties of life, as well as to the improvement of the intellectual faculties, the propenſity of the human mind to acquire knowledge

knowledge ought to be ſtrongly cheriſhed. As it is the duty of the ruſtic to work, ſo it alſo is the duty of the rich to explore the different regions of philoſophy in purſuit of uſeful truths. Nothing ſurely can point out a grovelling ſoul more than for a man of fortune not to have a cultivated mind *. This fact is deducible from this, that with every new

* What that moſt elegant and juſtly celebrated writer, Dr Blair, has obſerved, with reſpect to taſte, is equally applicable to the various branches of philoſophy.

" In the education of youth," ſays he, " no object has " in every age appeared more important to wiſe men than " to tincture them early with a reliſh for the entertain- " ments of taſte. The tranſition is commonly made with " eaſe from theſe to the diſcharge of the higher and more " important duties of life. Good hopes may be enter- " tained of thoſe whoſe minds have this liberal and ele- " gant turn. It is favourable to many virtues: Whereas, " to be entirely devoid of reliſh for eloquence, poetry, or " any of the fine arts, is juſtly conſtrued to be an unpro- " miſing ſymptom of youth; and raiſes ſuſpicions of their " being prone to low gratifications, or deſtined to drudge " in the more vulgar and illiberal purſuits of life."

" Theſe poliſh'd arts have humaniz'd mankind,
" Soften'd the rude, and calm'd the boiſt'rous mind.

new draught of knowledge, our thirst to acquire more is thereby increased.

— — — — — — But what need words
To paint its power? For this the daring youth
Breaks forth from his weeping mother's fondling arms
In foreign climes to rove. The pensive sage,
Heedless of sleep, or midnights hurtful vapour,
Hangs o'er the sickly taper.—Hence the scorn
Of all familiar prospects, though beheld
With transport once. Hence th' attentive gaze
Of young astonishment.
Such is the bounteous providence of Heaven,
In every breast implanting the desire
Of objects new and strange, to urge us on,
With unremitting labour, to attain
The sacred stores that wait the rip'ning soul
In truth's exhaustless bosom.—*Aikenside.*

The advantages resulting from philosophy may be deduced from the contemplation of that unbounded field of accessible knowledge in the works of creation. We there behold a world not consisting of detached objects but an universe, a system of beings all linked together with innumerable degrees of subordination and subserviency to each other, constituting one immense and glorious purpose.

That

That order, harmony, connection, beauty, and perfection which pervades every part of the universe, must warm the heart of him who contemplates them, though having but a spark of sensibility in it; and he must be overjoyed to find himself one of the most important parts of this wonderful machine, and will thence be led to adore the incomprehensible Artist, who contrived, created, and directs the whole by unerring laws. These general laws of nature, that concatenation and adjustment of every thing, both material and immaterial, which subsists in the universe, affords an example of infinite power and wisdom.

These are thy glorious works, parent of good,
Almighty! thine this universal frame;
Thus wondrous fair; thyself how wondrous then!

Milton.

A real knowledge of philosophy leads men to entertain a modest opinion of human attainments. For notwithstanding the great advances made in philosophy, and the fair prospect that there is of still greater and greater difcoveries coming to light; yet fuch are the limits of human intellect, that firft caufes or ultimate principles can never be afcertained by the philofopher.

Having only to judge by appearances, man muft content himfelf with attending to the fubordination of things; and thefe alone it is his bufinefs to inveftigate.

The means employed in carrying on the various movements in the heavens, and the other innumerable operations in nature, are fo few and fimple, and the effects which they produce fo tranfcendently beautiful and grand, that they overcome the powers of human conception. We have only to add, that a true knowledge of philofophy muft in general tend to give a bias to contemplation—to humanize the mind and polifh the manners—to lead to benevolence, generofity, and friendfhip—to a love of order and peace—to fortitude and magnanimity—to a love of truth and honefty—to lead to true patriotifm—to rivet the bonds of confanguinity—and, finally, lead to a love of God and religion, our greateft re-

fuge

fuge in pain and anguiſh, and our only hope and ſupport in the moments of diſſolution. *The unity of nature proves the unity of God.*

Law.

It would be incompatible with the limits of our preſent publication to enter at large on a ſubject which has given riſe to many thouſand volumes.

We ſhall therefore only,

1. Offer a few obſervations on the origin and nature of law.

2. Curſorily point out thoſe objects to which it would appear that laws ought chiefly to be directed, with the view of producing the beſt poſſible effects on ſociety and the government of a country, with ſome obſervations.

Had it accorded with the nature of a finite being, ſuch as man is, to have been perfect, there would have been no occaſion for the inſtitution of laws human or divine.

The

The fundamental principles of law are to be ſearched for in human nature.

There is no ſubject in the whole hiſtory of ſcience that has ſo much and ſo juſtly excited the attention of philoſophers in general, as the conſtruction of the human mind in as far as it relates to law. It has called forth the contemplation of the greateſt and wiſeſt of men, as well as the pens of the ableſt writers, who, with a noble enthuſiaſm in their ſublime deſcriptions on a topic of ſo high birth and tranſcendant dignity, have exhauſted all the powers of language.

The happineſs of man being the grand deſign of his exiſtence, there are impreſſed on his mind certain principles, by the regulation of which he is enabled to accompliſh ſo glorious a purpoſe. The inveſtigation of theſe intuitive powers and faculties of man will, we truſt, corroborate what we have juſt now advanced, as well as lead us to diſcover the true ſource and nature of law.

Thefe principles are,

1. Man is endowed with that eternal fpring of all action, termed felf-love, or with an unlimited and inceffant defire for his own happinefs.

2. He poffeffes a power by which he is enabled to conduct himfelf according to the freedom of his own will conftituting him a moral agent.

3. Man enjoys a faculty by which, whether in a favage or civilized ftate, he can difcriminate between actions which tend to promote the happinefs both of himfelf and his neighbour, and fuch as may abridge his own peace and comfort or that of his fellow creature.

Thefe two powers are denominated a knowledge of *good* and *evil*. An obfervance of the former conftitutes *virtue*, and a compliance with the latter *vice*.

Here are three diftinct powers whofe actions when united produce by far the moft wonderful and moft important phenomena in the

the moral world. We ſhall firſt conſider them ſeparately and then collectively.

1. The native impulſe of the mind to obtain happineſs being the chief ſpring of all human actions, mankind are kept in the cloſe purſuit of it through the whole of life. Every man, in proportion to the intenſity of this deſire, exerts himſelf more or leſs to accompliſh that end. It would do more than fill a volume to enumerate all the workings of this paſſion of the human breaſt to procure happineſs. All the world is activity and buſtle —all men are eager in the purſuit of what but few attain. This ariſes from the uſe of improper means to accompliſh it. Without this innate propenſity of the mind, however, how torpid an animal man!

2. By the exerciſe of the free-will man is at liberty either to purſue a courſe of virtue or vice, though not with impunity in the latter caſe, as will afterwards appear. He may adopt whatever plans he conceives to be moſt conducive to his happineſs. How miſerable would he have been provided had he been

born

born with useful and noble propensities without having an unrestrained power of gratifying them?

In such a state, no society could have existed. On the contrary, the great blessings resulting from this latitude given to human nature appear in this, that the Creator of the universe having in his wisdom endowed different men with various propensities, they are thereby impelled to follow different professions. Hence the great variety and multiplicity of human pursuits—the origin and support of society. Hence, according to the poet, " different minds incline to different objects."

Had all men possessed in this respect one and the same propensity, there only could have been one pursuit attempted to maintain human existence. The consequences would have been anarchy, misery, and the extinction of the human race.

3. That power which distinguishes between good and evil is of the highest utility to mankind: for without such a guide they would run

on

on promiſcuouſly, doing one hour what was right, and perhaps the very next what was wrong. In ſuch a ſtate of exiſtence (if it were poſſible there could be ſuch a one) there could be no law, no government, conſequently no adminiſtration of juſtice. This knowledge of good and evil, together with the power of volition, it may be here obſerved, conſtitute man an accountable being.

We ſhall now attempt to give a view of the operation of theſe three faculties combined together.

Happineſs implying the enjoyment of whatever is truly congenial to a man's natural feelings, or the moſt ample ſupply of all his neceſſary wants, the Almighty has impreſſed the purſuit of it on his nature as an immutable law; and, to aſſiſt him in the attainment of it, has endowed him with a free will, while his diſcriminating faculty of what is good and evil leads the van, and ſafely conducts man into the true and only paths where real happineſs is to be found, thus conſtituting what is called the law of nature.

It

It is a law, inaſmuch as it is a ſupreme unchangeable and uncontroulable rule of conduct, the violation of which is avenged by natural puniſhments, which inevitably flow from the conſtitution of things, and are as fixed as the order of nature itſelf.

This law of nature is ſo intimately connected and interwoven with the happineſs of man, that the latter cannot be attained but by obſerving the former; and, on the other hand, if the former be faithfully obeyed, it muſt as neceſſarily ſuperinduce the latter.

The exiſtence and force of this law of nature have led all civilized ſtates to look upon it hitherto as the only baſis of juſtice; and they accordingly have founded their civil laws upon it, calling them the *Laws* of *Nations*.

As all men are born with this law of nature engraven on their hearts, they are therefore all equally entitled to enjoy the benefits to be derived from it: Thus conſtituting the natural right of mankind. As human ſociety could not exiſt without civil laws, all men are intereſted in their conſtruction and adminiſtra-

 tion.

tion. In that caſe, every man is bound to bear a proportionate ſhare of the expence of the adminiſtration of public juſtice.

Where the laws and government of a country protect men's lives and properties, they are obliged to contribute to the ſupporting of theſe national inſtitutions as well as that of the ſtate. Hence the origin and propriety of *taxation.*

We have ſeen that, by the ſimplicity of the law of nature, man is not perplexed with a multiplicity of precepts. The only precept which the author of his exiſtence has preſcribed for him is to purſue his own happineſs. Accordingly, the celebrated *Juſtinian* has reduced the whole doctrine of law to theſe three general precepts, viz. " *That man ſhould* " *live honeſtly, hurt no body, and render to* " *every one his due.*"

We are now come to point out thoſe objects to which it would appear that laws ought to be chiefly directed, with the view of fulfilling the grand purpoſes of ſociety and the government of a country.

The

The object of all law is juſtice. It is the natural right of the governed to receive it from the diſtributive hand of government. As it would be impoſſible to hold ſociety together in amity and peace without laws founded on the principles of equity, it has therefore ever been a maxim with all wiſe legiſlators, to employ all their wiſdom in framing their laws. On their conſtruction and wiſe adminiſtration, the happineſs and glory of a nation depend: For no nation can riſe into power and greatneſs without wholeſome laws.

The moſt important and perplexing province of all legiſlatures appears to be the inſtitution of fundamental laws, and the laws of taxation. As the former proceeds on few and general principles, it is by no means ſo difficult as the latter. The ſubject of taxation, however, involves in it the inveſtigation of as many topics as would fill a volume. It requires the firſt rate abilities to develope its myſterious principles, and to demonſtrate their various effects.

There

There are three objects which appear of greater consequence to be attended to in the ruling of a nation than all others, religion and morality excepted. These are, property, marriage, character national as well as individual. Our limits will only permit us to make a very few observations on these most interesting topics.

In the primæval days of the world, the earth, by the express command of its Creator, was common to the human race. Property is therefore of divine original. By this mandate, and the laws of nature, the mere occupancy of any part of the globe, in these days of simplicity, constituted an absolute right while occupied; but, upon abandoning the premisses, they became the property of the next occupant.

This kind of tenure was only calculated for the rudiments of civil society, which would necessarily cease with the increase of population, and when the interests of men and established governments became complicated and their manners more refined. As for instance,

ſtance, what would be inconvenient or diſagreeable for one man to poſſeſs, might be highly ſuitable and pleaſant to another. Hence the exchange of one thing for another would frequently occur. By theſe means, commercial traffic would take its riſe as well as the transfer and permanency of property.

While the protection of property, together with the great diverſity in its extent, conſtitute two of the principal ſupports of ſociety and the government of a country, they at the ſame time demonſtrate the infinite goodneſs of omnipotence in not having created all men equally ambitious and induſtrious: For had this been the caſe, every ſort of pre eminence and rank, which might accrue to one man above thoſe in the ſame profeſſion with himſelf, depending on incidental cauſes alone, and this being alike the caſe with all other men in all the various purſuits of life, the different gradations of rank, which have been found to be abſolutely requiſite for the eſtabliſhing and maintaining of a well regulated government, could never have been produced.

It

It is demonſtrable, that where there is no ſuperior rank and power, there can be no controul or ſubordination, and where there is no ſubordination, there can be no adminiſtration of juſtice, and without the equal diſtribution of juſtice, no nation can exiſt but in a ſtate of barbarity.

As a ſecurity to the peaceable poſſeſſion of property, rank, and title, the human mind is ſo conſtituted, that men in the inferior ranks of life, in place of envying thoſe in exalted ſtations and poſſeſſing great riches, look up to them with admiration, complacency, and a ſecret awe. While it gratifies the pride of the dependent to be connected with the great, their intereſt in it, and a love of applauſe and fame, not only commands their ready obedience, but will even often carry them to ſhare in the greateſt hardſhips and dangers.

There are two principles in the human mind of the utmoſt conſequence to ſociety, and which are worthy of the attention of a nation.

They

They are, firſt, that ſpirit of emulation to excel which ſubſiſts more or leſs in the breaſts of thoſe in equal or ſimilar ſtations of life; and, 2dly, That ſympathy which is ſtrongly interwoven in the heart of man towards his fellow-creature, which leads him to acts of generoſity and a noble diſintereſtedneſs. The other various and important effects, individual as well as national, which reſult from the operation of theſe two principles, are ſo obvious as to ſuperſede the neceſſity of here pointing them out. It may be added, however, that the encouragement of that ſpirit of emulation, as well as the exerciſe of that heavenly principle, *ſympathy of ſoul*, conſtitute an object of the firſt moment to a nation.

In juſtice to Great Britain we cannot but here obſerve, that no nation on the face of the globe can boaſt of ſuch equal laws, of ſuch an extent of liberty, of ſo liberally rewarding real merit, and thereby encouraging a ſpirit of emulation in whatever relates to human happineſs as *herſelf.*

Marriage,

Marriage, consistent with its divine origin, is the wisest institution which could have been devised for accomplishing those objects of it, on which, in a great measure, the happiness, and, in a manner, the very existence of the human race depend. As it crowns all the common blessings of humanity with domestic peace and joy, that law which would annul matrimony, would rob the police of heaven of one of its brightest ornaments. The innumerable and complicated, individual as well as national miseries, which would inevitably result from the want of this institution, are so obvious as to render there being here pointed out unnecessary. On the other hand, the various and numerous advantages which flow from this institution, considered both individually and in a national point of view, are very great. As it is more agreeable to speculate on subjects which are apt to captivate the fancy, or to soothe the mind, than on those which may distress the spirits or horrify the imagination, we shall attempt to point out some of the most useful and important consequences

ſequences which in general are derived from marriage.

That man and woman who are united together in wedlock, and who are attached to each other by the bonds of true love, and afterwards farther rivetted by the ſtill ſtronger power of friendſhip, occupy the moſt enviable ſituation in human ſociety. The reciprocity of affection commanding an equal and correſponding attention on both ſides, their hours glide away in peace. Every difference of opinion is ſettled in cool and deliberate diſcuſſion. A common intereſt unites and directs their efforts to the attainment of the ſame objects. Happy in each others company, they prefer a retired life to one of buſtle and confuſion. On which account, they ſee no company but a few ſelect friends, whoſe agreeable converſation heighten every domeſtic enjoyment.

As a certain degree of wealth is requiſite to ſweeten the joys of life, they are led to be frugal and economic. By ſuffering few interruptions from the noiſe of the world, they have frequent opportunities of turning their converſation to the improvement of their minds, thus diſpoſing them to acts of charity and benevolence. By theſe means, their ideas and manners become aſſimilated, which, while it prevents all violent diſputes, it gives a zeſt to every enjoyment.

If they have children, the keeneſt intereſt is excited in every province of domeſtic and moral life. The rearing them up, under the hope of living to ſee them agreeably ſettled in the world, is accompanied with a thouſand endearments, though, at the ſame time, with ten thouſand cares and anxieties, but which, however, ſecure many important bleſſings to ſociety.

The eſtabliſhment of marriage is evidently calculated to promote happineſs in the utmoſt extent of the word; and as the ſtrength of a nation depends on the number of its inhabitants, it behoves every government to encourage and protect matrimony, while it *ſtrongly and markedly ſhould diſcourage celibacy.*

There

There is one incitement to enter into the married ſtate which, it is wonderful, has not operated more powerfully than, *a priori*, might have been expected.

As it is requiſite that, in every well regulated government, there ſhould be a head ruler, ſo man, from the great ſtrength of his body and active powers of his mind, has been appointed to govern, while woman, from the greater delicacy of her frame, and the extreme ſenſibility and tenderneſs of her mind, is commanded to obey. This conſtitutes the *pride* of *nature* dependent on man, and thus woman juſtly lays claim not only to his ſympathy but alſo to his matrimonial protection.

How inconceivable the contrivance!

How infinite the deſign!

The ſolace of domeſtic happineſs has been coveted and ſought after by the greateſt and wiſeſt of men. It calls forth the exerciſe of every power and faculty of the ſoul which can ennoble human nature. While it ſtimulates to a love of peace and order, to induſtry,

and

and an exemplary line of conduct, it at the same time alleviates all the miseries of life.

The nursery has been found to afford relief to the anxieties not only of the husbandman but also to those of the merchant, the pleader at the bar, the senator, nay even to those who sit on thrones.

The beauty, the accomplishments, and the helpless state of woman, are of themselves, independent of every other consideration, sufficient inducements to men of generous sentiments to marry. We are aware, however, that there are cases where it would be improper for some men to enter into the connubial state; but, unless for some particular reasons, it is surely criminal for man not to do so.

We conclude this subject with observing, that an institution which extends the limits of human felicity, that contributes to the support and stability of the government of a country, ought to be strongly cherished not only by its legislature but also by all ranks and denominations of men.

We

We have, laſtly, to conſider

Character.

Character, as applied to human life, conſiſts in that peculiarity of manners which diſtinguiſhes one man from another.

A *good character* is particularly applicable to that conduct which is regulated by morality and virtue; and, in the common acceptation of the word, it imports honeſty of dealing between man and man: Hence the great importance of an irreproachable character in the commerce of life.

From thoſe means which nature has taken to direct man in the paths of rectitude, may be inferred the beneficial conſequences to be derived from an upright conduct, as well as the inevitable evils which muſt accrue from unjuſt actions or depraved morals. For there are impreſſed on the human mind certain principles, the exerciſe of which powerfully counteract every tendency to depravity of character. Theſe are a knowledge of good and evil, a love of excellence, a ſenſe of remorſe,

morſe, an apprehenſion of infamy, and a fear of puniſhment.

To the man who has to puſh his way in the world, a reſpectable character is equally requiſite with addreſs and abilities.

The importance of character is deducible from the following conſiderations:

1. From that eſteem for excellence which is uſually obſerved to be long retained by the moſt depraved characters; and beſides that, though they may have loſt all their native reverence for virtue, yet that regard for their own intereſt and ſafety, which they ſeldom loſe, impel them, in all matters of importance, to importune the aid of thoſe whoſe integrity is unſullied.

2. If we wiſh to have the advice of a counſellor or a phyſician, a decided preference is always given to the man of character.

Theſe teſtimonies in favour of honeſty, ſet all the learning and eloquence of the ſchools at defiance to overturn them, and confirms the old proverb, that *honeſty is the beſt policy.*

National

National Character.

What constitutes a good character of a nation are equable laws, an impartial administration of justice, and a strict performance of all treaties.

On the contrary, a depraved character of a nation implies unjust and oppressive laws, a partial administration of justice, and a want of faith in fulfilling treaties; thus laying the foundation of the downfal of all empires.

If these are undeniable facts, as well as what has been advanced on the subject of individual character, it will thence appear of what immense consequence it must be for the government of a country to exert all its powers and influence in maintaining and protecting its national character, as well as to afford protection to individual reputation.

It would fill a volume, and require the pen of the ablest writer, to depict, with sufficient energy, that degree of turpitude and extent of the dreadful effects which attach themselves to the tongue of the keen slanderer.

What!

What! Shall human nature ſtill continue to diſgrace herſelf by glorying in malignant falſehood? In the invention of lies, whereby the innocent, the juſt, and the virtuous, are doomed to complicated miſeries? Alas! How pitiable is the ſtate of man, that he has not powers to cruſh this infernal ſpirit.

To contemplate the beautiful ſtructure and majeſty of man, the noble and generous faculties of his ſoul, and, at the ſame time, to behold him, by means of gratifying a diabolical principle, become the inſtrument of the ruin not only of individuals but even of whole families, the ſenſibility of human nature is put upon the rack.

The unfeeling ſlanderer, whoſe grovelling ſoul can derive no enjoyment but from his envenomed tongue, with ſneaking ſteps explores all the haunts of virtue, darting his ſhafts of malice on every ſide.

That even unprotected beauty and innocence itſelf ſhould not bridle the unhallowed lips of the ſlanderer; what a horrible picture of the depravity of human nature does it not preſent

present to mankind, which the utmoſt ſeverity of the law cannot adequately puniſh? For what compariſon would there be between taking away the life of a virtuous young woman, deſtitute of friends, and irretrievably ruining her character?

A defamer of ſuch atrocity as this, not ſatiated with the depredations of his neighbourhood in theſe reſpects, often ſallies forth to diſtant parts to employ his deadly weapon, and, if not checked in his courſe, he triumphantly extends his conqueſts, and perhaps, before he is diſcovered, has undermined the very props on which the exiſtence of his country depend.

The monſter, by his ſubtlety, having gained aſſociates, now aſſumes a daring aſpect, and ſtalks forth at noon-day diſſeminating the ſeeds of every infernal vice.

His inventive faculties are ever on the ſtretch. His deluſive harangues and ſecret machinations ſubvert the minds of the multitude, by which all the bleſſings of ſociety are blaſted.

All is anarchy and confuſion, miſery and deſpair. The powerful arm of the law is at laſt lifted up, which, if not ſucceſsful, the flames of war burſt forth, and, raging with increaſing fury, they ſpread from nation to nation, carrying along with them every ſpecies of accumulated miſery.

We conclude with obſerving, that in this ſcene of turbulence and confuſion, where the words and the actions of the beſt of men are apt to be miſunderſtood or miſrepreſented, where innocence and integrity are ſometimes not a ſufficient ſecurity againſt contempt, hatred, and reproach, it behoves mankind to do every thing in their power to preſerve their characters untainted. By this mean, they will be led to place their dependence for happineſs chiefly on the approbation of their own conſciences, as well as the advancement of their intereſts in that ſtate of exiſtence where liars and ſlanderers ſhall be cut off from beholding him, the effulgence of whoſe countenance ſhall impart inconceivable joys to the virtuous and the good.

Medicine

Medicine.

The great length which our work has already run out to obliges us greatly to abridge our intended obſervations on this ſubject *.

Notwithſtanding the great many diſcoveries which have of late years been made in the ſcience of medicine, there are many painful diſeaſes which ſtill baffle the ſkill of the moſt eminent phyſicians, and indeed there are ſome diſorders to which they cannot afford the leaſt alleviation. In fact, medicine, upon the whole, has made ſlower progreſs than any of the other ſciences. One great cauſe of this appears to be, that it has not been generally ſtudied by gentlemen of fortune, and proſecuted with that cloſe and unwearied aſſiduity which ſo ſublime a ſcience merits. On the contrary, it has in all countries been followed as a trade, and few practitioners can find leiſure to carry on a courſe of experiments

* Under the article diſeaſe we pointed out the importance of the healing art.

ments in chemiſtry, or to make deep reſearches in the vegetable kingdom.

Another ſource of retarding its improvement is, that myſterious cloak which more or leſs has ever veiled the practice, and thereby in a great meaſure concealed its principles. This illiberal plan, eſpecially when conjoined with an affectation of great abilities, as is generally the caſe, has often another bad effect, and which is, the monopoliſing of the profeſſion; and, farther, he who is ſucceſsful in that mean art generally triumphs over thoſe who are perhaps more honourable, and poſſeſs greater ſkill and knowledge than himſelf; but who, from their more ſimple and undiſguiſed mode in treating diſeaſes, have not ſo much attracted the public notice. Hence that credulity and love of myſtery which is ſo congenial to the multitude, is by ſuch practitioners ſometimes converted into a ſource not only of acquiring riches but alſo of obtaining fame. And alas! this at no leſs expence than retarding the improvement of a ſcience on which the happineſs and even the

lives

lives of mankind greatly depend, viz. an open, manly, and unaffected mode of practice.

We are ſorry to obſerve, that to theſe obſtructions to improving the healing art is to be added *jealouſy*, that bane of a liberal exchange of ſentiments and a reciprocal communication of knowledge, which, to the diſgrace of the medical profeſſion, has been found to ſubſiſt, more or leſs, every where among the faculty. This laſt circumſtance muſt ſometimes deter young men of exalted powers of mind, generous ſentiments, and fine feelings, from entering on the practice of medicine after that they have finiſhed their preparatory ſtudies.

As the ſtrength of a nation not only depends on the number of its inhabitants but alſo on their general healthineſs and robuſtneſs, ſo it may be inferred that every ſtate ought to direct its attention to prevent effeminacy among a people. Native effeminacy being generally accompanied with imbecility and puſillanimity of mind; an army compoſed of ſuch reptiles could but ill brave

the

the dangers either of the elements or the field. To what are thofe trophies of naval victory, which, under the bleffing of Heaven, have been won by the fons of proud Albion, to be afcribed but to the undaunted courage and Herculean arm of Britifh tars.

The Author, ftrongly impreffed with the importance of a race of heroes, drew up a letter to Sir John Sinclair, then Prefident of the Board of Agriculture, on the improvement of medicine, in November 1794.

The letter begins with adverting to the importance of the objects of the Board of Agriculture. It then takes notice of the ftill imperfect ftate of the healing art. After this a fhort fketch is given of the hiftory of medicine, together with fome of the caufes which have chiefly retarded its progrefs. This fcience is next pointed out as being of great national importance, and that every ftate ought to have an inftitution for carrying on a fyftem of improvement on a large fcale. In the courfe of thefe fpeculations, due attention is given to, and much praife is beftowed on individual

vidual exertions, as well as upon every medical inſtitution.

We ſhall here ſtate the above plan of improvement after premiſing a few general obſervations.

There ſtill exiſts a natural ſtate of medicine all over the globe, which is not unworthy of attention.

In the firſt ages of the world, ſome pious people would impute the art of curing diſeaſes to a revelation to the firſt man, but the truth is, we have no documents as to any ſuch divine original.

The heathens have imputed it to a particular inventor among men, but it was not poſſible for the ſagacity of one ſingle man to acquire ſo much knowledge as to deſerve the name of a ſcience. A more natural and probable account may be given of the matter.

It muſt have ariſen ſpontaneouſly among men like every other neceſſary art, which, from very ſimple and imperceptible beginnings, would in time conſtitute a conſiſtent ſyſtem of medicine.

Pain

Pain and ficknefs urge men to feek relief; inftinct directs to fome remedies. The random trials which pain fuggefts muft have difcovered others; and the conftitution of the body, by natural vomiting, haemorrhagy, and other evacuations effecting cures, would direct to more. And thefe means of obtaining fpontaneous cures muft have produced obfervations, and led to an imitation of them for conftituting an art of medicine.

When we look into the hiftory of medicine, we find that, in the early ages of the world, when no regular fyftem of practice was formed, the fick were expofed in the high ways and public places that they might have the opportunity of confulting the traveller as he paffed along. The feventh and laft period of the hiftory of medicine extends from the time of the difcovery of the circulation of the blood, in the middle of the 16th century, by the immortal Harvey, to the prefent day.

During this laft period, medicine has been taught upon a dogmatic plan, but has been more commonly practifed upon an empiric

fyftem,

ſyſtem, which proves the ſtill imperfect ſtate of the healing art. The Æſculapian ſuperſtition firſt obtained in Greece, from which country medicine and moſt of the other arts have been derived into all the ſtates of Europe.

It was common in thoſe days to have recourſe to the temples for advice, and alſo to hang up votive tables there, informing, by what means, the diſeaſed were cured or relieved, ſo that the temples became the repoſitories of the art, and the prieſts the moſt knowing in it. Cures were alſo recorded in thoſe times on ſtones, placed by the ſides of the public road.

It is well known that in ſavage countries the natives poſſeſs many ſpecific remedies for curing their diſeaſes. In order to take advantage of every poſſible means of acquiring a thorough knowledge of curing diſeaſes, we propoſed that there ſhould be a national inſtitution, either ſeparately or attached to that of the Board of Agriculture, for the improvement of medical ſcience. The means pointed out, for ſo glorious an end, were ſuch as aimed at a general reſearch in every province of nature. It was recommended, that beſides requeſting the communications of medical practitioners all over the world, that the miniſters, in their reſpective pariſhes, ſhould collect all the information in their power reſpecting the nature of the different diſeaſes, as they might occur, together with giving an account of the mode of treatment and the effects thereby produced. We do not mean that they ſhould tranſmit any circumſtance to the inſtitution but what is important; and that no remarkable cure, either made by nature or art, might not be loſt, they ſhould occaſionally requeſt of their hearers from the pulpit to make them acquainted with every extraordinary circumſtance which might occur relative to diſeaſe.

We adviſed that the inſtitution ſhould requeſt of ſome of the principal practitioners in each of the counties, to draw up yearly, or perhaps oftener, an account of the diſeaſes which have been moſt prevalent, with their apparent caufes, their fymptoms, and general termination, together with the modes of treatment adopted, and upon what principles founded: Alfo that all fpontaneous efforts of nature fhould be particularly noticed, as well as the effects of the particular remedies employed. The whole to conclude with obfervations not only on the different difeafes, but alfo upon the weather, the foil, climate, &c. By thefe means, the *vernacular* ftate of medicine of each county would be obtained, as alfo many extraordinary cafes would be more publicly made known, which might lead to the moft valuable difcoveries.

It was recommended to have an hofpital attached to the inftitution for fingular and defperate cafes. A botanical garden too was pointed out as being requifite for rearing fuch plants which might be difcovered by thofe botanifts whom the inftitution might fend throughout the kingdom, as well as to diftant countries. An elaboratory was, befides, recommended for carrying on a conftant courfe of experiments.

It

It was hinted that the ſale of the publications of the inſtitution, which would contain an infinite variety of important knowledge accumulated from every quarter of the globe, as well as from the works of individuals and ſocieties, would go far to defray the expence of maintaining this eſtabliſhment, which has been propoſed to be founded on that philanthropy which is truly worthy of the Britiſh Empire.

There was alſo incorporated in the addreſs, a plan for a national *Vetinerary College.*

To enforce the importance of publiſhing medical caſes, we ſtated *four*, which, in the courſe of a year and a half previous to the time of drawing up the above addreſs, had occurred to the author. We ſhall here ſtate them in a few words.

The firſt, a fiſtula in *ano*, which, from the great length of the ſinus *, could not be laid

* It may not be improper to ſtate here, that this diſeaſe has hitherto been deemed incurable except by laying open the ſinus its whole length.

laid open with ſafety, was cured by an irritating ſolution thrown into it three or four times a day. The ſubject of the diſeaſe was a young lad of about fourteen years of age. He is now a ſtout man free of all diſeaſe.

2. A large encyſted abſceſs, ſituated on the left lobe of the liver of a woman, was cured by one of the moſt extraordinary efforts perhaps that nature ever made. To give this fact credibliity, we muſt trouble the reader with a ſhort ſtatement of the moſt important circumſtances which attended this highly wonderful phenomenon.

The tumor, which gave the woman the appearance of being fully gone with child, by being ſituated on the left ſide of her body, had an unequal effect on the muſcles of the back, by which means the ſpine was ſomewhat diſordered, and ſhe was unable to ſtand upright or walk erect. She was greatly emaciated, had nocturnal perſpirations and other colliquative ſymptoms. Her pulſe, which was feeble, beat upwards of 100 in the minute. Having ſome years before this been ſucceſsful in a

ſimilar

ſimilar caſe by an operation, where there was diſcharged, from the opening made in the cyſt, ſeveral quarts of matter, beſides an incredible number of hydatids, I had reſolved on giving my patient a chance for her life, by making an inciſion into the tumour. As no ſuppuration had taken place in the parts covering the tumefaction of the liver, and as they were thick and rigid, it was directed, with a view to render the intended operation as free of pain as poſſible, to foment them frequently with a decoction of chamomile flowers, to lubricate them with warm unctuous and relaxing liniments three or four times a day. The rubbing the parts with theſe ſubſtances was ordered to be done before the fire, and continued for at leaſt half an hour each time. A warm poultice of bread and milk was directed to be kept conſtantly applied when the other applications were not making. She was allowed a light and nouriſhing diet, and a glaſs of red wine occaſionally. To leſſen the hectic ſymptoms, ſhe was put on a courſe of bark. Theſe directions were ſcrupulouſly attended

tended to. In about two weeks from the time of the woman's entering upon this plan of treatment, the author, accompanied with a military ſurgeon, went to her houſe to fix on a day for performing the operation. On inquiring into the ſtate of her tumour, they were ſurprized on being told, that it was not only ſofter, but that its ſize had diminiſhed as well as the pain had abated, which both the patient and her huſband ſuppoſed aroſe from matter having, within a few days paſt, begun to ooze out from the pores of the ſkin where the ſwelling was ſituated. On removing the poultice, we were aſtoniſhed to find a conſiderable quantity of glary yellowiſh matter upon it, which had iſſued from theſe cutaneous outlets. The woman was leſs hectic, and had acquired more ſtrength. Matters being ſo favourable, the idea of an operation for the preſent was given up, and a ſtill ſtricter perſeverance in the application of the ſeveral remedies enjoined. As this diſcharge increaſed by the friction, this was directed to be more frequently repeated, and continued

longer

longer at a time. The oozing at laſt increaſed to ſuch a degree, that upon ſome occaſions the viſcid ſtuff was ſeen bubbling out from the pores of the ſkin in the ſame manner that water iſſues from the ſurface of the earth. Some of her neighbours aſſured us that they had repeatedly been called to behold this extraordinary effort of nature. The tumour continued to diminiſh gradually, and in a few months nothing was to be found but a little thickneſs of the ſubjacent parts, which we aſcribed to the contracted ſtate of the cyſt. The woman recovered her wonted health, and ſince that period has had two children.

That this diſeaſe was an abſceſs we concluded from the hiſtory of the caſe, but particularly from a fluctuation of a fluid being felt in the tumor.

The wonder that ſo extraordinary a caſe excites is greatly heightened by this, that every recurrence of a great diſcharge was accompanied by a *niſus* in the tumor and ſurrounding parts.

This

This caſe affords the utmoſt ſcope both to the anatomiſt and phyſiologiſt. The author having the honour of being on a conſultation with that moſt learned phyſician, and moſt celebrated anatomiſt, Dr *Monro*, near to the place where the woman lived at the time of her illneſs, he ſent for her and ſhowed her to the doctor.

Soon after this I was conſulted on two caſes of *ſteatomatous tumors*, commonly called *wens*. One of them was ſeated on the knee of an old woman, and the other on the arm of a man far advanced in life.

As theſe kinds of tumours have been deemed incurable but by extirpation, the uſual operation was preſcribed; but as neither of the perſons would ſubmit to it, recourſe was had to the ſame practice which had been followed in the caſe of the woman juſt now deſcribed, and with complete ſucceſs. Since that time, we have been conſulted on other two caſes of ſteatom, and had the ſatisfaction of alſo curing them by the ſame means. We cannot carry our obſervations farther at preſent on this ſubject.

Theology.

As it would be incompatible with our limits to enter upon a full inveſtigation of this ſubject, all we propoſe, is,

1. To make a few obſervations on the nature and importance of Theology.

2. Curſorily to point out the great advantages that flow from religion.

Religion is divided into natural and revealed. The former relates to the being and attributes of God and thoſe duties which the light of nature enjoins. The latter again, in addition to theſe, relates to the original ſtate of man, the fall of Adam, and its conſequences, the doctrines of the trinity, and thoſe of faith and good works.

All other ſciences dwindle into inſignificance compared to that of natural and revealed religion: for without it we never could have acquired a competent knowledge of the

attributes

attributes of God, nor of the ſeveral relations in which he ſtands to man. Neither could mankind have diſcovered the ultimate ends of their creation: Hence we ſhould have wandered through life like beings groping in the dark, not knowing the road they are travelling, nor aware of the fate awaiting them at the termination of their journey.

If the ſubject of theology is of ſuch great importance to mankind in general, it muſt be of infinite more conſequence to him whoſe duty it is to explain its eſſential doctrines and to enforce the neceſſity of men conforming themſelves to thoſe religious tenets which are deduced from it.

The divine, therefore, conſiſtently with that reſponſibility which he owes to himſelf, to his flock, and to God, ſhould have a moſt liberal education. Before entering on the ſtudy of the ſacred ſcriptures, in addition to his claſſical literature, he ſhould receive a philoſophical education. In particular, we would recommend to him the ſtudy of mathematics, as there is no ſcience whatever which calls forth

forth the powers of the mind to so much advantage in point of argumentation and general induction as an intimate acquaintance with mathematical demonstration.

Without a knowledge of philosophy, it would in general be impossible for a preacher to convince the understanding, to affect the heart, and to arouse the passions to a proper pitch of pious fervour.

Theology, or revealed religion, is a law promulgated by the great Legislator of the universe, on the principles of eternal justice, for leading his creatures to happiness, most powerfully guarded and enforced by the dread of shame, disgrace, and misery.

Natural religion is enforced by the same sanction as revelation, thus constituting an irrefragable evidence of the truth of Christianity.

The advantages to be derived from the Christian religion divide themselves into two parts, the 1st is, that which relates to man as an individual, and, 2d, that which relates to society.

There

There is one incentive to this religion besides fear and ſelf-love, viz. gratitude to that Being who called man into exiſtence.

There are two points in religion which firſt preſent themſelves to the eye of the theological enquirer, and which are indiſpenſably neceſſary for eſtabliſhing and maintaining Chriſtianity, they are, 1ſt, The belief of a God. 2. The belief of a future ſtate of rewards and puniſhments.

To diſcuſs theſe topics would be entering on too wide a field at preſent.

All we ſhall here attempt, under a conviction of the truth of both theſe poſitions, will, 1ſt, be to point out the chief uſes which man as an individual reaps from religion, and, 2dly, Thoſe advantages which reſult to ſociety from this divine inſtitution.

The firſt and moſt natural exerciſes of a religious man, would appear to be the effuſions of a grateful heart to God for having placed him at the head of the creation, endowed with powers and faculties ſo noble and exalted as to enable him to contemplate with infinite

infinite ſatisfaction thoſe glorious works of nature which every where ſurround him.

Beſides this diſtinguiſhed privilege, there are others whoſe ſublimity raiſes man above himſelf, in as much as by the exerciſe of his contemplative powers, and a ſtrict obſervance of the duties of religion, he, in ſome meaſure, participates while on earth the joys of heaven.

The exerciſe of religion, by leading to the acquiſition of good diſpoſitions, fits man to act his part not only with propriety in this life, but alſo prepares him for that which is to come: Hence the truly religious man admires juſtice, order, harmony, and peace. He rejoices in charitable and generous actions. He is a faithful huſband and a loving parent. Abominating all evil, he delights in doing good, the rewards of which are the approbation of a good conſcience, the reſpect of man, and the favour of heaven.

If ſuch are the gifts of our religion; if ſuch are the ineſtimable bleſſings which ſhe confers on her votaries, the incalculable advan-

tages

tages which a nation may reap in her ſervice will be eaſily diſcovered.

Whoever wiſhes for a proof of the reality of natural religion, which correſponds in all points with that of revelation, has only to ſearch for it within his own breaſt.

All men, whether in a civilized or ſavage ſtate, are ſo impreſſed with the innumerable beauties and awful grandeur of the univerſe, that they irreſiſtibly attribute the creation of them to the power of an almighty being.

And finding that their exiſtence and happineſs depend on the preſervation of the world, or of that fitneſs, order, and harmony in the ſtupendous works of nature, thay have juſtly concluded that they are dependent beings, and are thence led to offer up grateful adorations to their Creator, as well as, upon all occaſions, to implore the continuance of his divine protection.

This veneration which ariſes from the belief of a ſupreme being, together with the dependent ſtate of man, lay the foundation of the greateſt bulwark in nature for the

ſecurity

ſecurity of life and property, as well as whatever is dear to ſociety. Without that ſolemn appeal made to heaven, in the preſence of men, by taking an oath, where would be the means of reſtraining, as well as of detecting and puniſhing the murderer—the robber—the liar—and the ſlanderer.

Without this, together with the puniſhment annexed to perjury, no ſociety could exiſt. Hence the importance of religion to ſociety.

We have ſhown the happy effects of religion to the individual; but as all ſocieties are compoſed of individuals, ſo they muſt be more or leſs happy as the individuals are more or leſs religious. Experience has long ſhown, that where religion is wanting vice prevails. Were it poſſible for a ſociety to exiſt without religion, it would neceſſarily be the moſt wretched that language could depict.

As religion is the chief ſupport of a ſtate, it ought to be moſt carefully attended to by every government; and, as example has a greater effect on the multitude than precept, the higher the rank which men hold in ſociety

ciety th emore diſtinguiſhed ſhould they be in the cauſe of religion. He who ſcoffs in reality at Chriſtianity, or affects to do ſo, is either groſsly ignorant, or miſerably depraved.

For we have found, in inveſtigating the laws of nature, that the Architect of the univerſe, in order to counteract every immoral impulſe of the mind, has ſo framed the ſoul of man, that he cannot, even in a ſavage ſtate, perform an action which, in its conſequences, has a tendency either to hurt himſelf, his neighbour, or the community, without ſuffering the reproach of his own conſcience.

Religion has ſuffered greatly from two ſets of people. The firſt are all thoſe who are not only indifferent about religion but alſo diſregard it altogether. How criminal is it, not even in a political point of view, to hold this ſacred inſtitution in deriſion, when men are aware of the dangerous conſequences to which ſo unpardonable a conduct may lead? Wherever ſuch an irreligious contamination ſpreads among men in power, or thoſe moving in the higher circles of life, the *glorious fabric* is in danger of being *levelled* with the *ground*, and unfortunate *man again* reduced to roam in the woods—the companion of *ſavages* and the *prey* of *wild beaſts*.

The other claſs are all thoſe who, from the moſt deteſtable motives, aſſume the appearance of the greateſt ſanctity, while, at the ſame time, they are only converting religion into a *maſk*, under which, with the ſubtlety of the ſerpent, they often perpetrate the worſt of crimes with impunity.

Their objects generally are mercenary—often ſlanderous, and frequently both are conjoined. This is the *vileſt* of all *hypocriſy*. It would fill a volume to deſcant at large on the unlimited havoc which ſuch a diſgraceful proſtitution of principle often occaſions. Theſe monſters failing in their views with one perſon, by being diſcovered, fly to another. Diſappointment only adds fuel to the flame, and ſpurs on their inventive faculties in order to enable them to enjoy a greater degree of *diabolical* gratification in the commiſſion of more atrocious wickedneſs. Who can withſtand the

the backbiter? Who can defeat the ſting of the ſlanderer? And who can abide the envenomed ſhafts of the malicious?

We cloſe this ſubject by obſerving, that religion teaches men to put a proper eſtimate on human life. It inclines them to ſubmit with patience to the various viciſſitudes incident to this tranſitory ſtate. It alſo inſpires them with fortitude, candour, and moderation; and, laſtly, gives them a bias to diſcretion, which, of all the qualities of the human mind, though not the moſt ſhining, is yet the moſt uſeful.

Diſcretion may be conſidered as the grand regulator of the ſoul. The moſt exalted abilities, or the moſt tranſcendant qualities of the mind without diſcretion, are of little uſe. It is diſcretion which gives a value to all the other mental qualities.

True diſcretion ſtands oppoſed to cunning. The former directs man to the nobleſt ends, and to purſue the moſt honourable means of attaining them; while the latter aims only at what is ſelfiſh, and ſticks at nothing to enſure ſucceſs. Diſcretion may be ſtiled the perfection of reaſon, or the helm by which men are to conduct themſelves through life with honour and reſpectability. This is a ſubject which would afford matter for a volume. It ought frequently to be inculcated from the pulpit, contraſted with that degrading quality peculiar to low minds, *cunning*.

CON-

CONCLUSION.

Advantages and Means of Improvement.

SECTION I.

Peculiar Advantages of Berwick in its present State.

THE local advantages which Berwick possesses are numerous and important, and of inestimable value to its inhabitants. In the *first* place, from what has been stated on the subject of disease, it appears that the town and liberties enjoy a healthful climate, and is not subject to contagious and epidemic diseases.

2.

2. From its being ſituated in the immediate neighbourhood of two rich and populous counties (Northumberland and Berwickſhire) the markets are moſt regularly and amply ſupplied with proviſions of every ſort and of the beſt quality, as hinted at above.

3. During the fiſhing ſeaſons ſalmon can be procured freſh from the river.

4. There is almoſt a conſtant ſupply of white fiſh, and of moſt excellent quality, as alſo of ſhell fiſh.

5. There is plenty of coal and lime in the immediate neighbourhood of the town.

6. From the great ſale of timber and iron in Berwick, and the working of free-ſtone quarries cloſe by the town, a great ſaving in expence of the carriage of wood, iron, and ſtone is obtained in the building of houſes and manufacturing works.

7. Thoſe peculiar advantages pointed out in article navigation and ſhipping.

8. It enjoys all thoſe conveniencies and advantages which are derived from places

ſituated

ſituated on the great London and Edinburgh poſt road.

9. Thoſe who manufacture wool can have it of the beſt quality, and in any quantity they chooſe, in the immediate neighbourhood. This circumſtance conſtitutes one of the principal local advantages that Berwick enjoys.

SECTION II.

Improvements of which it is capable in every reſpect.

IN the firſt place, *it is to be obſerved*, all thoſe who are engaged in manufactures in Berwick, are of opinion, that it is peculiarly well ſituated for manufacturing exertions. The Author will, therefore, content himſelf with giving little more than a bare enumeration of ſuch as have occurred to himſelf, and thoſe ſuggeſted to him by others.

An

An Woolen Manufacture.

The ſituation of Berwick with regard to wool, water, coals, ſhipping, and navigation, is allowed by every perſon to be of great conſequence, and peculiarly tempting to the eſtabliſhing of this branch of trade.

2. It is thought, by good judges, that a manufacture of cotton cloths, ſerges, &c. would anſwer well here.

3. A manufactory of thread, we are aſſured, could not fail to turn out to great advantage in Berwick. We know that ſuch a branch is at preſent in contemplation. By forming a ſmall canal, commencing at the river Whittader, a little below Gainſlaw bridge, and carrying it through the Low Haughs, and making it terminate in the Tweed, above New Water Haugh houſe, machinery to any extent might be erected for all manufacturing purpoſes whatever; and, beſides, it would be in the power of the corporation to accommodate manufacturers with any quantity of land they might chooſe. This canal might be made more than a mile in length, and the manu-

factured

factured goods would easily be carried down to the quay (a distance of about a mile and an half) either in boats or masted vessels. Mr Riddell of Gainslaw has, for two years past, carried potatoes down the river, a distance of nearly three miles, in a smack, carrying about 200 tons at a time. Houses built by the side of this canal would enjoy a most delightful situation and healthy climate. Were the corporation of opinion that the stuffs made use of in these manufactures might be hurtful to the fishing, it would be easy to prevent the impregnated liquor reaching the Tweed, by means of cuts similar to drains made into the land, such as is adopted at the blue manufacture in Spittal.

4. It is believed that a stocking manufacture might be carried on in Berwick or Tweedmouth upon a large scale with great advantage.

5. A brown ware manufacture might be established in Tweedmouth, as there is a stratum of clay for that purpose in the township.

This branch of trade was carried on there ſome years ago.

6. A manufacture of ſtone ware might be advantageouſly carried on in Tweedmouth or Spittal, ſimilar to the famous Staffordſhire ware. There is a ſtratum of clay between Tweedmouth and Spittal, of equal quality, we are told, with the Staffordſhire clay *.

7. A glaſs work might be eſtabliſhed at Spittal with very peculiar advantages.

8. It has been ſuggeſted to us, that a manufacture of ſugar might be carried on in Berwick.

9. It is to be preſumed, that a fiſhing whale company might ſucceed in Berwick. We

* Several years ago a gentleman was on the point of erecting a manufacture of this kind in Tweedmouth, when an occurrence took place which made him relinquiſh his plan. He had gone ſo far as to have employed a perſon who had been engaged in conducting ſuch manufactures, and upon making ſome experiments on the clay, he ſaid it deſerved the character above given it. How much more preferable would not this ſituation be to that of Staffordſhire, where the clay muſt be brought from a diſtance of ſeveral hundred miles.

We are informed, that the difference there would be between the expence of victualling a ſhip of 300 tons at Berwick, and one of the ſame burden in London river for Davis's ſtraits, would be about 300l.

10. It has alſo been ſuggeſted to the author, that ſhould manufactures of woolens, cottons, muſlins, &c. &c. be eſtabliſhed in Berwick, and carried on to any conſiderable extent, the opening a communication with the Weſt Indies by means of one or more veſſels carrying out theſe goods for ſale, and bringing others back in return, would bid fair to promote the proſperity of theſe manufactures.

The greateſt improvement of which Berwick is capable, is the rebuilding of Queen Elizabeth's Pier. From the deſcription we have given of its remains, and of the mouth of the harbour, it will appear evident, that were the pier rebuilt, it would both greatly widen and deepen the bed of the river as alſo the harbour mouth. Were this plan carried into execution ſhips might both ſail out of and into the harbour in any wind. To make this practicable it would be neceſſary to have a

gap

gap in the pier, in the ſame place where there is one at preſent, to allow veſſels to paſs into the meadow haven, or from the haven into the river. From the haven, veſſels might paſs into the ſea, either by the N. E. or the S. E. paſſage as the wind anſwered. There is a ſmall rock, however, near to the middle of the N. E. paſſage which would be requiſite to blow up in order to give ſufficient room for veſſels to ſail out to ſea. The gap might be ſo conſtructed as to prevent the river running through it. To aſcertain ſome idea of the expence of re-building the pier, we obtained an eſtimate from a builder of eminence, and who has built many piers in Scotland. He ſaid he would undertake to build it at the rate of ſeven ſhillings per cubic yard, which he averred was one half leſs than he has been paid for building ſome piers. The reaſon he aſſigned for the great difference of price was, that there were a great quantity of ſtones in the ſite of the pier, and what more might be requiſite, were to be got not many hundred yards diſtant. He declared that he never in his life ſaw a ſpot which exhibited ſo great

a

a temptation for building a pier as this; and added that the good effects were obvious to the meaneſt capacity. Upon the ſuppoſition that it would be neceſſary to carry the pier to the very mouth of the harbour, the expence would amount to 18000l. But he was clearly of opinion that 4000l. would build all that was neceſſary.

It has been ſaid it would hurt the fiſhery. In anſwer to this we have to obſerve, it has been ſtated to us by every fiſherman we have ſpoke to on the ſubject, that, if the river was widened, a great many more fiſh would enter it than at preſent. The reaſon aſſigned was, that when the river is ſmall and clear, Spittal Point deters the fiſh from entering the river: For it ſeems they are afraid of white bodies, ſuch as ſea ſand when it is dry.

If any fiſhing water was deſtroyed by erecting the pier, it might be purchaſed. Private property juſtly gives way to the public good.

Improvements of the Town.

The firſt improvement on this head which we would recommend to the corporation and the

the other inhabitants, is the paving, lighting, and cleaning of the ſtreets*. It is curious, that in Berwick, ſome years ago, the corporation uſed to give 60 and 70l. a year for cleaning the ſtreets, and though the contractors were entitled to the dung beſides, yet the object was unattained. For ſome years paſt, the price given for cleaning and ſweeping the ſtreets has been gradually decreaſing †.

The

* An act, as has been already noticed, was paſſed in Guild for petitioning Parliament for a bill to enable the corporation to light and pave the ſtreets.

† The following is extracted from the Agricultural Survey of Mid Lothian:

" From Edinburgh and Leith are obtained about 40,000 " cart load of ſtreet dung annually, which is commonly " expended on the lands within five miles of the town, " though there have been a few inſtances in which it has " been carried by ſea to a greater diſtance. For collect- " ing this manure, ariſing from the ſweepings of the " ſtreets, which are for this purpoſe arranged into diſ- " tricts, the town employs ſcavengers, and the farmers in " the neighbourhood furniſh carts to carry it daily to bye- " places without the walls of the city, laying it together " in dunghills, from which at their leiſure they drive it to

" their

The practice of the killing of cattle in the market place, which is situated in the middle of the town, constitute an intolerable nuisance. This will appear from the following facts and observations; and that, in consequence thereof, the expediency there would be in erecting a slaughtering house, some where disjoined from the town, will be demonstrated.

1. The blood runs in open gutters all the way from the shambles to the river, through a principal part of the town.

2. The excrementitious matter, mixed with blood, is allowed to lay in and around the shambles, until it accumulates to a great quantity, by which time it is in a high state of putridity.

3. That sometimes from a stoppage in the gutters

" their lands. It costs from 1s. to 1s. 6d. a load of about " a cubic yard each."

A plan similar to the above has lately been adopted by the Corporation in consequence of its having been recommended by Sir John Sinclair; and it is thought that the profits arising from the sale of the sweeping of the streets will at least defray the expence of keeping them clean. This manure is sold for 1s. 1d. per cart load.

gutters the blood is thrown upon the ſtreets, and there left to evaporate.

4. That there have been many inſtances of the blood of the ſhambles getting into the water pipes, on the great killing days, and coming out mixed with the water at the private pipes.

5. Every inhabitant of candor can give teſtimony, that often, in walking any where near to the ſhambles, his ſenſe of ſmelling is aſſailed in a moſt unpleaſant manner; and this is felt more or leſs in all the courſe the blood runs, particularly in hot weather.

6. It is well known, that the ſudden expoſure of a perſon to inſpire air, impregnated to a certain degree with exhalations, from an animal in a highly putrid ſtate, is inſtant ſuffocation and death; of which many melancholy inſtances ſtand on record.

7. That ſuch putrid exhalations, floating in the atmoſphere of a town, act as a remote cauſe of diſeaſe, which ſometimes alone, and at other times when combined with other cauſes, produces putrid fevers.

8. That the ſenſible effects of vitiated air, ariſing from putrid animal effluvia, are nauſea and ſickneſs, accompanied with a ſenſe of general laſſitude and debility of the whole body.

9. That in ſuch a ſtate of debility and relaxation, the human frame has been found, from long experience, to be more ſuſceptible of diſeaſe than when the body enjoys a ſtate of perfect health: hence ſound health and vigour of conſtitution are the greateſt preventatives to infectious maladies. It would be incompatible with the nature of this work to enter into a phyſical diſcuſſion on this law of the animal economy. However, it might be well for mankind were they, in conformity to this principle of the nature of their corporeal frame, to exert thoſe powers of their mind to preſerve inviolate all thoſe principles which ſtand diametrically in oppoſition to every vicious practice. Becauſe it is the ſame with the ſoul as the body in this reſpect: for where the ſtrength of the body is diminiſhed by any

exhaufting circumftances, and thereby render-ed more liable to difeafe, fo alfo is the mind of man more prone and more eafily led to the commiffion of crimes when its glorious bul-warks—the principles of virtue and morality, have been fhaken by former habits of vice. In inveftigating the nature of the foul ab-ftractedly, it appears, that purity of principle, accompanied with good works, as affording no fource for felf-accufation, is to the mind of man as wholefome food and falubrious air is to his body in imparting to it priftine health and athletic vigour.

10. Children playing about the fhambles while they have the infection of the fmall-pox in their bodies, the putrid inhalations might, by weakening the fyftem, add to the malignity of the difeafe.

A lady, fome years ago, far advanced in pregnancy, had nearly loft her life in Church ftreet by an ox which had broke loofe from the hands of the butchers. The poor animal was at laft killed in an entry adjoining to a

fhop

ſhop whether the gentlewoman had fled for refuge.

The fiſh market is alſo a great nuiſance in its preſent ſituation. It both hampers the ſtreet and vitiates the air, eſpecially in ſummer. The ſtones and fiſh guts too which are left by the fiſherwomen often occaſions accidents.

The next improvement recommended is of very conſiderable importance to the town and public at large. From the ſhort ſtreet that leads directly to the bridge going off at a right angle with Bridge ſtreet, and its being only twenty feet wide at this corner, there is much danger in riding ſmartly when making this acute turn, in either going out of or coming into town. A total ſtoppage of the ſtreet very often occurs at this place, ariſing from carriages meeting one another. Accidents frequently happen here, which might eaſily be prevented by pulling down that houſe in the corner of Bridge ſtreet ſituated on the ſouth ſide of it, by which means the ſtreet would

would be greatly widened, and inftead of having a fharp angular turn it would be femicircular. It would alfo render the ventilation of this part of Bridge ftreet more free, and would enliven the afpect of it and neighbouring buildings. There is another evident improvement that might be made in this quarter of the town, and that is, in leffening the afcent of the ftreet immediately before entering on the top of the bridge.

The weftern lane has, in fome part of it, an afcent forming nearly an angle of forty-five degrees with the level of Bridge ftreet. Some perfons of temerity venture to ride up and down this hill, and fome carters drive their empty carts down it to get to the fouth gate before their neighbours, who, on the other hand, have the caution to go round by Hide hill. We are told that this pull might be greatly leffened and at no great expence.

The main guard ftanding almoft in the middle of the high ftreet hampers it much, on which account it is complained of as a nuifance. In point of improvement, it ought to ftand ſtand cloſe to the ſide of the Scotch gate, in the ſame way as the guard houſe is placed by the ſide of the ſouth gate.

That area called the Parade, in its preſent ſtate, is a ſubject highly deſerving of our attention. Being appropriated to the purpoſe of exerciſing military troops on, it is neceſſary that it ſhould at all times be kept ſmooth and dry, which is by no means the caſe at preſent.

Were a ſpire to be erected on the church, it would add greatly to the grandeur of its appearance, and would conſtitute an object of great ornament to the town. The church ſtanding on the higheſt ground within the walls, the ſpire, if lofty, would be ſeen at a great diſtance at ſea, and thereby form an uſeful land mark. If a ſally port were opened in the walls in a line with Silver ſtreet, it would be productive of much convenience to all the inhabitants in the under part of the town, as it would afford a near road for their ſervants to carry out their clothes to dry

on

on the ſhore. It would alſo be advantageous to the public by opening a much nearer and better road to the lime kilns, and thoſe parts of the ſhore where ſea ware is thrown out.

It ſtrikes us that the adding of one or two ſtories to the Old Bell Tower, and the furniſhing of it with a proper teleſcope, would anſwer the purpoſe, 1ſt, of an uſeful obſervatory in time of war, 2dly, of an excellent land-mark for ſhips at ſea, and, 3dly, of a great ornament to the town.

The obſervations which we had made on the propriety of levelling Caſtlegate are now unneceſſary to print, as that great improvement has lately been made.

The ancient practice of ſhutting the gates in garriſon towns during night, to the great annoyance not only of the inhabitants within the gates, but alſo of thoſe in the ſuburbs, beſides to the public at large, ſtill prevails here. In order to make this poſition clearly underſtood by thoſe who are unacquainted with

with the ſubject, it will be neceſſary to ſtate thoſe circumſtances which give riſe to the aſſertion.

Phyſicians, ſurgeons, and midwives are exempted, as alſo perſons coming for them; but neither gentlemens' carriages, poſt chaiſes, carts, nor ſaddle horſes, are allowed to paſs through the gates during the time they are commanded to be ſhut.

If a perſon, upon his firſt coming up to the gate, quarrels with the guard, the greateſt importunities afterwards for admiſſion will more than likely be of no avail. Even medical people returning from the country, and though exhauſted by fatigue and the want of ſleep, are ſometimes detained for a long time at the gates. On ſome ſuch occaſions, the ſentry inſiſts that the perſon is uſing a fictitious name, and he will not even open the wicket to inform himſelf whether it is ſo or not, either by looking at his paſſport or his perſon.

It ſometimes happens, when they grant this indulgence in a rage, or in a ſtate of intoxication,

cation, that they let go the great wooden bar of the gate, the conſequence of which may be either the death of the rider or his horſe. We know of ſeveral perſons who, owing to that circumſtance, have made narrow eſcapes at theſe gates.

As for inſtance, two young girls were diſpatched in great haſte in the night time, from Caſtlegate, to requeſt of the author to give his inſtant attendance in a caſe of danger. When arrived at the Scotch gate, they told the urgency of their miſſion to the centinels, and ſtrongly importuned them for immediate admiſſion into the town; but, in place of inſtantly complying with their requeſt, they detained the girls at the gate for more than half an hour, ſometimes opening the wicket and again ſhutting it againſt them. The conſequence was, that before he could reach the place to which he was ſent for, a ſtout male child had ſuffered death for want of ſkilful aſſiſtance, and the poor mother of it had a near eſcape with her life. Had he arrived at the houſe fifteen minutes ſooner, the child might

have

have been eaſily ſaved, and the very imminent danger into which this poor woman was brought, by this delay, prevented. Theſe are not all the evils that ariſe from this etiquete of the garriſon. The gentlemen and farmers, in the county of Berwick, and who are under a neceſſity of ſending their waggons and carts to the Berwick and other coal hills, as well as to the lime kilns, in Northumberland, cannot procure leave for their ſervants to paſs the gates in the night-time.

From the end of the Draw Bridge, at the Scotch Gate, two walls project a conſiderable way; the diſtance between them is the ſame as the breadth of the Draw Bridge; this, with the gate-way, forms a very narrow paſſage of 200 feet in length.

From this deſcription, it will appear what unavoidable delay, danger, and confuſion, muſt always occur at this place from the conſtant ſucceſſion of carriages of all deſcriptions paſſing and repaſſing. There being no foot-way, perſons walking, when this paſſage is crowded, are in danger of being cruſhed to death. Many accidents have happened here, both to foot-paſſengers and perſons on horſeback getting entangled with carriages in endeavouring to paſs them. The utmoſt confuſion frequently occurs here in the night-time from this narrow paſſage being blocked up by carts when, at the time, either the mail coach comes up to it, medical people returning home, or in caſes of perſons coming for them on horſeback—in caſes of expreſſes to or from government, and alſo where perſons in a poſt-chaiſe or on horſeback, are anxious to paſs. It may be eaſily conceived what an untoward buſineſs it would be to prevail on a body of carters, ſtriving with each other in who ſhall firſt get through the gate, and whoſe carts have completely ſhut up all acceſs to it in that quarter, to force their horſes and carts backwards to clear the entry to the gate for a ſingle chaiſe or horſe, eſpecially when they know that, as ſoon as the traveller has been permitted to go into the town, the gate would

be

be ſhut againſt them. The temper and conduct of drivers in ſuch a ſituation, and under ſuch peculiar circumſtances, muſt always be doubtful, and much to be dreaded, and might, on certain occaſions, lead to the moſt ſerious conſequences. From the various circumſtances here ſtated on this head, it will appear obvious of what vaſt importance it would be to the public at large to have theſe two gates kept open at all times, and to have the two walls, which form the road leading from Scotch Gate, pulled down, and the road widened. That the inhabitants of ſo reſpectable a county and important a diſtrict of Scotland as Berwickſhire is, ſhould, by the ſhutting of theſe gates, which will ſurely be admitted by every perſon is now uſeleſs, (conſidered in point of defence), be ſubjected to vexatious inconvenience, loſs of time, and additional expence, and the riſk of loſing both men and horſes in bringing home their coals and lime, conſtitutes a galling burden upon them, which they never would ſubmit to without remon-

ſtrating

ſtrating againſt it in the ſtrongeſt terms, were it not for the high reſpect they entertain for the laws and government of the country. This aſſertion we are authoriſed in making by a reſpectable body of the gentlemen and farmers of that county.

If, upon a proper repreſentation of theſe accumulated evils being made to government, and thoſe propoſed improvements, in regard to the gates, meet with their approbation, and carry them into effect, it would afford to the world a ſtriking proof of that wiſdom, moderation, and ſound policy which has long diſtinguiſhed the legiſlature of Great Britain, and given it a decided pre-eminence among all other civiliſed nations.

We have written ſeveral more pages on theſe nuiſances, but which our room will not admit to be here inſerted.

We cannot cloſe our obſervations without adverting to that cruel and dangerous practice which carters in general have of over-driving their maſters horſes.

Theſe

Theſe obſervations are meant to apply in general to the cruel treatment of horſes, and, at the ſame time, to the unmanly and brutal cuſtom of beating of bulls and fighting of cocks. Notwithſtanding the various regulations that have hitherto been made for reſtraining drivers of carts from driving furiouſly, and to be always at their horſes heads, the object ſtill remains unattained. Scarcely a day paſſes but we hear of ſome accident happening from the careleſſneſs of drivers and their generally driving too faſt. Several lives have been loſt in Berwick and its ſuburbs within theſe few years paſt from theſe cauſes. Where is the pen that could deſcribe, in its true nature and full extent, that anguiſh of ſoul which a parent experiences for the loſs of a darling child by any accident, particularly if occaſioned by careleſſneſs or wantonneſs.—The truſt repoſed in carters is important in many reſpects; and when they diſcharge their duties with fidelity, ſobriety, and diligence, they form a reſpectable

part

part of the community, and are entitled to the esteem and encouragement of the public; but, when they conduct themselves contrary to these principles, they are not only reprehensible, but are just objects of the vengeance of the law. Few of them are able to pay a fine or to make retribution to their masters or others.

On the principle of the criminality of treating horses and other animals cruelly, we are of opinion, that a code of laws should be framed and carried into force for correcting and restraining the commission of this abominable vice—a vice which, by having been overlooked as yet by (as far as we know) even all the enlightened nations of Europe, tends to foster, in the wicked and vicious part of mankind, a spirit of cruelty which is disgraceful to human nature, and must always operate powerfully against the melioration of the human mind. Such a spirit savours of barbarism, and cannot fail more or less to lessen that inestimable value which every man ought to

put

put on the life and character of another. We do not mean that man is not to amuse himself occasionally with hunting or shooting—we only aim at checking wanton cruelty to the brute creation and licentiousness in the human mind; and we conceive, that if mankind were taught from their infancy to pay a tender and religious respect for the lives of dumb animals, it would naturally tend to blunt ferocity of temper, to soften the heart, and to render the mind more docile, placid, and humane.

P. S. A valuation of the parish of Berwick has been just now made, and the whole annual value of the real property, in lands, houses, fisheries, &c. within the town and liberties, is twenty-three thousand pounds.

OBSER-

OBSERVATIONS ON THE SURROUNDING COUNTRY.

Preliminary Obſervations.

WHEN we began to write the Hiſtory of Berwick, it was our intention to have delineated the moſt prominent features—the chief beauties—and the moſt remarkable improvements of the neighbouring counties; but the work having already exceeded the limits at firſt aſſigned to it, we ſhall confine ourſelves to a very few general obſervations only.

To ſome perſons all ſuch remarks may appear unneceſſary after the late very excellent publications of the Agricultural Reports of the Counties of Durham, Northumberland, and Berwick.

To give an account of cities or towns, without deſcribing the circumjacent countries, together with the various advantages which they

they derive from their agriculture, their commerce, and manufactures, &c. would, to the author at leaſt, appear extremely defective.

Were there ſuch a law as reſtricted one author from writing after another on the ſame ſubject, it would ſpeedily become the ſource of evils which would ſoon terminate in the deſtruction of all ſocial order, and in the complete extinction of the arts and ſciences.

The liberty of the preſs, therefore, conſtitutes one of the greateſt bleſſings which Britons enjoy as a free and a happy people, and is one of our moſt impregnable bulwarks againſt the incurſion of foreign foes.

We ſhall firſt glance at the adjacent country ſouth of the Tweed, and next at the county of Berwick.

There is a diſtrict of the county of Durham, called Norhamſhire, which we enter into after going along the bridge of Berwick, and beyond that is the county of Northumberland.

In deſcribing the ſcenery, it was pointed out, that the country adjoining to the ſouth ſide of the Tweed had but a bleak and barren profpect, owing to the fcarcity of plantings, and much of the lands being broken by coal-pits, lime-ftone quarries, and the roads leading to them. There are fome diftricts, however, in the extenfive county of Northumberland, which are entitled to the firft powers in defcriptive fcenery, or to the pencil of the beft delineator in landfcape.

The mountains of Cheviot, and the great number of verdant hills which beautifully furround them, conftitute the moft prominent feature of Northumberland.

The following is extracted from Meffrs John Bailey and George Culley's Agricultural Report of Northumberland: "The lower parts prefent a more pleafing profpect of inclofed country, extenfive farms, fcattered villages, populous towns, and bufy fcenes of trade, principally occafioned by the vaft refources of coal which this country in fo many parts abound with: It is alfo favoured with other valuable minerals, particularly lead ore, lime, and marl.

"Its

"Its greateſt length, from north to ſouth, is 64 miles, and breadth 48; and contains 1980 ſquare miles, which may be divided into lands that are, or may be, cultivated by the plough, - - 817,200 acres.

And mountainous diſtricts, improper for tillage, 450,000

Making in the whole 1,267,200.

"There are ſome tenants in the northern parts of the county that farm from 2000l. to 4000l. a year and upwards *."

Berwickſhire,

* "*The Wild Cattle*—are only found in Chillingham Park, belonging to the Earl of Tankerville, and as it is probable they are the only remains of the *true and genuine* breed of that ſpecies of cattle, we ſhall be more particular in our deſcription.

Their colour is invariably white, muzzle black; the whole of the inſide of the ear, and about one third of the outſide from the tip, downwards, red; horns white, with black tips, very fine, and bent upwards. Some of the bulls have a thin upright mane, about an inch and an half, or two inches long. The weight of the oxen is from 35 to 45 ſtone, and the cows from 25 to 35 ſtone, the four quarters;

Berwickſhire, which is partly bounded on the eaſt by the liberties of Berwick, is ſtated, in

Mr

quarters; 14lb. to the ſtone. The beef is finely marbled, and of excellent flavour.

From the nature of their paſture, and the frequent agitation they are put into, by the curioſity of ſtrangers, it is ſcarce to be expected they ſhould get very fat; yet ſix years old oxen are generally very good beef. From whence it may fairly be ſuppoſed, that in proper ſituations they would feed well.

At the firſt appearance of any perſon they ſet off in full gallop; and, at the diſtance of two or three hundred yards, make a wheel round, and come boldly up again, toſſing their heads in a menacing manner. On a ſudden they make a full ſtop, at the diſtance of forty or fifty yards, looking wildly at the object of their ſurpriſe; but upon the leaſt motion being made, they all again turn round, and gallop off again with equal ſpeed, but not to the ſame diſtance: forming a ſhorter circle, and again returning with a bolder and more threatening aſpect than before, they approach much nearer, probably within thirty yards, when they make another ſtand, and again gallop off. This they do ſeveral times, ſhortening their diſtance, and advancing nearer; till they come within a few yards, when moſt people think it prudent to leave them, not chuſing

to

Mr Home's Agricultural Report of the County, to be $31\frac{1}{4}$ in its extreme length, and its extreme breadth 17 miles.

In

to provoke them further, as it is probable that, in a few turns more, they would make an attack.

The mode of killing them was, perhaps, the only modern remains of the grandeur of ancient hunting. On notice being given, that a wild bull would be killed upon a certain day, the inhabitants of the neighbourhood came mounted, and armed with guns, &c. ſometimes to the amount of a hundred horſe, and four or five hundred foot, who ſtood upon walls, or got into trees, while the horſemen rode off the bull from the reſt of the herd, until he ſtood at bay; when the markſman diſmounted and ſhot. At ſome of theſe huntings, twenty or thirty ſhots have been fired before he was ſubdued. On ſuch occaſions, the bleeding victim grew deſperately furious, from the ſmarting of his wounds, and the ſhouts of ſavage joy that were echoing from every ſide; but, from the number of accidents that happened, this dangerous mode has been little practiſed of late years; the park-keeper alone generally ſhooting them with a rifled gun, at one ſhot. When the cows calve, they hide their calves, for a week or ten days, in ſome ſequeſtrated ſituation, and go and ſuckle them two or three times a day. If any perſon come near the calves, they clap their heads cloſe to the ground,

In viewing that part of county called the the Merſe from its higheſt grounds, it exhibits the appearance of a beautiful ſmooth plain, though in reality it abounds with many inequalities and eminences. Some of theſe riſe to ſuch elevations as to have obtained the names of hills and laws. Such as Lamberton and

ground, and lie like a hare in form, to hide themſelves. This is a proof of their native wildneſs, and is corroborated by the following circumſtance, that happened to the writer of this narrative, who found a hidden calf, two days old, very lean, and very weak. On ſtroking its head, it got up, pawed two or three times like an old bull, bellowed very loud, ſtepped back a few ſteps, and bolted at his legs with all its force: it then began to paw again, bellowed, ſtepped back, and bolted as before: but knowing its intention, and ſtepping aſide, it miſſed me, fell, and was ſo very weak, that it could not riſe, though it made ſeveral efforts. But it had done enough, the whole herd were alarmed, and, coming to its reſcue, obliged me to retire; for the dams will allow no perſon to touch their calves, without attacking them with impetuous ferocity.

When any one happens to be wounded, or grown weak and feeble through age and ſickneſs, the reſt of the herd ſet upon it, and gore it to death."

and Ayton hills, and Dunſe and Cockburn law.

Though this county is in general by far too thinly planted, yet there are many gentlemens ſeats in it, the plantations ſurrounding which not only exhibit great taſte, but they alſo evince a liberal and public ſpirit in the proprietors.

There is neither coal nor lime in the whole county. There is one mineral well in it. This ſpring is ſituated near Dunſe, and many years ago was the means of making that town a place of public reſort. The water contains iron diſſolved in fixed air, with a little ſea ſalt and bittern. Its effects have been found to be *diuretic* and *corroborant*.

In looking into the hiſtory of agriculture, we behold a miſerable picture of it in thoſe days, when, for mutual defence and ſecurity, every man's lands were ſo interwoven with thoſe of others as to reſemble the teeth of a comb.

This conſtituted what was called runrig, and formed one of the greateſt obſtacles to the improvement of agriculture. Next to that

were

were bad roads. Both these hindrances, to accelerate agricultural knowledge, we have forgot to state in the preliminary observations.

The practice of agriculture in this county, as well as in many others, about 50 years ago, was conducted on principles, and carried on by modes, which were infinitely less productive than results from the present improved system and modes of cultivation. From the great exertions of some landed gentlemen of this county, but more particularly from the unwearied and incessant applications of a few public spirited farmers in it, *agriculture* has arrived at as great a degree of perfection in Berwickshire as in any other county in the island. It has, indeed, by some been called the *Norfolk* of Scotland.

The Author having lived many years at Ayton, in the east end of the county, had an opportunity of observing the great improvements which were carried on with great success on the estate of Ayton, the property of John Fordyce, Esq; as well as in its neighbourhood.

Much

Much praiſe is due to Mr Fordyce for the liberal ſpirit he has long manifeſted in accelerating agricultural acquirements. In planting he has highly diſtinguiſhed himſelf, as, in the courſe of leſs than 30 years, he has planted upwards of 200 acres.

There is one improvement in the county which we cannot but recommend to the attention of the proprietors of Coldingham Moor, in the north eaſt part of the county, and that is, to plant it with fir trees.

As a proof that they would grow, there are ſeven or eight large roots of that ſpecies of wood, in the north part of the moor, ſtanding in the earth as when they were in a growing ſtate.

We beg leave to cloſe theſe obſervations by remarking, that low rented farms, by favouring the native indolence of the human mind, has in many inſtances proved a *quietus* inſtead of a *ſtimulus* to active exertion, which high rented ones generally produce. However juſt this remark may be, we are of opinion, that, for obvious cauſes, no gentleman ſhould let their farms at over-racked rents.

† APPENDIX.

APPENDIX.

THE

CHARTER

OF

BERWICK UPON TWEED.

JAMES by the grace of God King of England Scotland France and Ireland defender of the faith &c. WHEREAS our Borough of Berwick upon Tweed is an antient and populous Borough and the Burgeſſes of the ſaid Borough ſometimes by the name of Mayor Bailiffs and Burgeſſes of the ſaid Borough and ſometimes by other names have had uſed and enjoyed and have uſe and enjoy divers liberties franchiſes immunities cuſtoms preheminencies and other hereditaments as well by divers charters and letters patent of diverſe our progenitors and predeceſſors Kings and Queens of England as alſo by reaſon of divers preſcriptions and cuſtoms uſed and had within the ſaid Borough. And whereas our well beloved ſubjects the Mayor Bailiffs and Burgeſſes of the Borough of Berwick upon Tweed aforesaid have humbly beseeched us that we would exhibit and extend our royal grace and bounty to the said Mayor Bailiffs and Burgesses on their behalf And that we will vouchsafe for the better governing ruling and bettering of the said Borough by our letters patent to make reduce constitute and create a-new the said Mayor Bailiffs and Burgesses into one corporate and politick body by the name of Mayor Bailiffs and Burgesses of the Borough of Berwick upon Tweed with augmentation and addition of certain liberties privileges immunities and franchizes as to us shall seem most expedient We therefore willing that from henceforth for ever hereafter there be continually had and used one certain and undoubted mannor in our said Borough of in and about the keeping of the peace and for the ruling of our said Borough and of our people there inhabiting and others thither resorting and that the said Borough may be and remain in all future times a Borough of peace and quiet to the fear and terror of evil and the reward and nourishing of men And also that our peace and other facts of justice and good government may the better there be kept and done And hoping that if the Mayor Bailiffs and Burgesses of the said Borough and their successors may by our royal grant enjoy great and large dignities privileges jurisdictions liberties and franchises they will think themselves more especially and strongly obliged unto the performance and execution of their best service to us our heirs and successors And also at the humble petition and request of our right well beloved and faithfull counsellor Sir George Hume knight our

our treaſurer of our kingdom of Scotland chancellor of our exchequer of our ſpecial grace and of our certain knowledge and mere motion We have willed ordained appointed granted and declared and by theſe preſents for us our heirs and ſucceſſors do will ordain appoint grant and declare that our ſaid Borough of Berwick upon Tweed from henceforth for ever hereafter may be ſhall be and remain a free Borough of itſelf and that the men of the ſame Borough be free burgeſſes And that they may have all liberties and free cuſtoms to a free Borough belonging for ever And that the Mayor Bailiffs and Burgeſſes of the ſame Borough (whether they have been before this time lawfully incorporated or not) from henceforth for ever hereafter (without any queſtion or doubt to be made hereafter) may be and ſhall be one body corporate and politic in deed fact and law by the name of Mayor Bailiffs and Burgeſſes of the Borough of Berwick upon Tweed and them by the name of Mayor Bailiffs and Burgeſſes of the Borough of Berwick upon Tweed one body politick in deed fact and name fully for us our heirs and ſucceſſors We do erect make ordain conſtitute and declare by theſe preſents and that by the ſame name they may have perpetual ſucceſſion And that they by the name of Mayor Bailiffs and Burgeſſes of the Borough of Berwick upon Tweed may be and ſhall be in future times able and in law capable to have purchaſe receive enjoy and retain lands tenements liberties priviledges juriſdictions franchiſes and hereditaments whatſoever of what kind nature or quality ſoever they ſhall be to them and their ſucceſſors in fee

A free Borough.

fee and perpetuity or for term of years or year or otherwise howsoever And also goods and chattels whatsoever and also to give grant alien assign and dispose lands tenements and hereditaments and also goods and chattels whatsoever and unto all singular other deeds and things to be done and executed by the names aforesaid And that they may be able and of force by the same name of Mayor Bailiffs and Burgesses of the Borough of Berwick upon Tweed to plead and be impleaded to answer and be answered to defend and be defended in what courts and places soever before us our heirs and successors and before whatsoever our judges and justices and other persons and officers under us our heirs and successors and others whatsoever in all and singular actions pleas suits quarrels causes matters and demands whatsoever of whatsoever kind nature or quality they may be and shall be in manner and form as any other our leige people of this our kingdom of England personable and in law capable as any other body corporate and politick within our kingdom of England can and are able to have purchase receive possess enjoy plead and be impleaded answer and be answered defend and be defended do permit or execute And that the aforesaid Mayor Bailiffs and Burgesses of the Borough aforesaid and their successors may have for ever a common seal to serve during their and their successors causes and businesses whatsoever And that it may and shall be lawful to the said Mayor Bailiffs and Burgesses and their successors at their pleasures from time to time to break change and make new that seal as to them shall seem best

That they may have a commission seal and alter it at pleasure.

to

to be done And further of our abundant grace we will and by these presents for us our heirs and successors do grant to the said Mayor Bailiffs and Burgesses of the said Borough and their successors That the Mayor Bailiffs and Burgesses of the said Borough aforesaid or the greater part of them (whereof we will that the Mayor of the said Borough for the time being shall be one) shall have and by these presents may have full authority power and faculty of framing constituting appointing ordaining making and establishing from time to time such like laws statutes ordinances and constitutions which to them or the greater part of them (whereof we will that the Mayor of the Borough aforesaid for the time being be one) in their best discretion shall be thought to be good profitable wholesome honest and necessary for the good rule and government of the Mayor Bailiffs and Burgesses of the Borough aforesaid and all and singular other burgesses officers ministers artificers inhabitants and residents whosoever within the said Borough for the time being for declaration and orders how the Mayor Bailiffs and Burgesses and their successors and all and singular other officers ministers artificers inhabitants and residents for the time being within the said Borough shall behave carry and use themselves in those offices functions ministries trades and businesses within the said Borough and the liberties thereof for the more plentiful and public good common profit and good government of the said Borough for victualling the said Borough And also for the better preservation governing disposing letting and demising of the lands possessions revenues

That they may make laws for the good of the Borough.

venues

venues and hereditaments of the Mayor Bailiffs and Burgeſſes of the aforeſaid Borough and their ſucceſſors given granted and aſſigned and other things or cauſes whatſoever touching or any ways concerning the aforeſaid Borough or the eſtate right or intereſt of the ſame And that the Mayor Bailiffs and Burgeſſes of the Borough aforeſaid for the time being or the greater part of them (whereof we will that the Mayor of the ſaid Borough for the time being be one) as often as they ſhall frame make eſtabliſh or ordain ſuch like laws inſtitutions orders ordinances and conſtitutions in form aforeſaid may and may have power to make ordain limit and provide ſuch like pains puniſhment and penalties by bodily impriſonment or by fines and amerciaments or by either of them upon and againſt all offenders againſt ſuch the law inſtitutions decrees conſtitutions and ordinances or any of them as to the ſaid Mayor Bailiffs and Burgeſſes for the time being or the greater part of them (whereof we will that the Mayor of the ſaid Borough for the time being be one) ſhall be thought fit neceſſary or requiſite to be done for the obſervation of the ſame laws ordinances and conſtitutions and to levy and have the ſame fines and amerciaments to the uſe and behoof of the aforeſaid Mayor Bailiffs and Burgeſſes of the ſaid Borough and their ſucceſſors without hindrance of us our heirs or ſucceſſors or any other officers or miniſters of us our heirs or ſucceſſors and without any account therefore to be made to us our heirs or miniſters of us our heirs or ſucceſſors all and ſingular which laws ordinances and conſtitutions to be made as aforeſaid

Power to fine or impriſon ſuch as break laws ſo made.

aforeſaid we will ſhall be obſerved under the pains thereinto be contained ſo always that the ſaid laws ordinances inſtitutions conſtitutions impriſonments fines and amerciaments may be reaſonable and not repugnant or contrary to the laws ſtatutes cuſtoms or rights of our kingdom of England or reaſonable and laudable preſcriptions and cuſtoms in the ſaid Borough antiently uſed and accuſtomed And further we will and by theſe preſents for us our heirs and ſucceſſors do ordain that from henceforth for ever hereafter there may be and ſhall be in the Borough aforeſaid one Mayor of the Burgeſſes of the Borough aforeſaid in form of thoſe letters patent and below ſpecified to be elected and choſen And for the better execution thereof we will and grant on this behalf we have aſſigned named conſtituted and made and by theſe preſents for us our heirs and ſucceſſors do name conſtitute aſſign and make our well beloved Michael Sanderſon now Mayor of the Borough aforeſaid to be and remain the preſent Mayor of the ſaid Borough, willing that the ſaid Michael Sanderſon ſhall be and continue in the office of Mayor of the ſaid Borough from the date of theſe preſents until the feaſt of St Michael the Arch Angel next enſuing (if the ſaid Michael Sanderſon ſhall ſo long live) and from the ſame day until the ſaid Michael Sanderſon or ſome other Burgeſs ſhall in due manner be elected deputed and ſworn to that office according to the ordinances and proviſions hereafter in theſe preſents expreſſed and declared And further we will and by theſe preſents for us our heirs and ſucceſſors ordain that from henceforth for ever hereafter there

may

may be and ſhall be in the aforeſaid Borough four Bailiffs of the Burgeſſes of the Borough aforeſaid according to the form in theſe letters patent ſpecified to be elected and choſen and for the better execution of our will and grant on this behalf we have aſſigned named and conſtituted and by theſe preſents for us our heirs and ſucceſſors do aſſign name conſtitute and make our well beloved John Shotton Edward Haddleſey Leonard Fairly and Stephen Jackſon now Bailiffs of the Borough aforeſaid to be and remain the preſent Bailiffs of the aforeſaid Borough to continue in the office until the ſaid feaſt of St Michael the Arch Angel next enſuing (if the ſaid John Edward Leonard and Stephen ſo long live) and from the ſame day until the ſaid John Edward Leonard and Stephen or ſome other Burgeſſes of the ſame Borough in due manner ſhall be elected deputed and ſworn unto the office of Bailiffs of the Borough aforeſaid according to the ordinances and proviſions in theſe preſents hereafter ſpecified and declared And we will and grant by theſe preſents for us our heirs and ſucceſſors to the ſaid Mayor Bailiffs and Burgeſſes of the Borough aforeſaid and their ſucceſſors that they the ſaid Mayor Bailiffs and Burgeſſes or the greater part of them from time to time in all future times may have and ſhall have power and authority yearly and every year upon the feaſt of St Michael the Arch Angel to aſſemble and convocate themſelves together in the Guild Hall or Tolbooth of the ſaid Borough or in ſome other convenient places within the ſame Borough And the ſame Mayor Bailiffs and Burgeſſes of the ſaid Borough

or

or the greater part of them before they ſhall depart from thence may chuſe and nominate one of themſelves to be Mayor of the Borough aforeſaid for one whole year then next following and from thence until the ſame Mayor or ſome other Burgeſs of the Borough aforeſaid ſhall be choſen deputed and ſworn to execute that office which Burgeſs after that he ſhall be ſo elected and nominated as aforeſaid unto the Mayoralty of the aforeſaid Borough before he ſhall be admitted to execute that office ſhall take a corporal oath before the laſt Mayor his predeceſſor the Bailiffs and other the Burgeſſes of that Borough for the time being or ſo many of them as ſhall be the preſent rightly well and faithfully to execute that office in all things relating thereunto And we will and by theſe preſents for us our heirs and ſucceſſors do grant to the ſaid Mayor Bailiffs and Burgeſſes of the ſaid Borough and their ſucceſſors that the Mayor Bailiffs and Burgeſſes of the Borough aforeſaid or the greater part of them (whereof we will that the Mayor of the aforeſaid Borough be one) from time to time in all future times may have and ſhall have power and authority yearly and every year on the aforeſaid feaſt of St Michael the Arch Angel in the ſaid place within the ſaid Borough to elect and nominate four of themſelves to be Bailiffs of the ſaid Borough for one whole year next enſuing And that after they be ſo elected and nominated as aforeſaid to the office of Bailiffs of the ſaid Borough before they be admitted to execute the office of Bailiffs of the ſaid Borough ſhall take a corporal oath before the Mayor and laſt Bailiffs their predeceſſors and the reſt of the Burgeſſes of that Borough or ſo many of them as ſhall be then preſent rightly well and faithfully to execute the office of Bailiffs of the Borough aforeſaid in all things concerning that office And that after the ſaid oath ſo taken they may execute the ſaid office of Bailiffs of the ſaid Borough for one whole year next following And moreover we will and by theſe preſents for us our heirs and ſucceſſors do grant to the ſaid Mayor Bailiffs and Burgeſſes of the aforeſaid Borough and their ſucceſſors That if it ſhall happen that the Mayor of the ſaid Borough at any time within one year (after that he hath been elected to the office of Mayor) to die or to be removed from his office that then and ſo often it ſhall and may be lawful to the aforeſaid Bailiffs and Burgeſſes of the Borough aforeſaid for the time being or the greater part of them in convenient time after the death or remove of any ſuch like Mayor to elect and make another of themſelves to be Mayor of the Borough aforeſaid and that being ſo elected as aforeſaid to the office of Mayor of the ſaid Borough may have and exerciſe that office during the reſidue of that year taking firſt the corporal oath in form aforeſaid and ſo from time to time ſo often as the caſe ſhall ſo happen And moreover we will and by theſe preſents for us our heirs and ſucceſſors do grant to the aforeſaid Mayor Bailiffs and Burgeſſes of the Borough aforeſaid and their ſucceſſors that if it ſhall happen the Bailiffs of the ſaid Borough or any of them at any time within one year after they have been elected and ſworn to the office of Bailiffs of the ſaid Borough as aforeſaid to die or ſhall

Power to elect a new Mayor if one die or be removed.

ſhall be removed from that office that then and ſo often it and may be lawful to and for the ſaid Mayor and other Bailiffs of the ſaid Borough then ſurviving and remaining and the Burgeſſes of the ſame Borough for the time being or the greater part of them (whereof we will that the Mayor of the ſaid Borough for the time being ſhall be one) one other or two three or four others (as the caſe ſhall require) of themſelves to be Bailiff or Bailiffs of the ſaid Borough and that he or they ſo elected to the office or offices of Bailiffs of the ſaid Borough have and exerciſe that office during the reſidue of the ſame year their corporal oaths in form aforeſaid being firſt taken and ſo as often as the caſe ſhall happen We will alſo and by theſe preſents for us our heirs and ſucceſſors do grant to the ſaid Mayor Bailiffs and Burgeſſes of the Borough aforeſaid and their ſucceſſors that from time to time there may be and ſhall be in the ſaid Borough one honeſt and diſcreet man learned in the laws of England and ſhall be and ſhall be called Recorder of the ſaid Borough and ſhall do and execute all and ſingular thoſe things which do belong and ought to belong to the faithful doing and executing the office of Recorder within the ſame Borough. And alſo we have aſſigned named ordained and conſtituted and made and by theſe preſents do aſſign name declare ordain conſtitute and make Chriſtopher Perkinſon of Greys Inn in the County of Middleſex Gentleman to be preſent Recorder of the ſaid Borough to have and execute the ſaid office of Recorder of the ſame Borough according to the tenor and effect of the

grant

grant of the ſaid office of the new Mayor Bailiffs and Burgeſſes of the ſaid Borough to the ſaid Chriſtopher Perkinſon before made and to be made to be executed and executed by himſelf or his ſufficient deputy or deputies upon his oath juſtice and other things which do pertain or ought to pertain to the office of Recorder of the ſaid Borough faithfully to exerciſe and execute and that from time to time and at all times after the death of the ſaid Chriſtopher Perkinſon or his remove from that office the ſaid Mayor Bailiffs and Burgeſſes of the ſaid Borough for the time being and their ſucceſſors or the greater part of them (whereof we will that the Mayor of the ſaid Borough for the time being be one) may elect nominate and appoint one other honeſt and diſcreet man learned in the laws of England to be Recorder of the ſaid Borough And that he who ſhall be ſo elected and ſworn to the office of Recorder of the ſaid Borough as aforeſaid after the death or remove of the ſaid Chriſtopher Perkinſon may have enjoy and exerciſe that office of Recorder of the ſaid Borough aforeſaid according to the tenor and effect of the grant thereof to be made to him by the Mayor Bailiffs and Burgeſſes of the ſaid Borough for the time being and ſo often as the caſe ſhall ſo happen And we will and for us our heirs and ſucceſſors do grant to the ſaid Mayor Bailiffs and Burgeſſes of the ſaid Borough and their ſucceſſors that they and their ſucceſſors from henceforth for ever hereafter may have and hold and may be able to have and hold within the ſaid Borough one Court of Pleas every Tueſday in every ſecond week throughout the year to be holden before the Mayor Bailiffs and Recorder of the ſaid Borough for the time being or before any three of them (whereof we will that the Mayor of the ſaid Borough for the time being ſhall be one) in the Guild Hall or Tolbooth of the ſaid Borough and that they may hold in that court by plaints in the ſame court to be levied or otherwiſe according to the laudable and reaſonable cuſtoms before uſed and accuſtomed in the ſaid Borough All and all manner of pleas accounts ſuits complaints and demands as well real as perſonal and mixed of all perſonal tranſgreſſions whatſoever with force and arms and of whatſoever other tranſgreſſions done moved ariſing had or committed or hereafter to be done moved had or committed within the ſaid Borough ſuburbs liberties and precincts thereof And of all and all manner of intruſials tentures burgages lands tenements goods chattles debts pleas upon the caſe deceits accompts covenants detinues of charters eſcripts minuments and chattles the taking and detaining of beaſts and cattle and other contracts whatſoever of whatſoever cauſe or thing ariſing or in time to come happening to ariſe within the ſaid Borough ſuburbs liberties and precincts thereof to whatſoever ſum or value the ſaid tranſgreſſion debts accompts covenants deceipts detinues or other contracts they ſhall amount And that ſuch like pleas plaints quarrels ſuits and accompts may be there heard and determined before the ſaid Mayor Bailiffs and Recorder of the ſaid Borough for the time being or any three of them (whereof we will that the Mayor of the ſaid Borough for the time being ſhall be one) by ſuch and

ſuch

ſuch like proceedings ways and means according to the laws and cuſtoms of our kingdom of England or according to the ancient reaſonable and laudable cuſtoms of the ſaid Borough heretofore uſed and allowed in the ſaid Borough and in as large manner and form as in any court of pleas in any city borough or town corporate within this our kingdom of England or in our ſaid Borough of Berwick upon Tweed heretofore hath been uſed or accuſtomed or may or ought to be done

That they may have the recognizance of all Pleas.

AND FURTHER we will and by theſe preſents for us our heirs and ſucceſſors do grant to the ſaid Mayor Bailiffs and Burgeſſes of the ſaid Borough and their ſucceſſors That they and their ſucceſſors from time to time in all iſſuing times may have and may be of force to have the cognizance of all and all manner of pleas quarrels plaints accompts and demands whatſoever as well real as perſonal and mixed in what courts ſoever of us our heirs and ſucceſſors moved and begun or to be moved and begun of whatſoever things cauſes and matters happening ariſing or growing within the ſaid Borough ſuburbs liberties and precincts thereof as they have been anciently accuſtomed within the ſaid Borough

That the Mayor may be Eſcheator in the ſaid Borough.

AND FURTHER we will and by theſe preſents for us our heirs and ſucceſſors do grant to the ſaid Mayor Bailiffs and Burgeſſes of the ſaid Borough and their ſucceſſors that the Mayor of the ſaid Borough for the time being may be and ſhall be from henceforth for ever hereafter

eſcheats

efcheats and efcheator to us our heirs and fucceffors within the faid Borough the liberties and precincts thereof as before hath been ufed in the faid Borough And that he and his fucceffors fhall do and execute for ever all things which do belong to the office of efcheators within the faid Borough fuburbs liberties and precincts thereof to be done his corporal oath being firft taken for the faithful executing of the faid office of efcheator of the faid Borough fo that no efcheator or other minifter of us our heirs or fucceffors enter or interpofe himfelf into the faid Borough liberties or precincts thereof to do or execute any thing in the faid Borough which doth belong unto the faid office of efcheator unlefs it be in default of the Mayor for the time being

That they may have power to chufe a Coroner.

AND ALSO we will and by thefe prefents for us our heirs and fucceffors do grant to the faid Mayor Bailiffs and Burgeffes of the faid Borough and their fucceffors that from henceforth for ever hereafter there may be and fhall be in the faid Borough one honeft fit man who fhall be and fhall be called the Coroner of the faid Borough to ferve the office of Coroner in the faid Borough fuburbs liberties and precincts thereof and to do and execute every thing there which doth belong to the office of Coroner from time to time which faid Coroner fhall be appointed nominated and elected by the faid Mayor Bailiffs and Burgeffes or the greater part of them (whereof we will that the Mayor of the faid Borough for the time being fhall be one) And that the faid Coroner fo to be elected and nominated

nominated as aforeſaid faithfully to execute his office aforeſaid in due manner may and ſhall be ſworn before the Mayor Bailiffs and Recorder of the ſaid Borough or the greater part of them for the time being (whereof we will that the Mayor of the ſaid Borough for the time being ſhall be one) and that after ſuch oath ſo performed he ought and may have power to execute and exerciſe that office during the pleaſure of the ſaid Mayor Bailiffs and Burgeſſes of the ſame Borough or the greater part of them (whereof we will that the Mayor of the ſaid Borough for the time being ſhall be one

That they may have four Serjeants at Mace.

AND FURTHER we will and by theſe preſents for us our heirs and ſucceſſors do grant to the ſaid Mayor Bailiffs and Burgeſſes of the ſaid Borough and their ſucceſſors that from henceforth for ever hereafter there may be and ſhall be in that Borough officers not exceeding the number of four who ſhall be and ſhall be called Serjeants at Mace to ſerve in the court of the ſaid Borough for proclamations arreſting and executing of proceſs precepts and other buſineſſes belonging to the office of Serjeants at Mace in the ſaid Borough limits precincts and bounds thereof from time to time to execute and perform which Serjeants at Mace ſhall be appointed nominated and elected by the ſaid Mayor and the Bailiffs of the ſaid Borough or the greater part of them (whereof we will that the Mayor of the ſaid Borough for the time being ſhall be one) and they ſhall be attendant from time to time upon the Mayor and Bailiffs of the ſaid Borough for the time being.

being And the Serjeants at Mace to be elected and nominated as aforesaid for the faithful executing and exercising their offices aforesaid in due manner may and shall be sworn before the Mayor Bailiffs and Recorder of the said Borough or the greater part of them (whereof the Mayor of the said Borough for the time being to be one)

AND FURTHER we will by these presents for us our heirs and successors do grant to the said Mayor Bailiffs and Burgesses of the said Borough and their successors that they and their successors from henceforth for ever hereafter may have within the said Borough a Merchant Guild with house and all other liberties privileges and free customs belonging to that Guild in as ample manner and form as before they have had accustomed or ought to have so that none who is not of that Guild may make any merchandize in the said Borough liberties or precincts thereof but at the will and pleasure of the Mayor Bailiffs and Burgesses of the said Borough

Power to have a Merchant Guild.

AND ALSO we will and by these presents for us our heirs and successors do grant to the said Mayor Bailiffs and Burgesses of the said Borough and their successors That what merchant soever shall come into the said Borough with their merchandize of what place soever they shall be whether strangers or others who shall be of our peace or by our licence shall come into our land may come stay and depart in our peace doing the right customs of the same Borough

That any merchant may come in with his merchandize.

That the Burgeſſes may not be queſtioned in their declaration.

AND that the ſaid Burgeſſes or merchants may not be queſtioned for miſtelling in their declarations (that is to ſay) if they do not declare altogether ſo well

That no merchant go to meet any merchandize.

AND that no merchant may go to meet merchants coming by land or water with their merchandizes and victuals towards the ſaid Borough to buy or again to ſell until they be come to the ſaid Borough and there have ſet to ſale their merchandize upon forfeit of the things ſo bought and pain of impriſonment from whence without ſevere puniſhment he may not depart And that no ſtrange merchant who is not of the ſaid Merchant Guild and of the liberty of the ſaid Borough may make any contract or merchandize within the ſaid Borough ſuburbs liberties or precincts thereof to any other ſtrange merchant nor ſuch like ſtrange merchant may make ſuch merchandize with any other ſtrange merchant within the ſaid Borough upon forfeiture of the ſaid merchandize

That no ſtrange merchant may uſe any trad in the Borough.

No ſtrange merchant to ſell any thing but in groſs.

AND that no merchant which is a ſtranger and not of the Merchant Guild aforeſaid may ſell any merchandize in the ſaid Borough but in groſs We have granted alſo and by theſe preſents for us our heirs and ſucceſſors do grant to the ſaid Mayor Bailiffs and Burgeſſes of the ſaid Borough and their ſucceſſors that they yearly from time to time the ſaid Mayor Bailiffs and Burgeſſes of the ſaid Borough and their ſucceſſors may and may have power to enquire and make ſearch within the ſaid Borough ſuburbs liberties and precincts thereof if any Burgeſs of the liberty of

Power to examine if any Burgeſs colour any foreign goods.

of the ſaid Borough in his own proper name or in the name of any other Burgeſs of the ſaid Borough and as their proper goods and merchandize or as the goods and merchandize of any other Burgeſs of the ſaid Borough do ſell or ſet to ſale within the ſaid Borough any goods chattles or merchandize or the wares and merchandize of them who are not Burgeſſes of that Borough nor of the liberties of the ſame contrary to their oath in that behalf taken And that if any Burgeſs of the ſaid Borough ſhall be found guilty thereof and convicted according to the cuſtoms of the Guild of the ſaid Borough that ſaid Burgeſſes ſo offending ſhall utterly loſe his liberty in the ſaid Borough and therein ſhall be disfranchized for ever And that no ſtrange merchant may ſell or buy any wares or merchandizes which ought to be weighted or balanced but by our beam or weight upon forfeiture of the ſaid wares And alſo we will and by theſe preſents for us our heirs and ſucceſſors do grant to the ſaid Mayor Bailiffs and Burgeſſes of the ſaid Borough and their ſucceſſors that the cuſtomers weighters and other officers whatſoever who ſhall happen hereafter to be aſſigned in the ſaid Borough by us or by our heirs or ſucceſſors ſhall from henceforth continually be reſident and ſtay in the ſaid Borough upon their offices ſo that by their abſence or default merchants be not deferred or hindred about the delivery of their merchandizes And that no burgeſs of the ſaid Borough be detained or reſtrained for any debt or pledge unleſs to be debtor or pledge Furthermore we will and by theſe preſents for us our heirs and ſucceſſors do grant to the ſaid Mayor Bailiffs and Burgeſſes of the ſaid Borough and their

Burgeſſes colouring ſtrangers goods and thereof convicted to be disfranchiſed.

Burgeſſes not to be put upon juries, &c without the ſaid Borough.

their ſucceſſors that the ſaid Mayor Bailiffs and Burgeſſes of the ſaid Borough for the time being be not put in aſſize juries attaints or other recognizances by reaſon of any intruſials tenures or againſt their wills without the ſaid Borough and that the ſaid Burgeſſes of the ſaid Borough and their ſucceſſors be not conſtrained or compelled by us our heirs or ſucceſſors to go or be ſent to war without the ſaid Borough and ſuburbs liberties and precincts thereof but by the ſpecial commandment of us our heirs and ſucceſſors as before in the ſaid Borough hath been lawfully uſed and accuſtomed And that no man may take lodging within the ſaid Borongh by force or by livery of our Mayor our heirs and ſucceſſors we have granted moreovor and by theſe preſents for us our heirs and ſucceſſors of our ſpecial grace and of our certain knowledge and mere motion do grant to the ſaid Mayor Bailiffs and Burgeſſes of the ſaid Borough and their ſucceſſors that they may have the return of all our writs precepts and proceſs of us our heirs and ſucceſſors of whatſoever courts of us our heirs or ſucceſſors coming and ariſing within the ſaid Borough and the executions of them ſo that no Sheriff miniſter or Bailiff for us our heirs or ſucceſſors ſhall enter into the ſaid Borough ſuburbs liberties or precincts thereof to do any office there for any belonging to the ſaid Borough but in default of the Mayor and Bailiffs of the ſaid Borough

To have the return of all writs, &c.

AND FURTHER of our ſpecial grace and of our certain knowledge and mere motion we have given and granted and

No Burgeſs or cuſtom-houſe officer com-

and by thefe prefents for us our heirs and fucceffors do give and grant to the faid Mayor Bailiffs and Burgeffes of the faid Borough and their fucceffors that the faid Mayor Bailiffs and Burgeffes of the faid Borough or any of them or the cuftom-houfe weighters or officers of us &c within the faid Borough for the time being or any of them fhall not be employed nor fhall not be compelled to anfwer for any intrufials tenures or tranfgreffions debts contracts accounts or any other caufes or things within the faid Borough fuburbs liberties limits and precincts thereof done or to be done elfewhere than within the faid Borough before the Mayor and Bailiffs of the faid Borough and their fucceffors or before the Juftices of us our heirs and fucceffors affigned unto it within the faid Borough and not elfewhere And alfo we will and for us our heirs and fucceffors by thefe prefents do grant to the faid Mayor Bailiffs and Burgeffes of the faid Borough and their fucceffors that the faid Mayor Bailiffs and Burgeffes of the faid Borough and their fucceffors through our whole realm and power fhall be quit and exonered forever of toll pontage paffage marage pannage carnage laftage canage picage racage vinage and of all other fale achate rechate through our whole land and power with lock and fack and thole and theam ward and ward-penny and all other cuftoms to be performed of their own proper goods and merchandizes We have granted alfo to the faid Mayor Bailiffs and Burgeffes of the faid Borough and their fucceffors by thefe prefents quittance of murder within the faid Borough fuburbs liberties and precincts thereof And further we will

pellable to anfwer for intrufials or tenures done in the town, &c.

That they fhall be quit of toll, &c. through the whole realm.

Quittances of murder.

and

and do grant to the ſaid Mayor Bailiffs and Burgeſſes of the ſaid Borough and their ſucceſſors that the ſaid Mayor Bailiffs and Burgeſſes of the ſaid Borough and their ſucceſſors ſhall be free quit diſcharged and exonerated from all payments of ſuſidies taxes impoſitions tenths fifteenths and exactions whatſoever due or granted or hereafter to be granted to us our heirs and ſucceſſors as before in the ſaid Borough hath been uſed and accuſtomed And alſo from priſage of wines butleridge and priſage of wines for any wines carried unloaden or put to land or hereafter to be brought unloaden or put on land by the ſaid Mayor Bailiffs and Burgeſſes of the ſaid Borough or any of them within the ſaid port of the borough aforeſaid or the members and creeks of the ſaid port as before hath been uſed and accuſtomed And that the Mayor Bailiffs and Burgeſſes of the ſaid Borough and their ſucceſſors and every of them from henceforth for ever hereafter at their pleaſures may tranſport and convey over hides ſkins and all other things and merchandiſe whatſoever from the port of the ſaid Borough or from the members or creeks of the ſaid port into whatſoever place or places port or ports they will with the ſame liberties priviledges and immunities and in as ample and benefical manner and form as before time hath been uſed and accuſtomed in the ſaid Borough and as by divers laws ſtatutes and ordinances of our kingdom of England before publiſhed and provided hath been decreed and ordained And further of our more abundant grace and for the bettering of the ſaid Borough we will and for us our heirs and ſucceſſors by theſe preſents do grant

Free from all impoſitions, butleridge, and priſage of wines.

That they may tranſport corn, &c.

grant that the ſaid Mayor Bailiffs and Burgeſſes of the ſaid Borough and their ſucceſſors and every of them may at their pleaſure tranſport and convey corn and grain of every kind and quality being their proper goods and chattels from the port of the ſaid Borough and from any members and creeks of the ſaid port whereſoever they will according to the form and effect of certain ſtatutes in ſuch caſes provided and made without any other impoſition or exaction thereupon before impoſed or hereafter to be impoſed of us our heirs or ſucceſſors otherwiſe than in thoſe ſtatutes or any of them is ſpecified or contained.

AND FURTHER of our more abundant ſpecial grace and of our certain knowledge and meer motion we have given and granted and by theſe preſents for us our heirs and ſucceſſors do give and grant full free and lawful power faculty and authority to the ſaid Mayor Bailiffs and Burgeſſes of the ſaid Borough and their ſucceſſors that they and their ſucceſſors from time to time may ſhip burthen and load all and all manner of coals carried by ſea or Engliſh ſea coals and all other coals in Engliſh called ſtone coals and pit coals or by other name or names ſoever the ſame are called or named being digged or taken out of the earth into any ſhip craier or veſſel or into any ſhips veſſels or craier in the port of the ſaid Borough of Berwick or in any creeks or places belonging or appertaining to the ſaid port And that they may have power freely and without controul to convey and tranſport the ſaid coals ſo ſhipped burthened and loaded at their willand pleaſure into anyport creek And coals.

creek or place within this our kingdom of England or other our dominions or into any parts beyond the ſeas without this our kingdom of England without any impoſition taxes ſum or ſums of money therefore to be paid any way to us our heirs and ſucceſſors beſides the antient cuſtoms ſums of money and other duties to us our heirs and predeceſſors antiently due and payable for ſuch like kind of coals any ſtatutes acts ordinances or proviſos or any other thing cauſe or matter whatſoever in any thing notwithſtanding

Cuſtody of orphans appointed.

AND moreover we will and by theſe preſents for us our heirs and ſucceſſors do grant to the ſaid Mayor Bailiffs and Burgeſſes of the ſaid Borough and their ſucceſſors that if any Burgeſs of the ſaid Borough have any orphans begotten in lawful matrimony and that the ſaid Burgeſs happen to die the ſaid orphans with their chattels lands and tenements and poſſeſſions by the Mayor and Bailiffs of the ſaid Borough ſhall be put into cuſtody of ſome faithful burgeſs of the ſaid Borough next of kin to the ſaid orphan to whom the inheritance of the ſaid orphan cannot deſcend who ſhall give ſufficient ſecurity that he ſhall keep and defend the ſaid orphans their lands tenements without ſale waſte or ſpot and fully anſwer and reſtore all iſſues of the lands tenements and houſes of thoſe orphans in the time of their cuſtody ariſing (the reaſonable coſts and charges for the time of their cuſtody being deducted) to the orphans when they ſhall come to lawful years by the ſight and conſideration of the Mayor Bailiffs and

and Burgeſſes of the ſaid Borough together with the ſurpluſage of his expences We will alſo and by theſe preſents for us our heirs and ſucceſſors do grant to the ſaid Mayor Bailiffs and Burgeſſes of the ſaid Borough and their ſucceſſors that the Mayor Bailiffs and Burgeſſes of the ſaid Borough may have full power every year to ſurvey that the ſaid cuſtody be well and faithfully done to the profit of the ſaid orphans

Those that are free to be reſident in the Town.

AND we will and by theſe preſents for us our heirs and ſucceſſors do grant to the ſaid Mayor Bailiffs and Burgeſſes of the ſaid Borough and their ſucceſſors that all Burgeſſes of the ſaid Borough deſiring to enjoy the liberties immunities and free cuſtoms of the ſaid Borough be ſtaying inhabiting and reſident within the ſaid Borough and be at Guild and ſcot and lot and be partakers of all ceſsments and charges with the reſt of the Burgeſſes of the ſaid Borough as often as it ſhall happen that the ſaid Borough ſhall be taxed for the good ſtate and maintainance of that Borough and the liberties thereof according to their oaths in this behalf made when they were admitted to the ſaid liberty of the ſaid Borough and who ſhall refuſe to do ſo ſhall wholly loſe their liberty in the ſaid Borough ſuburbs liberties limits and precincts thereof And alſo that all other inhabitants not being Burgeſſes nor of the liberty of the ſaid Borough and the Stallingers of the Borough aforeſaid although they be not of the liberty of the ſaid Borough ſhall be partakes in all ceſsments and charges in the

Be at Guild and pay ſcot and lot, &c.

ſaid Borough reaſonably made or to be made for the ſtate and maintenance of the ſaid Borough

That all inhabitants that are not free ſhall be reaſonably aſſeſſed for the good of the Borough.

And that the Mayor Bailiffs and Burgeſſes of the ſaid Borough and their ſucceſſors or the greater part of them (whereof we will that the Mayor of the ſaid Borough for the time being to be one) for the neceſſity commodity and publick good of the ſaid Borough amongſt themſelves with their common aſſent of the goods and chattels of the Burgeſſes of the ſaid Borough and of whomſoever inhabiting within the ſaid Borough as well of the rents as of other things of the Burgeſſes and inhabitants within the ſaid Borough ſuburbs liberties and precincts thereof as ſhall beſt ſeem to them ſhall reaſonably tax and may impoſe taxes and tallages and taxations without let or hindrance of us our heirs or ſucceſſors or of our officers and miniſters of us our heirs and ſucceſſors whatſoever And that all ſum and ſums of money from time to time coming of and by theſe tallages may be to the uſe of the chamber of the ſaid Borough for the neceſſity profit and public good of the ſaid Borough and not otherwiſe to be diſburſed

That they may keep two markets every week.

And further we will and by theſe preſents for us our heirs and ſucceſſors do grant to the ſaid Mayor Bailiffs and Burgeſſes of the ſaid Borough and their ſucceſſors that they and their ſucceſſors may for ever have hold and keep within the ſaid Borough ſuburbs liberties limits and precincts thereof weekly two markets and whatſoever doth belong or ought to belong to a market every week (that is to ſay) one in and upon the Wedneſday and the other

other in and upon the Saturday in every week for ever in the ſaid Borough ſuburbs liberties limits and precincts to be holden.

That they may have one fair in every year.

AND that they may have one fair in every year in the ſaid Borough ſuburbs liberties limits and precincts thereof with all things thereunto belonging to continue from the feaſt of the invention of the Holy Croſs until the feaſt of the nativity of St John Baptiſt together with a court of pyepowders and together with all tolls cuſtoms liberties and free cuſtoms to ſuch like markets fairs marts and courts of pyepowder belonging or appertaining together with tolls thols tallages picage fines amerciaments and all other commodities profits and emoluments whatſoever of ſuch like markets and fairs or marts and courts of pyepowder coming having ariſing or growing and with all other free cuſtoms and liberties to ſuch markets fairs and marts and courts of pyepowder belonging or appertaining.

The Mayor to be Clerk of the Market.

AND we have granted and by theſe preſents for us our heirs and ſucceſſors do grant to the ſaid Mayor Bailiffs and Burgeſſes of the ſaid Borough and their ſucceſſors That the Mayor of the ſaid Borough for the time being for ever hereafter and from henceforth may be and ſhall be Clerk of the Market for us our heirs and ſucceſſors within the ſaid Borough ſuburbs liberties limits and precincts thereof And that the Mayor of the ſaid Borough for the time being may do and execute and may have power

power to and execute for ever all and whatsoever which there belongeth to the office of Clerk of the Market to be done and all and singular other deeds and things to be done or performed which do and belong to the doing and executing of that office within the said Borough suburbs liberties limits and precincts thereof as in former times hath been used in the said Borough so that the Clerk of the Market of our house of us our heirs and successors by no means shall come hereafter for the assize of bread wine and ale or the breaking of weights or measures into the same Borough suburbs liberties limits and precincts thereof to any thing which belongeth unto the office of Clerk of the Market Moreover we grant for us our heirs and successors to the Mayor Bailiffs and Burgesses of the said Borough and their successors That the said Mayor Bailiffs and Burgesses and their successors may have hold within the said Borough and the suburbs liberties and precincts thereof from henceforth for ever hereafter a court leet and view of frank-pledge of all the Burgesses inhabitants and residents within the said Borough and suburbs liberties and precincts thereof twice by the year to be holden in the Guild-hall of the said Borough at the same days and times which hath been agreeing to the laws and statutes of our kingdom of England and all and every thing that belongeth to view of frank-pledge in as ample manner and form as the Mayor Bailiffs and Burgesses of the said Borough or any of them before have holden it or have been able or ought to hold it And we also will and by these presents for us our heirs and successors do grant to

That they may hold Court Leet twice by the year.

The Mayor to have the keeping of

to the ſaid Mayor Bailiffs and Burgeſſes of the ſaid Borough and their ſucceſſors That the Mayors of the ſaid Borough and their ſucceſſors for the time being may have the cuſtody and government of the Gates Poſterns and Wickets of the ſaid Borough alſo the cuſtody of the Keys of the ſaid Gates

the Keys of the Priſon and Gates.

AND FURTTER we will and by theſe preſents for us our heirs and ſucceſſors do grant to the ſaid Mayor Bailiffs and Burgeſſes of the ſaid Borough and their ſucceſſors that the ſame Mayor Bailiffs and Burgeſſes and their ſucceſſors may have within the ſaid Borough or ſuburbs liberties limits and precincts thereof one Priſon or Goal for the priſoning or keeping of all and ſingular priſoners within the ſaid Borough liberties ſuburbs liberties and precincts thereof attached arreſted taken or apprehended or to be attached arreſted taken or apprehended or in the priſon or goal of the ſaid Borough for whatſoever cauſe or matter to be adjudged or committed there to ſtay and by the Mayor and Bailiffs of the ſaid Borough for the time being or miniſter or miniſters deputed or to be deputed by them to be ſafely kept as long and until they be delivered by lawful means ſo that the ſaid Mayor Bailiffs and Burgeſſes and their ſucceſſors may do judgment of infang theif and outfang theif as before in the ſaid Borough hath been uſed and accuſtomed

A Priſon.

AND FURTHER we will and by theſe preſents for us our heirs and ſucceſſors do grant to the ſaid Mayor Bailiffs

Power of Juſtices.

and

and Burgeſſes of the ſaid Borough and their ſucceſſors That the Mayor of the ſaid Borough for the time being and the Recorder of the ſaid Borough for the time being and ſuch Burgeſſes or Alderman of the ſaid Borough who have ſuſtained the office of Mayor of the ſaid Borough or hereafter ſhall ſuſtain it after they have executed the ſaid office of Mayoralty as long as they ſhall be Burgeſſes and Aldermen of the ſaid Borough and every one of them may and ſhall be for ever hereafter from henceforth within the ſaid Borough and within the ſuburbs liberties and precincts thereof our juſtices for us our heirs and ſucceſſors to keep and preſerve and cauſe to be kept and preſerved the peace of us our heirs and ſucceſſors within the ſaid Borough ſuburbs liberties and precincts thereof and alſo keep and cauſe to be kept all ordinances and ſtatutes for the good of our peace and for the preſervation of the ſame and for the quiet ruling and governing of our people publiſhed within the ſaid Borough ſuburbs liberties and precincts thereof in all their articles according to the force form and effect of ſuch ordinances and ſtatutes and to chaſtiſe correct and puniſh all and all manner of perſons whatſoever of what eſtate degree or condition ſoever they ſhall be offending againſt the form of thoſe ordinances and ſtatutes or any of them within the ſaid Borough ſuburbs liberties and precincts thereof or have been done againſt theſe ordinances and ſtatutes and to do that all thoſe within the ſaid Borough ſuburbs liberties and precincts thereof who ſhall threaten any of our people to hurt their bodies or burn their houſes to find ſufficient ſe-

curity

curity before them or any of them for the peace or good behaviour towards us or our liege people And if they ſhall refuſe to find ſuch ſecurity then to cauſe them to be ſafely kept in the goal or priſon of the ſaid Borough until they find ſuch ſecurity and that the Mayor Recorder and ſuch of the Aldermen or Burgeſſes of the ſaid Borough who have at any time borne the office of Mayor or hereafter ſhall bear it after that they have borne the ſaid office of Mayor of the ſaid Borough and as long as they ſhall be Burgeſſes or Alderman of that Borough or any three or more of them (whereof we will that the Mayor and Recorder of the ſaid Borough for the time being be two) may have and from henceforth for ever hereafter full power and authority from time to time to inquire hear and determine within the ſaid Borough ſuburbs liberties and precincts thereof of all and all manner of felonies murders homicides robberies aſſaults riots routs forces entries into lands and tenements treſpaſſes againſt the peace of us our heirs and ſucceſſors unlawful conventicles ambidexters conſpiracies contempts concealments and alſo of all miſpriſons offences miſdeeds defaults negligences cauſes and articles who do belong or hereafter may be able to belong to the authority or power of Juſtices or keepers of the peace of us our heirs or ſucceſſors in as ample manner and form as any Juſtices or keepers of the peace of us our heirs or ſucceſſors in any of our counties within this our kingdom of England by the laws and ſtatutes of the ſame kingdom for the offences ſo done and committed in the

ſaid

ſaid county as Juſtices of the Peace may be and may be able to hear and determine.

That the Mayor, Recorder, and Juſtices, may hold a goal delivery.

AND ALSO we will and by theſe preſents for us our heirs and ſucceſſors do grant to the ſaid Mayor Bailiffs and Burgeſſes of the ſaid Borough and their ſucceſſors That the Mayor and Recorder of the ſaid Borough for the time being and ſuch like Burgeſſes and Aldermen of the ſaid Borough who at any time have borne or hereafter ſhall bear the office of Mayor of the ſaid Borough after that they have borne the ſaid office as long as they ſhall be Burgeſſes and Aldermen of the ſaid Borough or any three or more of them (whereof we will that the Mayor and Recorder of the ſaid Borough for the time being ſhall be two) from time to time hereafter may be our Juſtices and every one of them from time to time may be Juſtices of us our heirs and ſucceſſors from time to time to deliver the goal of the ſaid Borough of the priſoners being therein And that the coroner for the time being ſhall make return from time to time of all juries inquiſitions pannels attachments and indentures by him taken or hereafter to be taken before the ſaid Mayor Recorder and the ſaid Burgeſſes or Aldermen of the ſaid Borough for the time being or any three or more of them (whereof we will that the Mayor and Recorder of the ſaid Borough for the time being ſhall be two) when and as often as they will deliver the ſaid goal of the priſoners being in that goal and be attending them in all things touching the ſaid goal delivery and the commandments of

That the Coroner ſhall make return of all juries.

the

for the time being or any three or more of them (whereof we will that the Mayor and Recorder of the ſaid Borough for the time being ſhall be two) ſhall execute from time to time in the ſame manner and form as any Sheriff of our kingdom of England have accuſtomed and ought to do return intend and execute any manner of way by the laws and ſtatutes of this our kingdom of England before the juſtices of goal delivery in any of our counties of the ſaid kingdom our heirs or ſucceſſors And that the ſame Mayor Recorder and Aldermen of the ſaid Borough for the time being or any three or more of them (whereof we will that the Mayor and Recorder of the ſaid Borough for the time being be two) may have and ſhall have and may erect from henceforth hereafter a gallows within the ſaid Borough ſuburbs liberties or precincts thereof to hang and execute felons murtherers and other malefactors within the ſaid Borough adjudged to death according to the laws of England And that the ſaid Mayor Recorder and ſuch like Burgeſſes or Aldermen of the ſaid Borough who at any time have born the office of Mayor of the ſaid Borough or hereafter ſhall bear it after that they have born the ſaid office as long as they ſhall be Burgeſſes or Aldermen of the ſaid Borough or any three or more of them (whereof we will that the Mayor and Recorder for the time being of the ſaid Borough ſhall be two) may take and arreſt whatſoever felons thieves or other malefactors within the ſaid Borough ſuburbs liberties and precincts thereof found or to be found by themſelves or by their miniſters or deputies conſtituted in the

Power to erect a Gallows.

ſaid Borough and that they may carry them to the goal within the ſaid Borough there to be kept in ſafe cuſtody until by due proceſs of law they ſhall be delivered any other ordinance decree or cuſtom to the contrary notwithſtanding Moreover we have granted and by theſe preſents for us our heirs and ſucceſſors of our ſpecial grace certain knowledge and mere motion do grant to the ſaid Mayor Bailiffs and Burgeſſes of the ſaid Borough and their ſucceſſors That they and their ſucceſſors from henceforth for ever hereafter may have enjoy and receive and may be able to have enjoy and receive to the proper uſe and behoof of the ſaid Mayor Bailiffs and Burgeſſes of the ſaid Borough and their ſucceſſors all and all manner of fines ranſoms and amerciaments whatſoever or for whatſoever treſpaſs or other offence or other matters and cauſes committed and to be committed within the ſaid Borough ſuburbs liberties and precincts thereof And all and all manner of fines iſſues amerciaments forfeitures profits and perquiſites of the ſaid courts ſo to be impoſed or forfeited before the ſaid Mayor Recorder and Bailiffs in the court of the ſaid Borough and before the ſaid Mayor Recorder and the ſaid Aldermen of the ſaid Borough or any three or more of them as aforeſaid as juſtices of the peace or of our goal delivery within the ſaid Borough liberties or precincts thereof for whatſoever cauſe or cauſes coming happening ariſing or growing as before hath been uſed and accuſtomed in the ſaid Borough And alſo all and all manner of goods and chattles whatſoever waived deodands chattles of felons and fugitives out-lawed and to be out-

That they ſhall have all fines, &c.

Forfeitures of felons goods.

lawed

lawed waived and to be waived condemned and to be condemned adjudged and to be adjudged attainted and happening to be attainted convicted and to be convicted of fugitives and men put in exigents of all and singular tenants inhabitants and now resident in the said Borough suburbs liberties and precincts thereof from time to time arising happening and coming and that it may and shall be lawful to the said Mayor Bailiffs and Burgesses of the said Borough and their successors the same fines issues amerciaments forfeitures and profits from time to time to levy and collect by the proper Ministers of the said Mayor Bailiffs and Burgesses of the said Borough according to the laws and customs of our kingdom of England or according to the antient customs of the said Borough And that the said Mayor Bailiffs and Burgesses of the said Borough and their successors from time to time may be the better able and of power to bear and import the charges and expences of the said Borough We of our special grace and of our certain knowledge and meer motion have granted and by these presents for us our heirs and successors as much as in use lies Do give and grant special licence free and lawful faculty power and authority to the said Mayor Bailiffs and Burgesses of the Borough and their successors to have purchase and receive to them and their successors for ever as well of us our heirs and successors as of our subjects and leige people whatsoever or of any other whatsoever or of any other person or persons whatsoever the mannors messuages lands tenements rectories tenths rents reversions services and other possessions

or

(that is to ſay) from the deep ſea to the river of Tweed aforeſaid by the ſaid bound road or other metts limits and bounds uſed and accuſtomed whereby the ſaid lands fields and bounds of Berwick aforeſaid are ſeparated and divided from our kingdom of Scotland and going and deſcending along by the river of Tweed aforeſaid eaſtward unto the ſaid port and haven of the ſaid Borough of Berwick and alſo all and ſingular our meſſages milns houſes orchards edifices buildings barns ſtables ſtorehouſes gardens curtelages ſhops cellars ſollars lands tenements meadows paſtures feedings commons and demeſn lands waſts heaths fairs marches fruits profits waters fiſhing places ſuit ſock rents proviſions and ſervices rent charges rents ſock and rents and ſervices as well of fee as cuſtomary tenants farmers or fee farmers annuities knight's fees wards marriages eſcheats releaſes heriot's fines amerciaments courts leet and views of frank pledge belonging chattels waived and eſtrained rights juriſdictions franchiſes priviledges profits commodities advantages emoluments and hereditaments whatſoever with every of their appurtenances of whatſoever kind nature or degree or by whatſoever names they be known or named ſituate lying and being coming growing or ariſing within the ſaid ſeigniory mannor Borough Town and ſock or in or within any of them or within the ſuburbs liberties limits and precincts thereof or within the metts limits and bounds above written or any of them to the ſaid ſeigniory mannor Borough Town and ſock and other the premiſſes laſt above by theſe preſents given and granted appertaining or belonging or as member

ber part and parcel thereof or any part thereof being heretofore had known accepted occupied or reputed And also the reversion or reversions whatsoever of all and singular the said seigniory mannor Borough Town and sock and all other the premisses above by these presents given and granted and every part and parcel thereof

Exceptions.

EXCEPTING always neverthelefs and out of these our letters patent and grant altogether reserved all that castle with all the appurtenances situate upon the walls of our said Borough of Berwick upon Tweed and all that house lately building within the said Borough and all buildings and edifices to the said castle and house lately built and to either of them belonging or appertaining or as part or parcel of the same castle house or either of them heretofore being known accepted or reputed and all that water miln situate and being near the walls of the said Borough of Berwick upon Tweed now or in the tenure or occupation of Mary Denton widow or her assigns And all tho lands tenements closes and other hereditaments whatsoever known or called by the several names of the Inner Castlehills inclosed and the Outer Castlehills not inclosed the New Water Haugh and Lumsden's annoy Gainslaw Cock Haugh the Snake and Maudlin fields the Cunney Garth and the Marshall Meadow near Lamberton And also except and out of these presents reserved altogether all that meadow called the Horseman's Batt and all those meadows now called or known by the name of the Horseman's Meadow and all that meadow called the Yellow Gowland adjoining near or upon Latham and extending

to

before the making of theſe our letters patent and notwithſtanding there is not full true and certain mention made of the names of tenants farmers or occupiers of the premiſſes or any parcel thereof and notwithſtanding the omiſſion or not declaration of the annual value of the premiſſes or any parcel thereof and notwithſtanding any the defects of the certainty of computation or declaration of the true annual value of the premiſſes or any parcel thereof or of the yearly rents reſerved of and upon the premiſſes or of and upon any parcel thereof in theſe our letters patent expreſſed and contained And notwithſtanding any other defects in the not naming or wrong naming any tenant farmer or occupier of the premiſſes or of any parcel thereof and notwithſtanding the ſtatute in parliament of King Henry VI. late King of England our predeceſſor made and publiſhed in the 18th year of his reign and notwithſtanding the ſtatutes of lands and tenements not to be given in mortmain and notwithſtanding any other defects in not right naming the nature kind ſort quantity or quality of the premiſſes or of any parcel thereof And further of our abounding ſpecial grace and of our certain knowledge and mere motion we grant and confirm for us our heirs and ſucceſſors to the ſaid Mayor Bailiffs and Burgeſſes of the ſaid Borough and their ſucceſſors all and all manner of lawful liberties grants franchiſes immunities priviledges exemptions quittances juriſdictions cuſtoms and free uſages as well by land as by water as well within as without the ſaid Borough ſuburbs liberties limits and precincts thereof through our whole land and power in

theſe

these our present charters or in any other charters of our progenitors or predecessors Kings and Queens of England expressed or not expressed And also all and singular those and such lands tenements hereditaments customs liberties priviledges franchises immunities quittances exemptions and jurisdictions which the Mayor Bailiffs and Burgesses of the said Borough or any of them by what names or name soever or by what incorporation soever or pretence of any incorporation heretofore they have had used or enjoyed or ought to have hold use or enjoy to them or their successors for ever of state of inheritance by reason or pretext of any charters or letters patent or of any use prescription or custom or by any other manner right or title heretofore had used or accustomed notwithstanding that any charter aforesaid were carried away and removed from thence by Robert a Bruce King of Scotland our progenitor And notwithstanding that the said Borough of Berwick hath come into the hands of our progenitors Kings of Scotland after the said grants of our said progenitors Kings of England and although the said Mayor Bailiffs and Burgesses of the said Borough or their predecessors or Burgesses of the said Borough or any of them whatsoever name or names or by whatsoever incorporation or pretext of any incorporation heretofore known or incorporated or not incorporated have used or enjoyed or not used or enjoyed the said liberties grants franchises immunities priviledges usages and free customs and we of our special grace all and singular the things above before granted and recited for us our heirs and successors to

the

AN ACT for Confirmation of the King's Majesty's Charter and Letters Patent granted to the Mayor Bailiffs and Burgesses of the Borough af BERWICK upon Tweed and their Successors and of the Franchizes Liberties Priviledges Jurisdictions and Customs of the said Borough.

IN ALL HUMBLENESS beseech your most Excellent Majesty your most bounden and most faithful subjects the Mayor Bailiffs and Burgesses of your Majesty's Borough of Berwick upon Tweed That whereas since such time as the said Borough of Berwick first became English your Majesty's most noble projenitor Kings and Queens of this land have successively by their charters and letters patent under the Great Seal of England granted and confirmed to the said Borough sundry franchizes priviledges jurisdictions liberties freedoms and immunities which together with other the rights customs and usages to the said Borough appertaining have been confirmed and saved to the said Borough by divers acts and statutes in sundry Parliaments of this Realm and are allowed and approved by sundry orders judgments and decrees in your Majesty's Courts at Westminster and elsewhere within this your Highness's Realm of England And whereas your Majesty since the beginning of this present Parliament by your Highness and letters patent under the Great Seal of England bearing date at Westminster the 30th day of April in the year of your reign of England France and Ireland the second

cond and of Scotland the ſeven and thirtieth hath given granted and confirmed unto the ſaid Mayor Bailiffs and Burgeſſes of the ſaid Borough of Berwick upon Tweed and their ſucceſſors for ever divers franchizes priviledges jurisdictions liberties freedoms immunities exemptions quietances rights uſages and cuſtoms And whereas alſo your Majeſty by your Highneſs's ſaid charter and letters patent bearing date as aforeſaid hath given and granted to the ſaid Mayor Bailiffs and Burgeſſes of the ſaid Borough of Berwick upon Tweed and their ſucceſſors for ever all that the ſeigniory mannor borough town and ſock of Berwick upon Tweed aforeſaid with all and ſingular the rights members and appurtenances thereunto belonging And alſo all thoſe lands and fields near unto the ſaid Borough adjoining commonly called the Fields and Bounds of Berwick and alſo all thoſe meſſuages houſes edifices buildings cottages lands tenements meadows paſtures feedings waſts commons ground and ſoyl and all the hereditaments whatſoever with the appurtenances ſituate lying and being within the ſaid ſeigniory mannor borough and ſock and in and within the ſaid Fields and Bounds of Berwick aforeſaid and the ſuburbs limits liberties and precincts thereof (excepting and reſerving as in your Majeſties ſaid charter and letters patent is excepted and reſerved) To have hold uſe and enjoy the ſaid franchizes priviledges jurisdictions liberties freedoms immunities exemptions quietances rights uſages and cuſtoms and the ſaid ſeigniory mannor borough town and ſock and the ſaid fields and bounds of Berwick aforeſaid and the ſaid meſſuages houſes

edifices

and fucceffors (other than your Majefty your heirs and fucceffors) all fuch eftate right title account leafe intereft condition fervice rent profit charge emoluments hereditaments and other demands whatfoever as they or any of them lawfully have or hereafter lawfully may have or claim of in to or out of the faid feigniory mannor borough town and fock and the faid fields and bounds of Berwick aforefaid and the faid meffuages houfes lands tenements and hereditaments and other things in your Majefties faid charter and letters patent granted contained mentioned and expreffed or any part thereof in as ample and beneficial manner to all intents and purpofes as if this act had never been made And your faid fubjects fhall dayly pray to God for your Majefty in all honour and profperity and fafety long to reign over us.

MATH. JOHNSON Clerk Parliamenter.